The New Global Terrorism

The New Global Terrorism

Terrorism

CHARACTERISTICS, CAUSES, CONTROLS

Edited by

CHARLES W. KEGLEY, JR.

PEARCE PROFESSOR OF INTERNATIONAL RELATIONS
THE UNIVERSITY OF SOUTH CAROLINA

Upper Saddle River, NJ 07458

Library of Congress Cataloging-in-Publication Data

The new global terrorism: characteristics, causes, controls /c edited by
Charles W. Kegley, Jr.
p. cm.
A sequel to, and derived from its predecessor, International terrorism, edited by
Charles W. Kegley, Jr. (c1990).
Includes bibliographical references.
ISBN 0-13-049413-5
1. Terrorism. 2. Terrorism—Prevention. 3. Social conflict. 4. Transnational crime.
5. Security, International. I. Kegley, Charles W. II. International terrorism.

HV6431 .N49 2003
303.6'25—dc21

2002029292

VP/Editorial Director: Charlyce Jones-Owen
Acquisitions Editor: Heather Shelstad
Associate Editor: Brian Prybella
Editorial Assistant: Jessica Drew
Production Liaison: Joanne Hakim
Project Manager: Rosie Jones
Prepress and Manufacturing Buyer: Ben Smith
Art Director: Jayne Conte
Cover Designer: Kiwi Design
Cover Art: DNA Helix: M. Freeman/Photolink/Getty Images/PhotoDisc, Earth
Observing Systems: Corbis Digital Stock, Mushroom Cloud: U.S. Department of
Defense Visual Information Center, World Financial Center: John Ortner/Getty
Images/Tony Stone Images
Cover Image Specialist: Karen Sanatar
Marketing Manager: Claire Rehwinkel

 © 2003 by Pearson Education, Inc.
Upper Saddle River, New Jersey 07458

Printed in the United States of America

Reprinted with corrections May, 2003.

ISBN 0-13-049413-5

Pearson Education Ltd., *London*
Pearson Education Australia, PTY. Limited, *Sydney*
Pearson Education Singapore, Pte. Ltd
Pearson Education North Asia Ltd, *Hong Kong*
Pearson Education Canada, Ltd., *Toronto*
Pearson Educacion de Mexico, S.A. de C.V.
Pearson Education—Japan, *Tokyo*
Pearson Education Malaysia, Pte. Ltd
Pearson Education, *Upper Saddle River, New Jersey*

Contents

Preface

The September 11, 2001 terrorist destruction of New York City's World Trade Center and the Pentagon in Arlington, Virginia, has stimulated much fresh thinking about the way collegiate instruction in international affairs and national security ought to be organized, and has culminated in reconstruction and revision of conventional coverage concerning the global terrorism now unfolding in the discourse about this problem. Understandably, in the wake of that horrendous 9/11 event and in response to the fear and interest that it provoked, the syllabi of many courses now give expanded coverage to global terrorism as a topic, and numerous new courses dealing exclusively with the subject have been added to the undergraduate and graduate curriculum. However, the available recent scholarship on terrorism arguably has not yet been assembled in a way that accommodates the need for instructional materials for use in the classroom, in light of the troubled new realities that now so stubbornly confront the entire world.

There is arguably a notable lag between the perceived new realities and the issues and topics addressed by much of the existing literature prepared primarily to orient students to the key points of debate about the nature, determinants, and means to combat the latest wave of terrorism. Moreover, the contemporary reader who wanders into a bookstore or library to find books and journal articles about international terrorism is likely to walk into a morass of contending views and competing prescriptions, and cannot help coming away feeling more puzzled than enlightened. It is my belief that the commentary regarding the rising threat of global terrorism needs to be put into perspective in a concise but representative sample of prevailing and divergent opinion that clarifies rather than adds to the confusion, while presenting a balanced assessment that allows for the spectrum of disagreement on the major issues to be considered.

This book is written primarily for instructors use to aid their students and help them to evaluate the key questions surrounding terrorism in the aftermath of 9/11. The collection has been assembled by selecting the world's leading experts and asking them to write original interpretations on particular topics. The goal is to provide an integrated anthology for instruction, written in the same accessible language that covers the most important topics and central arguments in the current debate about the nature of today's terrorist threats and methods of containing those multiple threats.

Obviously, no book on this topic can cover all issues, and this book is no exception. Without apologizing, this anthology seeks to sample the range of discussion without billing itself as providing a complete picture. Indeed, what has been included for student instruction is extracted from a huge nest of available research and commentary on the subject, and this book only provides a partial glimpse of the range of evaluation that exists. However, to assist instructors, it is important for them to note and to take advantage of the fact that the editor has written detailed introductions to each of the three parts. These essays summarize the key concepts and literature dealing with, respectively, the characteristics, causes, and control of today's terrorism. Each part introduction also provides a rationale for the essays that are presented as well as an overview of each chapter's theme and conclusion, placed into the context of other literature dealing with the same topic. Considerations of space precluded the publication of these extensive part introductions in the text, in the interest of making more space available for the authoritative essays deemed crucial for readers. However, the part introductions are available at the Prentice Hall website. All instructors are encouraged to exploit the information and critical comparative analysis provided by the editor's part introductions, which serves as a handy instructor's manual for the entire volume. They can be examined and retrieved at ***www.prenhall.com/politicalscience*** or can be located at Prentice Hall's "political science central."

The organization employed for *The New Global Terrorism* does not restrict the way the instructor might utilize the book. Though the text conveniently divides major issues and questions into three categories, the volume does not necessarily require that a particular sequence of presentation be followed for introducing the chapters pedagogically. Depending on the needs and preferences of the individual instructor, the parts (and the chapters selected and solicited for publication within them) may be reorganized without violating the meaning of the essays. Yet, the whole of *The New Global Terrorism* remains greater than the sum of its parts, for the ideas presented in each reading contribute synergistically to the understanding of the others.

Although there already exists an abundant technical (and often esoteric) literature on terrorism, and although the "new age of terrorism" since the atrocity of September 11 has generated an avalanche of new interpretative literature, *The New Global Terrorism* seeks to make a distinctive contribution. Assembling the major arguments, most authoritative statements, and most compelling empirical descriptions and normative interpretations, this book is designed to introduce students to key concepts to which they can refer for analyzing what may be anticipated with respect to future incidents of global terrorism. By design, therefore, the book is intended to do more than cover previous incidents of terrorism, such as the system-shattering events on September 11, 2001, which set the stage for a major reconfiguring of world politics similar in scope to the transformations provoked by the two World Wars and the Cold War in the twentieth century; the book provides a framework as well for analyzing present and future acts of terrorism.

The New Global Terrorism's major analytic contribution centers on its effort to expose the multifarious parts of a perplexing—and what promises to remain an enduring—puzzle. It might thereby allow the broad picture to be visualized, and illuminate the extensive range of opinion that can describe, account for, and combat terrorist activities in the aftermath of 9/11. Under this conviction, the analyst can see how the pieces to the puzzle fit by examining them when, as in the catastrophic events of September 11, 2001, they fell apart.

Specifically prepared for pedagogical purposes, *The New Global Terrorism* has been constructed to provoke interest, arouse controversy, and educate by demonstrating the inadequacy of simplistic theories and stereotypical images as well as by illustrating the tensions between contending interpretations and schools of thought. Given that the existing literature on terrorism is rife with ambiguity, impassioned rhetoric, and unsubstantiated claims, it is hoped *The New Global Terrorism* will demonstrate to students that how terrorism is defined will shape the conclusions reached about its causes and remedies. Similarly, the book seeks to illuminate how assumptions about terrorism's causes or the effectiveness of various counter-terrorism strategies will influence images of terrorism's essential defining characteristics. Thus, the text stresses the importance of studying terrorism with detached and dispassionate critical analysis from diverse perspectives. In so pursuing this educational principle, the book aims to expand awareness of the inherent limitations of efforts to reduce the subject to a single and simplistic account which overlooks the relationships between conclusions about terrorism's characteristics, causes, and controls.

No book can succeed without the help of many people. Intellectually, this book is a sequel to, and derived from, its well-received predecessor, *International Terrorism* (New York: St. Martin's Press, and London: Macmillan Education LTD, 1990). Much has changed in the eleven short years that have transpired until September 11, 2001, when the terrorist attacks created—and I say this without fear of hyperbole—a radically new international landscape darkened by the spectre of enduring global terrorism aimed at mass destruction. Accordingly, *The New Global Terrorism* has been designed to capture the sea changes in the conduct of terrorism that have occurred since 9/11, and this new anthology bears little resemblance to its 1990 predecessor, except in organization. All but two chapters have been replaced in this new text.

The development of this new book has been guided by advice from numerous experts in this area of specialization, and the text has also benefited from the helpful reviews provided for Prentice Hall by anonymous referees who evaluated earlier versions of the manuscript. But what has especially helped to make *The New Global Terrorism* so informed and informative was the willingness and ability of many scholars, regarded worldwide as experts in the study of terrorism, to graciously offer to author original chapters especially for this book. These authors include Martha Crenshaw,

Richard A. Falk, Ted Robert Gurr, David Held, Llewellyn D. Howell, James Turner Johnson, Loch K. Johnson, Mark Juergensmeyer, Michael T. Klare, David C. Rapoport, Gregory A. Raymond, Richard E. Rubenstein, Peter C. Sederberg, Michael Stohl, and Paul Wilkinson.

The editorial support offered by Heather Shelstad, Jessica Drew, Brian Prybella, and John Jordan at Prentice Hall and Rosie Jones, Silvia Freeburg and Holly Henjum at Clarinda Publication Services was instrumental in launching this project and steering it through expeditious production. Moreover, the editorial and administrative support for preparation of the manuscript provided by the staff of the Walker Institute of International Studies at the University of South Carolina—Linda Logan, Holli Buice, Long Wang, Min Ye, Wendy Halbert, and the Institute's Director, Roger Coate—is gratefully acknowledged, as is the support for the Institute and for this publication that was given by the dean of the College of Liberal Arts at the University of South Carolina, Joan H. Stewart. The admirable tolerance for my preoccupations while preparing this manuscript for publication—as displayed on the eve of our marriage by my fiancée, Debra Annette Jump—likewise is deeply appreciated. They don't cut them like this anymore, which is one (of the least important) reasons we exchanged vows to spend the rest of our lives together as this book was published for distribution.

About the Contributors

Timothy Garton Ash is Kurt A. Korber Senior Research Fellow in contemporary European history at the European Studies Center of St. Antony's College at Oxford University, and is a Senior Fellow in residence at the Hoover Institution at Stanford University. He is also a fellow of the European Academy of Arts and Sciences and the Royal Society of Arts. He is the author of *History of the Present* as well as *The File* and *In Europe's Name*.

Martha Crenshaw is John E. Andrus Professor of Government at Wesleyan University. She is the author of *Revolutionary Terrorism: The FLN in Algeria, 1954,* and editor of *Terrorism, Legitimacy, and Power.*

Richard Falk is Professor Emeritus of international law at Princeton University. A prolific author, Falk has most recently published *Law in an Emerging Global Village* as well as *Humane Global Governance.*

Ted Robert Gurr is Distinguished University Professor at the University of Maryland and is founder and director of the Minorities at Risk project, based at the university's Center for International Development and Conflict Management, which tracks the status and activities of more than 300 politically active ethnic groups world-wide. He has written or edited some twenty books and monographs on conflict including the award-winning *Why Men Rebel, Violence in America: Historical and Comparative Perspectives,* and *Peoples versus States: Minorities at Risk in the New Century.*

David Held is Graham Wallas Professor of Political Science at the London School of Economics. He is the author of many works including *Democracy and the Global Order: From the Modern State to Cosmopolitan Governance*, *Models of Democracy*, second edition and, as co-author, *Global Transformations: Politics, Economics and Culture*. He is currently working on *Cosmopolitanism: Globalization Tamed*.

Llewellyn D. Howell is Director of Executive MBA Programs, College of Business Administration, University of Hawaii, Manoa. He is the International Affairs Editor of *USA Today*. Dr. Howell has specialized in the areas of political risk assessment and analysis. His recent books include *The Handbook of Country and Political Risk Analysis*, (third edition), and *Political Risk Assessment: Concept, Method, and Management*.

Brian Michael Jenkins is Deputy Chairman of Kroll Associates. He is also former Director of RAND's Subnational Conflict Research Program. Jenkins is the author of several books and numerous articles including over one hundred RAND reports, and is editor-in-chief of *TVI Report*. His recent books include *A Hundred Wars; International Terrorism: A New Mode of Conflict Terrorism*, and *Personal Protection*.

James Turner Johnson is a Professor of Religion and Associate Member of the Graduate Department of Political Science at Rutgers, The State University of New Jersey. He has received Rockefeller, Guggenheim, and National Endowment for the Humanities fellowships and various other research grants and has directed two NEH summer seminars for college teachers. He is also a trustee, editorial board member, and former general editor of the *Journal of Religious Ethics*. His most recent books include *Morality and Contemporary Warfare*, and *The Holy War Idea in Western and Islamic Traditions*.

Loch Johnson is Regents Professor of Political Science at the University of Georgia. He has also served on the staffs of the U.S. Senate, the U.S. House of Representatives, and the White House. He is the author of *Bombs, Bugs, Drugs, and Thugs*, which was supported by a grant from the Understanding Government Foundation.

Mark Juergensmeyer is Professor of Sociology and Director of Global and International Studies at the University of California at Santa Barbara. He is the author of *Terror in the Mind of God: The Global Rise of Religious Violence*, and *The New Cold War? Religious Nationalism Confronts the Secular State*.

Michael T. Klare is Professor of Peace and World Security Studies at Hampshire College. He is the author of *Resource Wars: The New Landscape of Global Conflict*, and co-editor and contributor of *Light Weapons and Civil Conflict* as well as *World Security: Challenges for a New Century* (third edition).

Walter Laqueur is Chairman of the International Research Council at the Center for Strategic and International Studies in Washington, D.C. He has recently authored *The New Terrorism: Fanaticism and the Arms of Mass Destruction,* and *Fascism: Past, Present, and Future,* as well as *The End of the Century.*

Bernard Lewis is Cleveland E. Dodge Professor Emeritus of Near Eastern Studies at Princeton University. He is the author of numerous books on the Middle East, including, most recently, *What Went Wrong? Western Impact and Middle Eastern Response,* as well as *The Political Language of Islam* and *Race and Slavery in the Middle East: An Historical Enquiry.*

David C. Rapoport is a Professor of Political Science at the University of California at Los Angeles. He was the founding director of the Center for the Study of Religion, and is currently co-editor of the *Journal of Terrorism and Political Violence.* His books include *Assassination and Terrorism,* and four edited and co-edited volumes, including *The Democratic Experience and Violence.*

Gregory A. Raymond is director of the Honors College at Boise State University. He was selected as the Idaho Professor of the Year by the Carnegie Foundation for the Advancement of Teaching. His most recent books include co-authorship of *Exorcising the Ghost of Westphalia: Building World Order in the New Millennium,* as well as *From War to Peace: Fateful Decisions in International Politics.*

Richard E. Rubenstein is Professor of Political Psychology at the Institute for Conflict Analysis at George Mason University. A prolific writer, his books include *Alchemists of Revolution: Terrorism in the Modern World.*

Peter C. Sederberg is a Professor of Government and International Studies at the University of South Carolina, where he serves as Dean of the Honors College. His book publications include *The Politics of Meaning* as well as *Terrorist Myths: Illusion, Rhetoric, and Reality.*

Michael Stohl is Professor of Political Science at the University of California, Santa Barbara. He has published widely in the area of peace research, authoring more than fifty articles and book chapters, and has co-edited nine books including *The Politics of Terrorism,* in three editions.

Paul Wilkinson is Professor of International Relations and Director, Center for the Study of Terrorism and Political Violence, University of St. Andrews. His publications include *Political Terrorism, Terrorism and the Liberal State, The New Fascists, Aviation Terrorism and Security* (jointly edited with Brian Jenkins), and *Terrorism Versus Democracy: The Liberal State Response.* He has been joint-editor with David Rapoport of the academic journal *Terrorism and Political Violence* since its inception in 1989.

About the Editor

Charles W. Kegley is Pearce Professor of International Relations at the University of South Carolina. A past President of the International Studies Association (1993–1994), he has also taught at the Georgetown University School of Foreign Service, the University of Texas, Rutgers University as the Moses and Annuta Back Peace Scholar, and the People's University of China. In addition, he was a Pew Fellow at the John F. Kennedy School of Government at Harvard University and is a member of the Board of Trustees of the Carnegie Council on Ethics and International Affairs.

Kegley is Senior Editor of the *Prentice Hall Studies in International Relations: Enduring Questions in Changing Times* series devoted to the publication of serious scholarship addressing major problems and issues in international affairs. Among his four dozen book publications, he has recently published *From War to Peace: Fateful Decisions in International Politics, Exorcising the Ghost of Westphalia: Building World Order in the New Millennium, World Politics: Trend and Transformation; American Foreign Policy: Pattern and Process; How Nations Make Peace; The Global Agenda, Controversies in International Relations Theory: Realism and the Neoliberal Challenge; A Multipolar Peace? Great-Power Politics in the Twenty-First Century; The Long Postwar Peace: Contending Explanations and Projections; After the Cold War: Questioning the Morality of Nuclear Deterrence; When Trust Breaks Down: Alliance Norms and World Politics; International Terrorism;* and *The Nuclear Reader: Strategy, Weapons, War.* He has published articles in a wide range of scholarly journals, including *The Journal of Peace Research, The Journal of Conflict Resolution, International Studies Quarterly, Ethics and International Affairs, Cooperation and Conflict, The Bulletin of Peace Proposals, Alternatives, USA Today, Harvard International Review, Presidential Studies Quarterly, Comparative Political Studies, Conflict Management and Peace Science, International Interactions, The Journal of Politics,* and the *Political Research Quarterly.*

The New Global
Terrorism

THE CHARACTERISTICS, CAUSES, AND CONTROLS OF THE NEW GLOBAL TERRORISM: AN INTRODUCTION

CHARLES W. KEGLEY JR.

> Terrorism is dangerous ground for *simplificateurs* and *generalisateurs*. To approach it, a cool head is probably more essential than any other intellectual quality.
>
> WALTER LAQUEUR

The events of September 11, 2001, seem destined to remain permanently etched in the minds and memories of everyone. Few, if any, will ever forget where they were when they first heard the horrendous news that terrorists had attacked and destroyed the Twin Towers of the World Trade Center in New York and severely damaged the Pentagon in Washington. In a single flash the world was forced to confront grim new realities. Instantaneously, those absent towers became the symbol for the shapelessness of an apparent new world disorder; where once there had been complacent certainty about the stability of global interdependence, there were now pervasive uncertainties and pregnant fears.

The events of 9/11 shattered the preexisting, prevailing sense of personal, national, and international security. The presumed safety and euphoria of a peaceful and prosperous post–Cold War era were soon seen as an illusion. The primary product of 9/11 was the generation of fear. And that was precisely the purpose of the terrorists who perpetrated this atrocious violent act. "America is full of fear," proclaimed a jubilant Osama bin Laden in the taped message he broadcast in anticipation of the U.S. response to his slaughter of thousands of innocent people. "They cry for their children," he gleefully asserted, while warning "Nobody in the United States will feel safe."

Provoking fear is the name of the terrorist's game. It's an old game; "a new age of terrorism is dawning, but the old terrorism is far from dead."[1] However, terrorism after September 11 is now being practiced in what appear to be unprecedented ways. Terrorism is violence or the threat of violence undertaken to create alarm and fear. But the acts on 9/11 took the ancient practice to a new level, making terrorism something far more menacing than it customarily had been viewed. Terrorism was no longer a marginal problem, a nuisance in other countries to be watched on the evening news. It had become a sadistic assault on the principles and political culture of the United States and its allies—on their very way of life. September 11 exposed a previously complacent community to its vulnerability to an enemy who recognized no moral restraints, who was relentless in pursuit of violence, and who claimed to be poised to strike anyone, anything, anywhere, anytime.

What made September 11 an historic watershed arguably ushering in a new age is that it marked the advent of new rules for the old game of violence by the weak against the strong, but now conducted by ideological terrorists with grandiose revolutionary ambitions acting transnationally to transform the international status quo.[2] Prior to 9/11, the primary purpose of terrorism was publicity—to elicit attention and sympathy for the terrorist's cause. Accordingly, it was previously regarded as mainly theater, and it was often observed that "terrorists want a lot of people watching, not a lot of people dead." No longer. An awakened world began to recognize that terrorists had begun to engage in new practices for new purposes—intentionally seeking not simply to coerce changes in enemies' policies, but to annihilate enemies; they now want a lot of people dead. In the past, when terrorists hit targets, they killed small numbers of people with modest weapons; 9/11 was a transformative step in a new direction, killing twice the number of people that died in the December 7, 1941, Japanese attack on Pearl Harbor. "Between the jets, the fuel, and the kinetic force of the collapsing World Trade Center buildings, the southwestern tip of Manhattan had been struck with a force estimated at twice the size of the smallest U.S. tactical nuclear weapon. It was the most deadly attack on U.S. territory in history."[3] And 9/11 signaled the spectre of permanent terrorism throughout the globe, unless unchecked, with, as U.S. President George W. Bush pictured the scene in his January, 2002, State of the Union address, thousands of "dangerous killers"—"ticking time bombs"—roaming the globe and eager to destroy, especially dangerous because these networks of global terrorists "threaten us with the world's most destructive weapons."

How are we to think about the new circumstances that have now crystallized? How can the peace-loving people on the planet escape the plight that terrorizes them? How can people learn to walk daily in the valley of the shadow of death, without fear, but in knowledge that no government can protect everyone and everything, everywhere? And how are people expected to deal psychologically with U.S. Vice President Dick Cheney's warning in May 2002 that "The prospects of a future attack . . . are almost certainty. It's not a matter of if, but when"?

"The things that hurt, instruct," Benjamin Franklin once noted. Surprise and shock are effective teachers. Fear and terror can enlighten us to previously unappreciated dangers. Crisis, the Chinese proverb maintains, comprises both danger and opportunity. The opportunity before us is to understand the character of the new threats and to deal with them in ways that allow the world to adjust to the "new normalcy" of life in the midst of fear.

In a previous dark period of American history—at the height of the depression—President Franklin Delano Roosevelt on March 4, 1933, attempted to dispel the gloom of his time when he informed the American public that "The only thing we have to fear is fear itself—nameless, unreasoning, unjustified terror which paralyzes needed efforts to convert retreat into advance." In the wake of 9/11, in the new global topography, people have had to adjust to living *with* fear; recognition of the emergent and pervasive threat of terrorism is now a heightened state of awareness, and therefore reasonable rather than the paranoid. The basis for the validity of this pessimistic prediction is probably that after two grand towers 110 stories high were made to fall by terrorists on a clear, bright Tuesday morning in September 2001, the domestic and international climate of opinion shifted, perhaps permanently. Many people understandably began to ask, "When will life return to normal?" This turned out to be an unrealistic question, especially if the individuals who asked it really meant, "When will things be the way they were before September 11th?" Sadly, there appears to be only one realistic answer to such a question: This fear now *is* normal. Terror and the chronic threat it arouses have become constants. As U.S. Vice President Dick Cheney cautioned earlier, in January 2002, "Many of the steps we have now been forced to take will become permanent. . . . They represent an understanding of the world as it is, and dangers we must guard against perhaps for decades to come." Punctuating this dire prediction, President George W. Bush proclaimed in his January 2002 State of the Union address that "our war against terror is only beginning," signaling that the war to end global terrorism would be a long war. "Whatever it costs, we will pay it," Bush announced in proposing the largest increase in defense spending in two decades.

The Challenge

To bring intellectual understanding to the new threat now facing the world, we will be required to deal with the widespread view that after September 11th "everything has changed." This cliché has become so frequently voiced that it has gained the status of a new conventional wisdom. Although there may be an element of hyperbole in that claim, it does seem after 9/11 that in many ways the new age of global terrorism really has changed all the questions and all the answers. September 11 has pulled the global community into a maelstrom of anxiety and fear, transforming "the domestic and international landscape by making visible what was previously unrecognized—our own vulnerability to terrorism."[4] To U.S. President George W. Bush's way of thinking, September 11th has fundamentally changed the way America and both its friends and enemies hereafter should think about foreign policy and international politics. As George Bush put it, "Night fell on a different world," marking not only, in his words, "the first war of the twenty-first century," but also inaugurating a defining moment. "We have found our mission and our moment," he asserted in an effort to galvanize the concerted coalition needed to combat what he categorized as "evil" in the world. "Either you are with us, or you are with the terrorists," was the way the President defined the major cleavage he perceived that henceforth would define the new international realities created by a worldwide war between the forces of moral civilization against terrorism's evil. "The way I view this is that we're fighting evil, and I don't see any shades of gray," was how Bush pictured the new global war.[5]

To be sure, there are many elements of truth in all these claims about the sea change believed to have commenced. A new disease can now be said to stalk the face of the Earth, a disease highly resistant to control. That contagion will severely test the targets' perseverance and resolve. And it raises unfamiliar issues. Like terrorism in the past, today's terrorism stems from multiple causes whose roots are deep. What is different today is that the new age of terrorism is

- Global, in the sense that with the death of distance borders no longer serve as barriers to terrorism
- Lethal, because now terrorists have shifted their tactics from theatrical violent acts seeking to alarm for publicity to purposeful destruction of a target populated entirely by civilian noncombatants, to kill as many as possible for the purpose of undermining an enemy's entire society and culture
- Novel, in the sheer size, destructiveness, and professionally coordinated planning of the September 11 attack
- Waged by civilians without state sanction in ways and by means that erase the classic boundaries between terrorism and a declared war between states
- Reliant on the most advanced technology of modern civilization to destroy through those sophisticated technological means the modern civilization seen as posing a threat to the terrorist's sacred traditions
- Orchestrated by transnational non-state organizations through global conspiratorial networks of terrorist cells located in many countries, involving unprecedented levels of communication and coordination
- Pursued by fanatical extremists to annihilate through maximal bloodshed rather than to convince or persuade, by carrying out crimes against humanity by suicidal methods that require the terrorists to sacrifice their own lives, in acts that cannot be deterred or prevented through negotiated compromise
- Outside established moral and legal norms that were universally accepted and shared for centuries
- Predicated on the *realpolitik* principle that the power to destroy is equal to the power to change and control
- Driven by hatred of the target—by terrorists' desire to make the target suffer for what the target is, what it does, and the values for which the target stands

These changes require changes in strategy and tactics. A new compass is needed to travel through the new global landscape, even if the character of the new terrain has yet to take on clear definition and we do not as yet have an accepted name for the new international realities. The scale of change is awesome, and leaders must construct new frameworks for thought and analysis to chart a path to a new future. That will require great vision and insight. It will require observers to contemplate a congeries of questions:

> Will tomorrow's terrorist simply be a more bloodthirsty version of today's terrorist bent upon big bangs and body count, perhaps even more indiscriminate, but sticking with conventional explosives? Will tomorrow's terrorist turn instead to chemical, biological, or nuclear weapons to cause mass destruction? Or will tomorrow's terrorist be a sophisticated electronic warrior penetrating and sabotaging the information and communications systems upon which modern society increasingly depends? . . . While no one can predict the future course of terrorism with confidence, the history of terrorism counsels us to think broadly but at the same time to exercise caution.[6]

Contemplate how you, an innocent bystander yourself and a potential victim of another brutal act of atrocity like 9/11, can make sense of this seemingly senseless and powerless new predicament of having to face the possibility of constant fear and insecurity. A flood of emotions is certain to rush through your mind. However, your actions will probably appear limited because you are likely to perceive yourself as merely a helpless pawn in a deadly international showdown over which you are unable to exercise control. In addition, a number of deeper intellectual questions are bound to surface as you attempt to bring meaning to the pervasive trauma posed by the new global terrorism. Who are these people? What beliefs could they hold so strongly that they are willing to violate every ethical precept for their cause, and for which they were willing to die in an act of suicide? What psychological drives, ideological convictions, religious beliefs, institutional loyalties, cultural or ethnic affiliations, financial rewards, or sense of desperation leads such people to such barbarian acts? And why do terrorists act the way they do—killing innocents, advertising their crime to the entire world, and defining themselves as freedom fighters on a holy mission seeking justice? Why, indeed, is their message directed to particular governments and not just to those they claim deprive them of their legitimate rights? Why do their claims resonate with and inspire some, but fall on deaf ears to others? Do the terrorists receive external assistance for the acts they commit? And finally, why are such activities so resistant to prevention? What can be done to deter catastrophic terrorism's reoccurrence? Is there a solution available to control this menace, so that others will be spared in the future?

This chilling scenario of the 9/11 acts of terrorism does not stand alone. Unfortunately, the events of 9/11 followed a series of less dramatic terrorist acts in the 1980s and 1990s when, on a regular basis, headlines reported that jet-hijackings, kidnappings, hostage takings, and assassinations had become a prominent and horrifying feature of the times. Consider one real-world event, as described by the *Wall Street Journal*:

> The attractive couple and their young child appeared to be on vacation, flying on a Pan American World Airways jet from Hong Kong to Tokyo, on Aug. 11, 1982. But the man quietly and unobtrusively slipped a tiny, powerful bomb beneath his seat cushion before he and his family got off in Tokyo.

On the plane's next flight, as the Pan Am jet neared Honolulu, the bomb went off. The blast tore the legs off a Japanese teenager who happened to be in that seat, and he bled to death. Fifteen other passengers were injured.

The event brought new actors and increasingly sophisticated bombs onto the stage of international terrorism. The man who put the bomb beneath the seat allegedly is . . . a member of . . . terrorist groups that have since placed bombs in planes around the world.[7]

The unspeakable horror that surrounded this and other equally unsettling incidents of terrorism were not episodic products of imagination. The bombing of Pan Am flight 103 over Scotland on December 21, 1988—claiming 270 lives— provides another conspicuous real-world example of this kind of recurrent human tragedy, and exemplifies the potency of terrorism and the frustration and failure of efforts to contain it. Past acts of ruthless terrorism were real, having been committed on a regular basis, and their primary purpose was usually the production of alarm. To instill paralyzing fear—to terrorize—has unfortunately become a common way of expressing grievances and attempting to realize political objectives.

DEFINING GLOBAL TERRORISM

Since the 1960s, when they first became frequent, these kinds of nightmares have been termed, for lack of a better label, "terrorist." Terrorism, perversely like theater, had become "popular," attended by press and public. Its popularization has accelerated its growth as a political issue.

As acts of global terrorism began to increase, growing attention was paid to terrorists' existence and motives—just as its perpetrators intended. Since the 1960s, acts of international terrorism have recurred with sufficient frequency for terrorism to rise steadily on the global agenda as a primary topic of concern and debate. Regarded as a chronic condition of potentially epidemic proportions, it commanded increasing resources to combat during the last quarter of the twentieth century, and since 9/11, those costs have escalated exponentially (the U.S. government at the start of 2002 estimated the money to wage the war against terrorism to rise to as much as $160 billion annually). Because the September 11 attacks are widely perceived to be a "preview" to the security threats facing the international community in the twenty-first century, this "new and increasingly dangerous threat" has become the *top* international security priority, in part because the new global terrorism "is relatively inexpensive to conduct, and devilishly difficult to counter."[8]

As the affliction threatens to contagiously spread, global terrorism has changed from a problem previously overwhelmingly identified with obscure insurrectionists in remote areas to one that today might strike anyone, anyplace. In response, vigorous counterattacks against this pernicious new threat have been mounted, but these vigilant and expensive programs do not assure that they will meet with success in "extirpating terrorism from the force of the globe," as President George W. Bush defined the goal of the new "war on terrorism."

Global terrorism represents one of the defining elements of politics on the world's stage today. The ubiquitous threat of terrorism intrudes into the lives and thinking of people throughout the world. Its story is a human story, deeply personal and often tragic, that provokes great fear and intense outrage. It is high drama, the subject of widespread commentary. "These are circumstances in which only a fool is unafraid," is the way the editors of *The New Republic* captured—on October 29, 2001—the post-9/11 climate of opinion. Given its psychological impact, the extensive attention increasingly paid to the nature and roots of the new global terrorism is understandable, as is the recent frantic search for methods to control it.

The realization of the extent of vulnerability has stimulated the search for understanding and for a new organizing principle, and "we are already beginning to see some tectonic foreign policy changes as a result of the September 11 attacks."[9] However, despite this adaptation and analysis, global terrorism remains a phenomenon that is not clearly understood, adequately explained, or effectively controlled. Throughout the entire world, people are perplexed by and fixated on the frightening prospect that they, their neighbors, or their country will again be victimized by global terrorism; and they seek to understand the seemingly incomprehensible problems associated with and causing it. Governments, likewise, remain unable to forge an effective policy to combat this new menace, and have yet to agree on a definition of terrorism.[10] The scholarly literature that has emerged to deal with terrorism, while voluminous, has not produced a definitive conceptualization; policy makers remain in disagreement about the new global terrorism's character, causes, and antidotes.

Indeed, as hot as the topic is, global terrorism continues—even a year after 9/11—to be a topic surrounded by myth and cant. It is still a phenomenon that few people can ignore (and about which, it seems, everyone has an opinion, either ill or well informed). Polemics abound, and divergent interpretations compete for acceptance and dominance. But debate has failed to result in consensus about global terrorism's essential attributes, determinants, or cure.

It is not the purpose of *The New Global Terrorism* to resolve the many semantic, epistemological, and evaluative issues confronting its analysis, nor to propose preventive solutions to them. Instead, its educational mission is to illuminate these disagreements and the implications that result from alternate conceptualizations and diverse socially constructed images of the new terrorism's character, causes, and countermeasures. Global terrorism is a multidimensional concept; it refers to a diverse set of observable phenomena. Observers often bring very different assumptions to discussions of global terrorism, and their conclusions customarily spring from very different perceptions, beliefs, and preferences. As a result, the considerable disagreement that exists is unlikely to be resolved. Terrorism seems destined to remain a highly subjective, sensational, and emotional phenomenon, surrounded by polemics, double standards, and hypocrisy. Terrorism is a strategy consciously perpetrated to outrage the sensibilities of others, and terrorists are likely to continue to succeed in that goal. Because the concept of terrorism is inherently subjective, not scientific, this ambiguity invites ambivalence about observed individual acts of violence, an ambivalence that paradoxically increases terrorism's popularity as an instrument for propaganda.

To manage the task of comprehending terrorism in its diverse manifestations by reducing it to a single definition would mask complexities and thereby conceal its diverse and changing nature. It is the goal of this book to highlight, not minimize, this diversity by exposing the varying perceptions of and disagreements about the new global terrorism. Hence, this book aspires to evaluate a representative sample of the broad spectrum of opinion about the nature, sources, and solutions to the continuing problem in its latest form. Readers of this book are invited and challenged to evaluate for themselves the relative worth of incompatible ideas, and to refine their thinking by seeking to identify the criteria by which they make these assessments. *The New Global Terrorism* will provide discussion of the organizing concepts and interpretations necessary for engaging in these intellectual tasks.

Underlying the entire approach of this book is the premise that contemporary terrorism is primarily and intrinsically a *global* phenomenon. As Paul Wilkinson has argued, "Terrorism is inherently international in character, so that, paradoxically, the more individual states improve their national measures [to combat global terrorism] the more it becomes attractive for the terrorist to cross national frontiers."[11] In the age of growing global interdependence, customarily viewed as the process, product, policy and prescription for "globalization," terrorism may be seen as a phenomenon that increasingly colors every aspect of international relations, while simultaneously being facilitated by global trends toward the integration of international society in world politics. It is difficult to conceive of terrorism as a prominent problem in the absence of the pressures exerted by certain global developments, subsumed by the concept of "globalization." As Shirley Tilghman, President of Princeton University, admonished, "September 11th should alert us to what globalization really means."[12] Under conditions of globalization, everything becomes connected to everything else throughout the globe, so that conditions anyplace affect conditions everyplace; this means that "local tyranny and global terror go hand and hand."[13] This and other salient global trends[14] have created a hospitable environment for the practice of terrorist tactics and contributed to the transformation of terrorism from a subnational instrument of political change to one whose methods now almost invariably and inescapably transcend national boundaries. For these reasons, we shall inspect terrorism in this book as it typically unfolds through actions directed toward and addressed by actors beyond the home territory of those practicing terrorist acts. This follows the conceptualization of Brian Jenkins, who suggests that "what is called international terrorism may refer broadly to any terrorist violence that has international repercussions, or to acts of violence which are outside the accepted norms of international diplomacy and rules of war."[15]

This is not to deny the existence of occasional acts of terrorism that are primarily domestic in origin or orientation. Many terrorist movements undoubtedly are provincial in outlook and conceive of their activities exclusively as a response to internal circumstances. For this reason it has been conventional analytic practice to distinguish domestic and nationalist terrorism from global terrorism, with the former identified by activities confined within the borders of a single state and carried out, for example, by indigenous "Fourth World" minority nationalities who seek their own homelands within existing states, and the latter associated with attacks on third-party targets in foreign territory or supported by state sponsors. For example, one expert writing in the 1970s felt it useful to differentiate four types of terrorism: *international* (terrorism conducted by people controlled by a sovereign state), *transnational* (terrorism practiced by autonomous non-state actors, but not necessarily with the support of sympathetic states), *domestic* (terrorism involving the nationals of only one state), and *state terrorism* (terrorist tactics practiced by a state within its own borders, such as the genocide performed by Nazi Germany).[16] This classification allowed the *types* of terrorism to be isolated, as depicted in Table 1.

However interesting and informative, this kind of distinction has become increasingly difficult to draw. Since the 1970s, acts of terrorism have almost invariably transcended national borders in one way (violence on foreign soil) or another (through publicity communicated across international borders by the news media or by external sponsorship of terrorist activities abroad). Today, almost all acts of terrorism have international consequences. The increasingly global face of contemporary terrorism has blurred (if not totally erased) the distinction between national and international terrorism. Whereas it was once analytically useful to distinguish *intra*national from *inter*national aspects of terrorism, these categories increasingly refer to a distinction without a difference. It is exceedingly difficult to locate cases of terrorist activity— however defined and identified—that are not internationally supported, targeted abroad, fomented by prevailing global circumstances, global in their repercussions, or addressed to the global community in some manner.

Accordingly, despite the acknowledgment that terrorism may sometimes originate exclusively from internal conditions and be directed only at national governments, this type of purely indigenous terrorism today is statistically rare. Therefore, this book operates on the assumption that contemporary terrorism possesses a decidedly global character, and that terrorism's assessment requires exploration of the foreign implications of terrorist acts. Our object of analysis

TABLE 1   Four Forms of Terrorism*

Are Nationals of More than One State Directly Involved?

		YES	NO
Are Activities Controlled	*yes*	International	State
or Directed by Governments?	no	Transnational	Domestic

*Adapted from Edward Mickolus, "Trends in International Terrorism," in *International Terrorism in the Contemporary World*, ed. Marius H. Livingston et al., (Westport. Conn.: Greenwood Press, 1978), 45.

will be the generic phenomenon of global terrorism—those acts of terror that cross "national boundaries, through the choice of a foreign victim or target, the commission of the terrorist act in a foreign country, or an effort to influence the policies of a foreign government."[17] The inquiry undertaken will concentrate on those forms of terrorism international in scope, origin, and effects, wherein terrorism is seen as a particular "form of political violence, directed at governments but often involving ordinary citizens, whose aim is to create a climate of fear in which the [demands] of the terrorists will be granted by the government in question [but] extended to apply to acts perpetrated by governments themselves in order to instill a sense of fear."[18]

ORGANIZING PERCEPTIONS OF TERRORISM: BREAKING THE TOPIC INTO COMPONENTS

To organize thinking about the most recent wave of global terrorism, the book divides the subject into three parts, centered on three central questions: What is global terrorism? What are its predominant causes? What are the methods proposed for its control?

Part I is definitional and descriptive. It presents essays that provide alternative definitions of global terrorism and illuminate the different attributes of the phenomenon. The essays in this section place the new global terrorism in historical perspective and survey the properties commonly ascribed to it. Thus, the various ways in which contemporary global terrorism has been conceived are introduced so that the characteristics connecting it to other aspects of national and international politics can be appreciated. This coverage encourages the reader to contemplate the incompatible ways in which global terrorism has been defined, and to critically examine the implications of those differences.

Part II presents interpretations that address the sources or causes of global terrorism, as manifested recently in the events of 9/11 and in the precedents to that new epoch in the past. Here the focus shifts to the multiple causes commonly believed to have contributed to the growth of global terrorism. At issue is the question: What precipitant conditions and factors make the new global terrorism possible (and probable), and how do these preconditional stimuli threaten to make future global terror even more prevalent?

The competing interpretations offered here advance rival theories and evidence about the new terrorism's most probable causes, and evaluate popular and allegedly "mythical" beliefs about the panoply of sources claimed to promote its occurrence. The readings were selected to stimulate debate about contending propositions regarding the new global terrorism's determinants.

To most, global terrorism is appropriately likened to a disease, and to them the contagious disease requires a remedy. For those of this persuasion, essays are presented here whose insights enable the reader to play the role of a physician in an attempt to diagnose the causes of the disease and to separate the immediate or precipitating symptoms from the underlying sources. To this end, it is important to balance the interpretation by appreciating that others see terrorism as a legitimate response to unjustified repression, and accordingly view it not as a curse but as a cure; to understand terrorism's origins, it is helpful also to consider the perspective of global terrorism's perpetrators and defenders if we are to appreciate the diverse mentalities, ideologies, and circumstances which may motivate terrorists' actions. Without awareness of the roots from which acts of global terrorism spring, it is extremely unlikely that a cure to its outbreak and spread will be found (however ambitious the effort). The coverage is designed to treat not only the background factors, beliefs, and circumstances that lead individuals to become involved in terrorist movements, but especially the internal (national) and external (global) conditions that stimulate terrorist activity. The former include indigenous sources of terrorism, such as discontent emerging from perceived political, social, and economic inequities within states, as well as the resentments that fuel efforts by terrorists to repel the foreign cultural and material influences they perceive to intrude on their cultural traditions and thereby to oppress them. The latter include the transnational links between terrorist groups such as the networks among these transnational movements and their state sponsors (for example, the alleged support of Muslim dissidents in Palestine and the Philippines by Iraq, Iran, Somalia, Libya, and other Arab states).

A key assumption of this and other parts is that the observer's definition of global terrorism is inevitably tied to underlying inferences made about terrorism's cause(s); and, vice versa, one's presumptions about terrorism's causes will shape images of its characteristics and how it should be defined. For example, those who perceive terrorism as undertaken primarily by the impoverished or persecuted will tend to see terrorism as rooted in conditions of oppression and inequality, whereas those who characterize it as merely another mode of violent conflict will tend to attribute terrorist activities to ideologies that justify aggression for political purposes. And likewise those who maintain that with the new global terrorism after September 11, "we are faced with a special variety of terrorism carried out by suicidal maniacs,"[19] causation resides in pathological impulses of psychopaths that make terrorist acts difficult to deter.

Finally, **Part III** deals with the various solutions proposed to bring the most recent phase of global terrorism under control and to arrest its spread. Here the discussion focuses on debate about how the new global terrorism might be most effectively combated, and considers the limitations and dangers inherent in the various proposals that have been considered or practiced for the control of the new global terrorism. These range from counter-terrorist tactics using force to nonviolent remedies, with a host of institutional, legal, and political responses in between. Again, the reading selections highlight contending arguments in order to enable readers to understand the motives underlying efforts to combat violence with violence or to counter threats to freedom by restricting citizens' freedom. Moreover, the interpretations frame the debate about how a moral response to the new global terrorism might be fought, in terms of competing conceptions the means and ends of a just war. Accordingly, an inventory of specific policy programs and counter-terrorist measures is provided, along with the relevant ideas and information required to consider the problems and controversies those responses to terrorism entail.

By breaking them into separate categories, this tripartite organizational design allows the most important issues to be introduced and ordered in a way that makes the consideration of rival ideas manageable. In many respects, however, this separation is misleading. Whereas the organization divides these three dimensions into distinct categories, their inherently overlapping nature should be recognized. The reader is encouraged to contemplate the ways in which characteristics, causes, and controls are intimately linked. The readings provide a rich set of materials demonstrating that how global terrorism is defined will necessarily shape the conclusions reached about its causes and remedies. Similarly, the readings will suggest how inferences about terrorism's causes will structure images of both its character and the best policy response to it. And, to round out the circle, the ways in which counter-terrorist policy options are viewed will shape, and be shaped by, views of its character and the factors that produce it. The "tyranny of assumptions"—the way in which prior beliefs and expectations may lead to divergent conclusions—is thus revealed by the discordant messages presented by the diverse interpretations published in *The New Global Terrorism*.

This overriding theme follows J. Bowyer Bell's warning that "the posture of the investigator quite often determines the result of his or her analysis."[20] As he notes, there "has at times been more interest in accumulating sympathetic 'evidence' or defining the nature of terrorism so as to buttress long-held positions, than in value-free investigation." To illustrate this (inevitable?) deficiency in the analysis of terrorism, Bell notes the inescapably tight relationship between analysts' definitions of terrorism and their recommendations for its control. He warns that "a number [of analysts] have begun at the end, with prescription, rather than at the beginning," with description and definition, and that their positions can be collapsed into

> . . . two general postures. At one extreme are those who feel that most terrorists are warped, their politics pathological and consequently unamenable to accommodation. Since (terrorists') demands are essentially nonnegotiable . . . the appropriate response is placed on coercion, protection, and punishment. . . . At the other pole are those who concentrate on the reasoned demands of the revolutionaries, who believe that in many cases accommodations or at least a dialogue is possible. They stress the reasons behind the massacres, the roots of violence, and the remedies to ease real frustration. They put less stress on maintaining order by coercive law and more on the necessity for justice.[21]

Obviously, the tension between these two incompatible approaches increases as fears increase, as they have since 9/11.

Another way of illustrating this connection among controls, characteristics, and causes is to note that those who think that global terrorism demands a retributive militant response are prone to define terrorism as a substitute form of warfare caused primarily by the foreign sponsorship of external supporters. This has occurred since 9/11 when the view gained proponents that counter-terrorism is essentially a "war" against a general evil global phenomenon promoted by evil perpetrators. U.S. President Bush, in November 2001, described the "mad, global ambitions" of the new terrorist as a "threat to civilization" requiring waging "the first war of the twenty-first century."[22] There exist many other examples in which conclusions about one facet of global terrorism are colored and contaminated by the premises embraced about the others. Take, for example, the argument that "since terrorism is always a political instrument, the right way to combat it is always political. Solve the problem that breeds terrorism and you get rid of the terrorism."[23] If we recognize and take into account the inherent overlap of analysts' beliefs about terrorism's characteristics, causes, and controls, we can gain better understanding of the intellectual barriers to unlocking the mystery of the new global terrorism and better avoid reaching erroneous conclusions about what the latest wave of global terrorism is, what produces it, and what can be done about it. In reading the essays in *The New Global Terrorism,* it is essential to critically inspect how each analysis has been influenced by the assumptions of the interpreter. The reader is urged to evaluate the validity and logic of the assumptions made by each author, and to consider the extent to which the interpretation advanced in each chapter is supported or undermined by alternative interpretations in the unfolding debate and discourse in other literature on the subject.

This tripartite organizational scheme, it might be noted, parallels the scholarly convention to separate the analysis of international behavior into three tasks: description, explanation, and prescription. But again, this division, though common in the study of interpersonal and international behavior,[24] is artificial; for how a subject is observed and described is closely related to explanations of the factors that cause it. Likewise, the efficacy of prescriptions about how people *ought* to deal with a perceived phenomenon is contingent on the accuracy with which those phenomena are observed and the validity of the causes identified to explain them. Hence the descriptive, explanatory or causal, and prescriptive policy analyses of global terrorism are heavily intertwined; none of these analytic tasks can be conducted wholly in isolation from the others, and the adequacies of each influence the adequacy of the others.

To introduce the contents, let us turn to the descriptions, explanations, and prescriptions presented in the readings. We shall expose the themes and contending interpretations by following the organizational scheme just described, so as to treat sequentially—in three discrete parts—leading ideas about the characteristics, causes, and control of contemporary global terrorism in the wake of September 11, 2001. (Readers are encouraged to consult the editor's extensive thematic introduction to each part and the chapters presented in them at **www.prenhall.com/politicalscience**).

Notes

1. Walter Laqueur, *The New Terrorism* (New York: Oxford University Press, 1999):32.
2. See Mark N. Katz, "Osama bin Laden as Transnational Revolutionary Leader," *Current History* 101 (February 2002):81–85.

3. Linda Rothstein, "After September 11," *Bulletin of the Atomic Scientists* (November–December 2001):44.

4. James Schlesinger, "A Test by Terrorism," *The National Interest* 65-S (Special Issue, Thanksgiving 2001):5.

5. Cited in Kenneth T. Walsh, "Taking on the 'Axis of Evil,'" *U.S. News & World Report* (11 February 2002):20.

6. Michael Brian Jenkins, "Foreword," in *Countering the New Terrorism*, ed. Ian Lesser et al. (Santa Monica, Calif.: RAND, 1999):x.

7. William M. Carley, "Terrorist Blueprint," *Wall Street Journal*, 27 February 1989:Al.

8. L. Paul Bremer, III, "A New Strategy for the New Face of Terrorism," *The National Interest* 65-S (Special Issue, Thanksgiving 2001):25.

9. Charles Krauthammer, in "After September 11," *The National Interest* 65-S (Special Issue, Thanksgiving 2001):6a.

10. David L. Philips, "Wanted, a Covenant to Define and Fight Terrorism," *Wall Street Journal*, 4 January 2002:6.

11. Paul Wilkinson, "Trends in International Terrorism and the American Response," in *Terrorism and International Order*, ed. Lawrence Freeman et al. (London: Routledge and Kegan Paul, 1986):49.

12. In *Christian Science Monitor* (28 December 2001):10.

13. William Safire, "Cozying Up to Iran Won't Help America's War on Terrorism," *International Herald Tribune*, 1–2 December 2001:8.

14. For a recent survey, see Charles W. Kegley Jr. and Eugene R. Wittkopf, *World Politics: Trend and Transformation*, 9th ed. (Belmont, Calif.: Wadsworth, 2003).

15. Brian Jenkins, *International Terrorism: A New Mode of Conflict* (Los Angeles: Crescent Publications, 1975):11.

16. Edward Mickolus, "Trends in International Terrorism," in *International Terrorism in the Contemporary World*, ed. Marius H. Livingston, with Lee Bruce Kress and Marie G. Wanek (Westport, Conn.: Greenwood Press, 1978):45.

17. Robert A. Fearey, "Introduction to International Terrorism," in Livingston et al., 25.

18. David Miller, ed., *The Blackwell Encyclopedia of Political Thought* (New York: Basil Blackwell, 1987):514.

19. Richard Perle, "After September 11," *The National Interest* 65-S (Special Issue, Thanksgiving 2001):83.

20. J. Bowyer Bell, in Livingston et al., 1978, 42.

21. Ibid., 42.

22. Brian Knowlton, "Bush Sees Threat to 'Civilization' from Terrorists," *International Herald Tribune*, 7 November 2001, 1, 8; Karen De Young and Michael Dobbbs, "Evolving Terror Tactics Join Old Theology with New Technology," *International Herald Tribune*, 17 September 2001, 1, 6.

23. Uri Avnery, "To Understand Terrorism, Trace Its Bloodline," *USA Today*, 21 (November 2000): A17.

24. For a critical discussion and application, see William D. Coplin and Charles W. Kegley Jr., eds., *Analyzing International Relations: A Multimethod Introduction* (New York: Praeger, 1979); and Charles W. Kegley Jr. and Gregory A. Raymond, *From War to Peace* (Belmont, Calif.: Wadsworth, 2002).

PART ONE

The Changing Characteristics of Twenty-First Century Global Terrorism

•

Chapter 1

INTERNATIONAL TERRORISM: THE OTHER WORLD WAR

BRIAN M. JENKINS

"The Third World War has started," the notorious terrorist Carlos told his hostages in Vienna in 1975. A french soldier in Beirut, a survivor of the suicide terrorist bombing that killed 58 of his comrades, made a similar observation: "Our 58 comrades are perhaps the first deaths of the Third World War." Unlike the wars of the past, this war did not begin with one identifiable event. Indeed, no one can say for certain when or where it began.

It is not the war the . . . military [of national governments] has trained for. There are no massed armor formations pouring across a central front, no divisions on the march, no scramble of fighter aircraft. It is, rather, a hundred wars waged by elusive and ruthless foes. They operate under diverse banners: the Red Army Faction, the Red Brigades, the Armed Forces of National Liberation, the Revolutionary Armed Forces, the Revolutionary Army of the People, the Popular Front, the Holy War.

It is a conflict for which we are inadequately prepared . . . [Embassies] have been destroyed, . . . citizens have been kidnapped and killed . . . jet fighters have been blown up on the ground. . . .

If [the] losses are numerically small compared to those suffered in more conventional combat, they are nevertheless symbolically and politically significant. Terrorists have . . . demonstrated the difficulties . . . in striking back. They have compelled us to divert increasing resources to protect ourselves and our facilities against their attacks. [In the United States, the] Joint Chiefs of Staff, the Secretary of Defense, the Secretary of State, and even the President live behind concrete barriers, visible reminders of [their] vulnerability.

The Definition of Terrorism

When we talk about terrorism, what exactly are we talking about? How does terrorism differ from ordinary crime? Is all politically motivated violence terrorism? Is terrorism synonymous with guerrilla war, or is the term properly reserved for those trying to overthrow governments? Can governments also be terrorists? What is the distinction between driving a truck loaded with explosives into an embassy and dropping high explosives on a city? How do we make useful distinctions? Virtually all discussions about terrorism sooner or later wander into the swamp of definition.

The term "terrorism" has no precise or widely accepted definition. If it were a mere matter of description, establishing a definition would be simple: Terrorism is violence or the threat of violence calculated to create an atmosphere of fear and alarm—in a word, to terrorize—and thereby bring about some social or political change. This is pretty close to the definition offered by a South American jurist more than [35] years ago, i.e., terrorism consists of acts that in themselves may be classic forms of crime—murder, arson, the use of explosives—but that differ from classic crimes in that they are executed "with the deliberate intention of causing panic, disorder, and terror within an organized society."

But while this definition puts terrorism in the realm of crime, we live in a world that recognizes the legitimacy of war and the right of revolution. At the turn of the 20th century, socialist revolutionaries in Russia were proud to call themselves terrorists. They had a terrorist arm called appropriately the Terrorist Brigade, and they hoped through selective assassination to inspire terror among Russia's ruling elite. They were careful not to injure bystanders, and if their intended victim was accompanied by members of his family, they would abort their attack. Ironically, today's terrorists are less fastidious about their actions and more concerned about their public image. In the age of mass media, *terrorism* has become a pejorative term. Terrorists now call themselves anything but terrorists.

Nobody is a terrorist who "stands for a just cause," Yasir Arafat told the United Nations. If we accept Arafat's statement, the problem of definition is further complicated, since the validity of causes must be inserted into the criteria. As a result, only to the extent that everyone in the world can agree on the justice of a particular cause is there likely to be agreement that an action is or is not a terrorist action.

Some governments are prone to label as terrorism all violent acts committed by their political opponents, while antigovernment extremists frequently claim to be the victims of government terror. Use of the term thus implies a moral judgment. If one group can successfully attach the label *terrorist* to its opponent, then it has indirectly persuaded others to adopt its moral and political point of view, or at least to reject the terrorists' view. Terrorism is what the bad guys do. This drawing of boundaries between what is legitimate and what is illegitimate, between the *right* way to fight and the *wrong* way to fight, brings high political stakes to the task of definition.

Terrorism in recent years has become a fad word that is promiscuously applied to a variety of violent acts which are not necessarily intended to produce terror. It is important to distinguish between actions that are intended to terrorize and actions that just happen to terrify. Muggers may terrify the population of a large urban area, but they produce terror as a by-product of their crimes; their objectives are wallets and watches, not alarm.

The difficulty in defining terrorism has led to the cliché that one man's terrorist is another man's freedom fighter. The phrase implies that there can be no objective definition of terrorism, that there are no universal standards of conduct in conflict. However, civilized nations have through law identified modes of conduct that are criminal. Homicide, kidnapping, threats to life, and the willful destruction of property appear in the criminal codes of every country. True, some of the prohibitions may legally be violated in times of war— the law against killing, for example, may be violated by those we call "lawful combatants." Terrorists claim to be not criminals, but soldiers at war who are therefore privileged to break ordinary laws. But even in war, there are rules that outlaw the use of certain weapons and tactics.

The rules of war grant civilian noncombatants who are not associated with "valid" targets at least theoretical immunity from deliberate attack. They prohibit taking hostages. They prohibit violence against those held captive. They define belligerents. They define neutral territory. These rules are sometimes violated—and in these cases, those responsible for the violations become war criminals. But violations in no way diminish the validity of the rules.

Some international lawyers see the laws of war as a possible solution to the dilemma of definition. They suggest that rather than trying to negotiate new treaties on terrorism which are not likely to be ratified or enforced, nations should apply the laws of war, to which almost all have agreed. Terrorists, they say, should be dealt with as soldiers who commit atrocities. Nearly all countries have agreed to try or extradite soldiers who commit atrocities in international armed conflicts. Why should persons not explicitly granted soldiers' status be given greater leeway to commit violence than soldiers have? Under the laws-of-war approach, terrorism would comprise all acts committed in peacetime that, if committed during war, would constitute war crimes.

Terrorism can be objectively defined by the quality of the act, but not by the identity of the perpetrators or the nature of their cause. All terrorist acts are crimes, and many would also be war crimes or "grave breaches" of the rules of war if we accepted the terrorists' assertion that they wage war. All involve violence or the threat of violence, sometimes coupled with explicit demands. The violence is frequently directed against civilian targets. The purposes are political. The actions are often carried out in a way that will achieve maximum publicity. The perpetrators are usually members of an organized group. Their organizations are by necessity clandestine, but unlike other criminals, terrorists often claim credit for their acts. And finally—the hallmark of terrorism—the acts are intended to produce psychological effects beyond the immediate physical damage.

While these criteria do not eliminate all ambiguity, they enable us to draw some limits and answer some of the questions. Terrorism differs from ordinary crime in its political purpose and in its primary objective. Neither the ordinary bank robber nor the man who shot President Reagan is a terrorist. Likewise, not all politically motivated violence is terrorism. The Minuteman of the American Revolution and the rebel in Central America both have political motives, but they are not automatically terrorists. Terrorism is not synonymous with guerrilla war or any other kind of war, and it is not reserved exclusively for those trying to overthrow governments. The leftist assassin and the right-wing death squad secretly working under the direction of a Ministry of Interior both use the same tactics for the same purpose—to instill fear and alter a political situation.

Differing Concepts of Conflict

International terrorism comprises those terrorist incidents that have clear international consequences: incidents in which terrorists go abroad to strike their targets, stay at home but select victims because of their connections to a foreign state (e.g., diplomats or the executives of foreign corporations), or attack international lines of commerce (e.g., airliners). It excludes the considerable amount of terrorist violence carried out by terrorists operating within their own country against their own nationals and in many countries by governments against their own citizens. For example, Irish terrorists blowing up other Irishmen in Belfast would not be counted as international terrorists, nor would Italian terrorists kidnapping Italian officials in Italy.

This definition of international terrorism reflects the particular concern of the United States and the handful of other governments frequently targeted by terrorists abroad. The issue here is not the general problem of political violence or terrorism, or the causes of the conflicts that give rise to terrorist violence. These are domestic matters. The unit of measure is the spillover of this violence into the international domain. But why, terrorists might ask, should they play by the established rules of diplomacy and war when these rules were contrived by a small group of primarily Western nations for their own advantage, and when they deprive groups without recognized governments, territory, or armies from exercising their "right" to resort to violence?

The terrorists of today see no essential difference between the local authority they fight against and the diplomatic and commercial representatives of foreign powers. All terrorists, from the urban guerrillas in South America to the Palestinian fighters in the Middle East, have incorporated the Marxist concept of imperialism. It has become an article of faith in Third World thinking. The banker in Manhattan, the embassy in Montevideo, the local subsidiary of the multinational corporation, the President in his office are all links in a chain of economic exploitation and political repression. It is a concept shared also by the "irregulars" in North America, Western Europe, and Japan who consider themselves to be the auxiliary forces of a Third World revolution.

Many Third World governments, particularly those in Africa and Asia, do not always cooperate with American and European efforts to identify and combat international terrorism, not because these governments approve of terrorist tactics, but because they see the antiterrorist efforts as part of a broader campaign aimed at outlawing the irregular methods of warfare that were developed in the Third World during the civil war in China and the anti-colonial struggles in Asia and Africa. Not a few of the Third World's insurgent chiefs—and today's leaders—were once called terrorists themselves. Their governments, particularly the ones that lack the tools of modern conventional war, therefore deliberately exclude from their definition of terrorism other means of struggle—"wars of liberation," or guerrilla warfare—which they once employed or which are now being employed on behalf of causes they support.

The position of international terrorism taken by the Third World governments is consistent with the position they took at the Geneva negotiations to revise the laws of war. There, they sought to extend the rights and protections of the original Geneva Conventions to irregular forces as well as regular soldiers in international wars. They noted that the Geneva Conventions and other treaties regulating war had been drafted by Europeans to regulate warfare among Europeans, but that they omitted from "international warfare" military force used by the Europeans in gaining and maintaining colonies. In other words, when Europeans shot at Europeans, it was a closely regulated affair, but when Europeans shot at Africans or Asians, they could do what they wanted. The Third World governments feared that the Americans and Europeans now wanted to brand the irregular methods used by the natives to fight back as "terrorism" and thereby outlaw them.

Their rejection of this unequal state of affairs was reflected in the long-winded definition of international terrorism proposed by a group of non-aligned nations in 1973, which included "acts of violence and other repressive acts by colonial, racist and alien regimes against peoples struggling for their liberation . . . ; tolerating or assisting by a State the organizations of the remnants of fascists or mercenary groups whose terrorist activity is directed against other sovereign countries; acts of violence committed by individuals or groups of individuals which endanger or take innocent human lives or jeopardize fundamental freedoms, [provided this definition does] not affect the inalienable rights to self-determination and independence of all peoples under colonial and racist regimes and other forms of alien domination."

It must be remembered that this debate about what constitutes international terrorism originally began in the early 1970s, when guerrilla armies still fought for independence in Portugese Angola and Mozambique, against white supremacist governments in Rhodesia and South Africa, for "national liberation" in Indochina, and for the recovery of a Palestinian homeland in the Middle East—causes which evoked considerable support in the Third World.

Even though governments have not been able to agree on a common definition of terrorism, they have achieved a modest degree of cooperation in dealing with certain aspects of the problem. This has been attained by avoiding definition altogether and identifying specific terrorist tactics that concern all nations. For example, most nations have signed and generally have abided by the various international conventions against hijacking and sabotage of aircraft. Not surprisingly, the world's diplomats have been able to agree that diplomats should not be targets of terrorist violence and have signed the *Convention on the Prevention and Punishment of Crimes Against Internationally Protected Persons*. A broader degree of cooperation has been achieved in smaller international forums, such as the [G-8 Summit or the European Union], where political consensus is more easily reached.

The Theory of Terrorism: Aimed at the People Watching

Present-day terrorism derives largely from twentieth century theories of guerrilla warfare, for which Mao Zedong deserves the most credit, although his paramount concern for winning the support of the masses would probably have made him reject the tactics of contemporary terrorism. During the civil war in China, Mao formulated a series of relationships that differed both from conventional military strategies and from earlier Marxist theories of revolution. He placed greater emphasis on military power than the earlier Marxists did. They relied primarily on political organization, seeing the military portion of the revolution as a final assault on government buildings. This had not worked in China. Mao had to wage a long war, but because his forces were numerically and technologically inferior to those of his opponents, he had to substitute political power for conventional military power. With superior political motivation, Mao reasoned, guerrillas strengthened by the support of the Chinese peasants could survive military reverses and wage a protracted military campaign that would wear down their opponents.

Mao's concept of a "people's war," elaborated in the insurgent movements of the 1950s and 1960s, freed strategists from thinking about warfare exclusively in terms of more soldiers and better armaments. It allowed determined revolutionaries who lacked conventional military power to take on militarily superior forces, with some hope of ultimately defeating them. Perhaps it accorded too much weight to political motivation and determination—both very subjective factors—because it has convinced later revolutionaries that a few pistols and their own political convictions (which they always judge superior to everyone else's) could guarantee them eventual victory.

Mao suggested that guerrillas must aim for and depend upon the political mobilization of people who are mere bystanders in a conventional military conflict. Mao thus introduced a relationship between military action and the attitude and response of the audience. This added a new dimension to armed conflict: Instead of gauging success primarily in terms of the physical effect that military action had on the enemy, strategists could now say that the effect a violent action has on the people watching may be independent of, and may equal or even exceed in importance the actual physical damage inflicted on the foe. Terrorism is that proposition pursued to its most violent extreme, though terrorists have not been very good at explaining it.

"Political power grows from the barrel of a gun," wrote Mao, a phrase contemporary terrorists are fond of repeating. Their own thinking apparently stops at the muzzle. In recent years, terrorists have turned out thousands of pages of manifestos, manuals, assessments, directives, claims, communiqués, commentaries, critiques, and self-criticisms, but they have yet to articulate a clear and convincing theory to explain just how laying a bomb here or pulling a trigger there relates to the achievement of their objectives. What emerges from this vast body of angry literature are declarations, slogans, exhortations, unjustified assumptions, unproved assertions, and generally poor analysis. Carlos Marighella's *Mini Manual of the Urban Guerrilla,* which is supposed to have inspired and instructed the first generation of terrorists in Latin America and Western Europe, offers at best a discussion of terrorist tactics. (Marighella, a renegade from the Brazilian Communist Party, died in a gun battle with Brazilian police—hardly a model of success to be emulated.) Today's terrorists offer no theory, no doctrine, no strategy, not even an inspiring vision of the future.

Most outsiders find it difficult to understand how the killing of Olympic athletes in Munich or the hijacking of an airliner in Rome is supposed to ease the plight of Palestinians in the Middle East, or how blowing up an office in Manhattan will help topple a dictator in Latin America. And terrorists themselves may argue with each other over whether a particular action helps or hurts their cause. Some terrorist attacks may appear to be random or directed against targets that are not directly related to the terrorists' cause. For this reason, terrorist acts are often dismissed as *mindless* violence, *senseless* violence, or *irrational* violence; but terrorism is seldom mindless or irrational.

If it is not mindless, terrorism must have purpose—but what? To answer that question, we must try to think like terrorists and see beyond the apparent meaninglessness—sometimes even the tragic absurdity—of a single terrorist act, to discern its objectives.

The objectives of terrorism are not those of conventional combat. Terrorists do not try to take and hold ground or physically destroy their opponent's forces. They usually lack the kind of power needed to pursue such goals. Instead, terrorists attempt by their acts to inspire and manipulate fear, for a variety of purposes.

Terrorism may be aimed at gaining publicity. Terrorists hope that dramatic and shocking incidents of violence will attract attention to their cause and make them appear to be a force to be reckoned with. The atmosphere of fear and alarm they create frequently causes people to exaggerate the importance of the terrorists' cause and the strength of their forces and their movement. Because most terrorist groups are small and weak, the violence they carry out must be all the more dramatic and deliberately shocking.

Terrorist attacks are often carefully choreographed to attract the attention of the electronic media and the international press. The victims themselves often mean nothing to the terrorists. Terrorism is aimed at the people watching, not at the actual victims. Terrorism is theater.

Individual acts of terrorism also may be aimed at extracting specific concessions, such as the payment of ransom, the release of prisoners, or the publication of a terrorist message. Terrorists often seek to improve their bargaining power by creating a dramatic hostage situation that might coerce a government into meeting their demands.

The seizure of Israeli athletes at the 1972 Munich Olympiad had two objectives: publicity and concessions. The terrorists demanded that the government of Israel release a number of their imprisoned comrades. Israel rejected the demands, but the millions of people watching the Olympics on worldwide television guaranteed the terrorists the publicity they sought. Abu Iyad, the reputed architect of the attack, summarized the results: "The sacrifices made by the Munich heroes were not entirely in vain. They didn't bring about the liberation of any of their comrades imprisoned in Israel . . . but they did obtain the operation's other two objectives: World opinion was forced to take note of the Palestinian drama, and the Palestinian people imposed their presence on an international gathering that had sought to exclude them."

Terrorism also may be aimed at causing widespread disorder, demoralizing society, and breaking down the existing social and political order. These objectives are typical of revolutionary, nihilistic, or anarchistic terrorists. Terrorists condemn society's normal rules and relationships as intolerable complacency. Dramatic acts of terrorism, they think, will awaken an army of potential supporters who slumber in apathy. If the benefits of political obedience are destroyed, if the complacency of uninvolvement is not allowed, if the government's inability to protect its citizens (which is the origin of and basic reason for the existence of government) is revealed, if there is no place to hide in the ensuing battle, if people are forced to choose sides, then, terrorists presume, the "people" will join the opponents of the government and a revolution will be carried out.

Impatient at the reluctance of the "people" to join them, terrorists may deliberately aim at provoking repression. In the terrorists' mind, the government, alarmed by continued terrorist attacks, will be compelled to strike back brutally, and perhaps blindly. The heavy hand of repression will fall upon the masses, whose discontent can then be mobilized by the terrorists.

This idea was colorfully expressed by the Basque terrorists who wrote, "The enemy, as a massive animal, stung by many bees, is infuriated to the point of uncontrollable rage, and strikes out blindly to the left and right—on every side. At this point we have achieved one of our major objectives, forcing him to commit a thousand atrocities and brutal acts. The majority of his victims are innocent. Then the people—to this point more or less passive and waiting—become indignant and in reaction turn to us. We could not hope for a better outcome."

Another powerful motivation for terrorist actions is revenge. Small groups who have lost close comrades are particularly likely to strike back ferociously. A Puerto Rican separatist group detonated a bomb in a Wall Street restaurant in an obvious effort to cause casualties. The attack was in revenge for a bomb that was allegedly detonated by government authorities in a cafe frequented by separatists in Puerto Rico. Revenge becomes less important in larger organizations, where the deaths of comrades are accepted as losses in combat.

Finally, terrorism may be used to enforce obedience. This is the usual purpose of state or official terrorism, but terrorists themselves may also employ violence against their own members to discourage betrayal. The outcome desired is a prescribed pattern of behavior: obedience to the state or to the cause, and full cooperation in identifying and rooting out infiltrators or enemies. In recent years, governments have extended their reach to émigrés and exiles, hiring terrorists or employing their own agents to attack foes of the regime in other countries. Libya openly avowed its campaign to murder "traitors living abroad" as a warning to all dissidents. Syria, Iran, Yugoslavia, Bulgaria, and Romania have all been accused of killing defectors and troublesome exiles in Western Europe.

The success of such terrorism again depends on the creation of an atmosphere of fear, reinforced by the seeming omnipresence of the internal security or terrorist apparatus. Like other forms of terrorism, that aimed at enforcing obedience contains elements of deliberate drama: defectors are abducted or mysteriously assassinated, stories (often real) are spread of dungeons and torture. The objective is to frighten and alarm the target audience. In contrast to other forms of terrorism, however, terrorism for the purpose of enforcement seldom involves victims chosen at random, and the terrorists do not usually seek widespread publicity. It aims at the influence and control of its "own" population or organization....

Terrorist Tactics: A Limited Repertoire

Terrorists operate with a limited tactical repertoire. Six basic terrorist tactics comprise 95 percent of all terrorist incidents: bombings, assassinations, armed assaults, kidnappings, barricade and hostage situations, and hijackings. No terrorist group uses all of them. Bombings, generally the least demanding of the tactics, predominate. Explosives are easy to obtain or manufacture, and a bombing requires little organization—one person can do the job, with little risk. Bombings alone account for roughly half of all international terrorist incidents.

This tactical repertoire has changed little over time. Terrorists appear to be more imitative than innovative, although their tactics have changed in response to new defenses. For example, seizing embassies, a popular terrorist tactic in the 1970s, declined in the 1980s for several reasons. Nations began turning their embassies into virtual fortresses, making takeovers more difficult. Governments also changed their policies. Whereas they were initially inclined to yield to the demands of terrorists holding hostages, governments began to adopt hardline policies as terrorist kidnappings and hostage seizures continued. Officials refused to release prisoners (the most frequent terrorist demand) or make other serious concessions.

The Israeli government refused to offer concessions to the terrorists holding Israeli athletes hostage at the Munich Olympics in 1972. In 1973, the United States refused to yield to the demands of terrorists holding American diplomats in Khartoum. In 1975, the German government refused to yield to the demands of terrorists holding the German embassy in Stockholm, the Irish government refused to yield to the demands of the surrounded kidnappers of a Dutch businessman, the Dutch government refused to yield to terrorists who had seized the Indonesian consulate, and the British government refused to yield to the terrorists holding hostages in London. There were exceptions, of course; terrorists occasionally won concessions. But overall, the likelihood that their demands would be met declined almost 50 percent in the latter half of the 1970s.

Unwilling to make concessions or stand by and do nothing while terrorists shot hostages, governments increasingly resorted to force to end barricade and hostage episodes at home and abroad, using forces they had created for the task. In the wake of the 1972 Munich incident, which ended in a disastrous shootout and the deaths of all of the hostages, governments began to develop specialized hostage-rescue units.

The tide turned in the second half of the 1970s. In 1976, Israeli commandos successfully rescued hostages held at Entebbe Airport in Uganda. In 1977, German commandos successfully rescued passengers aboard a hijacked airliner in Mogadishu. That same year, Dutch commandos successfully stormed a hijacked train and a school both held by South Moluccan terrorists. In 1980, British commandos rescued hostages held in the Iranian embassy in London. Some of the rescue attempts failed, notably the American attempt to rescue U.S. hostages held in Iran. But the message was clear: Terrorists who barricaded themselves with hostages risked capture or death.

As security measures improved, the terrorists' chances of obtaining concessions declined, and the probability of their being captured or killed went up. Not surprisingly, seizing embassies declined as a terrorist tactic. At the same time, however, terrorist attacks in general, and attacks on diplomats in particular, increased. Terrorists merely changed their tactics, turning to assassinations and bombings.

This ability to switch tactics is a major reason why defending against terrorism is so difficult. Security measures can protect one set of targets against one type of attack, but terrorists can alter their tactics or shift their sights to other targets, obviating rather than overcoming the security measures, thus requiring new security measures to be devised. Unfortunately, the situation is asymmetrical. Unlike regular soldiers, terrorists do not have to attack at a certain time and place. Since many possible targets will satisfy their political needs, terrorists can strike practically anything or anyone they decide is a suitable target; they can attack almost anywhere, at any time. Because of limitations on resources, however, and because they prefer not to become garrison states, governments cannot protect everything, everywhere, all the time. This asymmetry also means an inequality of effort between terrorist attackers and anti-terrorist defenders. The amount of resources required for defense against terrorism is determined not by the very small number of the terrorists, but rather by the virtually unlimited number of targets to be defended. This makes terrorism a cheap way to fight and a costly kind of threat to defend against....

State-Sponsored Terrorism: A New Mode of Conflict

[State] sponsorship of terrorism [represents another disturbing trend]. A growing number of governments are using terrorist tactics themselves or employing terrorist groups as a mode of surrogate warfare. These governments see in terrorism a useful capability, a "weapons system," a cheap means of waging war against domestic foes or another nation rather than against a political or social structure. Terrorists offer a possible alternative to open, interstate armed conflict. Modern conventional war is increasingly impractical—it is destructive, it is expensive, and it is dangerous. World, and sometimes domestic, opinion imposes constraints. Some nations that are unable to mount a conventional military challenge see terrorism as the only alternative: an "equalizer."

Growing state sponsorship of terrorism has serious consequences. It puts more resources in the hands of the terrorists: money, sanctuary, sophisticated munitions, intelligence, and technical expertise. It also reduces the constraints on them, permitting them to contemplate large-scale operations without worrying so much about alienating their perceived constituents or provoking public backlash, since they need not depend on the local population for support.

Without the need to finance themselves through bank robberies or ransom kidnappings, and without the need to carry out operations just to maintain group cohesion, state-sponsored terrorist groups operate less frequently than groups that receive little or no state support, but they are many times more lethal and have far greater operational reach.

Middle Eastern groups like Black June (*Al-Assifa*), which has carried out assassinations in Western Europe, the Middle East, and Asia, and Islamic Jihad, the Shi'ite Moslem extremist group that claimed credit for the suicide bombings of the American and French embassies in Beirut and Kuwait and the U.S. Marine barracks, fall under the heading of state-sponsored groups. The 1983 bombing that killed 17 South Korean officials in Rangoon was an example of a country, in this case North Korea, sending its own agents to assassinate another country's leaders.

We may be on the threshold of an era of armed conflict in which limited conventional warfare, guerrilla warfare, and international terrorism will coexist, with governments and sub-national entities employing them individually, interchangeably, sequentially, or simultaneously—and having to defend against them.

Warfare in the future may be less destructive than that in . . . the twentieth century, but it may also be less coherent. Warfare will cease to be finite. The distinction between war and peace will become more ambiguous and complex. Armed conflict will not be confined by national frontiers. Local belligerents will mobilize foreign patrons. Terrorists will attack foreign targets both at home and abroad. It will be necessary to develop capabilities to deal with—if not wage—all three modes of armed conflict, *perhaps simultaneously.* . . .

Chapter 2

THE NEW FACE OF COMBAT: TERRORISM AND IRREGULAR WARFARE IN THE 21ST CENTURY

MICHAEL T. KLARE

The September 11 terrorist assaults on New York and Washington, no less than the 1941 Japanese attack on Pearl Harbor and the 1945 nuclear strikes on Hiroshima and Nagasaki, have fundamentally altered the landscape of global conflict. Before September 11, most analysts assumed that the next major American war would entail all-out combat with the well-equipped armies of a modern state, such as Iran or China; instead, U.S. forces are now engaged in a global struggle against a secretive, multinational terrorist organization backed by a clique of religious fanatics. What we are seeing, in fact, is an entirely *new system* of warfare. The industrial-style fighting methods that prevailed in most of the wars of the 20th century have been replaced by a different mode of combat: post-industrial warfare.

Post-industrial warfare is distinguishable from earlier systems of combat in a number of ways. Most important, it relies on irregular forces (often of a non-state character) plus unconventional methods of fighting to inflict disproportionate damage on more powerful conventional forces. In place of traditional, "heavy metal" weapons—tanks, combat planes, warships, and so on—it employs cheap, low-tech weapons and commercially-available technologies (including biotechnology) to defeat an opponent. And, while the practitioners of such combat often espouse backward-looking ideologies, they seek to exploit every innovation of modern technology to their advantage.

All of these characteristics were evident in the September 11 terror attack. The perpetrators of the assault were self-made warriors, not professional soldiers in an established state's armed forces. In place of firearms, they carried penknives and box-cutters; instead of combat planes, they used civilian airliners filled with aviation fuel to obliterate their targets. While motivated by an extremely conservative form of Islam, they employed e-mail, computers, and other modern systems to expedite their operations.

Of course, guerrillas, outlaws, and revolutionaries have always relied on unconventional means of warfare to defeat more powerful foes. In this sense, the September 11 attack was but a modern variant of a familiar form of combat. But there is much about this event, and the larger terror campaign of which it is a part, that distinguishes it from similar episodes in the past. This is not the work of a localized insurgency against a particular ruler or authority; it is a global assault on the very structure of modern, Western society. And yet, for all of its anti-Western ideology, it is a campaign that is thoroughly rooted in the high-tech, transnational processes of globalization.

Nor is Al Qaeda, the terror organization believed responsible for the September 11 attack, the only violent group to exhibit these characteristics. Around the world, many other insurgent and outlaw entities that employ a similar mix of post-industrial tactics. In Sri Lanka, for example, the rebel Tamil Tigers have utilized a sophisticated, world-spanning procurement network to obtain advanced explosives for a relentless campaign of suicide bombings at important sites in Colombo, the nation's capital. In Sierra Leone, rebel forces use machetes to maim and mutilate civilians caught in their path while using globalized trade channels to sell their diamonds on the international market. The drug cartels and their guerrilla partners in Colombia have established an international banking system as sophisticated as those employed by the large multinational corporations.

The U.S. Department of Defense uses the term "asymmetrical operations" to describe tactics of this sort. Such operations, the Department's 1999 *Annual Report* states, represent an attempt by America's adversaries "to circumvent or undermine U.S. strengths while exploiting its weaknesses, using methods that differ significantly from the usual mode of U.S. operations." President George W. Bush and Secretary of Defense Donald Rumsfeld have made frequent use of this term to describe the September 11 assault and other terrorist attacks by Al Qaeda. But "asymmetry" only describes one aspect of these attacks—the use of unconventional methods by a weaker party against the strong. It fails to capture other aspects of the emerging combat milieu, including the anti-modern, anti-Western ideology of many outlaw forces combined with the use of "off-the-shelf" commercial technologies to foil the industrial-era weaponry of the major powers.

The United States military is now engaged in a global "war against terrorism"—a campaign that by definition entails a clash between industrial and post-industrial modes of combat. Other wars of the future are also likely to exhibit this sort of confrontation. As a result, future battles will look very different from those of the past, with surprising and possibly disturbing outcomes.

The New Combatants

For most of the twentieth century, the practice of warfare—as it was commonly understood—entailed a clash between the regular armed forces of established states. To prevail in such contests, most nations sought to assemble modern military forces and to provide those forces with as many guns, tanks, aircraft, and ships as it could afford. This, in turn, required the mobilization of the nation's scientific and industrial capabilities for the design, development, and production of ever-more potent military systems—a process that culminated in the introduction of the nuclear bomb. Following the 1945 nuclear strikes on Hiroshima and Nagasaki, every major power sought to acquire nuclear weapons of their own, or to align themselves with a nuclear-armed superpower. Under these circumstances, it was widely assumed that any major war of the future—a World War III—would produce human casualties on an unprecedented scale.

The end of the Cold War greatly diminished the risk of a global nuclear exchange, but did not erase the common association between the concept of "war" and the mobilization of industrial resources for the development and production of modern weapons. Since 1990, however, the emphasis has been on the development of high-tech conventional munitions rather than nuclear weapons and ballistic missiles. America's concentrated use of airpower and "smart" munitions during the Persian Gulf war of 1991 and the Kosovo campaign of 1999 has become the new standard of combat that all other major powers seek to emulate.

These state-based efforts to develop increasingly capable professional armies have had a paradoxical effect: as the costs and risks of a major military encounter between the regular forces of established states have risen, the inclination of most governments to engage in such action has greatly diminished. As a result, the outbreak of interstate warfare has become a relatively rare occurrence. Of the 50 armed conflicts that broke out in the 1990s, only four entailed combat between two or more states, and only one—the Persian Gulf war—involved all-out fighting between large numbers of air, ground, and sea forces. "As the 20th century approached its end," Martin van Crevald wrote in the *Naval War College Review,* "major interstate wars appeared to be on the retreat."

Although interstate combat has become rare, internal conflict involving non-state actors—insurgents, terrorists, brigands, warlords, ethnic militias, and so on—has become quite common. Such conflict can take several forms: revolutionary (or fundamentalist) struggles to replace existing authorities with more ideologically (or religiously) "correct" regimes; nationalistic campaigns by repressed minorities in multi-ethnic states to break off a piece of territory and create an ethnically pure state of their own; and efforts by local warlords to gain control of valuable resources—gold mines, diamond fields, rare timber stands, and the like—for their personal benefit. Almost all of the wars now under way around the world fit into one or another of these categories.

Conflicts of this sort may arise from distinctive local conditions, but most exhibit certain characteristics in common. Typically, the forces involved are composed of non-professional soldiers who are recruited from the local population on the basis of ideological or religious fervor, unabashed greed, or a lust for combat—or some combination of all three. Most of these combatants are young men (in many cases, teenage boys) who are attracted by the camaraderie and sense of purpose of such forces, or the opportunity to earn a regular income (in what are often economically depressed areas). The ranks of both the Taliban and the Northern Alliance forces were full of such men and boys. Combatants of this sort rarely possess the learning or skills to operate high-tech weapons, but are perfectly capable of wielding a club or firing an AK-47 assault rifle into a crowd of unprotected civilians.

Unconventional forces of this type usually operate in a remote and inaccessible part of the country, or in urban slums and shantytowns. Given their outlaw status, they cannot draw on the state's financial and industrial resources, and so must arm themselves with the limited weaponry at hand—hunting weapons, stolen pistols and rifles, black-market firearms, common explosives, and so on. Armies equipped in this manner are no match for the professional forces of an established state, and so normally avoid combat with them. Instead, they seek to undermine government authority by attacking isolated police and army outposts, by disrupting economic activity, and by conducting terrorist strikes on symbolically important urban facilities (such as train stations, banks, and post offices). Because the state in developing countries is often viewed as an agent of modernization, every manifestation of the modern—especially industrial facilities—is considered a legitimate target of attack. As a result, the recent wars in Chechnya, Congo, Liberia, Sierra Leone, and Sri Lanka have become, in effect, wars of de-industrialization.

These conflicts often share another distinguishing characteristic: the marriage of political and religious objectives with criminal forms of resource acquisition. Because non-state combatants are normally barred from participation in the open, legal economy, they must rely on illegal forms of activity to obtain funds to purchase arms and pay their soldiers. This can mean engagement in the illegal drug trade, as is in the case of some local militias in Afghanistan and the various guerrilla groups in Colombia. Other irregular forces, such as the Revolutionary United Front (RUF) of Sierra Leone and the National Union for the Total Independence of Angola (UNITA), rely on illicit sales of diamonds to meet their operating expenses. Still other groups have engaged in kidnaping, extortion, or the sale of protected timber and animal products.

To conduct their illicit endeavors, these non-state actors have been forced to insert themselves, one way or another, in the global underground economy. And because the underground economy operates as a hidden branch of the legal economy, insurgent forces have had to learn to mimic the operating techniques of multinational corporations: opening offshore banking accounts, moving money around the world by wire transfers, establishing foreign offices, using satellite phones and fax machines to transmit instructions, and so on, no matter how opposed to the effects of globalization, these forces have become dependent on the continuing operation of its financial and communications infrastructure. Al Qaeda "is a well-oiled, well-financed organization," Defense Secretary Rumsfeld told reporters in November 2001. "It's got bank accounts, it's got businesses, it's got the ability to talk in codes, it's got all kinds of . . . technologies that were developed in the West."

Low-Tech Weapons/Unconventional Tactics

Non-state actors possess neither the means nor the capacity to operate modern, high-tech weapons of the types found in the arsenals of established nation-states. In any face-to-face battle with a state's regular forces, non-state armies are likely to come out on the losing side. But belligerents of this sort rarely engage in this type of combat, preferring instead to slip away in the night whenever the state marshals its forces for attack. To achieve their objectives— or just to stay alive—rebel and insurgent forces must rely on low-tech weapons and unconventional tactics to overcome the advantages of their more powerful opponents.

In any firefight between a rifle and a tank, the rifle carrier is likely to perish. This has led most modern strategists to denigrate the importance in combat of basic infantry weaponry. But in an internecine struggle over the control of isolated towns and villages, modern assault rifles and rocket-propelled grenades (RPGs) can be employed with devastating effect. According to some estimates, 80 to 90 percent of all casualties inflicted in recent wars have been caused by small arms and light weapons—a category that includes rifles, RPGs, machine guns, lightweight mortars, and man-portable anti-tank weapons. Light weapons of these types can also be used to assassinate government officials, protect illegal drug facilities, and expedite the "ethnic cleansing" of targeted neighborhoods.

Insurgent forces have also made effective use of common explosives to destroy military installations and terrorize civilian populations. Terror bombings in crowded urban settings have, in fact, become an all-too-common feature of contemporary conflict. The Irish Republican Army (IRA), for example, conducted a wave of bombings in major English cities in the late 1990s—one of which, the massive 1996 blast at Canary Wharf in London, killed over one hundred people. The Tamil Tigers of Sri Lanka have made this kind of terror attack a standard technique. The Tigers generally use teenage boys and girls who are persuaded (through promises of eternal fame) to slip into public areas and detonate the explosive charges hidden beneath their clothes—killing themselves in the process.

Suicide bombings have also occurred with regular frequency in the Middle East and achieved their most spectacular results in the World Trade Center attacks of September 11, 2001. But such assaults are just one of the unconventional tactics employed by insurgent and terrorist groups to inflict pain and damage on their more powerful opponents. The systematic assassination of government officials—police officers, tax collectors, school teachers, or anyone else who presents the public face of governmental authority in slums or rural areas—is another common tactic. By eradicating government authority in this manner, the insurgents seek to undermine ordinary people's faith in the ability of the government to provide day-to-day protection, and thus force people to submit to the guerrilla's demands for food, cash, and recruits. This has long been the practice in Colombia's guerrilla-dominated areas, and was a noted feature of the recent fighting in Sierra Leone. Some rebel organizations, such as the Armed Islamic Group of Algeria, have slaughtered the entire population of isolated rural villages in order to demonstrate the impotence of the national government.

Economic warfare is another tactic employed by rebel groups seeking to undermine the power and authority of the established government. In Egypt, for example, militant fundamentalists have attacked foreign visitors at well known archaeological sites—thus producing a sharp drop in tourist income (a major factor in the Egyptian economy). The 1997 raid at the Temple of Hatshepsut in Luxor, for example, resulted in the death of 58 foreigners. (This attack has been attributed to the Islamic Group of Egypt, one of the entities associated with Al Qaeda.) In Colombia, the guerrillas of the National Liberation Army (ELN, by its initials in Spanish) bombed the 480-mile Cano Limón-to-Covenas pipeline 79 times in 1999, causing millions of dollars in damage and lost oil revenues. And while there is no proven case of an insurgent or terrorist group spreading computer viruses to paralyze the information and financial systems of the advanced industrial nations, it is widely believed that "cyber war" of this sort will be a common feature of unconventional warfare in the future.

Most of these techniques, and others like them, have been employed by Al Qaeda in its campaign to undermine pro-Western governments in the Middle East and to eject U.S. forces from the region. Terrorist bombings were conducted on U.S. facilities in Saudi Arabia (1995 and 1996), U.S. embassies in Kenya and Tanzania (1998), and the USS *Cole* in Yemen (2000). Al Qaeda has also been linked to guerrilla and terrorist activities in other locations, including Egypt, Indonesia, Kashmir, the Philippines, Somalia, Uzbekistan, and Yemen. To finance its operations, Al Qaeda has engaged in various forms of licit and illicit commerce, including the sale of illegal narcotics. But it was the September 11 assault on the Pentagon and the World Trade Center that most dramatically revealed the organization's capacity for daring and improvisation, entailing the use of civilian airliners as flying super-bombs.

The September 11 attacks are also revealing in terms of the terrorists' approach to technology. While supposedly disdaining everything Western, the soldiers in Osama bin Laden's multinational army (and others like it) are fully prepared to make use of modern, Information Age technologies—cell phones, computers, e-mail, the Internet, international banking networks, mass communications—whenever it suits their purpose. "The new wars make use of new technology," Mary Kaldor of the London School of Economics wrote in 1997. "In particular, modern communications are crucial in coordinating horizontally organized military units, for propaganda, and for connecting transnational [terror] networks."

Insurgent and terrorist organizations have also sought to employ modern pharmaceutical technologies to manufacture biological warfare (BW) agents. Although no firm link had been established by early 2002 between the terrorists responsible for the September 11 hijack attacks and the anthrax outbreaks that plagued parts of the United States in the following weeks, it is believed that Al Qaeda and other extremist groups have considered the use of BW agents in attacks on civilian populations. The Aum Shinrikyo cult in Japan, for example, experimented with the use of anthrax as a terror weapon before deciding to release chemical weapons in the Tokyo subways. The technologies used to produce BW weapons are closely related to those used in non-military pharmaceutical research efforts; because these technologies have been widely disseminated in recent years, it is possible for underground organizations like Al Qaeda to obtain BW-related equipment and materials from scores of locations around the world.

Globalization and Its Discontents

The use of modern technology by insurgent and terrorist organizations is part of another distinctive aspect of post-industrial warfare: the close relationship between economic globalization and the emergence of new forms and foci of revolt.

Globalization has influenced the outbreak and character of conflict in a number of ways. The creation of a global market has resulted in a growing divide between rich and poor, with new pockets of affluence arising in areas of widespread poverty and stagnation. Rapidly changing class dynamics are often a source of friction but become especially explosive when new class disparities correspond to long-standing ethnic and religious divisions. Thus, while globalization has improved living conditions in some areas, it has also increased the risk of conflict in others. As noted by the U.S. Defense Department-funded Institute for National Security Studies (INSS) in its *Strategic Assessment* for 1999, "forces associated with economic globalization have threatened near-term stability in several key countries, aggravated social and economic tensions, and increased the potential for backlash against globalization."

This tendency is especially prevalent in parts of Africa, the Middle East, and Southeast Asia, where economic growth has lagged behind other regions or has left some populations in a stagnant or declining position. When the 1997 Asian economic crisis spread to Indonesia, for example, many indigenous Indonesians turned against the resident Chinese community, which was viewed (not always accurately) as having benefitted disproportionately from the "crony capitalism" of the Suharto era. More recently, continuing economic decline appears to have exacerbated tensions between Indonesian Muslims and Christians in the Moluccas, and between the Acehenese and other inhabitants of Sumatra. Economic grievances have also contributed to the antagonism between Israelis and Palestinians, and between the Tamils and the Sinhalese in Sri Lanka. Similarly, Islamic fundamentalist groups in Egypt and Saudi Arabia have created significant grassroots support by denouncing the lavish lifestyles of the ruling elites.

Economic discontent can also lead to the demonization of globalization itself. "Many nongovernment groups see globalization as serving large corporate interests at the expense of the poor," the INSS reported in 1999. Indeed, precisely such views were articulated by anti-globalization protesters at World Bank meetings in Seattle and Washington D.C. A similar assessment can be seen in the statements of many insurgent organizations, such as the Zapatistas of Mexico and the Revolutionary Armed Forces of Colombia (FARC, by its initials in Spanish).

Globalization is also associated with the intrusion of Western values and behavior patterns into traditional societies, producing anxiety and resentment among those who feel alienated from (or threatened by) the emerging, consumer-based world culture. For some, this has led to nostalgia for an earlier, supposedly more just and puritanical epoch. Many militant followers of Islamic fundamentalism, for example, would like to recreate what they believe to have been the utopian world of the early Muslim era. Some of these believers, including the leaders of the Taliban, are prepared to use armed violence to achieve this purpose.

In some cases, anti-globalization campaigns have taken on a decidedly anti-American character. "Although economic globalization is not the same as Americanization, it is largely driven by Americans," the INSS observed. "U.S. companies are at the forefront of global trade, investment, finance, and information technology." Inevitably, this leads to anti-American sentiments on the part of those who remain immured in poverty. As suggested by the INSS, "The social and economic strains associated with globalization give rise to the charge that the United States is advancing its own commercial interests under a global banner at the expense of the poor."

Globalization is thus a contributing factor in the outbreak of conflict and often determines its particular targets. But, however strongly they may oppose the effects of globalization, many insurgent and terrorist groups rely on its various manifestations to further their revolutionary or reactionary purposes. As noted, this entails the use of modern information and communications technologies such as e-mail and the Internet, as well as advanced biotechnology. Indeed, it is striking just how closely transnational terror groups like Al Qaeda and the Tamil Tigers have come to resemble large multinational corporations, with their far-flung communications, information-processing, and financial networks. It is this, more than anything, that distinguishes the new insurgencies from those of the past.

Implications

The new, post-industrial system of warfare described above poses a significant challenge to the international community and to status-quo powers like the United States. Transnational terrorist organizations like Al Qaeda, and the transnational criminal organizations with which they are often associated, have successfully breached long-standing defense mechanisms to inflict great harm on Western societies. Given their proven capacity for stealth and improvisation, moreover, it is likely that these groups will continue to evade and circumvent the determined efforts now being made to incapacitate them. Political violence and organized criminality will thus remain significant features of the international landscape.

Clearly, to successfully address this challenge it will be necessary to acquire a better understanding of the new system of combat and the development of strategies capable of counteracting its effects. This, in turn, will require a deeper investigation into the various phenomena described above, along with their respective causes and consequences. Ultimately, it will also require a more rigorous effort to chart the many complex links between economic globalization and violent conflict.

Although many belligerents have begun to appreciate—and take advantage of—the distinctive characteristics of the emerging military environment, strategic theory and practice in the United States (and other advanced industrial nations) has not kept pace with developments on the ground. Only by studying and adapting to the exigencies of post-industrial warfare can we successfully overcome the challenges that surely lie ahead.

Chapter 3

THE FOUR WAVES OF REBEL TERROR AND SEPTEMBER 11[1]

DAVID C. RAPOPORT

September 11, 2001, is the most destructive day in the long, bloody history of rebel terrorism. The casualties and the economic damage were unprecedented. It could be the most important day, too. President Bush declared a "war" to eliminate terror,[2] galvanizing a response that could reshape the international world.

Exactly 100 years ago, we heard a similar appeal. An anarchist assassinated President William McKinley in September 1901, moving the new president—Theodore Roosevelt—to summon a worldwide crusade to exterminate terrorism everywhere.[3]

Will we succeed this time? No one knows, but even a brief acquaintance with the history of terrorism should make us more sensitive to the difficulties ahead. To this end, I will briefly describe rebel terrorism in the last 135 years to show how deeply implanted it has become in modern culture. The discussion is divided into two sections. The first describes the four waves of modern terror, and the other focuses on the international ingredients in each. I will discuss the political events triggering each wave, but lack space to enumerate the great and persistent domestic impacts.

Every state affected in the first wave, for example, radically transformed its police organizations. Plainclothes police forces were created as indispensable tools to penetrate underground groups. The Russian *Okrahana,* the British *Special Branch,* and the American FBI are conspicuous examples.[4] The new organizational form remains a permanent, perhaps indispensable, feature of modern life.

Terrorist tactics invariably produce rage and frustration, often driving governments to respond in unanticipated, extraordinary, illegal, and destructive ways. Because a significant Jewish element, for example, was present in the several Russian terrorist movements, the Okrahana organized pogroms to intimidate the Jewish population, compelling many to flee to the West and to the Holy Land. Okrahana fabricated *The Protocols of Zion,* a book that helped stimulate a virulent anti-Semitism that went beyond Russia and continued for decades and influences the Christian and Islamic terrorist worlds still.[5]

Democratic states overreact too. President Theodore Roosevelt proposed sending all Anarchists back to their countries of origin, though many had not committed crimes and were opposed to terror. Roosevelt's proposal was not acted upon; but President Wilson in 1919 authorized Attorney-General Palmer to round up all Anarchists, though many committed no crimes, to ship them to the Soviet Union. That led to the 1920 Wall Street Bombing, which then became the impetus for an immigration quota law making it much more difficult for persons from Southern and Eastern European states (the original home of most anarchists) to immigrate to America for several decades.

The Waves

In the 1880s, an initial "anarchist wave"[6] appeared that continued for some 40 years. Its successor, the "anti-colonial wave," began in the 1920s and by the 1960s had largely disappeared. The late 1960s witnessed the birth of the "new left wave," which dissipated largely in the 1990s, leaving a few groups still active in Sri Lanka, Spain, France, Peru, and Colombia. The fourth or "religious wave" began in 1979, and if it follows the pattern of its predecessors, it still has twenty to twenty-five years to run.

Revolution was the overriding aim in every wave, but revolution was understood differently in each. Most terrorist organizations have understood revolution as secession or national self-determination. That principle, a people should govern itself, was bequeathed by the American and French Revolutions. (The French Revolution also introduced the term *terror* to our vocabulary.[7]) In leaving open the question of what constitutes a "people," the principle is very ambiguous and can lead to endless conflict.

Revolution is also seen to be a radical reconstruction of authority, and this objective was often combined with efforts to create a new state by destroying two or more existing ones. Often the three conceptions were combined in different ways, and all were affected by different preexisting contexts, which makes it useful to give each wave a distinctive name.[8]

The first three waves lasted approximately 40 to 45 years, but the new left wave was somewhat abbreviated. The pattern suggests a human life-cycle pattern, where dreams that inspire fathers lose their attractiveness for the son. Clearly, the life cycle of the waves does not correspond to those of organizations. Organizations normally dissipate before the wave does, though sometimes an organization survives its associated wave. The IRA, for example, is the oldest terrorist organization of the modern world; it began the anti-colonial wave in the 1920s and is still here. By way of comparison, the average life of organizations in the third or new left wave is two years.

The lineage of rebel terror is ancient, going back at least to the first century. Hinduism, Judaism, and Islam produced the Thugs, Zealots, and Assassins respectively; these names are still used to designate terrorists.[9] Religion determined every *purpose* and *each tactic* of this ancient form.

Significant examples of secular rebel terror appeared before the anarchist wave began. The United States, for example, experienced two major successful ones. The Sons of Liberty, provoked by the Stamp Act, organized mobs to tar and feather colonists still loyal to the king,[10] forcing many to flee the country and settle in Canada. The Ku Klux Klan (KKK) forced the federal government to end Reconstruction. But the two American examples were *time and country specific*. They had no contemporary parallels and no emulators, because they "did their dirty work in secret and kept their mouths shut afterwards."[11]

But the Russian experience in the 1880s spread rapidly to other parts of Europe, the Americas, and Asia before reaching its peak and receding. Despite this extraordinary spread of activities and unlike the American examples, *no first-wave group achieved its goal*. The three subsequent waves show similar, though not identical, patterns. Each begins in a different locale and the participating rebel groups often share purposes and tactics that distinguish them from participants in other waves. Local aims are common in all waves, but the crucial fact is that other states are simultaneously experiencing similar activities. The anti-colonial wave produces the most successes, but they are few in number and in every example, the achievement falls short of the stated aim as we shall elaborate below.

Why does the first wave begin in the late nineteenth century? There may be many reasons, but two stand out—doctrine and technology. Russian writers, particularly Nechaev, Bakunin, and Kropotkin, created a doctrine or strategy for terror, an inheritance for successors to use, improve, and transmit. Participants, even those with different ultimate objectives, were now able to learn from each other. The distinctiveness of this pattern is brought home by comparing it with those of the ancient religious terrorists who always stayed within their own religious traditions. Each religious tradition produced its own kind of terrorist, and sometimes their tactics were so uniform that they appear to be a form of ritual. But if one compares Nechaev's *Revolutionary Catechism* with the *Training Manual* Osama bin Laden wrote for Al Qaeda, the paramount desire to learn from the experiences of both friends and enemies is clear.[12] The greatest tactical difference between them is that Nechaev understands women to be priceless assets, while Osama bin Laden defers to the Islamic tradition and employs men only.[13]

The transformation in communication and transportation patterns is the second reason to explain the timing and spread of the first wave. The telegraph, daily mass-distributed newspapers, and railroads flourished in this period; and subsequently throughout the twentieth century technology continued to shrink time and space.

Strangely enough, the characteristics and possibilities of modern revolutionary terror were partly inspired by studying the intrigues of the Russians in the Balkans. The Czars employed assassins against Turkish officials. The Turks responded by massacring Christian subjects, massacres that provoked Christian uprisings, a war fever in Russia. *Publicity* and *provocation*, not pure terror, were the objectives of the Czarist atrocities, and these objectives were incorporated in systematic anarchist efforts to put atrocities at the service of revolution.

Narodnaya Volya ("the People's Will"), the first terrorist group in the first wave, inherited a world where traditional revolutionaries seemed obsolete or irrelevant. No longer could pamphlets, books, meetings, and demonstrations produce mass uprisings. Even revolutionaries described themselves as "idle word spillers!" A "new form of communication" was needed, one that would be heard and command respect. Terror filled that need; no one could ignore it, and repeated acts of terror would generate the polarization necessary for revolution.

The Anarchist doctrine has four major points: (1) Modern society contains huge reservoirs of latent ambivalence and hostility;[14] (2) society muffles and diffuses them by devising moral conventions to generate guilt, provide channels for settling some grievances and securing personal amenities; (3) however, moral conventions that subjugate can be challenged, and our children will hail these endeavors as noble efforts to liberate humanity; and (4) terror is the quickest and most effective means to destroy conventions. The perpetrator frees himself from the paralyzing grip of convention to become a different sort of person and society's defenders will respond in ways that undermine the rules they claim are sacred.[15]

An incident, often identified as the inspiration for the turbulent decades to follow, illustrates the process visualized. Vera Zasulich wounded a Russian police commander who abused prisoners taken in a demonstration. Throwing her weapon to the floor, she proclaimed that she was a terrorist *not* a killer."[16] In effect, the ensuing trial quickly became that of the police chief. When the court freed Zasulich, crowds greeted the verdict with thunderous applause. "Society seemed to say through the court: yes it is legitimate and necessary to resort to violence to shake up the autocracy."[17] The vivid scene was quickly described in mass newspapers throughout Europe and America, convincing Russian revolutionaries laboring in obscurity in the countryside that only in the city would they be noticed.

A successful campaign entailed learning how to fight and how to *die*, and the most admirable death occurred as a result of a court trial where one accepted responsibility using the occasion to indict the regime. The Russian writer Stepniak described the terrorist as "noble, terrible, irresistibly fascinating uniting the two sublimities of human grandeur, the martyr and the hero." Dynamite, a recent invention, was the weapon of choice for the *male* terrorist, because it usually killed the person who threw the bomb also, demonstrating that he was not an ordinary criminal.[18]

Terror-was extra-*normal* violence, or violence beyond the moral conventions regulating violence. Most specifically, the conventions violated were the rules of war designed to distinguish combatants from noncombatants. Invariably, most onlookers would label the acts atrocities or outrages.

The rebels described themselves terrorists, not guerrillas, tracing their lineage back to the French Revolution, and sometimes to the Order of Assassins in medieval Islam. They sought political targets with the potentiality to shake up public attitudes.[19] Terrorism was a strategy, not an end. The specific tactics used depended on both the context and the rebel's political objectives. Judging a context so often in flux was both an art and a science.

What gave the creators of this strategy confidence that it would work? In this case, as in the later waves, the moving forces were major *political* events, which unexpectedly exposed new vulnerabilities of government. Hope was excited, and *hope* is always an indispensable lubricant of rebel activity. The turn of events that gave rebels evidence of Russian vulnerability was the dazzling effort of the young Czar Alexander II to transform the system virtually overnight. In one stroke of the pen (1861), he freed the serfs (one-third of the population) and gave them funds to buy land. Three years later he established limited local self-government, "westernized" the judicial system, and relaxed censorship powers and control over education. Hopes were aroused but could not be fulfilled quickly enough; and in the wake of inevitable disappointment, systematic assassination campaigns largely against prominent officials began, culminating in the death of Alexander II himself.

Soon other groups in the Russian Empire emerged, focusing on assassinations and robbing banks to finance their activities. The Armenians (Hunchaks) and the Poles were first. Then the Balkans exploded where many groups (i.e., Internal Macedonian Revolutionary Organization, Young Bosnia, and the Serbian Black Hand) found the boundaries of states recently torn out of the Ottoman Empire unsatisfactory. In the West, revolutionary Anarchists mounted assassination campaigns and helped stimulate comparable ones in India (i.e., the *Maniktala* Secret Society in 1905).[20]

The Versailles Peace Treaty concluding World War I sparked the hope for the second or anti-colonial wave. The empires of the defeated states (which were mostly in Europe) were broken up by applying the principle of self-determination. Where independence was not immediately feasible, territories were understood to be "mandates" ultimately destined for independence. But the victors could not articulate the principle without also raising questions about the legitimacy of their own empires. The IRA emerged in the 1920s, and terrorist groups developed in all imperial domains except the Soviet after World War II. A variety of new states (i.e., Ireland, Israel, Cyprus, Yemen, Algeria, etc.) emerged, and the wave receded as the empires it swept over dissolved.

Second-wave tactics differed in some respects from those of first. Bank robberies were less common, partly because diaspora sources this time contributed more money. Most conspicuous was the lesson learned that assassinating prominent political figures was often counterproductive, and few attacks on the prominent occurred. One organization continued the old practice—*Lehi* (a Zionist revisionist group the British labeled the "Stern Gang")—and it proved much less effective than competitors in the struggle for independence. Martyrdom so often linked to assassinating the prominent seemed less significant too. The new strategy was to eliminate via systematic assassinations the police first, a government's eyes and ears. Military units would replace them and would prove too clumsy to cope without producing counter-atrocities, increasing social support for the terrorists. If the process of atrocities and counter-atrocities was well planned, it worked nearly always to favor those perceived to be weak and without alternatives.[21]

Major energies went into guerrilla-like (hit and run) actions against troops, attacks that went beyond the rules of war, however, because weapons were concealed and the *assailants* had no identifying insignia.[22] Some groups (i.e., *Irgun* and IRA) made efforts to give warnings in order to limit civilian casualties. In some cases (i.e., Algeria), terror was one aspect of a more comprehensive rebellion depending on guerrilla forces. Although an important ingredient in colonial dissolution, terrorist groups rarely achieved their original purposes. The IRA gained an Irish state but not one extending over the whole island. EOKA fought to unify Cyprus and Greece but had to settle for the state of Cyprus, which split in two afterward and has remained so ever since. Begin's *Irgun* fought to gain the entire Palestine mandate but settled for partition rather than risk civil war among Jews.

Anti-colonial causes were legitimate to many more parties than the causes articulated in the first wave, and that created a definition problem. The term *terrorist* had accumulated so many abusive connotations that those identified as terrorists found they had enormous political liabilities. Rebels stopped calling themselves terrorists. Lehi (the last organization to rely on assassinations) was also the last to characterize itself as a terrorist group. Menachem Begin, leader of the *Irgun* (Lehi's contemporary and rival), concentrating on purpose rather than means, described his people as "freedom fighters" struggling against government terror. So appealing did this self-description prove to be that all subsequent terrorist groups followed suit. Governments appreciated the political value of "appropriate" language too, and began to describe *all* violent rebels as terrorists. The media corrupted language further, refusing to use terms consistently, hoping to avoid being seen by the public as blatantly partisan. Major American newspapers, for example, often described the same individuals in the *same* account, indeed sometimes in the same paragraph, alternatively as terrorists, guerrillas, and soldiers.[23]

The agonizing Vietnam War produced the psychological requisites for the third or new left wave. The effectiveness of Vietcong terror against the American Goliath armed with modern technology kindled hopes that the Western heartland was vulnerable too. The war also stimulated an enormous ambivalence about the value of the existing system, especially among the young in the West.

Many groups in the "developed world" (i.e., American Weather Underground, West German RAF, Italian Red Brigades, Japanese Red Army, and the French *Action Directe*) saw themselves as vanguards for the masses of the Third World, where much hostility to the West already existed. The Soviets encouraged these groups in many different ways. In Latin America revolutionary groups repeated a pattern visible in the first wave; they abandoned the countryside and came to the city, where they would be noticed. Carlos Marighella, a major figure on the Latin American scene produced *The MiniManual of the Urban Guerrilla,* a handbook of tactics, comparable to Nechaev's earlier *Revolutionary Catechism* in the first wave.

In the third wave, radicalism was often combined with nationalism—the Basque Nation and Liberty (ETA), the Armenian Secret Army for the Liberation of Armenia (ASALA), the Corsican National Liberation Front (FNLC), and the IRA. The pattern reminds us of the first wave where anarchists sometimes linked themselves to nationalist aspirations (i.e., Indian, Armenian, and Macedonian groups). Although every early effort failed, the linkage was renewed for the obvious reason that self-determination always appeals to a larger constituency than radical aspirations do, and over time self-determination obscured the radical programs initially embraced. Nonetheless, most failed quickly. The survivors did not make much headway, because the countries concerned (i.e., Turkey, Spain and France) did not understand themselves to be colonial powers or did not display the ambivalence necessary for the separatists to succeed.

When the Vietnam War ended in 1975, the Palestine Liberation Organization (PLO) became the heroic model. Originating after three Arab armies collapsed, its very existence was a statement that terror offered more hope than conventional military forces. The central position of the PLO was augmented by three powerful circumstances; Israel, its chief enemy, was an integral part of the West, the PLO got strong Soviet support, and was able to provide facilities in Lebanon to train terrorists from many countries.

The term *international terrorism* (commonly used during the Anarchist wave) was revived to describe new left wave activities.[24] The revolutionary ethos created significant bonds between separate national groups. The PLO had provided extensive training facilities for other groups. The targets chosen reflected international dimensions. Some groups conducted more assaults abroad than on their home territories; the PLO, for example, were more active in Europe than on the West Bank, and sometimes more active in Europe than many European groups themselves were. On their own soil, groups often struck targets with special international significance, especially Americans and their installations. Teams composed of different national groups cooperated in attacks; the 1972 Munich Olympics massacre, the 1975 kidnapping of OPEC ministers, and 1975 hijackings to Uganda and to Somalia in 1977. Libya, Iraq, and Syria also employed terrorists in other countries as foreign policy instruments.

Airline hijacking was the most novel tactic in this wave, and over a hundred hijackings occurred during the 1970s. Hijacking had an international character because foreign rather than domestic landing fields were more available to hijacked planes. Hijacking also reflected an impulse for spectacular acts; a first-wave theme was abandoned in the second for more effective military-like strikes.

Planes were taken to get hostages, and hostage crises of various sorts dominated the era. The most memorable was the 1979 kidnapping of Italian Prime Minister Aldo Moro by the Red Brigades. When his government refused to negotiate, Moro was brutally murdered and his body dumped in the streets. The Sandinistas took Nicaragua's Congress hostage in 1978; the act was so audacious that it sparked the popular insurrection that brought the Somoza regime down a year later. In Colombia the M-19 tried to duplicate the feat by seizing the Supreme Court, but the government killed more than 100 people, including 11 justices, rather than yield.

Strikes on foreign embassies began in the third wave when in 1973 the PLO attacked the Saudi Embassy in Khartoum. The most recent was the attack in 1996 of the Peruvian Tupac Amaru (which held 72 hostages in the Japanese Embassy for more than four months until a rescue operation killed every terrorist in the embassy).

Kidnappings occurred in at least seventy-three countries and were especially important in Italy, Spain, and Latin America. In the fourteen years after 1968, there were numerous international incidents—409 kidnappings and 951 hostages.[25] Initially, hostages were taken to gain political leverage. But it was soon apparent that hostages (especially company executives) could provide much cash. Companies insured their executives, and one unintended consequence was that it made kidnapping more lucrative and easier to consummate on the kidnappers' terms. Informed observers estimate that some $350 million were gained from the practice in the period.

Although bank robbing was not as significant as it was in the first wave, some striking examples materialized. In January 1976 the PLO, together with their bitter rivals the Christian Phalange, hired safe breakers to help them loot the vaults of the major banks in Beirut. Estimates range between $50 and $100 million stolen. "Whatever the truth the robbery was large enough to earn a place in the *Guinness Book of Records* as the biggest bank robbery of all time."[26]

The third wave began to ebb in the 1980s. Revolutionary terrorists were defeated in one country after another. Israel's invasion of Lebanon in 1982 eliminated PLO facilities to train terrorist groups, and international counter-terrorist cooperation became increasingly effective.

The "religious wave" began in the same decade. In the three earlier waves, religious identity was always important because religious and ethnic identities often overlap as the Armenian, Macedonian, Irish, Cypriot, Israeli, and Palestinian struggles illustrate. But the aim earlier was to create secular sovereign states, in principle no different from those present in the international world. Religion has a vastly different significance in the fourth wave, supplying justifications and organizing principles for the New World to be established.

Islam is the most important religion in this wave and will get special attention below. But we should remember that other religious communities produced terrorists too. Sikhs sought a religious state in the Punjab. Jewish terrorists attempted to blow up Islam's most sacred shrine in Jerusalem and waged an assassination campaign against Palestinian mayors. One religious settler in 1994 murdered 29 worshippers in Abraham's tomb in Hebron, and in 1995 a fundamentalist assassinated Israeli Prime Minister Rabin. 1995 was also the year in which *Aum Shinrikyo,* a group that combined Buddhist, Christian, and Hindu religious themes, released nerve gas on the Tokyo subway—killing 12 and injuring 3,000. A worldwide anxiety materialized over expectations that a new threshold in terrorist experience had materialized because various groups would be encouraged to use chemo-bio weapons soon, and that each separate attack would produce casualties numbering in the tens of thousands.

Christian terrorism, based on racial interpretations of the Bible, emerged mostly in the amorphous American Christian Identity movement. In true millenarian fashion, armed rural communes composed of families would withdraw from the state to wait for the Second Coming and the great racial war that event would initiate. So far the Christian level of violence has been minimal, although some observers have associated the Identity movement with the 1995 Oklahoma City bombing.

Three events in the Islamic world provided the dramatic political turning point, or necessary condition, for a new wave. The Iranian Revolution was the first. Street demonstrations disintegrated the Shah's armies and provided proof that religion now had more political appeal than the prevailing revolutionary ethos. Significantly, Iranian Marxists also active against the Shah could muster only meager support.

The Iranians inspired and helped Shi'ite terror movements elsewhere—in Iraq, Saudi Arabia, Kuwait, and Lebanon. Most important were the events in Lebanon where Shi'ites, influenced by the self-martyrdom tactic of the early Assassins, introduced suicide bombing. The result was surprising, perhaps even to the Lebanese themselves. American and other foreign troops that had entered the country after the 1982 Israeli invasion quickly left and never returned.

Later in Afghanistan, Muslim resistance (partly due to U.S. aid in bringing Sunni volunteers to the battlefield)[27] forced the Soviets out, an event which became a crucial step in the stunning, unimaginable disintegration of the Soviet Union itself. Religion now manifested the ability to eliminate a secular superpower.

Iranian and Afghan events were unexpected, but a third ingredient to give religion its special significance was fully anticipated by believing Muslims. The year 1979 was the beginning of a new century, according to the Muslim calendar, and the tradition is that a redeemer would come at that time, a tradition that had regularly sparked uprisings at the turn of earlier Muslim centuries. This tradition influenced the Iranian Revolution itself, which occurred in the crucial expected year and may even have intensified Afghan resistance. Certainly, it affected other events. Sunni Muslims stormed the Grand Mosque in Mecca in the first minutes of the new century, and 10,000 casualties resulted. Whatever the specific local causes, Sunni terrorism soon appeared in many states with large Islamic populations—Egypt, Syria, Tunisia, Morocco, Algeria, the Philippines, and Indonesia. Sunni groups competed with the PLO in strikes against Israel. Afghan veterans, who had volunteered from all parts of the Islamic world, returned home with the will, confidence, and training to begin terrorist operations against weak home governments.

Assassinations and hostage taking, common features of the third wave, persisted; but "suicide bombing" was the most striking and deadly tactical innovation. It reasserted the martyrdom theme of the first wave, neglected by its two successors. The achievements in Lebanon inspired one remaining secular group, the Tamil Tigers in Sri Lanka, who used suicide bombing to give their ailing movement new life. The most spectacular Tamil act killed Indian

Prime Minister Rajiv Ghandi. Despite the conventional wisdom that only a vision of rewards in Paradise could inspire such acts, the Tamils have used "suicide bombers" more than all Islamic groups put together.[28]

Fourth-wave groups, much more than their counterparts in the third wave, have made massive attacks against military and government installations. Americans, in particular, became frequent targets. An ambush in Somalia forced American troops who evacuated Lebanon to abandon another mission. Suicide bomb attacks on military posts in Yemen, Saudi Arabia, and an American destroyer went unanswered. Similarly, embassies in Kenya and Tanzania were struck, occasioning heavy casualties in the local populations. The responses were ineffective cruise missile strikes against suspected targets. In 1993 the first successful attack by foreign terrorists on American soil occurred—the first World Trade Center bombing. It was followed by unsuccessful efforts to coincide new attacks on America on the eve of the new millenium.[29] Finally, the massive assaults on September 11 occurred, and the "war" against terror was launched.

The fourth wave produced an organization with a purpose and recruitment pattern unique in the history of terrorism, namely, Al Qaeda—led and financed by the Saudi Osama bin Laden. Al Qaeda seeks to create a single state for all Muslims, a state that once existed, and one that would be governed by the *Sharia,* Islamic law. The aspiration resonates in Sunni populations throughout the Middle East, Africa, and Asia. In the past, every terrorist *organization* recruited from a single national base or people. Al Qaeda seeks members from all parts of the vast Sunni world, including those who have gone to live in the West, though Arabs especially from Egypt and Saudi Arabia supply most recruits. Its unity is enhanced by the Afghan experiences, during which virtually all recruits had trained. The first step in achieving Al Qaeda's goal would be to strengthen rebel Islamic groups in various states of the Sunni world, an effort Americans helped frustrate by supporting existing states organized on national lines, which many see as residues of collapsed colonial empires. Eliminating American influence in these states is a precondition of re-unification. Forcing the Americans to withdraw troops from Islam's holiest shrines is the first step, and the second is to exploit a general anger over the American influence in the Palestinian and Iraqi questions. Because Al Qaeda achieved none of its objectives and the early attacks produced virtually no response, the September 11 attacks could be understood as a desperate attempt to rejuvenate a failing cause, by triggering indiscriminate American reactions.

A Closer Look at Global Dimensions

Although their relationships vary in each wave, there are four major international audiences for each terrorist group—foreign terrorist groups, diaspora populations, liberal sympathizers, and foreign governments. Vera Figner, who organized the foreign policy of Narodnaya Volya, appealed directly to three audiences. She identified totally with an international revolutionary tradition of socialists and Anarchists,[30] developing good contacts with the Russian diaspora community—an element hitherto "lost to the revolutionary tradition." By expressing her regret for the assassination of President Garfield, Figner tried to reach out to Western liberals, taking the occasion to emphasize that terror was always wrong in democratic states.[31] (The statement alienated many radicals supporting her; indeed, it failed to convince all interested parties that she truly meant what she said.) She made no direct efforts to shape the policies of foreign states, but diaspora and liberal communities worked to make their governments more sympathetic to the Russian terrorists. Russian foreign policies and its political system in any case irritated other states. The offer of the Japanese to finance Russian terrorists during the Russo-Japanese War in 1905 encouraged Indian terrorists to believe that the Japanese would help them too.[32]

The 1890s became the "Golden Age of Assassination" in the West; monarchs, prime ministers, and presidents were struck down one after another. Most assassins were anarchists who moved easily across international borders to assassinate foreign leaders, compelling affected governments to conclude that they had to share police information and cooperate to control borders. President Theodore Roosevelt seized the opportunity to call for the first international crusade to safeguard civilization: "Anarchy is a crime against the whole human race, and all mankind should band together against the Anarchist. His crimes should be made a crime against the law of nations . . . declared by treaties among all civilized powers." But three years later, when Germany and Russia urged states to convene in St. Petersburg to sign an international protocol to share police information, the United States refused to come. Hostility to Germany, anxiety about involvement in European politics, and the fact that it had no federal police force shaped that U.S. decision. Italy refused too, for a different but very revealing concern. If anarchists were returned to their countries of origin, Italy's domestic troubles might be worse than its international ones.

The first great effort to deal with international terrorism failed largely because the interests and priorities of states pulled them in different directions, and indeed as the twentieth century began, some states actively helped terrorist groups. Bulgaria gave substantial support to Macedonian terrorists in the Ottoman Empire, and the suspicion that Serbia helped in the assassin of Archduke Franz Ferdinand was an important ingredient in launching World War I. Ironically, that assassination was crucial in stemming the first terrorist wave, and the deed might not have happened if Roosevelt's crusade had been successful a decade earlier.

The international ingredient in the next wave had a different shape. Terrorist leaders of different national groups acknowledged common bonds and heritage, but the heroes their literature invoked were overwhelmingly national ones.[33] The underlying assumption was that if one strengthened ties with foreign terrorist groups, abilities to use other international assets would be weakened.

The League of Nations drafted two conventions in 1937 to cope with terrorism, but they were "political theatre," not serious efforts to deal with the problem, and never came into effect.[34] After World War II, the United Nations (UN) inherited the League's authority over international terror and over the mandates governed by colonial powers, territories that were now scenes of extensive terrorist activity. As the UN grew by admitting new states, virtually all of which were former colonial territories, that body gave the anti-colonial sentiment more structure, focus, and opportunities. Significantly, UN debates regularly described anti-colonial terrorists as "freedom fighters."

Diaspora groups displayed abilities not seen in earlier waves.[35] The IRA received money, weapons, and volunteers from the Irish overseas, especially those in America. The support of the U.S. government for Irish independence was partly dependent on Irish-American influence too. Israeli groups got similar support from similar, especially American, diaspora sources. The Arab world gave the Algerian FLN crucial political support, and Arab states adjacent to Algeria offered sanctuaries and allowed their territories to be used as staging grounds for attacks. The Greek government sponsored the Cypriot uprising against the British, and as the revolt grew more successful, the more enraged Turkish Cypriots who looked to Turkey for aid and received it. The Cyprus problem is still unresolved nearly a half century later.

The different Irish experiences illustrate how crucial influences are shaped by foreign perceptions of purpose and context. The first effort in the 1920s, seen simply as an anti-colonial movement, gained the foreign support needed from Irish Americans and the U.S. government to secure an Irish state. The supporting parties abandoned the IRA during its brief campaigns to bring Northern Ireland into the Republic during World War II when a more important concern prevailed. Support from abroad did not materialize in the 1950s during the Cold War. IRA activities in the early part of the new left wave had a Marxist element that alienated the usual sources of diaspora support. The Cold War had to end before an American government showed serious interest in the issue again, when it initiated moves that may resolve the conflict.

The third wave had one strikingly new international feature. Never before had one people been the favorite target of most groups. Approximately one-third of the international attacks involved American targets. American economic, diplomatic, and military activities were visible in Latin America, Europe, and the Middle East. The support the United States gave governments under terrorist siege only intensified this proclivity.

The conventional wisdom about the third wave is that international connections provided participants with enormous advantages. This wisdom is deeply flawed. One important—and not fully understood—reason the third wave was the shortest was that it was so dependent on unreliable international connections. The emphasis on the revolutionary bond alienated potential domestic and liberal constituencies, particularly during the Cold War. Soon it was found that the effort to foster cooperation between terrorist groups posed serious problems for the weaker ones. Thus the German Revolutionary

Cells, partners of the Palestine Front for the Liberation of Palestine (PFLP) in a variety of hijacking efforts, tried to get help from its partner to release German prisoners. But the Germans found themselves wholly "dependent on the will of Wadi Haddad and his group," whose agenda was very different from theirs after all, and the relationship soon terminated.[36] A member of another German group (2nd June) suggests that the group's obsession with the Palestinian cause induced it to attack a Jewish synagogue on the anniversary of *Kristall Nacht,* a date often considered the beginning of the Holocaust. Such "stupidity," he says, alienated potential German constituencies.[37]

Palestinian raids from Egyptian-occupied Gaza helped precipitate a disastrous war with Israel in 1956, and Egypt was led to prevent the possibility that fidayeen raids would be launched from its territories ever again. A Palestinian raid from Syria brought the latter into the Six-Day War, and Syria ever afterward kept a tight control on those operating from its territories.

From its inception in 1968 the PLO, a loose confederation, often found international ties unexpectedly expensive because they complicated existing divisions within the organization. In the 1970s Abu Iyad, founding member and intelligence chief, wrote that the Palestinian cause was so important in Syrian and Iraqi domestic politics that those states captured organizations within the PLO to serve their own ends. The result was that it was even more difficult to settle for a limited goal, as the *Irgun* and the EOKA had done earlier. Entanglements with Arab states created other problems for both parties similar to those in 1956 and 1967. When in 1970 a PLO faction hijacked British and American planes to Jordan in the first effort to target non-Israelis, the Jordanian army devastated the Palestinians and the PLO lost its home. Finally, an attempt to assassinate an Israeli diplomat in Britain sparked the 1982 invasion of Lebanon, forcing the PLO to leave the home that gave it so much significance among foreign terrorist groups.

To maintain control over their own destiny, states began to sponsor their own groups—an activity unknown in the second wave, and a very costly one to the sponsors. In the 1980s Britain severed diplomatic relations with Libya and Syria for sponsoring terrorism on British soil, and France broke with Iran when Iran refused to let the French interrogate its embassy staff about assassinations of Iranian émigrés. The limited value of state-sponsored terror was emphasized by Iraqi restraint during the Gulf War, despite widespread predictions that Iraqi terrorists would flood Europe. If terror had materialized, it would have made bringing Saddam Hussein to trial for crimes a war aim, and the most plausible explanation for Hussein's uncharacteristic restraint is the desire to avoid that result.

During the third wave, states for the first time cooperated openly and formally in counter-terror efforts. The international cooperation of national police forces sought so desperately in the 1904 St. Petersburg Protocol finally materialized in the mid-1970s, when Trevi and Interpol were established. The Americans, with British aid, bombed Libya in 1986 for the terrorist attacks it sponsored, and the European Community imposed an arms embargo. Two years later, some evidence that Libya's agents were involved in the Pan Am crash in Lockerbie, Scotland, led to a unanimous UN Security Council decision obliging Libya to extradite the suspects; and a decade later, when collective sanctions had their full effects, Libya complied. When compared with League and UN activities during the anti-colonial wave, the UN action in the Libya case signified a dramatic change.

Nonetheless, sometimes even close allies could not cooperate. France refused to extradite PLO, Red Brigade, and ETA suspects to West Germany, Italy, and Spain respectively. Italy spurned American requests to extradite a Palestinian suspect in the seizure of the *Achille Lauro* cruise ship in 1984. The United States in its turn has refused to extradite some IRA suspects. In 1988 Italy refused to extradite a Kurd sought by Turkey because Italian law forbids capital punishment and Turkish law does not. Events of this sort will not stop until the laws and interests of separate states are identical.

Finally, the breakdown of the Lebanese government gave the PLO an opportunity to become the first terrorist organization to train foreign groups. When the PLO fled Lebanon, its host afterward (Tunisia) refused to let it continue that activity, and to a large extent the PLO's career as an effective terrorist organization was over. Ironically, as the Oslo Accords demonstrated, the PLO achieved more of its objectives when it became less dangerous.

Religion (the basis for the fourth wave) transcends the state bond. But groups from different mainstream religious traditions do not cooperate. Even traditional cleavages within a religion—Shia and Sunni for example— sometimes are intensified.

Within the same religion, particularly the same branch of that religion, the potentialities for cooperation affecting many interests may be great, particularly in the Islamic world where so many states exist. Whether or not the religious tie was crucial, the first successful strategic example of state-sponsored terror occurred during the fourth wave. Iran facilitated the suicide (self-martyrdom) bombings, which compelled foreign withdrawals in Lebanon. Inasmuch as the attacks were made by local elements on their own terrain, the targeted parties did not make retaliatory strikes at the sponsor. Al Qaeda's tactical strikes at the American installations and embassies were protected by the Afghan Taliban government's refusal to accept the UN ultimatum to force Al Qaeda to leave its bases. The religious ties may have been a crucial element in the decision. But whatever the reason, when the Taliban again refused to comply after September 11, it suffered the consequences.

Resemblances between Al Qaeda and the PLO exist, but the differences are significant. While the PLO prior to the Oslo Agreements targeted Americans more than any other non-Israeli people, the United States was not the principal target, as it seems to have been for Al Qaeda from the very beginning. The PLO trained elements of pre-existing groups, but those groups retained their identity; Al Qaeda trains individuals committed to its goal from various places in the Sunni world, including the West. The PLO had a loose, divided form that caused it enormous trouble but gave it an ability to persevere. While Al Qaeda has created unique "sleeper cells" in areas to be targeted, it does seem like a single unit, and hence much more dangerous. But there is a flip side to this structural difference. Once their centers are destroyed, better-organized groups are more likely to quit fighting.[38]

Conclusion

My conclusion is brief. The September 11 attack has created a resolve in America and elsewhere to end international terror once and for all. The first step, the unexpectedly quick and decisive success of the Afghan intervention, was impressive. At this writing, Al Qaeda seems destroyed. Certainly a few attacks by existing cells may yet occur, but much more important is the fact that the territory to regroup elsewhere as an organization will not be available, because no host will accept the inherent risks. The extraordinary unwillingness of the Taliban and Al Qaeda to fight will also have its effect on the ability to generate successor movements from Islamic fundamentalism.

But an acquaintance with modern history does not inspire confidence that there will be many more striking successes. Previous international efforts have always been difficult to sustain over time, and the present coalition may be running into similar problems now. Different state interests and priorities will have their effects, as the resistance of other countries to the American effort to pinpoint Iran, Iraq, and North Korea as the "axis of evil" shows. Members of the coalition do not agree on how to apply the term. The issues of Kashmir and Israel are cases in point, and it is clear that some states will encourage groups that others abhor.

Even if the fourth wave follows the path of its three predecessors soon, another inspiring cause for hope is likely to emerge *unexpectedly,* as it has four times in the past. That history shows that the inspiration for a terrorist wave may dry out in time, and that resistance can destroy organizations or make them ineffectual. But, alas, it also demonstrates that terrorists regularly invent new ways to conduct their activities.

Notes

1. An earlier version of this essay was published in *Current History* 100 (December 2001);419–425.
2. On September 20, the President told Congress that "any nation that continues to harbor or support terrorism will be regarded as a hostile regime. . . . The war would not end until every terrorist group of *global reach* has been found, stopped, and defeated." [My emphasis]
3. See Richard B. Jensen, "The United States, International Policing the War against Anarchist Terrorism," *Terrorism and Political Violence* 13 (Spring 2001):15–46.
4. The Russian police prior to the rise of rebel terror also were not armed; they carried ceremonial sabers only.

5. Pope Leo XII blamed Jews, Anarchists, Socialists, and Freemasons for the stream of assassinations that occurred in the 1890s (*New York Times*, September 6, 1901).

6. Anarchists were the most dominant element in the first wave. But in the Balkans, Poland, the Ottoman Empire, and India, those influenced by anarchist strategy largely had separatist ends.

7. The term *terror* originally referred to actions of the revolutionary government that went beyond the rules regulating punishment to make a people fit to govern itself.

8. We will ignore "single issue" groups, that is, some suffragette elements at the beginning of the century or contemporary elements of the antiabortion and green movements.

9. See my "Fear and Trembling: Terror in Three Religious Traditions," *American Political Science Review* 78 (No. 3, 1984):658–677.

10. Henry Dawson, *The Sons of Liberty* (New York: Private Publication, 1959).

11. Most groups in every wave except the fourth cite the American Revolution as worth emulating. But I know no reference to the Sons of Liberty or its tactics.

12. See Jerry Post's edited versions of the bin Laden work in *Terrorism and Political Violence* 14 (Summer 2002), forthcoming. It took time for this attitude to develop in Islam. If one compares bin Laden's work with Faraj's *Neglected Duty,* a work used to justify the assassination of Egyptian President Sadat in 1981, the two authors seem to be in two different worlds. Faraj cites no experience outside the Islamic tradition, and his most recent historical reference is to Napoleon's invasion of Europe. See my "Sacred Terror: A Case from Contemporary Islam" in *Origins of Terrorism,* ed. Walter Reich (Cambridge: Cambridge University Press, 1990), 103–130.

13. The traditional still binding Islamic view is that women may participate in fighting only when no men are available.

14. For the revolutionary, the French Revolution in making us aware of the potentialities for perfection was for the anarchists the functional equivalent of the unredeemed divine promise for religious groups.

15. An equivalent for this argument in religious millennial thought is that that the world must become impossibly bad before it could become unimaginably good.

16. Adam B. Ulam, *In the Name of the People* (New York: Viking Press, 1977), 269. [My emphasis]

17. Ulam, *In the Name of the People,* 74.

18. The bomb was most significant in Russia. While Russian women were crucial in the organization, they were not allowed to throw the bomb, presumably because most bombers did not escape from the scene. Other terrorists used the bomb extensively, but chose other weapons as well.

19. A guerrilla force has political objectives, as any army does, but it aims to weaken or destroy the enemy's military forces first. The terrorist strikes directly at the political sentiments that sustain his enemies.

20. Peter Heehs, *Nationalism, Terrorism, and Communalism* (Delhi: Oxford University Press, 1998), Chapter 2.

21. The strategy is superbly described in the film *Battle of Algiers,* which is based on the memoirs of Yacev Saadi who organized the battle. Attacks against the police occur whose responses are limited by rules governing criminal procedure. In desperation the police set a bomb off in the Casbah, inadvertently exploding an ammunition dump and killing Algerian women and children. A mob emerges

screaming for revenge, and at this point the FLN has the moral warrant to attack civilians.

There is another underlying element that makes rebel terrorism in a democratic world often have special weight. The atrocities of the strong always seem worse than those of the weak because it is believed the latter have no alternatives.

22. Guerrillas carry weapons openly and wear an identifying emblem, and we are obliged therefore to treat them as soldiers.

23. For a more detailed discussion of the definition problem, see my "Politics of Atrocity," in *Terrorism: Interdisciplinary Perspectives,* ed. Y. Alexander and S. Finger (New York: John Jay Press, 1997), 46.

24. Most people using the term *international terrorism* thought that it was a product of the 1960s and 1970s.

25. James Adams, *The Financing of Terror* (New York: Simon and Schuster, 1986), 192.

26. Adams, *Financing of Terror,* 94.

27. This was not the first time secular forces would help launch the careers of those who would become religious terrorists. Israel helped Hamas to get started, thinking that it would compete to weaken the PLO, and to check left-wing opposition, Egyptian President Anwar Sadat released religious elements from prison who later assassinated him.

28. From 1983 to 2000 the Tamils used suicide bombs 171 times while the combined total for all 13 Islamic groups using the tactic was 117. The figures were compiled by Yoram Schweitzer and cited by Ehud Sprinzak, "Rational Fanatics," *Foreign Policy* (October 2002): 69.

29. Those attacks, as well as the expected ones that did not materialize, are discussed in a special forthcoming volume of *Terrorism and Political Violence* 14 (Spring 2002), edited by Jeffrey Kaplan.

30. For a more extensive discussion of Figner, see my "The International World as Some Terrorists Have Seen It: A Look at a Century of Memoirs," in my *Inside Terrorist Organizations,* 2nd ed. (London: Frank Cass, 2001).

31. A disappointed office seeker, not an anarchist, assassinated Garfield.

32. Heehs, *Nationalism, Terrorism, and Communalism,* 4.

33. See my "The International World."

34. Martin David Dubin, "Great Britain and the Anti-Terrorist Conventions of 1937," *Terrorism and Political Violence* 5 (Spring 1993):1.

35. Irish-Americans have always given Irish rebels extensive support. The Fenian movement was born in the American Civil War and sparked a rebellion in Ireland.

36. Hans J. Klein, in Jean M. Bourguereau, ed. *German Guerrilla: Terror, Rebel Reaction and Resistance* (Orkney, U.K.: Sanday, 1981):31.

37. Michael Baumann, *Terror or Love* (New York: Grove Press, 1977), 61.

38. The Spaniards, for example, conquered the Incas and Aztecs easily, but the United States had much more difficulty with the less powerful but highly decentralized native American peoples resisting it. Contrary to the argument above, Steven Simon and Daniel Benjamin contend that that Al Qaeda is a uniquely decentralized organization and therefore less likely to be disturbed by destroying the center. "America and the New Terrorism," *Survival* 42 (September 2000): 156–77.

Chapter 4

A DUAL REALITY: TERRORISM AGAINST THE STATE AND TERRORISM BY THE STATE

RICHARD A. FALK

The official American response to September 11 has been to initiate a Great Terror War, indicating a national resolve to rid the world of "terrorism." From the statements of President Bush and others it is evident that the idea of terrorism is being used exclusively to refer to violent enemies of sovereign states. The U.S. Government has won a victory in Afghanistan on such a basis, and proposes expanding the scope of the war to a series of other countries associated with terrorism. Some governments have also been warned by Washington because of their alleged links with organizations that are engaged in wars over the future of Palestine or Kashmir.

Such a posture invites moral confusion and partakes of political incoherence. The confusion arises because the essence of terrorism, going back to its origins in the French Revolution, is the calculated use of violence for political ends against civilian society to induce widespread and intense fear. Governments are as likely as their adversaries to rely on such tactics. It is self-serving and opportunistic for the United States after being victimized by the attacks of September 11 to so restrict our understanding of terrorism. With such an understanding, for instance, the violence used by the Sharon government in Israel against the Palestinian people is exempted from the stigma of terrorism, and it makes sense then to condemn as terrorism only the Palestinian suicide bombing directed at Israeli civilians.

Such a one-eyed definition is also politically incoherent. It overlooks the degree to which the United States has itself backed anti-state political violence, as in relation to *contra* opposition to the established government in Nicaragua during the 1980s and with respect to the Cuban exiles operating with thinly disguised official support from their base in Miami.

To act effectively against terrorism, we must first learn to think clearly about what it is. There exists great confusion, some genuine, some insidious, about the true character of terrorism in our world. As well, there are several strange, even startling, inconsistencies between what the government in Washington tells its citizens about terrorism and the actual policies it pursues.

So far, the subject matter of terrorism has been dominated, with a few notable exceptions, by polemical treatments of the topic that encourage the illusion that terrorism is something alien to American patterns of conduct in the world, that it is done unto us, and that what we do violently unto others is legitimate counterterrorism, or, in the language of the polemics, "fighting back."

The general view is that the deepest roots of terrorism involve some mixture of desperation and depravity within dispossessed political extremists, especially those on the Left. My claim is that this mainstream image of terrorism is dangerously misleading. It overlooks the often calculating character of recourse to wanton and indiscriminate political violence from a variety of sources, including the deepest recesses of governmental bureaucracy operating in an entirely cool, calculating, rational style.

My argument is that it is futile and hypocritical self-deception to suppose that we can use the word *terrorism* to establish a double standard pertaining to the use of political violence. Unless we are consistent and self-critical in our use of language we invite the very violence we deplore.

Terrorism, then, is used here to designate any type of political violence that lacks an adequate moral and legal justification, regardless of whether the actor is a revolutionary group or a government. Of course, such a definition is open to interpretation. The word *adequate* suggests that legal and moral judgments are unavoidably somewhat subjective and that the process of justification is necessarily grounded in the realms of private morality and partisan ideology. To justify political violence adequately means seeking a generally persuasive and objective interpretation of prevailing community norms as embodied in international law and in a shared ethos that restricts political violence to a defensive role and unconditionally protects those who are innocent. Seeking such an objective interpretation is not easy in a world of rival belief systems and cultural backgrounds, but neither is it impossible.

A pitfall of repudiating terrorism is the question of its effectiveness, especially in war. So long as terrorist methods are relied upon by states to avoid defeat or hasten victory in war, bolstered by the claim of saving lives, terrorists of all persuasions gain validation, provided only that they express some plausible justification that an indiscriminate attack or a sacrifice of innocent lives is reasonably consonant with their political goals. Programs of counter-terrorism must renounce certain forms of political violence even if they seem effective and even if they are selected by leaders of governments or battlefield commanders in the heat of war.

It is foolish moralism to suppose that revolutionary groups would be prepared to follow a higher morality than that accepted by states. And it is hypocritical to insist that they do so; besides, it has no effect, except possibly as an example of self-deluding propaganda. On occasion, revolutionary groups adopt a higher morality, either renouncing violence altogether or being much more careful than their governmental adversaries about the protection of innocents. A comparison between the tactics of the African National Congress and the South African government over the course of several decades discloses such a persistent normative gap favorable to the revolutionary group in relation to the role of political violence in the South African struggle. Similar claims have been advanced on behalf of the conduct of the Sendero Luminoso ("Shining Path") in Peru, both as to its care in confining violence to appropriate targets given the reality of revolutionary struggle and its relatively greater care as to the protection of innocents as compared to the government of Peru, especially during the period of Fernando Belaúnde Terry's presidency (1980–1985).

Similarly, we cannot argue conclusively that terrorism never works, and that therefore its renunciation on all sides could be undertaken as a practical political step. It is true that terroristic methods often harden opposition and alienate the perpetrators from the citizenry. But it is also true that acts of terrorism under certain circumstances focus attention on grievances and may induce an adversary to back down. Arguably, the British decisions to quit Ireland after World War I and Palestine and Cyprus after World War II were influenced by the terrorist tactics of their opponents, and surely the French defeat in Algeria was a consequence, in part, of terrorist challenges by revolutionary nationalists. Similarly the Allied powers in World War II may have weakened the will of Germany and Japan to resist by large-scale indiscriminate air attacks against heavy concentrations of the civilian population on cities.

The embodiment of terrorism in the modern war-fighting mentality is, at present, a fact of international life. Without using the word *terrorism,* Thomas Schelling accurately and typically associates the essence of military strategy with calculated recourse to terrorism:

> Military strategy can no longer be thought of, as it could for some countries in some eras, as the science of military victory. It is now equally, if not more, the art of coercion, of intimidation and deterrence. The instruments of war are more punitive than acquisitive. Military strategy, whether we like it or not, has become the diplomacy of violence.

The essence of our problem is that terrorism has been routinized on every side of the main political equations of our day.

In various forms, terrorism is as old as government and armed struggle, and as pervasive. The modern torment over terrorism arises because our lives and societies are more interconnected than ever before through mass media and because we live in an era of pervasive turmoil and high-technology weaponry that threaten the very idea of a human future.

It is too easy to blame the terrorist menace on the evil other. To end terrorism, in my view, requires a cultural resolve to avoid indiscriminate and unjustified political violence and to respect the integrity of civilian life at all costs. As soon as the choice of violent means is entrusted to human evaluations of effectiveness in supporting a political cause in a given setting, a terrorist ethos is bound to hold sway in circumstances of crisis and pressure.

Another strong temptation is to turn from terrorism to pacifism. After all, our world is saturated with violence, and we seem locked into a series of cultural patterns that sustain spirals of violence within and between nations. To move from violence to nonviolence is also to solve the problem of ambiguity.

We do away with the dilemmas of assessment if we agree that violence is *never* justified. And further, nonviolence enjoys a strong mandate in several leading world religions, including Christianity and Buddhism, providing a basis for challenging the war system at a time of great jeopardy to the entire human species.

Yet pure nonviolence is not the course proposed here. For one thing, the opposite of terrorism is not nonviolence, but permissible violence. In other words, we don't want to claim that a war fought in self-defense is an instance of terrorism. That would be abuse of language as damaging as that of now associating terrorism only with the political violence of enemies while reserving to ourselves the right to engage in comparable practice.

Furthermore, given the way the world is organized—repressive governments, aggressive foreign policies—it is unrealistic and arrogant to insist that victims acquiesce in injustice. We may be exceedingly skeptical about violent strategies, and yet there does not seem to be either an ethical basis or a political structure that could sustain an invariable practice of nonviolence.

What we can do, and need to try, although it is difficult, is to oppose at the very least those forms of political violence that seek to gain their ends by striking fear into hearts and minds and that refuse to respect the innocence of civilian life. Such a position demands a lot, including the practice of warfare in a principled way. But unless we demand this much we are fooling ourselves if we think we are opposing terrorism. How can we claim to be anti-terrorists unless we have ourselves renounced terrorism?

In the end there are two principal ways to frame the debate on terrorism: the mainstream focus on the political violence of revolutionary groups and their supporters and the emphasis placed here on impermissible forms of political violence, regardless of the identity of the actor. The attempt here is to persuade readers of the importance of moving from the narrow to the broader conception of terrorism.

One notices that the torch of dignity is kept lit among suppressed and mutilated nationalist causes by terrorist practices. Whether among the Irish, Croatians, Basques, Moluccans, Ukrainians, Sikhs, Palestinians, Puerto Ricans, or others, the common impulse seems to be an incredibly deep urge to keep faith with the past and with one's specific identity. The mode of doing this is to make the victors or their representatives share some of the pain. Such recourse to terrorism is not mainly instrumental (a means to a political end), but rather symbolic or expressive (seeking to register a statement of grievance as powerfully as possible, by inducing shock, even trauma). In some settings, the main terrorist purpose is to mobilize the victims, challenging their indifference and ignorance. Recovering a sense of cultural identity need not require such violence: witness efforts to revive cultural identity by encouraging language study, music and art, and observance of folk rituals. Powerful experiences of national recovery have taken place among various indigenous peoples throughout the world. Among these peoples there is no project to dispossess the settler civilization, nor does such a capability exist, but there is a sense that cultural vitality can overcome the humiliations of the historical past. Some indigenous peoples, such as the Maoris in New Zealand, have made impressive progress despite the great difficulty of reestablishing cultural identity in opposition to the whole weight of modern industrial civilization.

But there is another distinctive source of terrorism in the modern world. It is the general suspension of limits with respect to political undertakings by, for, or against the state. The state claims for itself an unconditional security rationale, a rationale that culminates in making preparations to wage nuclear war and in envisioning a nuclear winter or other forms of catastrophic collapse. Many leading states have established intelligence agencies that engage in covert operations against foreign enemies without respect to the limits of law or morality. Analogously, those who aspire to statehood regard their nationalist aspirations as unconditional, therefore not subject to limits on their tactics.

But it is not only extremists who reject limits on their tactics, including recourse to violence. The pervasiveness of the terrorist phenomenon reflects a generalized breakdown of moral and legal inhibition to violence throughout society. To the extent that terrorism is perceived by the players to be "useful" it will be authorized even by liberal democracies that proclaim their *raison d'être* to be human dignity and the worth of the individual. In a quasi-official publication of the RAND Corporation, Brian Michael Jenkins (a prominent specialist on terrorism) summarizes his belief that the United States government must use terrorism to fight terrorism, as part of its need to engage in what he calls "indirect forms of warfare:"

> Indirect forms of warfare include clandestine and covert military operations carried out by other than the regular armed forces of a nation, providing asylum and support for guerrillas in an adjacent country, *providing support—and sometimes operational direction—to terrorist groups opposing a rival or enemy regime, and governmental use of terrorist tactics, such as assassinating foreign foes or troublesome exiles.* [emphasis added]

Only ignorance could excuse the view that the United States or other major governments renounce terrorist practices even when they serve accepted foreign policy goals. All that is unusual about the Jenkins formulation is its candor. Any examination of official practices would disclose the adoption of a wide series of terrorist undertakings, veiled in secrecy and disguised by the antiseptic semantics of covert operations, low-intensity warfare, and indirect modes of conflict.

So it is misleading in the extreme to characterize a few Arab states as international pariahs because they alone sponsor terrorist activities. It was equally misleading during the Cold War to construct an elaborate conspiracy theory that linked instances of terrorism with a network masterminded and financed in Moscow. Opportunistic support of terrorist activity is an ingredient of geopolitical rivalry. No one would deny that the Soviet government lent support to groups using political violence in a manner that qualified it as terrorism under most accepted definitions, and that these groups had transnational links. But it is equally undeniable that the United States was similarly engaged. Indeed, given the relative openness of the American political system, it was impossible to mount a denial. The attempt was rather to provide a justification, in the form of either promoting democracy or resisting the expansion of Soviet interests. The debate over the Nicaraguan Contras did not seriously draw into question the reality of U.S. official support for political violence against civilians that could generally be identified as terrorism. The attempt was rather to provide an abstract justification for support by reference to democracy and strategic interests.

This second source of terrorism is the absolutism of secular politics, whether statist or antistatist. Terrorism is deployed (more or less intelligently and successfully) as a rational instrument by policymakers on *all sides* of the political equation.

This kind of idolatry finds its theoretical validation in a tradition of Western realist thought, especially that of Niccoló Machiavelli, Thoms Hobbes, and Karl von Clausewitz. The terrorist sensibility is only one manifestation of the Machiavellian mind-set that proclaims the absolute primacy of state interests. We condemn the political adversary who engages in indiscriminate violence as a barbarian and outlaw and reward our own officials with accolades for their "statecraft," even conferring a Nobel Peace Prize from time to time on those who oversee this second type of terrorism.

I believe that it has become as essential to eliminate terrorism from our world as it is to eliminate nuclear weapons, and that it is possibly more difficult. To overcome terrorism we must respond to both of its sources: the unrelieved pain of groups who are victims of severe abuse and the unconditional pretension that political goals associated with state power can be pursued without respect for the limits of law or morality. In the foreground of this undertaking is a new consideration of the place of political violence in human affairs.

Admittedly, there are additional types of terrorism that do not flow from the two sources discussed, as well as depraved behavior that exerts a terrorist impact on the community even if it is derived from purely personal motives. There is the kind of nihilistic violence that is directed at modern societies by alienated intellectuals who feel betrayed on all sides, not least of all by the collapse of a viable Left project for the seizure of state power.

There is also the kind of pseudo-political private pathology that is associated with drug-induced, anti-social random violence that was frighteningly displayed by "the Manson family" in the Sharon Tate murders. This is not terrorism, but it spreads fear and acute anxiety throughout the society and may also be self-aggrandizing in the sense of seeking personal notoriety, even leadership among those sharing the same antisocial ethos.

Although pain and abuse seem to lie in the background of the terrorist personality in both these instances, the problems these individuals pose can usually be dealt with locally by standard law enforcement techniques. True, this kind of normative breakout is not nearly so likely to occur in societies that aspire actively to social justice and that sustain the social fabric of child development and community, but neither can complex societies tolerate expressive and symbolic violence, nor are such activities likely to put down deep roots. Unlike the two sources of terrorism, these variants cannot acquire potency from the notion of a sacred struggle, mutilated or thwarted by oppressive political arrangements that may currently have ascendancy, but not in the hearts and minds of those vanquished.

In any event, those forms of political violence that are tied to the existence of states *and* to the vitality of nationalist strivings must be emphasized. Hence the two critical terrorist types for my purpose are revolutionaries (who act to oppose the state or to gain control over the state) and functionaries (who act on behalf of the state). There is a period of overlapping identity that occurs in the time after revolutionaries acquire control of the state and functionaries lose control. Some of the worst orgies of political violence occur in the aftermath of revolution when the fear of counterrevolution is both a pretext and explanation for bloody terror.

The new global context associated with terrorism makes it more important than ever that we clarify our understanding of terrorism. Even from a narrow nationalistic perspective we may be haunted in the future by conceptions of terrorism that exempt states. And in relation to our international campaign for support in an effort to destroy the Al Qaeda network a more balanced and nuanced view of terrorism is indispensable. The goal of anti-terrorist undertakings should be to eliminate all forms of political violence directed at civilian society regardless of source. States that engage in such violence whether against their own citizens or overseas are acting in a terrorist mode as much as are their non-state adversaries.

Chapter 5

IS THERE A GOOD TERRORIST?

TIMOTHY GARTON ASH

Have you heard that Osama bin Laden is coming to Macedonia?
No. Why?
Because we've declared an amnesty for terrorists.

This Macedonian joke, told to me recently in Skopje, invites us to reflect on one of the most important questions in the post–September 11 world: Who is a terrorist? It is a question to which the international community sorely needs an answer.

Slav Macedonian nationalists insist that they face their own Osama bin Laden in an Albanian Macedonian guerrilla leader called Ali Ahmeti.[1] Yet, they say, the United States and NATO have been making deals with this terrorist, and pressing the Macedonian government to grant him amnesty. Of course, nationalist regimes around the world have always played this semantic card— Russia denounces Chechen "terrorists:" Israel, Palestinian "terrorists:" China, Tibetan "terrorists:" and so on—with widely varying degrees of justification. In this case, however, it is not just the local nationalists who have taken a dim view of Mr. Ali Ahmeti.

On June 27, 2001, President George W. Bush signed an Executive Order freezing all U.S.-based property of, and blocking donations to, a list of persons engaged in or supporting "extremist violence in the Former Yugoslav Republic of Macedonia" and in other parts of the Western Balkans. "I find," said the presidential order, "that such actions constitute an unusual and extraordinary threat to the national security and foreign policy of the United States, and hereby declare a national emergency to deal with that threat." Near the top of the list of persons thus dramatically stigmatized is "AHMETI, Ali, Member of National Liberation Army (NLA)," born in Kicevo, Macedonia, on January 4, 1959. The presidential order does not actually use the word "terrorist," yet it treats him as such. In May that year, the NATO secretary-general, Lord (George) Robertson, described the National Liberation Army that Ahmeti leads as "a bunch of murderous thugs whose objective is to destroy a democratic Macedonia."

In mid-August, however, under heavy pressure from the United States, NATO, and European negotiators, representatives of the Slav and Albanian Macedonians signed a peace deal. In return for constitutional and administrative changes designed to secure equal rights for Albanian Macedonians in the Macedonian state, the NLA would stop fighting and hand in many of its weapons to NATO. As part of the deal, the Macedonian president, Boris Trajkovski, committed himself to giving amnesty to the insurgents, a commitment effectively guaranteed to Ahmeti by NATO. As President Trajkovski memorably explained to me: "I signed an agreement with the Secretary-General [of NATO] and the Secretary-General's representative signed an agreement with the terrorists."

I found some confusion among Western representatives in Skopje about the proper characterization of Mr. Ahmeti. One senior British military officer, who had spent years fighting the IRA in Northern Ireland, told me with emphasis and passion that Ahmeti and his colleagues in the NLA are terrorists. "If you take the NATO definition of terrorism, they absolutely fit," he said.[2] Other senior civilian and military NATO representatives described the NLA action as an "insurgency" and expressed admiration for the restraint exercised by Ahmeti and his men in their astonishingly successful seven-month campaign. On paper, international organizations had characteristically taken refuge in a euphemism wrapped in an acronym. "EAAG," said the documents— short for Ethnic Albanian Armed Group.

I felt it might be useful to ask Mr. Ahmeti himself. So, with an Albanian driver and interpreter, I drove up high into the beautiful wooded mountains of western Macedonia, past Macedonian police checkpoints, past well-built hillside villages with gleaming minarets, past a makeshift road sign saying "STOP: NLA," to the village of Sipkovica. Dodging mules carrying great loads of straw up the steep and narrow cobbled street, we made our way to a large house guarded by young men in jeans and dark glasses. While we waited, they proudly pointed to a black Audi "captured" from the deputy speaker of the Macedonian parliament. Inside, Ahmeti, a weary-looking man with sweptback silver-gray hair and fingers heavily stained with nicotine, seated himself cross-legged on a weary-looking armchair and offered me what he called a "very good" whiskey—a fifteen-year-old Bowmore from the Scottish island of Islay. He drank some too. (In the Balkans, Islay trumps Islam.)

After a few minutes of preliminary conversation, I told Ahmeti that there was much discussion since September 11 about terrorism and that "some people would say *you* are a terrorist." How would he answer them?

As my question was translated, his bodyguards shifted slightly in their seats. Ahmeti replied calmly and quietly. I expected him to say words to the effect "No, I'm a freedom fighter," but his response was more thoughtful. "That person cannot be a terrorist," he said, "who wears an army badge, who has an objective for which he is fighting, who respects the Geneva Conventions and the Hague Tribunal, who acts in public with name and surname, and answers for everything he does. . . . Someone who is aiming for good reforms and democracy in the country—and that people should be equal before the law."

Now of course one can't simply say "Oh well, that's all right then!" One has to look at what the NLA actually did, and may still do. Nor should we retreat into the weary relativism of the phrase I have heard so many times in

Europe over the last few weeks: "One man's terrorist is another man's free-dom fighter." To be sure, on this matter there are blatant double standards throughout the world. The Kurds are freedom fighters in Iraq and terrorists in Turkey, or vice versa, depending on where you sit. To be sure, the kind of sudden shifts that we have often seen in Western policy and language invite cynicism. The banned terrorist Ahmeti becomes a valued partner in a peace process. The CIA-funded, heroic, anti-Soviet fighter Osama bin Laden becomes the world's most wanted terrorist. The former terrorist (or was it freedom fighter?) Menachem Begin wins the Nobel Peace Prize.

Yet it is also true that people change. They spiral downward into bru-tality like Conrad's Kurtz, or they reemerge from darkness as they conclude that their political purposes are best served by moving on from armed strug-gle, as did the former German terrorist Horst Mahler, the Sinn Fein leader Gerry Adams, and Nelson Mandela. It is also true that there are many differ-ent terrorisms, and not all forms of using violence to achieve political ends are properly described as terrorism. If we are not to lose the global "war against terrorism," proclaimed by President Bush after September 11, we need a sophisticated understanding of the differences.

Identifying Terrorists

Here are four things to look at in deciding whether someone is a terrorist, and, if they are, what kind of terrorist: Biography, Goals, Methods, and Context. Only a combination of the four will yield an answer. I will use the example of Ahmeti and the NLA, but the template can be used anywhere.

BIOGRAPHY

Who are they, where are they coming from, and what do they really want? Why did fifteen of the nineteen assassins of September 11 come from Saudi Arabia? Does Osama bin Laden really want to destroy the West, to purify Islam, to top-ple the Saudi royal house, or merely to change the Saudi succession? The clas-sic questions of intelligence work are also the first intelligent questions about any suspected terrorist. Biography may not be at the heart of all History—but it certainly is for this patch.

To anyone who has spent time in Kosovo and Macedonia, what we know of Ali Ahmeti's life story feels quite familiar. He comes from the vil-lage of Zajas, near the town of Kicevo, in the mountainous western part of Macedonia that is largely inhabited by Albanians, but he studied at the University of Pristina, in Kosovo. (It was then all Tito's Yugoslavia.) He was a student radical. Like many others at that time, he combined Albanian nationalism and Marxism-Leninism. He was imprisoned for a few months. He was, aged twenty-two, an active participant in the 1981 uprising of Albanian students in Pristina. Then he fled to Switzerland. Not having access to clas-sified intelligence reports. I do not know exactly what his "studies" and "work" in Switzerland consisted of, but he remained politically active. In exile he reportedly joined the Movement for an Albanian Socialist Republic in Yugoslavia, and formed a Macedonian subcommittee of the Marxist-Leninists of Kosovo. His style during our long conversation spoke to me of many hours spent debating revolutionary politics in smoke-filled rooms. He read many books, he told me, "for example, about psychology and guerrilla warfare."

While the rural population among whom he operates is largely Muslim, at no point in our conversation did he even mention Islam, let alone give any hint of fellow feeling for Islamic terrorist groups such as Al Qaeda. It is a reasonable assumption that a whiskey-drinking, ex–Marxist-Leninist, Albanian nationalist does not see himself as part of any Muslim international.

His movements during the 1990s are unclear. He told me that he was back in Macedonia in 1993, when he found his Albanian compatriots still hoping for peaceful recognition of their rights inside the newly independent Macedonia. An unconfirmed report speaks of him being in Tirana, the capital of Albania, in 1997, attempting to organize guerrilla groups. A great influence on him was his uncle, Fazli Veliu, a former schoolteacher from the same village of Zajas (and another name on President Bush's exclusion list of June 27). Ahmeti joined a small political party called the LPK, which uncle Fazli had been instrumental in founding. The LPK was the main precursor of the Kosovo Liberation Army (KLA).[3] They also organized the Homeland Calling fund, which raised money among Albanians living abroad for the armed struggle in Kosovo.[4] How much of that money derived from the drug trade, prostitution, or protection rackets we shall never know, but some of it certainly came from ordinary Albanians making patriotic contributions.

Obviously, the military campaign of the KLA in Kosovo in 1998–1999 was a formative experience for him. Ahmeti told me he was in Kosovo at that time, but did not actually fight. Other reports say he fought. Not accidentally, the Albanian initials of the National Liberation Army in Macedonia are the same as those of the Kosovo Liberation Army: UCK.[5] Some of the leading figures of the NLA came from the KLA. So did some of the weapons. But above all, there was the immediate example. I asked Ahmeti if he thought Albanian Macedonians would have been ready to fight for their rights in 1998. No, he said, "because of the situation in Kosovo." But after the West had come in to Kosovo and—as most Albanian Macedonians saw it—the KLA had "won" as a result, there were enough people ready to heed the call to arms in Macedonia at the beginning of [2001]. Most of the ordinary fighters of the NLA were Albanian Macedonians, many of whom had bought their own guns.

Summarizing what he told me, I would say that the now forty-two-year-old Ahmeti drew two main conclusions from the Kosovo war. First, you could win more by a few months of armed struggle than Albanian politicians had achieved in nearly a decade of peaceful politics. As in Kosovo, so in Macedonia. Second, that you could do this only if you got the West involved. That was the great tactical goal—and the great unknown. He told me that when the insurgency took off in February. "I knew that without the help of the West we couldn't win. But we didn't know how much they would help. . . ." So he had to do everything possible to bring the West in. That meant being deliberately restrained in both their goals and their methods. This was Albanian Macedonia's chance. This was Ali Ahmeti's chance.

GOALS

Whatever the tangle of biographically conditioned motives—and human motives are often unclear even to ourselves—one also has to look at the proclaimed goals of a terrorist goal or movement. Sometimes, as in the case of Al Qaeda or the German Red Army Faction, the overall goals are so vague, apocalyptic, and all-embracing that they could never be realized in any real world. But sometimes they are clear and—as much as we deplore tactics that shed the blood of innocents—in some sense rational objectives, which may sooner or later be achieved in the real world. The KLA wants independence for Kosovo; the IRA, a united Ireland; ETA, independence for the Basque Country, and so on.

The NLA was remarkable for the clarity and relative modesty of its proclaimed goals. From the outset, its leaders insisted that they only wanted what Albanian Macedonian politicians had been arguing for since Macedonia became independent in 1991: equal status and equal rights for the Albanian Macedonians. Albanians should be recognized as a constitutive nation of the Republic of Macedonia. The Albanian language should be accepted as an official language, in parliament and the public administration. Albanians should have the right to higher education in their own language. Albanians should be proportionately represented in the bureaucracy, the courts, and, especially, the police, who should stop harassing them. There should be more devolution of powers to local government—with obvious implications for those areas with an Albanian majority. But Macedonia should remain a unitary, multiethnic state.

Compared with the demands of the KLA, Bosnian Serbs and Croats, the IRA, or the ETA, these look as if they were drafted by Amnesty International. Most Western representatives regard them as reasonable, and believe that the Macedonian state should have conceded most of them years ago. Now you may say: but these demands are tactical, designed to appeal to the West. Certainly they are. Altogether, I found Ahmeti guarded, elusive, even evasive on these political questions—which is to say, he spoke as a politician. Like the old Marxist-Leninist comrade that he is, he stuck firmly to the party line: equal rights in a unitary, multiethnic state, nothing more! But, it seemed to me, he did so with some personal conviction—and good arguments.

Why, I asked, could one not envisage a federal solution for Macedonia? He smiled: "In a country with just two million people and 25,000 square kilometers?" It would be ridiculous. Federalism would mean new territorial borders and competition between the constituent parts. How could you draw the lines in a country where Albanian and Slav Macedonians live so mixed up together? "Either we're in the twenty-first century and thinking of integration into Europe, or we do it as they did one hundred years ago. . . ." Putting his hand on his heart, he said, "My country is Macedonia."

Not all his colleagues agree. I spoke to another NLA commander, Rafiz Aliti, known as "Teacher" because he was, until the spring uprising, the village physical education teacher. He told me that he favored the federalization and "cantonization" of Macedonia. A unitary state could not work. If the Macedonian side did not implement the mid-August "framework agreement," which on paper fulfills the Albanians' moderate demands, then they would go to war again. And this time it would be a war for territory. What territory? "The territory where Albanians live."

Yet there is a substantial body of evidence that most of the Albanian political elite in Kosovo and Macedonia have agreed that the medium-term strategic goal should be different in each place: independence for Kosovo, equal rights in Macedonia. And, incidentally, not Greater Albania for either. Not for the foreseeable future anyway.

There is a very good reason for Albanian Macedonians to take this gradualist path. According to the Macedonian authorities, some 23 percent of the Macedonian population is Albanian, but unofficial estimates put the number as high as 35 percent. The "framework agreement" provides for a new, internationally supervised census, and it will be interesting to see what figure it comes up with. Whatever the result, everyone knows that the Albanian Macedonians have many more children than the Slav Macedonians. At current birth rates, the Albanians will probably become a demographic majority in about 2025. And then the majority might elect the sixty-six-year-old Ali Ahmeti president of Macedonia . . .

METHODS

This is the single most important criterion. An old man who stands on a soapbox at Speakers' Corner in London on a rainy Saturday afternoon demanding that the Lord raze to the ground all branches of Marks & Spencer is not a terrorist. He is a nut at Speakers' Corner. The Scottish National Party has goals much more far-reaching than the NLA—it wants full independence for Scotland—but it works entirely by peaceful, constitutional means.

Does the individual or group use violence to realize their personal or political goals? Is that violence targeted specifically at the armed and uniformed representatives of the state, or does the terrorist group also target innocent civilians? Does it attempt to limit civilian casualties while spreading panic and disruption—as Irish paramilitaries have sometimes done, by telephoning bomb warnings—or does it aim for the mass killing of innocent civilians, as Al Qaeda plainly did on September 11?

Ahmeti and the NLA deliberately chose violence. The lesson they learned from Kosovo was: if you play your cards right, a little well-calculated violence achieves what years of nonviolent politics had not. Which, once again, it did. But, Ahmeti and others claim, they never targeted civilians. They observed the Geneva Conventions, were mindful of the Hague Tribunal, and so on. Most international observers agree that the NLA did much less harm to Slav Macedonian civilians than the KLA did to Serbian civilians in Kosovo. This was especially true in the areas most directly under Ahmeti's command. But Human Rights Watch and Amnesty International have documented several cases of kidnapping, torture, and abuse by members of the NLA.

I spoke with a group of young Slav Macedonian men who had fled from their villages in western Macedonia. However, they had done so—even by their own account—after themselves having taken up arms against the NLA. They told the dreadfully familiar story of how neighbors who had lived and worked peacefully together for years suddenly turned guns on each other (as in Kosovo, as in Bosnia, as in Croatia . . .). According to the Macedonian government, some 70,000 people fled or were expelled from their homes as a result of the fighting. International observers suggest the number is much lower. They also say that the worst damage to civilians was done by the Macedonian army and security forces. The guns of an incompetent army indiscriminately pounded rebel villages—the textbook way *not* to fight an insurgency. Paramilitaries called the Lions, working, as in Milosevic's Serbia, under the interior ministry, attacked Albanians in the shadows. And there is no doubt that ordinary Albanians have for years been subjected to harassment by a police force that is overwhelmingly Slav Macedonian.

Coming down from my mountain meeting with Ahmeti, our car was stopped by a man in the uniform of a police major and a paramilitary soldier with a large wooden cross around his neck. The major verbally abused my interpreter. When I tried to intervene, saying (rather pompously) that I had that morning spoken to President Trajkovski and I was sure the President would wish us to be given fair passage, he said to my interpreter, "Tell your man I don't give a fuck about the President." When I smiled, he said, "Tell him to stop smiling." This Macedonian policeman was a fine propagandist for the Albanian cause.

Afterward, my Albanian driver was physically trembling with rage. "You see how they treat us," he cried, in his broken German. "If I had not seen the policeman waving us down at the roadside, they would have shot us. That is not *korrekt*." Not *korrekt*, indeed.

This was a messy little low-level civil war, in which neither side was very *korrekt* and neither very brutal, by the low standards of the Balkans. The NLA started it, but the Slav Macedonian side behaved rather worse during it. This brings us to our last criterion: context.

CONTEXT

Basic Principle 1.1 of the *Framework Agreement for Macedonia* says, "The use of violence in pursuit of political aims is rejected completely and unconditionally."

An admirable principle. But not to be taken too literally. After all, in bombing Afghanistan, America and Britain are pursuing political aims through the use of violence. You may say: but that is justified by all the time-honored criteria of "just war," and legitimated by international coalitions, organizations, and law. Anyway, to use political violence from inside and against a legitimate state is a quite different thing. But who decides if a particular state is legitimate?

Even within an internationally recognized state, there can be such oppression that armed resistance may be considered legitimate. This is the claim expressed with incomparable force in the words that Schiller puts into the mouth of Stauffacher in his *Wilhelm Tell*. When the oppressed man can find justice in no other way, says Stauffacher, then he calmly reaches up into the sky and pulls down his eternal rights that hang there, inalienable and, like the stars, imperishable. When no other means remains, then he must . . . take up the sword.[6] Such, perhaps, were the Polish uprisings for freedom in the eighteenth and nineteenth centuries. Such was the American War of Independence.

It therefore matters hugely what kind of state you're in. It is one thing for groups like the IRA and ETA to use political violence in states like Britain or Spain, where the means of working for peaceful change are equally available to all in a mature democracy. It is another thing for Palestinian groups to use political violence against an oppressive military occupation in the Gaza strip or the West Bank. Another again for the ANC against the South African apartheid regime. Yet another for the violently repressed Kosovo Albanians to take up arms against the Milosevic regime in Serbia. We may want to uphold the universal principle "No violence!" but we all know that these are, in political fact and in moral content, very different things, and some violent political actions are—shall we say—less unjustified than others.

"So far as I know," President Boris Trajkovski smilingly informed me, "world leaders are all praising Macedonia." Well, I have news for President Trajkovski (who is a nice, decent, personally uncorrupt, and well-intentioned man, but not perhaps possessed of the world's strongest intellect or character). They're not. In private, many of them are cursing it. I remarked to a very senior Western negotiator who has had much to do with Macedonia that I had never encountered a more pigheaded, shortsighted political elite than the Slav Macedonian one. "Amen to all that," the negotiator said, "except that I would question your use of the word 'elite.'" Just as they fought the war against the NLA in a way that rebounded against themselves, so they are still—at this writing—pigheadedly holding out against amendments to the constitution that most international observers regard as wholly reasonable.

A particular sticking-point is a wording in the preamble that refers (in my official English translation) to "the historical fact that Macedonia is established as a national state of the Macedonian people. . . ." Understandably, the Albanians don't like this reference to a national state, especially since the word for "people" in this context is *narod*, implying ethnic community, rather than the broader and more civic *nacija*. The Slav Macedonian side agreed to a rewording in the summer peace deal, but now the parliament is threatening to renege on it.

Extraordinary Western pressure—almost weekly visits by the EU foreign policy representative Javier Solana and NATO secretary-general George Robertson (who might have a few other things on their minds), the withholding of international aid to the crippled Macedonian economy until the amendments are passed—seems incapable of budging them. The sledgehammer is defied by the nut. And at lower levels, the bureaucracy, the army, and the police seem as stubborn, corrupt, and incompetent as their politicians.

There are explanations for all this. Looking back over the last decade one must have sympathy with Slav Macedonians too. There are peoples that aspire to statehood and peoples that have statehood thrust upon them. The Macedonians had statehood thrust upon them, as former Yugoslavia collapsed in 1991. Well into the twentieth century, all of the country's four neighbors had claims on its territory: Serbia between the wars treated it as part of Southern Serbia, Bulgaria regarded it as part of Bulgaria (and the Macedonian language as just a dialect of Bulgarian), Albanian nationalists wanted great chunks of it for Greater Albania, and Greeks said Macedonia is really Greek.

None of these claims were fully, unambiguously laid to rest in 1991. Their already battered economy was then shattered and corrupted by Western sanctions on Milosevic's Serbia, and a Greek blockade of international recognition for Macedonia because, said the Greeks, there is already a Macedonia in Greece. (Hence the state's awkward international name, the Former Yugoslav Republic of Macedonia, though it calls itself plain Republic of Macedonia.) Then it had to cope with the vast Albanian refugee influx from Kosovo. Western promises of economic aid and investment have remained largely that—promises. Oh yes, and the Slav Macedonians will soon be a minority in their own country. A little existential *Angst* is understandable. This helps to explain, but it does not excuse. Most of the changes now being made (or not being made) under pressure from the NLA and the West should have been made years ago.

All that being said, the fact remains that the position of the Albanians in Macedonia at the beginning of this year was nothing like the one unforgettably evoked in *Schiller's Wilhelm Tell*. There were still possibilities for peaceful change. Established Albanian political parties were in the government as well as parliament (as they still are), and they were pressing for most of the same reforms. They were not getting there very fast (partly because both Slav Macedonian and Albanian Macedonian parties harbor impressive levels of corruption), but in time, with Western and especially European pressure, they would have got there. However relatively restrained the NLA was in its goals and methods, it willfully chose the path of violence when other paths were still open. As a result, it has accelerated the necessary reforms on paper, but it may also have impeded their practical realization. For the war has resulted in further alienation of the Albanian and Slav Macedonian communities, and political radicalization on both sides.

The Definitional Challenge

So: was I drinking whiskey with a terrorist? Well, certainly with a former revolutionary politician and a guerrilla leader who deliberately reached for the gun when other means were available. Perhaps the moderation of his proclaimed goals, and the fact that he tried not to target civilians, pulls him just the right side of the line. Just. Perhaps. Certainly, he has moved on to become an impressively consistent advocate of change through political negotiation inside an undivided, multi-ethnic state. So maybe it is all right to drink whiskey with a reformed terrorist? If it were not, the consumption of whiskey by world leaders would have been reduced by quite a few bottles over the last fifty years.

Will the United Nations give us some further guidance on this matter? For a long time, the UN has avoided any definition of terrorism. Recently, it has tiptoed toward one. A November 2000 report by the UN's Sixth Committee came close to a general definition when it declared:

> Criminal acts intended or calculated to provoke a state of terror in the general public, a group of persons or particular persons for political reasons are in any circumstances unjustifiable, whatever the considerations of a political, philosophical, ideological, racial, ethnic, religious or other nature that may be used to justify them.[7]

But that is unsustainably broad. Isn't the Taliban a "group of persons" among whom we hope to provoke a state of terror? Who decides what is a criminal act?

Since September 11, support has been growing for a UN convention on terrorism. One wonders how useful any definition it comes up with can be, both because member states will have such widely differing views of what should count and because of the intrinsic difficulties for even the most neutral, independent analyst. Realistically, the best one can hope for may be that as wide as possible a spectrum of states, including states from different "civilizations," in [Harvard Professor] Samuel Huntington's sense, may reach agreement on the description of as many particular cases as possible. At the very least, Europe and America should agree—which is by no means guaranteed, if one thinks of differing approaches to Iraq, for example, or to Israel and the Palestinian question. Even then, a common policy might not follow, but at least there would be a common analysis to start from.

To this end, my four headings—Biography, Goals, Methods, Context— may serve as a modest template, but the content in each case will be very different and there will be no universal guidelines for judging the combination. As the great Bishop Butler once unshallowly remarked, every thing is what it is and not another thing.

Notes

1. The point was made to me, vociferously, by a group of nationalist demonstrators outside the Macedonian parliament. A Macedonian Web site makes a tabular comparison of the two men (Occupation: Leader of a terrorist organization; Leader of a terrorist organization; Islamic? Yes; Yes; and so on). See www.realitymacedonia.org.mk.

2. But what is the NATO definition of terrorism? This officer could not remember exactly. Subsequent inquiries reveal that NATO does not have one, not least because its member states cannot agree on one—which again indicates the difficulties. Probably this officer was thinking of a working distinction made in British military doctrine between "terrorism" and "insurgency."

3. On this, see Tim Judah, *Kosovo: War and Revenge* (Yale University Press, 2000), and my review essay on the Kosovo war in *The New York Review*, September 21, 2000. I quote there US special envoy Robert Gelbard characterizing the KLA in February 1998 as "without any questions, a terrorist group."

4. The Homeland Calling fund may be compared with the US-based Noraid fund, which raised money in the US for the IRA—except that the Noraid fund was long tolerated by the US authorities. The Albanian-American vote was of course, rather smaller than the Irish-American one.

5. The Kosovo Liberation Army was Ushtria Clirimtare e Kosoves (UCK); the National Liberation Army is Ushtria Clirimtare e Kombetare (UCK). Thus, when my driver was asking for the location of Ahmeti's headquarters he asked, "Where is the headquarters of the UCK?"

6. I cannot resist quoting these marvelous lines in full:

   Nein, eine Grenze hat Tyrannenmacht:
   Wenn der Gedrückte nirgends Recht kann finden,
   Wenn unerträglich wird die Last—greift er
   Hinauf getrosten Mutes in den Himmel
   Und holt herunter seine ew'gen Rechte,
   Die droben hangen unveräusserlich
   Und unzerbrechlich, wie die Sterne selbst—
   Der alte Urstand der Natur kehrt wieder,
   Wo Mensch dem Menschen gegenübersteht
   Zum letzten Mittel, wenn kein andres mehr
   Verfangen will, ist ihm das Schwert gegeben.

7. I owe this quotation, and my summary of what the UN has done, to my Oxford colleague Professor Adam Roberts.

Chapter 6

THE EVOLVING STRATEGIES OF POLITICAL TERRORISM

GREGORY A. RAYMOND

Shortly after the September 11, 2001, attacks on the World Trade Center and the Pentagon, Governor Dirk Kempthorne of Idaho initiated a series of security measures to counter an unspecified terrorist threat against what he called "trophy targets" in Boise. Besides closing all of the roads around the Capitol and encircling the building with massive concrete barricades, he ordered 24 National Guardsmen and over a dozen state troopers to patrol the Statehouse grounds. Traffic soon clogged those streets in the city center that remained open, shoppers began avoiding downtown businesses, and county sheriffs complained that they had to cover for state police who were baby-sitting buildings rather than patrolling highways. As the cost of these new security measures mounted and an economic recession plunged the state into a budgetary crisis, law enforcement officials rented an expensive condominium next to the governor's residence to give him around-the-clock protection. Though ridiculed for his bunker mentality, Kempthorne insisted that he was merely being prudent. Terrorist attacks were just as likely in Idaho, he maintained, as they were anywhere else.

What would lead the governor of a state located over 2,000 miles away from the attacks on New York and Washington to take such controversial security precautions? How was Osama bin Laden, the Saudi Arabian dissident who orchestrated the attacks from his base in Afghanistan, able create fear and alarm among government officials in the northern Rocky Mountains? Questions of this sort raise important issues about the military logic underpinning terrorism. Over the past century and a half, much has been written by those who countenance terrorism regarding how violence should be used to achieve political goals. The purpose of this essay is to examine that body of thought, tracing its evolution through a series of debates about strategic objectives, tactics, and operational art.

Terrorism can be employed to support or change the political status quo. Repressive terror, which is wielded to sustain an existing political order, has been utilized by governments as well as by vigilantes. From the Committee of General Security in Jacobin France to the death squads in various Latin American states, establishment violence attempts to defend the prevailing political order by eliminating vexatious individuals and intimidating virtually everyone else. Although repressive terror has a long, gruesome history, the focus of this essay will be on the evolving strategies of those dissidents who use terror to change the political status quo.

In analyzing the military logic of dissidents who use terrorism to attack an established political order, we shall do three things: (1) identify their strategic objectives; (2) examine the repertoire of tactics at their disposal; and (3) compare contending paramilitary doctrines that link strategic objectives to terrorist tactics.

The Strategic Objectives of Terrorism

Political terrorism entails the deliberate use or threat of violence against noncombatants, calculated to instill fear, alarm, and ultimately a feeling of helplessness in an audience beyond the immediate victims. Because perpetrators of terrorism often strike symbolic targets in a horrific manner, the psychological impact of an attack can exceed the physical damage. The campaign of assassinations in Judea conducted by the Sicarii during the first century CE illustrates the atmosphere of collective vulnerability that can be created by terrorism. As Josephus Flavius wrote in *The Jewish War*: "The panic [they] created was more alarming than the calamity itself; nearly everyone . . . hourly expected death. Men kept watch at a distance on their enemies and would not trust even their friends when they approached."

A mixture of drama and dread, political terrorism is not senseless violence; it springs from a premeditated, coldly calculated strategy of extortion. Strategies are plans of action, blueprints linking military means to political ends. A common feature in the strategies embraced by different terrorist groups is an attempt to induce acute feelings of insecurity within targeted populations. To borrow a phrase from Paul Wilkinson, terrorism is a "mode of unconventional psychological warfare." It presents people with a danger that seems ubiquitous, unavoidable, and unpredictable.

Beyond seeking to change the political status quo, the long-term goals of those who resort to dissident terrorism vary considerably. Some groups, like the MPLA (Popular Movement for the Liberation of Angola), used it to expel colonial rulers; others, such as ETA (Basque Homeland and Liberty), adopted terrorism as part of an ethnonational separatist struggle; still others, including the Islamic Jihad, the Christian Identity Movement, the Sikh group Babbar Khalsa, and Jewish militants belonging to Kach, placed terror in the service of what they saw as religious imperatives; finally, groups such as the Japanese Red Army and Italian Black Order turned to terrorism for left or right-wing ideological reasons. In short, dissident terrorism may be grounded in anticolonialism, separatism, religion, or secular ideology. Although the ultimate goals of individuals and groups that employ terrorism differ, they seek similar intermediate objectives as a means of attaining their goals.

One way to conceptualize the multilayered, intermediate aims of terrorism is to differentiate among three categories of strategic objectives: agitational, coercive, and organizational. Let us briefly discuss each in turn.

The agitational objectives of terrorism include promoting the dissident group, advertizing its agenda, and discrediting rivals. Shocking behavior makes people take heed, especially when performed at a time and place imbued with symbolism. Nineteenth century anarchists such as Carlo Pisacane and Peter Kropotkin were among the first to emphasize the propaganda value of terrorism. One stunning act, they believed, would draw more attention than a thousand leaflets. Perhaps no group embodied their ideas more than the Tupamaros, who undertook a campaign of "armed propaganda" in Uruguay during the mid to late 1960s. In addition to cultivating a Robin Hood image by commandeering groceries and distributing them in poor neighborhoods, they seized radio and television stations to broadcast inflammatory proclamations and harangue their opponents. As is often the case, the successful initiatives of one terrorist group are emulated by others. Among those copying the armed propaganda techniques of the Tupamaros were the ERP (People's Revolutionary Army), FAL (Liberation Armed Forces), and FAP (Peronist Armed Forces) in nearby Argentina.

Once such groups win notoriety and have their cause widely acknowledged, they can exert significant leverage over established authorities. The primary coercive objectives of terrorism include disorienting a target population, inflating the perceived power of the dissident group, wringing concessions from authorities, and provoking a heavy-handed overreaction from the police and military. Launching vicious, indiscriminant attacks at markets, cafes, resorts, and other normally tranquil locations can create a paralyzing sense of foreboding within the general public. Anything, it seems, can happen to anyone at anytime. As doubts about the ability of the government to protect innocent civilians spread, civil society becomes atomized. Communal life gives way to isolated, demoralized individuals who feel exposed to arbitrary, capricious dangers. Believing they are alone, people easily exaggerate the strength of the terrorists. At first, political leaders may relent to terrorist demands. But once the demands escalate, the government may respond with brutal repression, which the terrorists insist will drive the population to their side of the struggle.

The organizational objectives of terrorism include acquiring resources, forging group cohesion, and maintaining an underground network of supporters. Although terrorist groups are not all alike, they face common problems stemming from their need for secrecy. To guard against infiltration, they are usually compartmentalized into small, clandestine cells. Command and control within such decentralized structures are difficult; however, terrorism can fortify these groups in several ways. First, it can finance training and logistical support for field operations when used to rob banks, obtain ransom for hostages, and collect protection money from businesses. Second, it can elevate morale, particularly when employed to win the release of imprisoned group members. Third, since high initiation costs tend to lower group defections, it can increase allegiance when recruits are required to participate in violent acts. Finally, terrorism can enforce obedience when used to punish anyone who collaborates with the enemy. According to psychiatrist Franz Fanon, violence has both bonding and therapeutic effects; it builds solidarity among those fighting together as it frees them from feeling inferior to their enemy. Terrorism, wrote Bhagwat Charan of the Hindustan Socialist Revolutionary Army in *The Philosophy of the Bomb*, "gives self-confidence to the wavering." It is a "safety valve," added Algerian FLN (National Liberation Front) leader Amar Ouzegane in his *Le Meilleur Combat*. It allows its users "to liberate themselves from an unconscious psychological complex, to keep cool heads, to respect revolutionary discipline."

In summary, practitioners of dissident terrorism despise the political status quo. Although they may differ on what should replace it, they agree that remorseless acts of violence directed against noncombatants will accomplish certain agitational, coercive, and organizational objectives that facilitate attaining their ultimate goals. Moreover, a single act of terrorism may simultaneously accomplish several objectives. To illuminate how they attempt to reach these objectives, we shall now consider their tactics.

The Repertoire of Terrorist Tactics

The most common tactics employed by practitioners of terrorism are bombing, arson, assault, hijacking, kidnapping, and taking hostages. Bombing alone accounts for roughly half of all recorded terrorist incidents. Not only can terrorists sabotage electrical power grids and other utilities with explosives, but they can kill and maim large numbers of people, especially if nails and other metal objects are packed around the bomb's core. When combined with a timing mechanism, bombs allow even solitary terrorists to cause enormous damage with little risk of being apprehended. Theodore Kacynski (the Unabomber), Muharem Kurbegovic (the Alphabet Bomber), and Eric Rudolph, the anti-abortion activist charged with planting a bomb at the 1996 Atlanta Olympic Games, exemplify the havoc that can be created by a single individual.

Over time, rudimentary fragmentation devices like the pipe and letter bombs favored by many lone terrorists have given way to incredibly powerful blast weapons, some of which can be crafted with off-the-shelf technology. The truck bomb that devastated the Alfred P. Murrah Federal Building in Oklahoma City during 1995 contained a simple mixture of ammonium nitrate fertilizer and fuel oil. More sophisticated bombs are available from states that sponsor terrorism, as well as from black market vendors with access to weapons from former Warsaw Pact members. Shaped charges, constructed from plastic explosives such as Semtex, can be molded to fit inside of books, letters, suitcases, and other items. Pan Am flight 103, for example, was brought down over Lockerbie, Scotland, in 1988 by plastic explosives hidden inside a radio.

Although incendiary devices are not used as frequently as blast and fragmentation weapons, arson can also be a tool of terror. From the Molotov cocktail to explosives attached to propane tanks, firebombs are inexpensive and easily fabricated from chemicals available at pharmacies, hardware stores, and other commercial outlets.

Armed assaults range from attacking hardened targets from afar with mortars and portable rockets to attacking soft targets at short range with easily concealed sidearms that possess high rates of fire and good penetration power. As the assassinations of Italian Premier Aldo Moro, German industrialist Hans-Martin Schleyer, and President Malcolm Kerr of the American University of Beirut indicate, one aim of armed attacks is to liquidate key government officials, corporate executives, and other highly visible figures. Another aim is to attack symbols of a country's prestige. Armed groups have stormed airports, embassies, police stations, post offices, and country clubs. On July 30, 1970, the FAR (Revolutionary Armed Forces) of Argentina briefly occupied the town of Garín. Not only are these kinds of assaults embarrassing to an incumbent regime, they also have serious economic repercussions when launched against oil pipelines, transportation hubs, or tourist sites.

Hijacking, kidnaping, and hostage-taking generally involve more complex operations than planting a bomb in a crowded department store or gunning down travelers in an airport lounge. An example of such careful planning can be seen in the coordinated hijacking of five airliners by Palestinians during September 1970, which eventually led to one airliner being blown up in Cairo and three others at Dawson Field in Jordan. To be successful, these kinds of seizures require detailed preparation, vigorous bargaining, and the capacity to guard captives for long periods of time. Tupac Amaru, a Peruvian group, seized the Japanese ambassador's residence in Lima on December 17, 1996, and held 72 hostages for four months before they were rescued.

While the risk of capture by government commandos is significant, seizures like the one in Lima rivet media attention on a dissident group. Recognizing the opportunity to speak on a worldwide stage, some groups have become adept at manipulating coverage to serve their purposes. The Lebanese architects of the 1985 hijacking of TWA flight 847, for instance, excelled at using U.S. television networks to articulate their grievances to the American public, which had the effect of circumscribing the options that the Reagan administration entertained while searching for a solution to the crisis. The Tupamaros illustrate yet another approach to amplifying a political message. To maximize their public exposure, they incarcerated kidnap victims in secret "People's Prisons" and released cassette tapes of subsequent trials. From their perspective, the resulting publicity conveyed a message of "dual" sovereignty: the government was not the only power center; the Tupamaros were a viable, rival political authority within Uruguay.

Beyond the conventional tactics of bombings, arson, assaults, hijacking, and the like, two other threats could become part of the terrorist repertoire. First, dissidents may acquire weapons of mass destruction, to shatter the complacency of a desensitized audience. Violence can become routinized. What once was considered a shocking act of terror may no longer garner sufficient attention. An apocalyptic world view, like that held by the Aum Shinrikyo cult responsible for the 1995 sarin gas in the Tokyo subway, is not necessary for dissident groups to seek weapons of mass destruction. They may have more pragmatic aims in mind, such as commanding attention, demonstrating their prowess, and delivering a mortal blow to detested enemies.

Nuclear armaments are the ultimate terror weapons. Their blast, thermal, and ionizing radiation effects are catastrophic, even if produced by small atomic demolition munitions—so-called suitcase bombs. While most people fear nuclear terrorism, they often forget that radiological, chemical, and biological weapons pose extraordinary dangers. Crude radiological weapons can be fabricated by combining ordinary explosives with nuclear waste or radioactive isotopes, which could be stolen from hospitals, industrial facilities, or research laboratories. Rudimentary chemical weapons can be made from herbicides, pesticides, and other toxic substances that are available commercially. Primitive biological weapons based on food-borne pathogens are also easy to concoct, as the Rajneeshees cult in Oregon demonstrated during 1984 when they applied a solution containing salmonella to restaurant salad bars. Biological weapons based on viral agents are more difficult to produce, though the dispersal of anthrax spores through the mail during the fall of 2001 illustrated that low-technology attacks with bacterial agents in powder form are a frightening possibility.

The second tactical innovation on the horizon is cyberterrorism. Not only can the Internet be used by extremists as a recruiting tool and a means of coordinating their activities with like-minded groups, but it allows them to case potential targets by hacking into a foe's computer system. Viruses and other weapons of "information warfare" could cause havoc if they disabled financial institutions, power grids, air traffic control systems, and other key elements in a country's communication infrastructure. Disrupting vital streams of data flowing between and within highly interdependent societies offers extremist groups an attractive, inexpensive way to besiege their more powerful enemies.

In summary, the specific tactics employed by practitioners of terrorism depend on their capabilities and strategic objectives. Whereas some groups have access to such sophisticated weaponry as surface-to-air, heat-seeking missiles, others rely on a modest arsenal of pistols and pump shotguns. For individuals obsessed with offensive action, creativity and meticulous planning compensate for a lack of firepower. As the September 2001 attacks on the World Trade Center and the Pentagon reveal, everyday tools like box cutters may become potent weapons under the right conditions. A 1994 Philippines Airline flight from Manila to Tokyo was crippled by a bomb that used an ordinary digital wristwatch as a timing device. Even toys and automotive accessories can be adapted to terrorist purposes. The Provisional Irish Republican Army, for example, has used model aircraft remote controls and radar detectors to trigger explosives. When seen in this light, it is clear that absolute security from terrorism is a chimerical aspiration. In target-rich environments, it is always possible for the perpetrator of terrorism to eschew quarry defended by robust safeguards and, as the 1985 *Achille Lauro* incident reminds us, strike with stealth and ingenuity where the risks are lower.

Paramilitary Doctrines Linking Strategic Objectives to Terrorist Tactics

Having described the objectives and tactics common to practitioners of political terrorism, we turn now to debates over how tactical encounters should be managed during a sustained campaign of terror to achieve strategic objectives. Among the issues of contention are geographic focus, organizational design, and situational ripeness. Where should attacks be made? What should be the relationship between political and military forces? When should violence be intensified or curtailed? Whereas defenders of the established political order must constantly protect every potential weakness against many different types of attack, perpetrators of terror only need to concentrate on the most vulnerable point, striking with a configuration of forces tailored to exploit their adversary when and where his guard is down.

Terrorism and Urban Insurrection

The systematic use of modern, dissident terrorism originates in the nineteenth century. Daggers, poisons, and pistols were its primary weapons until the invention of dynamite in 1867. More stable than nitroglycerin and requiring smaller amounts than black powder, dynamite seemed to be the answer to the German radical Karl Heinzen's call for an instrument by which a few militants could destroy thousands of reactionaries. Advocates of terrorism from Johann Most in North America to O'Donovan Rossa in Europe saw opportunities for this new technology. Within Russia, an organization called People's Will began a campaign of bombing during the late 1870s to bring down the Czarist regime. "All the terroristic struggle really needs," boasted Nikolai Morozov in his *Terrorist Struggle,* "is a small number of people and a large material means." The *Catechism of the Revolutionist,* a chilling revolutionary tract variously ascribed to either Mikhail Bakunin or Sergey Nechaev, described such people as implacable enemies of the state, devoid of sentiment and dedicated to merciless destruction.

Although some implacable enemies of the state accepted the socialist Louis August Blanqui's argument that a small group of conspirators could seize power on behalf of the "masses" in a lightening strike, others were skeptical. They believed that large-scale, popular participation in revolutionary movements was imperative, but doubted it would occur automatically. In their opinion, the masses were politically inert; exemplary action by a few terrorists was needed to galvanize the populace into a revolutionary force. On the one hand, acts of terror revealing weaknesses in the established order would raise popular consciousness and empower people to see through the facade of state power. On the other hand, pummeling the state apparatus with incessant terrorist attacks would provoke a spasm of massive, indiscriminate retaliation by a frustrated military, which would ignite a popular uprising.

Metropolitan areas were considered ideal for terrorist campaigns. First, they contained high concentrations of targets, ranging from symbolic buildings to high-level officials. Second, their size and demographic diversity provided terrorists with security by allowing them to come and go anonymously. Third, equipment and supplies were readily available. Fourth, the mass media maintained a sizable presence in urban centers. Finally, the population density of cities neutralized the regime's advantages in firepower and troops. Terrorists operating in neighborhoods crowded with civilians cannot be attacked with artillery. Instead of fighting the mass, set-piece battles for which it was trained, the military must deploy small, lightly armed units to skirmish in narrow, unfamiliar streets and back alleys.

The paramilitary doctrines of these nineteenth-century dynamiters did not win universal acceptance within radical circles. Karl Marx, for example, scoffed at the idea that a small group of terrorists could overthrow an entire socioeconomic system. Deriding them as "alchemists of the revolution," he claimed that they confused the violent symptoms of revolution with its causes. "A single isolated hero," Leon Trotsky would later write in *Against Individual Terrorism*, "cannot replace the masses." Terrorists might kill a tyrant, Vladimir Lenin added, but only a vanguard of skilled professionals doing day-to-day political work with the industrial proletariat could lead a revolution. Whereas Marx rejected terrorism in principle, Lenin's qualms hinged on practical matters. In *"Left-Wing" Communism, An Infantile Disorder,* he rejected individual terrorism as inexpedient, but in *Partisan Warfare* he maintained that terror organized by the vanguard party might be necessary under certain circumstances. Indeed, Lenin was not hesitant to use repressive terror when consolidating Bolshevik rule after the 1917 October Revolution.

Though criticized during the first half of the twentieth century by classical Marxists, the idea of using terrorist tactics in cities to raise the political consciousness of the working class and provoke an overreaction by the state returned from the 1960s through the 1980s under the guise of "urban guerrilla warfare." Carlos Marighela, author of the *Minimanual of the Urban Guerrilla,* asserted that "Terrorism is an arm that the revolutionary can never relinquish." It must be used "with the greatest cold bloodedness" against "the government, the big capitalists, and foreign imperialists." When the regime attempts to institute political reforms, "the urban guerrilla must become more aggressive and violent, resorting without let-up to sabotage, terrorism, expropriations, assaults, kidnapings, executions, etc." *The Urban Guerrilla Concept,* ostensibly written by Ulrike Meinhof of the Red Army Faction in Germany, summarized the purpose of terrorism as destroying the myth of the state's invulnerability. Once its frailties were exposed, the masses could be mobilized. As expressed in *Prairie Fire,* a 1974 manifesto of the Weather Underground in the United States: "Revolutionary action generates revolutionary consciousness; growing consciousness develops revolutionary action."

Both ideological and ethnonationalist groups gravitated to the urban guerrilla doctrine. Italy's Red Brigades, an example of the former, hoped to mobilize their country's industrial workers by sabotaging manufacturing facilities, assassinating business leaders, "knee-capping" (shooting a victim's knee) union officers who allegedly had been co-opted by management, and kidnapping what it saw as henchmen of corporate capitalism, such as NATO Brigadier General James Dozier. The Basque group ETA, an example of the latter, used bombing and armed attacks against Spanish police and government installations for consciousness-raising purposes, as well as to wear down the patience of officials in Madrid. *Insurrection in Euskadi,* a pamphlet outlining their tactics, predicted that Spanish political leaders would overreact to terrorism, and thus generate sympathy in the Basque population for ETA's aims.

Still, questions about the efficacy of terrorism remained. Neither ideological nor ethnonationalist urban guerrillas enjoyed the success that they had predicted. Leftist groups like the New World Liberation Front and Symbionese Liberation Army in the United States fared the worst, alienating the very people they had sought to rally. In *Philosophy of the Urban Guerrilla,* Abraham Guillén, a leading proponent of fluid, hit-and-run street fighting, concluded that urban guerrillas "must not fall prey to terrorism." Similarly, João Quartim, a member of the Brazilian VPR (Popular Revolutionary Vanguard), argued that urban guerrillas had overestimated the value of terrorist attacks as a means of mobilizing the masses.

Terrorism and Rural Guerrilla Warfare

In contrast to the urban focus of some paramilitary doctrines, other strategies emphasize the countryside as a geographic medium, with peasants playing an important role in a lengthy guerrilla struggle. Although the modern word *guerrilla* derives from the resistance by Spanish partisans to Napoleon's invasion of the Iberian Peninsula in 1808, guerrilla wars have been waged throughout recorded history. They normally involve military operations by irregular forces against the rear or flanks of regular army units. Guerrillas rely on maneuver and surprise, preferring ambushes to fixed lines of battle. T. E. Lawrence, who led Arab guerrillas against Ottoman forces between 1916 and 1918, described their strengths as speed and time, not hitting power. Rather than overwhelming the enemy with one bold stroke, they sap his will through attrition. In *The Art of War,* Sun Tzu expressed the essence of the guerrilla creed in the following terms: "When the enemy advances, we retreat; when the enemy halts, we harass; when the enemy seeks to avoid battle, we attack; when the enemy retreats, we pursue."

Although guerrilla warfare is not synonymous with terrorism, various paramilitary doctrines combine guerrilla and terrorist tactics in a protracted, multi-phased campaign. Mao Zedong, for example, proposed three stages. During the first stage, a zone of guerrilla operation in rugged, easily defended terrain is converted into a base area once the enemy within that locale has been defeated. In addition to providing an opportunity to recruit local peasants to the cause, the base area offers a safe haven from which small, mobile units can mount further attacks. Not knowing where or when the next attack will occur immobilizes enemy troops, who must guard numerous transportation and communication facilities. Mao predicted that an exhausted, overextended enemy would eventually withdraw from some contested regions in order to consolidate its hold elsewhere. At this point, the war entered a second stage, during which a regular army is raised while guerrillas strike behind enemy lines to destroy supplies and undermine morale. Terror, he noted, would be necessary to suppress counter-revolutionaries in newly liberated regions, but it must be used with care so as not to alienate peasant support. Finally, as momentum gradually shifted toward the insurgents, the war moved to a third stage. With guerrilla cadres now integrated into the body of the regular army, Mao recommended a massive counteroffensive to vanquish the enemy.

The North Vietnamese General Vo Nguyen Giap modified Mao's approach to guerrilla war. Like his Chinese counterpart, Giap believed that active support from the agrarian population was essential. Peasant-based fighting forces needed to seize the military initiative, using terror when expedient. But in his *Banner of People's War, The Party's Military Line*, he departed from Mao by suggesting that a decisive victory against a symbolically important target could shorten the war, as illustrated by his successful siege of Dien Bien Phu in 1954 which precipitated the French withdrawal from Vietnam. Quoting Ho Chi Minh, he claimed that "Come the right moment, a pawn can bring you victory."

An alternative model of rural guerrilla warfare emerged from the Cuban Revolution. According to Ernesto "Che" Guevara, it was not necessary to wait for all the objective conditions for making revolution to exist; a small group of guerrillas (a *foco,* or nucleus) could create them through exemplary military action. Whereas the Chinese experience dictated that extensive preparatory political work by a vanguard party was indispensable for beginning an uprising, Guevara urged immediate military action. The guerrilla foco would be the party in embryo. Echoing the anarchists of the nineteenth century, Régis Debary wrote in his *Revolution in the Revolution?* that the foco was the "small motor" that set the "large motor" of the masses in motion.

Most Latin American countries lacked the size and topography for a large, secluded base area; consequently, the security of the foco would have to be rooted in secrecy, mobility, and flexibility. In *Guerrilla Warfare*, Guevara declared that terrorism would undermine the foco by making victims of innocent people and destroying lives that would be valuable to the revolution. However, his associate Debray disagreed, asserting that urban terror could help the rural struggle by functioning as a diversion, tying down government troops in guard duty.

To sum up, the first half of the twentieth century witnessed the emergence of several schools of thought that considered rural areas fertile ground for insurgency, despite peasants living far from the nerve centers of society. Unlike in earlier urban-based doctrines, terrorism played a subsidiary role to partisan attacks on regular army units. While disagreements raged over whether political mobilization should precede or follow military action, a consensus existed on the need for guerrilla tactics to be employed for a prolonged period. Amílcar Cabral, one of Africa's most significant revolutionary theorists, believed that by raising revolutionary consciousness guerrilla movements could attain their political goals even without achieving immediate military victory.

In recent years, debates over whether insurgents should rely on urban versus rural-based doctrines have given way to a more eclectic attitude. For example, the Peruvian group Sendero Luminoso began with a rural strategy based in the isolated, impoverished Ayacucho region, but added terrorist operations in Lima and other cities. Similarly, the New People's Army (NPA) of the Philippines has combined urban terror tactics with rural guerrilla war. The death of Che Guevara in an ill-conceived attempt to organize a rural guerrilla foco in Bolivia led many theorists of political insurgency to conclude that the flexibility of combined urban-rural operations held greater prospects for success than a rigid reliance on a single paramilitary doctrine.

Terrorism and Asymmetric International War

During the mid-1990s, two notorious individuals were apprehended, tried, and convicted for acts of political terrorism. The first, Illich Ramírez Sánchez (alias Carlos the Jackal), epitomized a form of terrorism that was based on a secular agenda, a relatively hierarchical command structure, and, as Brian Jenkins once put it, a desire to have a lot of people watching, not a lot of people dead. The second, Ramzi Ahmed Yousef, represented a form of terrorism based on a religious agenda, a more horizontal organizational structure, and a desire to kill as many people as possible. Their capture symbolized a transition in the evolution of terrorist strategy. Whereas the former was steeped in older paramilitary doctrines geared to expelling a colonial power, overthrowing an incumbent regime, or emancipating a region from central government control, the latter embodied newer ideas that suggested terrorism was a potent weapon in asymmetric international warfare.

Asymmetric war is organized violence conducted between political units of vastly unequal military capability, where the weaker side relies on relatively low-tech means to attack its more powerful high-tech opponent. The belligerents may be states, or they may involve some combination of state and non-state actors. When Osama bin Laden announced his 1996 "Declaration of War Against Americans Occupying the Land of the Two Holy Places" and issued a *fatwa* (or religious ruling) two years later calling for Americans to be killed anywhere in the world, he laid the rhetorical foundation for an asymmetric international war between the United States and a non-state actor known as Al Qaeda. Loosely tied together by the Internet, e-mail, and cellular telephones, Al Qaeda (or "Base") is a shadowy network of terrorist cells and front organizations that operate semi-autonomously. Rather than serving as a commander, Osama bin Laden functions as a coordinator who provides financial and logistical support to extremist groups fighting a jihad against enemies of the Muslim community. Prior to September 11, 2001, he sponsored a series of vicious, indiscriminate attacks on U.S. citizens and facilities, including suicide truck bombings of the Khobar Towers military housing complex in 1996 near Dhahran, Saudi Arabia, and the American embassies in Nairobi, Kenya, and Dar es Salaam, Tanzania in 1998, as well as a suicide boat bombing of the USS *Cole* in Aden, Yemen in 2000.

Osama bin Laden's spectacular attacks are part of a multi-pronged effort to compel the United States to disengage from Muslim lands stretching from North Africa to South Asia. Without an American presence in the region, Israel and apostate Arab regimes could be swept away by what he has termed a "guerrilla war . . . [of] fast-moving, light forces that work under complete secrecy." Islamic militants have traditionally emphasized rooting out apostates, heretics, and other internal enemies. In *The Neglected Duty*, for example, Abd Al-Salam Faraj, leader of the group responsible for assassinating Anwar Sadat, advocated using more vigorous methods against apostates than those used against infidels. In contrast, bin Laden has urged Muslims to suspend their intramural quarrels and concentrate on punishing the United States—the invidious infidel state he charged with responsibility for myriad problems within the Islamic community.

Pointing to the withdrawal of U.S. military forces from Lebanon following the 1983 bombing of the Marine barracks in Beirut, and their withdrawal from Somalia a decade later after losses were sustained while fighting in Mogadishu, bin Laden envisions terror as a proven instrument in asymmetric conflicts with the United States. Just as the mujahadeen evicted the Soviet Union from Afghanistan through a combination of resourcefulness, resolve, and unrelenting pressure, so too will a legion of holy warriors oust the United States from the realm of Islam. Every spectacular attack Osama bin Laden engineers increases his prestige, and every major incidence of collateral damage from retaliatory strikes has the potential to add new recruits to his movement.

What makes organizations such as Al Qaeda, the Algerian GIA (Armed Islamic Group), and other messianic groups more lethal than their older, secular counterparts is their propensity to conceptualize acts of terror on two levels. At one level, terrorism is a means to change the political status quo by punishing those culpable for felt wrongs. At another level, terrorism is an end in itself, a sacrament performed for its own sake in what Mark Juergensmeyer describes as an eschatological confrontation between good and evil. Functioning only on the first level, most secular terrorist groups rarely employ suicide missions. Operating on both levels, religious terrorist groups see worldly gain as well as transcendent importance in a martyr's death. As a result, groups like the Lebanese Hezbollah have not shied away from suicide missions. Ramadan Shalah of the Palestinian Jihad is reported to have explained the military logic of suicide tactics within asymmetric warfare in the following way: "Our enemy possesses the most sophisticated weapons in the world. . . . We have nothing . . . except the weapon of martyrdom. It is easy and costs us only our lives." A suicide bomber, added Israeli Internal Security Minister Uzi Landau in a recent interview, "is a two-legged missile. Once it's launched, it is very difficult to intercept."

Conclusion

An analysis of terrorist incidents over the past century and a half indicates that there is no terrorist orthodoxy on strategic questions, no canon with strict precepts neatly running from ultimate political purpose to intermediate objectives to specific tactics. Strategic thinking about use of terrorism has evolved in response to new technologies, new targets of opportunity, and new counterterrorist policies.

Ingenuity and incrementalism describe the evolution. Take, for instance, the problem of aviation security. Malcolm Gladwell has studied how following the rash of airline hijackings during the late 1960s, X-ray machines and metal detectors were installed at airports to screen passengers and their carry-on baggage. In 1985, he points out, terrorists on TWA flight 847 circumvented screening devices in Athens by having workers hide weapons in the aircraft lavatory, thus prompting airlines to undertake background checks of ground crews. A year later, El Al employees in London discovered explosives in a woman's luggage, which had been secretly placed there by her boyfriend. Airlines responded by asking passengers if they had packed their own bags. Terrorists, notes Gladwell, reacted to this new procedure by checking explosive-laden luggage themselves and then not boarding the flights for which they had tickets. In response, airlines started matching checked bags to boarded passengers, under the assumption that terrorists would not undertake suicide missions. In December 2001, Richard Reed discredited that assumption by attempting to bomb an American Airlines flight from Paris to Miami with explosives concealed in his sneakers. It is a cat-and-mouse game, concludes Ariel Merari in *Aviation Terrorism and Security*, "where the cat is busy blocking old holes and the mouse always succeeds in finding new ones."

As the case of aviation security illustrates, the perpetrators of political terrorism are not mindless. They have long-term goals, and they carefully calculate how different tactical operations may facilitate accomplishing the strategic objectives they believe are necessary for attaining those goals. Indeed, it is their ability to plan, execute, and learn from these operations that makes them so dangerous.

Chapter 7

THE MYSTERY OF THE NEW GLOBAL
TERRORISM: OLD MYTHS,
NEW REALITIES?

MICHAEL STOHL

The initial response to the events of 11 September 2001 beyond the shock and the horror is to declare that everything is different and the world will never be the same again. In many important ways, that is true. In the short run certainly Americans will never again feel the sense of security that its two oceans had provided from the U.S. revolution until the Cold War, and then again after. One cannot erase the insecurity and doubts that have resulted from these attacks.

But, in many important ways, that is not true. There are some things we knew before the attacks that are still valid, and while no one can really claim to have expected what happened to happen, we have to go back and explore why we should not be as surprised as we were and continue to be and what we know that can help us to cope with and respond to the events of that week. We need also to reflect on how we have responded and how what we understood before about the hows and whys of terrorism can continue to guide our understanding.

Part of coping is trying to understand what the terrorists were likely trying to achieve, why these targets, how they were able to do what they did, and, in general, how terrorism "works."

There is clearly much we don't know, but at the same time there is much we do know. What was sophisticated about this attack was the organization and coordination, not the techniques.

Four airplanes, all hijacked within less than 45 minutes. While it took careful training to fly the planes, the plan did not require sophisticated weaponry. In the first 100 days after the attack we learned of the enormous extent of the network which Al Qaeda had created and of the great numbers of persons involved, and wonder more how they were not noticed during the many months and, as it seems likely, years that this event was planned. We have also learned that the suicide bombers expected from previous incidents were quite different from those who operated on 11 September. The profile of the suicide bomber prior to September 11 was that of an uneducated, poor, psychologically troubled, young male—not mature, middle-class, university graduates who had pilot training.

The Purpose of Terrorism

The most important thing to remember about what happened on September 11 is that as horrific as the carnage was, those victims and all that destruction were not as important to the perpetrators as the audience around the world that viewed the destruction. That is, the victims of the attacks were not the targets of those who planned and carried out the acts—the targets were the rest of us. It is how we, individually and collectively, in the United States and around the world have reacted and continue to act that will determine the impact of the attacks.

It is always the case that how the audience reacts and the political effects of the reactions and response to the acts are the core of the process of terrorism. The victims are the instrument of the terrorist.

At the very least, 9/11 demonstrated that in terms of scope of perpetrators, victims, and target locations, these particular terrorists were very different from the terrorists that we knew best over the past three decades.

In the past most scholars of terrorism have agreed with the 1975 observation of Brian Jenkins of RAND that terrorists want a lot of people watching, not a lot of people dead, and there have been very good reasons for that.

Indeed, we know now from Osama bin Laden's November 8, 2001, interview with Pakistani journalist Hamid Mir, subsequently rebroadcast on the American media, that the perpetrators did not expect the level of death that occurred, but rather planned for what bin Laden characterized as the "spectacular damage and audacity." What was different then was that the terrorist attackers did not "care" and were not much concerned with the horrific loss of life because the "center" of the attack was the demonstration that the terrorists could bring the "war" against the United States to the territory of the United States itself. Further, bin Laden's interviews in May 2001 with the Arab journalists also indicated that he was hoping for an unrestrained U.S. government response that would clamp down on the domestic public and limit civil liberties and "normal" American life. In short, bin Laden understood that it was the reaction to the act, both immediate and long term, that was the primary purpose of the attack, not the original attack itself. (So this terrorist act on September 11 was similar to many acts of the past; however, what was different was its scope and intensity.)

Let us return for the moment to how it could be that the United States government and public were not being prepared for this type of attack. In short, how was it possible for most experts not to expect what happened? As we shall see, the experts were unprepared for the scope of victims in a terrorist attack that used conventional means, for the location of such attacks, and for the wide array of types of perpetrators associated with these attacks. The best place to begin is with some summary statistics of the past thirty years' experience with acts of global terrorism.

At the heart of the fear generating the capacity of terrorism is terrorism's threat to life. Mention terrorism, and the images that immediately come to mind are large-scale tragedies, the bombings in Oklahoma City or Moscow, or the embassies in Nairobi and Dar es Salaam, and after September 11 the World Trade Center and the Pentagon, for example. However, relatively few incidents of global terrorism in the past actually ended with deaths. So it is not surprising that experts would not expect such a large-scale attack. Thus we need to look at the recorded past patterns of global terrorism. According to the ITERATE data produced originally by the Central Intelligence Agency, about 11,650 international terrorist incidents occurred between 1968 and 2001. The total number of recorded deaths from incidents of global terrorism for the past thirty years before 11 September was just over 10,000. Of these, 85.5 percent of global acts of terrorism did not result in fatalities. Another 8 percent resulted in a single death. In total, fatality-free and single-death incidents accounted for 93.6 percent of all global terrorist incidents. In the same thirty years, according to the same estimating procedure, there were approximately twice as many people wounded as killed.

In the vast majority of international terrorist incidents (over 82 percent) nobody was wounded, and in another 685 (6.3 percent) only one person was wounded per incident. In almost 90 percent of these recorded terrorist events, one or no persons were even injured. Thus, big events with many deaths and injuries are in our consciousness; however, none or few deaths and injury-free events are the "reality" for most incidents. Furthermore, in general according to the ITERATE data most incidents of international terrorism produce no property damage at all.

Despite a relatively high frequency of international terrorist incidents in the United States (678), the majority (93.9 percent) of these did not produce fatalities or major property damage. Outside of Oklahoma City, fewer than 100 persons were killed on U.S. soil during the past thirty years. Many of these were connected to anti-Castro Cubans. Most events involved no fatalities and have caused little damage. Since terrorists had discovered that they could gain access to the American media and thus communicate their message by "simply" attacking American targets and people abroad, and since it was assumed that was easier than actually attacking on U.S. soil, most experts expected that future attacks would continue, as in the past, to occur outside the territorial boundaries of the United States rather than within the United States.

Many scholars had also noted the increasing threat that the rise of religious-based terrorist organizations posed and the greater willingness to sacrifice innocent lives for a religious cause, and many understood the particular danger of Osama bin Laden and Al Qaeda, who had been linked to the embassy bombings in August 1998 in Kenya and Tanzania and the attack on the USS *Cole* in October 2000. Bin Laden had made quite clear his explanation for his focus on the United States. But while many will claim that they expected bin Laden and his followers to perpetrate an attack like this one on the United States, the reality of the literature of the past few years is that the attack that was "expected" was that coming from weapons of mass destruction. The concern with chemical, biological, radiological, or nuclear attacks—not a large-scale "conventional" act—dominated not only the scholarly literature but also U.S. government hearings and reports. It was customarily assumed that large-scale conventional attacks were simply more likely on an overseas target than in the United States. In addition, while the rise of other religious-based terrorist actors were noted, the fear of these attacks continued to be centered on overseas targets.

This brief introduction provides one picture of the changing character of global terrorism disclosed by a measure of the magnitude and nature of international terrorism. It shows that misunderstandings of the true nature of terrorism can result from a misreading of how terrorism is defined and how its frequency and magnitude is measured. Misinterpretations lead to accepted "myths"—fallacious attributes commonly ascribed to terrorism's character. In fact, looking at terrorism prior to 9/11, ten[1] erroneous images or myths can be identified which rest on mistaken assumptions:

1. Political terrorism is exclusively the activity of nongovernmental actors.
2. All terrorists are madmen.
3. All terrorists are criminals.
4. One man's terrorist is another man's freedom fighter.
5. All insurgent violence is political terrorism.
6. Terrorism's purpose is to produce chaos.
7. Governments always oppose nongovernmental terrorism.
8. Political terrorism is exclusively a problem relating to internal conditions.
9. Contemporary terrorism is caused by the evil actions of one or two major actors.
10. Terrorism is a futile strategy.

Since September 11, three new myths about international terrorism have become prominent, which should now also be questioned. To provoke discussion about the meaning of post-September 2001 terrorism and the responses to the threat of the new global terrorism, we shall here look at these new myths.

Myth One: Terrorism Is Random and Lacks Specific Direction

To the innocent bystander caught in the crossfire or explosion connected to a terrorist incident, there is no doubt that the 9/11 incident and the targets' victimization was random, and hence even more terrifying. However, the reality of terrorism is that it is purposeful and involves selectivity in its execution. Confirmation of this assertion can be found in further analysis of the events-based CIA data of the patterns of both the theater of operations and targeting of global terrorism introduced above. These inventories continue to reveal a distinctive set of patterns that suggest that factors such as environment and terrorist-group composition play significant roles in the nature of the terrorism that transpires. More specifically, terrorist groups develop their modus operandi based on where they originate, who supports them, who their enemies are, what their likelihood of success will be, and a host of other tactical and strategic considerations.

Such terrorist groups engage in terrorist activity for a predetermined political purpose, and their goals are not furthered by random attacks, which the public (their audience) cannot interpret. Although the last three decades have witnessed thousands of global terrorist incidents, they have more often than not been of a deliberate rather than random nature. In the context, the United States—the very center and symbol of globalization (both of foes and advocates)—made it the deliberate target of choice.

Terrorism and counter-terrorism have historical contexts and realities. As difficult as it is to understand or even try to understand how and why these innocents could be chosen as targets, we need to understand why the 9/11 terrorism was directed at the United States, and why the World Trade Center, the Pentagon or, as apparently planned, the White House, were chosen as the targets.

The twin towers symbolized more than anything else what many scholars and journalists summarize as "globalization." This globalization is identified by many as the spread of the American commodity culture and capitalism as well as all the cultural apparatus of modernity. It challenges traditional society and social relationships. There are many who object to this challenge. The vast majority who object, like the Amish in the United States, try to avoid the changes or to make small adjustments, and to live peacefully within such societies but outside and aside. Some, however, have chosen to fight what they see as objectionable and have announced their intentions in the past to do so.

The World Trade Center was both a symbolic and real representation of that globalization. We know that the victims of the attacks included some of the 50,000 citizens of European, Asian, Australian, Middle Eastern, and Latin American countries as well as Americans who were working in those towers for companies both American and international. The towers attracted an additional 90,000 visitors every day.

Osama bin Laden and his followers in Al Qaeda are also enraged by the presence of the American military on what is conceived of as sacred soil in Saudi Arabia. The Saudi dynasty has the responsibility to guard the holiest sites in Islam, and bin Laden had made it clear that he judged them to have violated that trust. He sought to overthrow their regime, destroy the Israeli state (which also occupies Muslim holy sites), and destroy the United States.

In the case of Osama bin Laden, there is a record of explanation which benefits from substantial empirical support, and it is absolutely crucial to understand why this message of hate and destruction resonates with supporters, why it is that wealthy Saudis as well as poor Pakistanis, Indonesians, Egyptians and, we now learn, Americans and Australians, responded to Osama bin Laden's message. This answers the question, Why in America?, regardless of whether we accept the reasoning or the data as valid.

At the same time we must remember that as significant as the attacks by Al Qaeda on 9/11 were, there are many other political organizations that turn to terror around the globe. The point to remember is that terrorism is a weapon, a behavior of choice, not a group's identity. It is always important to identify the sources of the political dispute to determine if the problem can be ameliorated—not to excuse the terrorism but to work on eliminating future attacks and support for them. One does not have to accept either the political interpretation or the choice to engage in terrorism to try and see the world from the vantage of the "other." We must try and understand the choices made to employ the weapon. Such an attempt should never be equated with justification of the actions, but rather must be seen as a necessary step in the process of response and the separation of those who acquiesce to the actions of the terrorist because they share their "understanding" of the political struggle from the perpetrators of terrorism. It is necessary to find the means to communicate with such acquiescers rather than hope to either destroy them or frighten them into submission if the cycle of support for terrorism is to be broken.

Myth Two: Governments Always Oppose Nongovernmental Terrorism

This myth leads to miscalculations about who would be terrorist actors and the relations among them. It is important to recognize that it is not only the states in the "evil axis" identified in President Bush's first State of the Union Address that have supported or acquiesced to terrorism. Unfortunately, there are numerous instances where the terrorism of non-state organizations coincide with the national interests of sovereign states. State support in this respect generally depends on a cost-benefit analysis that calculates the benefit thought possible from the desired outcome, the believed probability with which the action will bring about the desired state of affairs, and the believed probable cost of engaging in the action. For example, many have noted that the Saudi state habitually acquiesced to the transfer of funds and other means of support for groups engaged in terrorism as long as those groups did not target the Saudi state. Similarly, Pakistan's security service was intimately involved with Kashmiris engaged in struggle against India. To engage in a "war" against all such support for as well as use of "terrorism," the United States (which, many would argue, has its own skeletons in the closet) will need to convince states not only to end their support for all forms of terrorism but also to cease their acquiescence to those acts which serve what are often conceived of as in the U.S. national interest, acts with which expected deniability have been in the past seen as quite useful.

Myth Three: The Source of Contemporary Political Terrorism May Be Found in the Evil of One or Two Major Actors

The political expediency of identifying terrorism with evil and to focus on one particular evil such as Osama bin Laden is clear in the mobilization of political support. The ability to equate the horrors of terrorism with the newly defined satanic character of the state or group or person engaged in it creates a powerful tool in the arena of international public opinion and also enables people in opposition to ignore the potential sources or political causes behind the terrorists' acts, which are rightly condemned. The nature of terrorism, as abhorrent as it may be, has not precluded its use by a wide spectrum of actors, and has not prevented millions of persons from supporting those actions. The crusade to respond to the threat will not be successful if the United States and those joining it in a global war against terrorism simply write off those responsible and those who support the acts as evil. Naturally, the terrorists' actions are reprehensible and cannot be justified, but counter-terrorists cannot conclude that all acts of terror have one source, one core, or simply spring from "evil." There is danger if the myth is accepted that terrorism stems from the acts of one or two evil actors, because an underestimation of the scope of a terrorist network will miscalculate the actual perpetrators and thereby misrepresent the true magnitude of the threat. It will also fail to aid in combating and defeating global terrorism. In this context, the elimination of bin Laden and the core of his organization will not completely eliminate the threat of terrorism. In parallel the leaders in this war against terrorism should not slip into the trap of equating the bin Laden, Al Qaeda network with a mythical grand network of global terrorism.

We also need to understand that the changes in the past decade in information technology have enabled terrorist organizations to move from vertical to horizontal organizations and to communicate across secure cells in ways that only closely knit family units could in years past. Understanding networks and its marriage with information technology is an important key to understanding the "power" of this new organization. It allowed widely distributed cells to communicate effectively, channel resources, and maintain a very high degree of security. Of course, at present we cannot know how much of this network strategy was reliant on anything more than email and the use of Internet cafes, laptops, local ISPs, or buried communiqués on Web sites.

While recognizing the existence and organizational sophistication of bin Laden's network, let us be careful also to distinguish from among those closed networks of Al Qaeda collaborators and the global networks created out of the very globalization that bin Laden and his supporters condemn. Globalization has brought the ability to move money, people, and goods to anyone with access to the capital to do so. Globalization has meant much greater travel and migration flows. The normality of the expansion of interstate travel means that terrorists as well as business travelers, tourists, or drug dealers can move quite easily across borders. Greater interconnectedness makes migration more plausible (and more difficult to detect the terrorists from the students, businessmen, and others looking for greater opportunity). The expansion of international trade and finance makes the transfer of money simple for anyone with an ATM card and an account in a financial institution with foreign corresponding financial institutions or branches. In addition, the same networks that have existed for decades for those with the money to buy weapons, information, passage, or money laundering continue to provide such "services." The existence of such networks and the existence of other terrorist groups and states that support them does not mean that they are all part of a vast conspiracy or stem from a single evil. If they did, it would make responding to them and the problem much easier.

The most important lessons we can continue to draw from the actions of Al Qaeda and the response to September 11 are that there are no simple solutions to terrorism. The potential targets and the potential perpetrators are in the millions. It is how we structure our response to the new globalized threat of terrorism that will be most important.

It is impossible to completely eliminate the threat of terrorism. Security can be improved, but the threat cannot be completely eliminated. To do so, the cost in time and money to make things safer must be increased, from arriving at the airport earlier, having all luggage more carefully checked, being inspected more closely at numerous points within the airport, and so forth. Immigration and customs will take much longer. Visas will be more difficult to obtain and take longer. Universities will now be asked to track their international students, and it will be much more difficult to predict the arrival of each new class of students.

Counter-terrorism and foreign policy actions and interests are inseparable. If the United States is going to sustain a grand coalition against terrorism, it must be prepared to join coalitions with other countries to respond to other global problems identified by its partners in that global alliance as important, such as the environment, land mines, child soldiers or development aid.

Further, the United States will need to engage in multilateral responses within the context of existing international organizations, and understand that while others will not have the capacity to contribute to the military means that are necessary in the campaign that international cooperation on non-military means will provide the greater long-term effect in the campaign against the political sources of support for terrorist actions. Unlike the terrorists, the United States globally and other counter-terrorists regionally or locally can deliver that power anywhere at any time without fear of being stopped. What the United States and other states cannot do is necessarily deliver that power in a way that will automatically provide protection. It is that which must be discovered how to do.

Note

1. See Michael Stohl, "Demystifying the Mystery of International Terrorism", in Charles W. Kegley Jr., ed., *International Terrorism* (New York: St. Martin's, 1990), 81–96.

The Causes of Terrorism, Past and Present

●

Chapter 8

●

THE CAUSES OF TERRORISM

MARTHA CRENSHAW

In focusing on terrorism directed against governments, we are considering the premeditated use or threat of symbolic, low-level violence by conspiratorial organizations for purposes of political change. Terrorist violence communicates a political message; its ends go beyond damaging an enemy's material resources. The victims or objects of terrorist attack represent an audience from whom terrorists seek a reaction.

The study of terrorism can be organized around three issues: causes, processes, and effects. Here the objective is to outline an approach to the analysis of the causes of terrorism.

We can begin explaining terrorism by establishing a theoretical order for different types and levels of causes. We initially approach terrorism as a deliberate choice. A comprehensive explanation, however, must also account for the environment in which terrorism occurs and address the question of whether political, social, and economic conditions make terrorism more likely in some contexts than in others. What sort of circumstances lead to the formation of a terrorist group? On the other hand, only a few people with similar experiences practice terrorism. Not even all individuals who share the same ends agree that terrorism is the best means. Psychological variables may encourage or inhibit individual participation in terrorist actions. The analysis will consider first situational variables, then strategies of terrorism, and last individual participation.

This essay represents only a preliminary set of ideas about the problem of causation; historical cases of terrorism are used as illustrations, not as demonstrations of hypotheses. The historical examples referred to here are significant terrorist campaigns since the French Revolution of 1789; terrorism is considered as a facet of secular modern politics, principally associated with the rise of nationalism, anarchism, and revolutionary socialism. The term *terrorism* was coined to describe the systematic inducement of fear and anxiety to control and direct a civilian population, and the phenomenon of terrorism as a challenge to the authority of the state grew from the difficulties revolutionaries experienced in trying to recreate the mass uprisings of the French Revolution. Most references are drawn from the best-known examples: Narodnaya Volya and the Combat Organization of the Socialist-Revolutionary party in Russia from 1878 to 1913; anarchist terrorism of the 1890s in Europe, primarily France; the Irish Republican Army (IRA) and its predecessors and successors from 1919 to the present; the Irgun Zvai Leumi in Mandate Palestine from 1937 to 1947; the Front de Libération Nationale (FLN) in Algeria from 1954 to 1962; the Popular Front for the Liberation of Palestine from 1968 to the present; the Rote Armee Fraktion (RAF) and the 2nd June Movement in West Germany since 1968; and the Tupamaros of Uruguay, 1968–1974.

The Setting for Terrorism

The absence of significant empirical studies of relevant cross-national factors is an obstacle to identification of propitious circumstances for terrorism. There are a number of quantitative analyses of collective violence, assassination, civil strife, and crime, but none of these phenomena is identical to a campaign of terrorism. Little internal agreement exists among such studies, and the consensus one finds is not particularly useful for the study of terrorism.[1]

To analyze the likely settings for terrorism, we must distinguish different types of factors. *Preconditions* are factors that set the stage for terrorism over the long run, while *precipitants* are specific events that immediately precede the occurrence of terrorism. Preconditions can be enabling or permissive, providing opportunities for terrorism to happen, or situations that directly inspire and motivate terrorist campaigns.[2]

Modernization produces an interrelated set of factors that is a significant permissive cause of terrorism, as increased complexity on all levels of society and economy creates opportunities and vulnerabilities. Sophisticated networks of transportation and communication offer mobility and publicity to terrorists. The terrorists of Narodnaya Volya would have been unable to operate without Russia's newly established rail system, and the Popular Front for the Liberation of Palestine could not indulge in hijacking without the jet aircraft. In Algeria, the FLN only adopted a strategy of urban bombings when they were able to acquire plastic explosives. In 1907, the Combat Organization of the Socialist-Revolutionary party paid 20,000 rubles to an inventor who was working on an aircraft in the futile hope of bombing the Russian imperial palaces from the air.[3] Today we fear that terrorists will exploit the potential of nuclear power, but it was in 1867 that Nobel's invention of dynamite made bombings feasible.

Urbanization is part of the modern trend toward aggregation and complexity which increases the number and accessibility of targets and methods.

The popular concept of terrorism as "urban guerrilla warfare" grew out of the Latin American experience of the late 1960s. Yet, cities became the arena for terrorism after the urban renewal projects of the late nineteenth century such as the boulevards constructed by Baron Haussman in Paris made them unsuitable for a strategy based on riots and the defense of barricades.[4] Cities may be significant because they provide an opportunity (a multitude of targets, mobility, communications, anonymity, and audiences) and a recruiting ground among politicized and volatile inhabitants.[5]

Social habits and historical traditions may sanction the use of violence against the government by making it morally and politically justifiable, and may even dictate appropriate forms of resistance, such as demonstrations, coups, or terrorism. In Ireland, for example, the tradition of physical force dates from the eighteenth century, and the legend of the Irish Republican army in 1919–1921 still inspires and partially excuses the much less discriminate and less effective terrorism of the contemporary Provisional IRA in Northern Ireland.

Moreover, the attitudes and beliefs that condone terrorism are communicated transnationally. Revolutionary ideologies have always crossed borders with ease. In the nineteenth and early twentieth centuries, such ideas originated in Europe, stemming from the French and Bolshevik Revolutions. Since the Second World War, Third World revolutions—China, Cuba, Algeria—and intellectuals such as Frantz Fanon and Carlos Marighela have significantly influenced terrorist movements in the West.

The most salient political factor in the category of permissive causes is probably the government's inability or unwillingness to prevent terrorism. The absence of adequate prevention permits the spread of conspiracy. However, since terrorist organizations are small and clandestine, prevention is extremely difficult. Inefficiency or leniency can be found in a broad range of all but the most brutally efficient dictatorships, including incompetent authoritarian states such as tsarist Russia as well as modern liberal democratic states whose desire to protect civil liberties constrains security measures.

Turning to the direct causes of terrorism, we focus on background conditions that encourage resistance to the state. These instigating circumstances go beyond creating an environment in which terrorism is possible; they provide motivation and direction for the terrorist movement. We are dealing here with reasons rather than opportunities.

The first possible direct cause of terrorism is the existence of grievances among a subgroup of a larger population, such as an ethnic minority discriminated against by the majority. A social movement develops in order to redress these grievances and to gain equal rights or autonomy; terrorism is then the resort of an extremist faction of this broader movement.

This is not to say, however, that dissatisfaction is a necessary or sufficient cause of terrorism. Not all those who are discriminated against turn to terrorism, nor does terrorism always reflect deprivation. In Germany, Japan, and Italy, for example, terrorism has been the chosen method of the privileged, not the downtrodden. Some theoretical studies have suggested that the essential ingredient that must be added to real deprivation is the perception on the part of the deprived that this condition is not what they deserve or expect, in short, that discrimination is unjust. An attitude study, for example, found that "the idea of justice or fairness may be more centrally related to attitudes toward violence than are feelings of deprivation. It is the perceived injustice underlying the deprivation that gives rise to anger or frustration."[6]

A second condition that motivates terrorists is lack of opportunity for political participation. In this case, grievances are primarily political, without social or economic overtones. Discrimination is not directed against any subgroup of the population. The terrorist organization is not necessarily part of a broader social movement; indeed, the population may be largely apathetic. In situations where paths to the legal expression of opposition are blocked, but where the regime's repression is inefficient, revolutionary terrorism is doubly likely, as permissive and direct causes reinforce each other. An example is Russia in the 1870s.

Terrorism is the result of elite disaffection; it represents the strategy of a minority, who may act on behalf of a wider popular constituency who have not been consulted about, and do not necessarily approve of, the terrorists' aims or methods. There is considerable relevance in E. J. Hobsbawn's comments on the secret societies of post-Napoleonic Europe: "All revolutionaries regarded themselves, with some justification, as small elites of the emancipated and progressive operating among, and for the eventual benefit of, a vast and inert mass of the ignorant and misled common people, which would no doubt welcome liberation when it came, but could not be expected to take much part in preparing it."[7]

Perhaps terrorism occurs precisely where mass passivity and elite dissatisfaction coincide. Discontent is not generalized or severe enough to provoke the majority of the populace to action against the regime, yet a small minority, without access to the power resources that would permit overthrow of the government through coup d'état or subversion, seeks radical change. Terrorism may thus be a sign of a stable society rather than a symptom of fragility and impending collapse.

We must also ask whether a precipitating event immediately precedes outbreaks of terrorism. Although it is generally thought that precipitants are unpredictable, there does seem to be a common pattern of government actions that act as catalysts for terrorism. The resort to unexpected and unusual force in response to protest or reform often invites retaliation. The development of an action-reaction syndrome then establishes the structure of the conflict between the regime and its challengers. There are numerous historical examples of a campaign of terrorism precipitated by a government's reliance on excessive force to quell protest or squash dissent. The tsarist regime's severity in dealing with the populist movement was a factor in the development of Narodnaya Volya in 1879. The French government's persecution of anarchists was a factor in subsequent anarchist terrorism in the 1890s. The British government's execution of the heroes of the Easter Rising set the stage for Michael Collins and the IRA. The Protestant violence that met the Catholic civil rights movement in Northern Ireland in 1969 pushed the Provisional IRA to retaliate. In West Germany, the death of Beno Ohnesorg at the hands of the police in a demonstration against the Shah of Iran in 1968 contributed to the emergence of the RAF.

The Reasons for Terrorism

Campaigns of terrorism may be considered to depend on political choice. As purposeful activity, terrorism is the result of an organization's decision that it is politically useful. The argument that terrorist behavior should be analyzed as "rational" is based on the assumption that radical organizations possess internally consistent sets of values and regularized procedures for making decisions. Terrorism is seen collectively as a logical means to advance desired ends. The terrorist organization engages in decision-making calculations that an analyst can approximate.

Terrorism is not restricted to any particular ideology. Terrorists may be revolutionaries (such as the Combat Organization of the Socialist-Revolutionary Party in the nineteenth century or the Tupamaros in the twentieth); nationalists fighting against foreign occupiers (the Algerian FLN, the IRA of 1919–1921, or the Irgun); minority separatists combating indigenous regimes (such as the Corsican, Breton, and Basque movements, and the Provisional IRA); anarchists or millenarians (such as the original anarchist movement of the nineteenth century and modern millenarian groups such as the Red Army faction in West Germany, the Italian Red Brigades, and the Japanese Red Army); or reactionaries acting to prevent change from the top (such as the Secret Army Organization during the Algerian war or the contemporary Ulster Defence Association in Northern Ireland).[8]

Saying that extremist groups resort to terrorism in order to acquire political influence does not mean that all groups have equally precise or realistic objectives. The leaders of Narodnaya Volya, for example, lacked a clear conception of how the assassination of the tsar would force his successor to permit liberalization. Other terrorist groups are more pragmatic: the IRA of 1919–1921 and the Irgun, for instance, understood the utility of a war of attrition against the British. Degree of skill in relating means to ends seems to have little to do with ideological sophistication. The French anarchists of the 1890s, for example, acted in light of a well-developed philosophical doctrine but were ambiguous about how violence against the bourgeoisie would bring about freedom.

However diverse the long-run goals of terrorist groups, there is a common pattern of proximate or short-run objectives, defined in terms of the reactions that terrorists want to produce in different audiences.[9] A basic reason for terrorism is to gain recognition or attention—what Thomas P. Thornton called advertisement of the cause. Violence and bloodshed always excite human curiosity, and the theatricality, suspense, and threat of danger inherent in terrorism enhance its attention-getting qualities. Publicity may be the highest goal of some groups. Today, in an interdependent world, the need for international recognition encourages transnational terrorist activities, with escalation to ever more destructive and spectacular violence. As the audience grows larger, more diverse, and more accustomed to terrorism, terrorists must go to extreme lengths to shock.

Terrorism is also often designed to disrupt and discredit the processes of government. As a direct attack on the regime, it aims at producing insecurity and demoralization. An excellent example is Michael Collins's campaign against the British intelligence system in Ireland in 1919–1921. This form of terrorism often accompanies guerrilla warfare, as insurgents try to weaken the government's control.

Terrorism aims at creating either sympathy in a potential constituency or fear and hostility in an audience identified as the "enemy." These two functions are interrelated, since intimidating the "enemy" impresses both sympathizers and the uncommitted. At the same time, terrorism may be used to enforce obedience in an audience from whom the terrorists demand allegiance.

Terrorism may also be intended to provoke a counterreaction from the government, to increase publicity for the terrorists' cause, and to demonstrate that criticism of the regime is well founded. The terrorists mean to force the state to show its true repressive face, thereby driving the people into the arms of the challengers. For example, in Brazil, Carlos Marighela argued that the way to win popular support was to provoke the regime to measures of greater repression and persecution.[10] The FLN against the French, the Palestinians against Israel, and the RAF against the Federal Republic all appear to have used terrorism as provocation.

In addition, terrorism serves internal organizational functions of control, discipline, and morale building within the terrorist group and even becomes an instrument of internecine rivalry. Factional terrorism has frequently characterized the Palestinian resistance movement. The victims are Israeli civilians or anonymous airline passengers, but the immediate goal is influence within the resistance movement.

Terrorism is a logical choice when oppositions are extreme and when the power ratio of government to challenger is high. The observation that terrorism is a weapon of the weak is hackneyed but apt. Terrorism is initially the strategy of a minority that by its own judgment lacks other means. When the group perceives its options as limited, terrorism is attractive because it is relatively inexpensive and simple and its potential reward is high.

Weakness and consequent restriction of choice can stem from different sources. Weakness may result from the regime's suppression of opposition. Resistance organizations who lack the means of mounting more extensive violence may then turn to terrorism because legitimate expression of dissent is denied. Lack of popular support initially does not mean that the terrorists' aims lack general appeal. Over the course of the conflict they may acquire the allegiance of the population. For example, the Algerian FLN used terrorism to mobilize mass support.

Yet, it is wrong to assume that terrorism is always a sign of oppression. An extremist organization may reject nonviolence and adopt terrorism because they are impatient with time-consuming legal methods of eliciting support or advertising their cause, because they distrust the regime or are not capable of, or interested in, mobilizing majority support. Most terrorist groups operating in Western Europe and Japan in the 1970s are cases in point.

Thus, the weakness of some groups is imposed by the political system on others, by unpopularity. In some cases resistance groups are genuinely desperate; in others they have alternatives to violence. Nor do we want to forget that nonviolent resistance is a choice in some circumstances; Gandhi and Martin Luther King made this choice. Terrorists may argue that they have no alternative, but their perceptions may be flawed.[11]

In addition to weakness, an important reason for terrorism is impatience. For a variety of reasons, the challenge to the state cannot be left to the future. Given limited means, the group often sees the choice as between action as survival and inaction as the death of resistance.

One reason for haste lies in the situation; the historical moment seems to present a unique opportunity. For example, the resistance group facing a colonial power recently weakened by a foreign war exploits a temporary vulnerability: the IRA against Britain after World War I, the Irgun against Britain after World War II, and the FLN against France after the Indochina war. We might even suggest that the stalemate between the United States and North Vietnam stimulated the post-1968 wave of anti-imperialist terrorism, especially in Latin America.

A sense of urgency may also develop when similar resistance groups have apparently succeeded with terrorism. The contagion effect of terrorism is partially based on an image of success that recommends terrorism to groups who identify with the innovator. The Algerian FLN, for example, was pressured to keep up with nationalists in Tunisia and Morocco, who won independence in 1956. Terrorism spread rapidly through Latin America after 1968 as revolutionary groups worked for a continental solidarity.

Dramatic failure of alternatives may also fuel a drive toward terrorism. The Arab defeat in the 1967 war with Israel led Palestinians to realize that they could no longer depend on the Arab states to further their goals. Extreme weakness, traditions of violence, and the intolerability of the status quo made it likely that militant nationalists should turn to terrorism. Since international recognition of the Palestinian cause was a primary aim (given the influence of outside powers in the region) and attacks on Israeli territory were difficult, terrorism developed into a transnational phenomenon.

These external pressures to act are often intensified by internal politics. Leaders of resistance groups act under constraints imposed by their followers. They are forced to justify the organization's existence, quell restlessness among militants, satisfy demands for revenge, enforce unity, and maintain control.

In conclusion, terrorism is an attractive strategy for groups of varied ideological persuasions who challenge the state's authority. Groups who want to dramatize a cause, demoralize the government, gain popular support, provoke regime violence, inspire followers, or dominate a wider resistance movement, who are weak vis-à-vis the regime, and who are impatient to act, often find terrorism a reasonable choice. This is especially so when conditions are favorable, providing opportunities and making terrorism a convenient and economical option, with immediate and visible payoff.

Individual Motivation and Participation

Terrorism is neither an automatic reaction to conditions nor a purely calculated strategy. Terrorists are only a small minority of people with similar personal backgrounds and experiences who might be expected to reach identical conclusions about the utility of terrorism. What psychological factors motivate the terrorist and influence his or her perceptions? What limited data we have on individual terrorists suggest that the outstanding common characteristic is normality. Terrorism often seems to be the connecting link among dissimilar personalities. Franco Venturi observed that "the policy of terrorism united many very different characters and mentalities" and that agreement on using terrorism was the cement that bound the members of Narodnaya Volya together.[12] The West German psychiatrist who conducted a pretrial examination of four members of the RAF concluded that they were "intelligent," even "humorous," and showed no symptoms of psychosis or neurosis and "no particular personality type."[13]

In his study of the pre-1933 Nazi movement, Peter Merkl abandoned any attempt to classify personality types and instead focused on factors such as level of political understanding.[14] An examination of conscious attitudes might be more revealing than a study of subconscious predispositions or personalities. If terrorists see the state as unjust, morally corrupt, and violent, then terrorism may seem legitimate and justified. The evidence also indicates that many terrorists are activists with prior political experience in nonviolent opposition to the state. How do these experiences in participation influence later attitudes?

Analyzing these issues involves serious methodological problems. As the Blumenthal study emphasizes, there are two ways of analyzing the relationship between attitudes and political behavior.[15] If our interest is in identifying potential terrorists by predicting behavior from the existence of certain attitudes, then it would be best to survey a young age group in a society determined to be susceptible. If terrorism subsequently occurred, we could then see who became terrorists. (A problem is that the preconditions would change over time and that precipitants are unpredictable.) The easier way of investigating the attitudes-behavior connection is to select people who have engaged in a particular behavior and ask them questions about their opinions. Yet attitudes may be adopted subsequent to behavior and serve as rationalizations, rather than as motivations. These problems would seem to be particularly acute when the behavior in question is illegal.

Another problem is that terrorists are recruited in different ways. Assuming that people who are in some way personally attracted to terrorism actually engage in such behavior supposes that potential terrorists are presented with an appropriate opportunity, which is a factor over which they have little control. Moreover, terrorist groups often discourage or reject potential recruits who openly seek excitement or danger. William Mackey Lomasney, a member of the Clan na Gael or American Fenians in the nineteenth century (who was killed in 1884 in an attempt to blow up London Bridge) condemned the "disgraceful" activities of Jeremiah O'Donovan Rossa:

> Were it not that O'Donovan Rossa has openly and unblushingly boasted that he is responsible for those ridiculous and futile efforts . . . we might hesitate to even suspect that any sane man, least of all one professedly friendly to the cause, would for any consideration or desire for notoriety take upon himself such a fearful responsibility, and, that having done so, he could engage men so utterly incapable of carrying out his insane designs.[16]

Lomasney complained that the would-be terrorists were:

> . . . such stupid blundering fools that they make our cause appear imbecile and farcical. When the fact becomes known that those half-idiotic attempts have been made by men professing to be patriotic Irishmen what will the world think but that Irish revolutionists are a lot of fools and ignoramuses, men who do not understand the first principles of the art of war, the elements of chemistry or even the amount of explosive material necessary to remove or destroy an ordinary brick or stone wall. Think of the utter madness of men who have no idea of accumulative and destructive forces undertaking with common blasting powder to scare and shatter the Empire.[17]

Similarly, Boris Savinkov, head of the Combat Organization of the Socialist-Revolutionary party in Russia, tried to discourage an aspirant whom he suspected of being drawn to adventure:

> I explained to him that terrorist activity did not consist only of throwing bombs; that it was much more minute, difficult and tedious than might be imagined; that a terrorist is called upon to live a rather dull existence for months at a time, eschewing meeting his own comrades and doing most difficult and unpleasant work—the work of systematic observation.[18]

Similar problems in linking attitudes to behavior arise from role differentiations within organizations. Degree of organization varies from the paramilitary hierarchies of the Irgun or the IRA to the semiautonomous coexistence of small groups in contemporary West Germany or Italy or even to the absence of central direction in the nineteenth century anarchist movement in France. There are thus likely to be psychological or background differences between leaders and cadres. If there is a predisposition to terrorism, the terrorism-prone individual who obtains psychic gratification from the experience is likely to be a follower, not a leader who commands but does not perform the act.

An alternative approach to analyzing the psychology of terrorism is to use a deductive method based on what we know about terrorism as an activity, rather than an inductive method yielding general propositions from statements of the particular. What sort of characteristics would make an individual suited for terrorism? What are the role requirements of the terrorist?

One of the most salient attributes of terrorist activity is that it involves significant personal danger. Furthermore, since terrorism involves premeditated, not impulsive, violence, the terrorist's awareness of the risks is maximized. Thus, although terrorists may simply be people who enjoy or disregard risk, it is more likely that they are people who tolerate high risk because of intense commitment to a cause. Their commitment is strong enough to make the risk of personal harm acceptable and perhaps to outweigh the cost of society's rejection, although defiance of the majority may be a reward in itself. In either case, the violent activity is not gratifying in itself.

Terrorism is group activity, involving intimate relationships among a small number of people. Interactions among members of the group may be more important in determining behavior than the psychological predispositions of individuals. Furthermore, the group operates under conditions of stress and isolation.

Terrorists can only trust each other. The nature of their commitment cuts them off from society; they inhabit a closed community that is forsaken only at great cost. Isolation and the perception of a hostile environment intensify shared beliefs and make faith in the cause imperative. A pattern of mutual reassurance, solidarity, and comradeship develops, in which the members of the group reinforce each other's self-righteousness, image of a hostile world, and sense of mission. Because of the real danger terrorists confront, the strain they live under, and the moral conflicts they undergo, they value solidarity. Terrorists are not necessarily people who seek "belonging" or personal integration through ideological commitment; but once embarked on the path of terrorism, they desperately need the group. Isolation and the need for internal consensus explain how the beliefs and values of a terrorist group can be so drastically at odds with those of society at large. An example of such divergent conceptions is the idea of the RAF that terrorism would lead to a resurgence of Nazism in West Germany that would in turn spark a workers' revolt.

In their intense commitment, separation from the outside world, and intolerance of internal dissent, terrorist groups resemble religious sects or cults. Michael Barkun has explained the continued commitment of members of millenarian movements, a conviction frequently expressed in proselytizing in order to validate beliefs, in terms of the reinforcement and reassurance of rightness that the individual receives from other members of the organization. He also notes the frequent practice of initiation rites that involve violations of taboos, or "bridge-burning acts," that create guilt and prevent the convert's return to society. Thus the millenarian, like the terrorist group, constitutes "a community of common guilt."[19] J. Bowyer Bell commented on the religious qualities of dedication and moral fervor characterizing the IRA: "In the Republican Movement, the two seemingly opposing traditions, one of the revolution and physical force, and the other of pious and puritanical service, combine into a secular vocation."[20]

If a single common emotion drives the individual or group to terrorism, it is vengeance. A government that creates martyrs encourages terrorism. Anger at what is perceived as unjust persecution inspires demands for revenge.

There are numerous historical demonstrations of the central role of vengeance. It is seen as one of the principal causes of anarchist terrorism in France in the 1890s. The infamous Ravachol acted to avenge the "martyrs of Clichy," two possibly innocent anarchists who were beaten by the police and sentenced to prison. Subsequent bombings and assassinations, for instance that of President Carnot, were intended to avenge Ravachol's execution. In Russia, the cruelty of the sentences imposed for minor offenses at the "Trial of the 193," the hanging of eleven southern revolutionaries after Soloviev's unsuccessful attack on the tsar in 1879, and the "Trial of the 16" in 1880 deeply affected the members of Narodnaya Volya. During the Algerian war, the French execution of FLN prisoners; in Northern Ireland, British troops firing on civil rights demonstrators; in West Germany, the death of a demonstrator at the hands of the police—all served to precipitate terrorism.

Willingness to accept high risks may also be related to the belief that one's death will be avenged. The prospect of retribution gives the act of terrorism and the death of the terrorist meaning and continuity, even fame and immortality. Vengeance may be not only a function of anger but of a desire for transcendence.

Shared guilt binds members of the terrorist group together. Almost all terrorists seem compelled to justify their behavior, and this anxiety cannot be explained solely as public relations. Justifications include past suffering, the glorious future to be created, and the regime's illegitimacy and violence. Shared guilt and anxiety increase the group's interdependence and mutual commitment and may also make followers more dependent on leaders and on the common ideology as sources of moral authority.

Guilt may also lead terrorists to court danger. The motive of self-sacrifice influenced many Russian terrorists of the nineteenth century. Kaliayev, for example, felt that only his death could atone for the murder he committed. A member of the Irgun High Command felt "high spirits" and "satisfaction" when arrested by the British because he now shared the suffering that all fighters had to experience. He almost welcomed the opportunity to prove that he was prepared to sacrifice himself for the cause. In fact, until his arrest he had felt "morally uncomfortable," whereas afterwards he felt "exalted."[21] Vera Figner of the Narodnaya Volya insisted on participating in terrorism, although her comrades accused her of seeking personal satisfaction instead of allowing the organization to make the best use of her talents. She found it intolerable to bear a moral responsibility for acts that endangered her comrades. She could not encourage others to commit acts she would not herself commit; anything less than full acceptance of the consequences of her decisions would be cowardice.[22]

Willingness to face risk may be related to what Robert J. Lifton has termed "survivor-guilt" as well as to feelings of group solidarity or of guilt at harming victims.[23] Sometimes individuals who survive disaster or escape punishment when others have suffered seek relief by courting a similar fate. This may explain why terrorists often take enormous risks to rescue imprisoned comrades, as well as why they accept danger or arrest with equanimity or even satisfaction.

Once a group embarks on a strategy of terrorism, whatever its purpose and whatever its results, psychological factors make it very difficult to halt. Terrorism gathers an independent momentum.

Conclusions

Terrorism need not reflect mass discontent or deep social cleavages. More likely it represents the disaffection of a fragment of the elite who take it upon themselves to act on the behalf of a majority unaware of its plight, unwilling to take action to remedy grievances, or unable to express dissent. Terrorism is an attractive strategy for small organizations that want to attract attention, provoke the government, intimidate opponents, appeal for sympathy, impress an audience, or maintain the adherence of the faithful. Whether unable or unwilling to perceive a choice, the group reasons that there is no alternative. The ease, simplicity, and rapidity of terrorism strengthens its appeal, especially since terrorist groups are impatient. Traditions that sanction terrorism against the state further enhance its attractiveness.

There are two fundamental questions about the psychological basis of terrorism. The first is why the individual takes the first step and chooses to engage in terrorism: why join? Does the terrorist possess specific psychological predispositions, identifiable in advance, that suit him or her for terrorism? That terrorists are people capable of intense commitment tells us little, and the motivations for terrorism vary immensely. To explain why terrorism happens, a second question is more useful: Why does involvement continue? What are the psychological mechanisms of group interaction? We are not dealing with a situation in which certain types of personalities suddenly turn to terrorism in answer to some inner call. Terrorism is the result of a gradual growth of commitment both to political objectives and to a group. The psychological relationships within the group—the interplay of commitment, risk, solidarity, loyalty, guilt, revenge, and isolation—discourage members from altering the course they have taken. This may explain why opposition persists even after grievances are met or nonviolent alternatives opened.

Notes

An earlier version of this article was published in *Comparative Politics* 13 (1981): 370–99.

1. A sampling would include Douglas Hibbs, Jr., *Mass Political Violence: A Cross-National Causal Analysis* (New York, 1983); William J. Crotty, ed. *Assassinations and the Political Order* (New York, 1971); Ted Robert Gurr, *Why Men Rebel* (Princeton, 1971), and Ted Robert Gurr, Peter N. Grabosky, and Richard C. Hula, *The Politics of Crime and Conflict* (Beverly Hills, 1977). For a summary of these findings, see Gurr, "The Calculus of Civil Conflict," *Journal of Social Issues* 28 (1972):27–47.

2. A distinction between preconditions and precipitants is found in Harry Eckstein, "On the Etiology of Internal Wars," *History and Theory* 4 (1965):133–62. Kenneth Waltz also differentiates between the framework for action as a permissive or underlying cause and special reasons as immediate or efficient causes. In some cases we can say of terrorism, as he says of war, that it occurs because there is nothing to prevent it. See *Man, the State and War* (New York, 1959):232.

3. Boris Savinkov, *Memoirs of a Terrorist*, trans. Joseph Shaplen (New York: A. & C. Boni. 1931):286–87.

4. E. J. Hobsbawm, *Revolutionaries: Contemporary Essays* (New York, 1973):226–27.

5. P. N. Grabosky, "The Urban Context of Political Terrorism," in Michael Stohl, ed., *The Politics of Terrorism* (New York, 1979):51–76.

6. Monica D. Blumenthal et al., *More About Justifying Violence: Methodological Studies of Attitudes and Behavior* (Ann Arbor: Survey Research Center, Institute for Social Research, University of Michigan, 1975):108. Similarly, Peter Lupsha, "Explanation of Political Violence: Some Psychological Theories Versus Indignation," *Politics and Society* 2 (1971):89–104, contrasts the concept of "indignation" with Gurr's theory of relative deprivation, which holds that expectations exceed rewards (see *Why Men Rebel*, especially 24–30).

7. E. J. Hobsbawm, *Revolutionaries*, 143.

8. For a typology of terrorist organizations, see Paul Wilkinson, *Political Terrorism* (New York, 1975).

9. Thomas P. Thornton, "Terror as a Weapon of Political Agitations," in *Internal War*, ed. Harry Eckstein (New York, 1964):82–88.

10. Carlos Marighela, *For the Liberation of Brazil* (Harmondsworth: Penguin, 1971): 94–95. The West German RAF apparently adopted the idea of provocation as part of a general national liberation strategy borrowed from the Third World.

11. See Michael Walzer's analysis of the morality of terrorism in *Just and Unjust Wars* (New York, 1977):197–206. See also Bernard Avishai, "In Cold Blood," *New York Review of Books*, 8 March 1979:41–44, for a critical appraisal of the failure of recent works on terrorism to discuss moral issues.

12. Franco Venturi, *Roots of Revolution: A History of the Populist and Socialist Movements in Nineteenth Century Russia* (London, 1960):647.

13. Quoted in *Science* 203 (5 January 1979), 34, as part of an account of the proceedings of the International Scientific Conference on Terrorism held in Berlin, December 1978. Advocates of the "terrorist personality" theory, however, argued that terrorists suffer from faulty vestibular functions in the middle ear or from inconsistent mothering resulting in dysphoria. For another description see John Wykert, "Psychiatry and Terrorism," *Psychiatric News*, 14 (2 February 1979):1 and 12–14.

14. Peter Merkl, *Political Violence Under the Swastika: 581 Early Nazis* (Princeton, 1974):33–34.
15. Blumenthal, et al., 12.
16. Quoted in William O'Brien and Desmond Ryan, eds. *Devoy's Post Bag,* vol. II (Dublin: D. J. Fallon, Ltd., 1953):51.
17. Ibid., 52.
18. Savinkov, *Memoirs,* 147.
19. Michael Barkun, *Disaster and the Millenium* (New Haven, 1974):14–16. See also Leon Festinger, et al., *When Prophecy Fails* (New York, 1964).
20. J. Bowyer Bell, *The Secret Army* (London, 1970):379.
21. Ya'acov Meridor, *Long Road to Freedom* (Tujunga, Calif.: Barak Publications, 1961):6 and 9.
22. Vera Figner, *Mémoires d'une révolutionnaire,* trans. Victor Serge (Paris: Gallimard, 1930):131 and 257–62.
23. Such an argument is applied to Japanese Red Army terrorist Kozo Okamoto by Patricia Steinhof in "Portrait of a Terrorist," *Asian Survey* 16 (1976):830–45.

Chapter 9

WHY MODERN TERRORISM? DIFFERENTIATING TYPES AND DISTINGUISHING IDEOLOGICAL MOTIVATIONS

PAUL WILKINSON

Terrorism is the systematic use of coercive intimidation, usually to service political ends. It is used to create and exploit a climate of fear among a wider target group than the immediate victims of the violence, often to publicize a cause, as well as to coerce a target into acceding to terrorist aims. Terrorism may be used on its own or as part of a wider unconventional war. It can be employed by desperate and weak minorities, by states as a tool of domestic and foreign policy, or by belligerents as an accompaniment or additional weapon in all types and stages of warfare. A common feature is that innocent civilians, sometimes foreigners who know nothing of the terrorist political quarrel, are killed or injured.

The weapon of terror can be used for an almost infinite variety of causes and purposes. Hence although it is quite wrong to regard terrorism as synonymous with violence in general, it is a rather broad politico-strategic concept and is therefore useful to distinguish between basic forms and contexts of terrorism, and to employ a basic typology of contemporary perpetrators of terrorism based on their underlying causes or political motivation.

One basic distinction is between *state* and *factional* terror. The former has been vastly more lethal and has often been an antecedent to, and contributory cause of, factional terrorism. Once regimes and factions decide that their ends justify any means, or that their opponents' actions justify them in unrestrained retaliation, they tend to become locked in a spiral of terror and counter-terror. *Internal* terrorism is confined within a single state or region while *international* terrorism, in its most obvious manifestation, is an attack carried out across international frontiers or against foreign targets in a terrorists' state of origin. But in reality, most terrorist campaigns of a protracted and intensive character have international dimensions as the groups involved look abroad for finance, weapons, safe haven, and political support.

In the brief survey that follows the emphasis will be on the underlying aims and motivations of different types of contemporary terrorism, and some of the major trends. However, it is important to bear in mind that the categories proposed are not meant to be mutually exclusive. For example, many groups employing the weapon of terror combine religious, ethnic, and political aims and motivations, and generally this tends to make them more durable and effective than those groups founded entirely on the basis of ideological affinity or the influence of a charismatic individual.

State Terror

If we are to gain an adequate understanding of the broader historical and international trends in the use of terror violence, we need to recognize that throughout history it is regimes and states, with their overwhelming preponderance of coercive power, which have shown the greatest propensity for terror on a mass scale, both as instrument of internal repression and control and as a weapon of external aggression and subjugation.

Nineteenth-century idealists and utopians hoped that the march of reason and progress would banish tyranny and dictatorship and usher in a new age of universal democracy and peace. Such dreams were shattered in the mid-twentieth century with the rise of totalitarian regimes using mass terror on an unprecedented scale. The rise of the totalitarian state has been brilliantly anatomized by Hannah Arendt,[1] and many valuable studies exist dealing with the distinctive and complex features of the Nazi and Soviet terror apparats.[2] The more one examines these regimes, the more one is struck by the fact that although they developed on the basis of very different ideologies there are some remarkably close parallels in the organizational structure and modus operandi of terror they employed.

The ending of the Cold War and the overthrow of communism in Eastern Europe and the former Soviet Union may have led many observers to assume that this presaged the general demise of the one-party terror regime and the rapid acceptance of western concepts of democracy, freedom, and human rights throughout the international system.[3] Millions of people have been liberated from the tyranny of communist dictatorship in the former Soviet Union and in the former Warsaw Pact states. For the first time in the lives of most of their citizens, these countries can enjoy the political and economic freedoms we have for so long taken for granted in the West. These are huge gains in human rights terms. Moreover, we should not underestimate the enormous significance of this "velvet revolution" for world peace.[4] With breathtaking speed the bipolar confrontation between the superpowers was removed, and the risk of a general nuclear war was enormously reduced if not completely eliminated.

The ending of the Cold War contains another important lesson with positive implications for the future of international relations: The "revolution" in the communist world that had gathered pace with such speed in the 1980s and early 1990s was in truth "velvet;" that is to say, it was carried out without any recourse to violence by the anti-communist opposition and without any armed intervention on their behalf by outside powers.[5] Hence, the really good news is that despite decades of state repression and terror, the desire for democratic freedoms and human rights could not be extinguished. The velvet revolution revealed that even powerful modern states using the full repertoire of techniques of totalitarian control and backed up by allied states are not invincible. George Orwell's nightmare vision of *1984* has shown that it cannot succeed over the determined will of the people seeking democratic change.

But of course it would be, to say the least, premature to assume that the demise of communist rule in the former Soviet Union and Eastern Europe means the end of state terror. From a Far Eastern perspective the totalitarian one-party state depending extensively on its own terror apparat for internal control is an ever-present reality. The Chinese People's Republic is notorious throughout the world for its ruthless suppression of the students' pro-democracy movement in the Tiananmen Square massacre of 1989, and in recent months, prior to this book going to press, the authorities have continued to crack down ruthlessly both against pro-democracy activists and against ethno-religious separation in Tibet and Sinkiang.[6] China's neighbor, North Korea, is even more of a Cold War dinosaur, a totalitarian state complete with personality cult and one of the most repressive systems of internal control in the world.[7]

However, terror is not a weapon exclusive to communist one-party states. There are numerous military regimes and other forms of dictatorship where the use of terror for internal control is routine. One of the clearest indicators that a regime of terror is operating is a high level of torture, the archetypal form of state terror. It has been estimated that in 1995 torture *and/or* other cruel, inhuman, or degrading treatment or punishment existed in 151 out of the UN's then 185 members.[8] But torture is widespread or commonly used only in around a third of these countries. For example, it has been employed extensively in countries such as Iraq and Syria in the Middle East; Burundi, Rwanda, and Zaire in Africa; Myanmar and Indonesia in Asia; and Serbia and Chechnya in Europe— all countries that have suffered high levels of both regime and factional terror.[9]

It is of course no accident that such countries have frequently experienced both regime and sub-state terror and the horrors of civil war. Very often it is repressive terror of the regime that provokes a campaign of counter-terror, or vice versa. It is also no accident that regimes which routinely use terror as a weapon of domestic policy also have a tendency to employ it as a tool of foreign policy. Hence state sponsorship of terrorist clients operating abroad is likely to remain a feature of the international system as long as regimes of state terror exist. As we shall see later in this chapter, there are elements in the post–Cold War international environment that may both discourage and provoke further state sponsorship and support of terrorism. A further paradox is that the sharp reduction in the number of states actively involved giving sponsorship, safe haven, and other forms of support makes the role of the remaining state sponsors all the more critical to the survival of their terrorist group clients.

However, while there are some effective multilateral measures that can be taken to discourage and reduce state sponsorship of terrorism as a weapon of intervention in foreign states, the international community generally and the major democracies in combination have precious little power to influence those regimes that are inflicting major human rights violations on their own populations by waging state terror.[10] For most states, almost certainly including the majority of liberal democracies, the international norms of nonintervention in internal affairs of other states are a highly convenient rationale for restricting themselves to expressions of humanitarian concern, condemnatory resolutions at the UN, and *perhaps* support for international economic sanctions against the offending regime.

However, in the 1990s there were signs that in particularly egregious cases of mass terror—as in the cases of the plight of the Kurds in Northern Iraq, the "ethnic cleansing" or genocide in Bosnia, the genocide in Rwanda and Burundi, and the Serbs' campaign of massive ethnic cleansing against ethnic Albanians in Kosovo—the international community may be persuaded to override the norms of nonintervention and to make strenuous efforts to bring those guilty of crimes against humanity and war crimes before the International Tribunal. This is already happening in the cases of the former Yugoslavia, Rwanda, and Burundi. The UN establishment of an International Criminal Court (ICC) to begin dealing with war crimes, genocide, and crimes against humanity are further evidence of this trend.[11]

The creation of an ICC for such purposes has been discussed by jurists for decades, and was surely long overdue. If we believe in the universal applicability of the UN Human Rights Declaration and in strengthening the rule of law internationally, it is both a logical and eminently desirable development. Nevertheless, many important issues about the ICC must be satisfactorily resolved: Why should crimes of international terrorism, including state-sponsored terrorism, be excluded from its remit? Surely the terrorist sabotage bombings of Pan Am 103 over Lockerbie and UTA 772 over Niger, for example, constitute massive human rights violations by any standards? In the Lockerbie bombing 270 innocent persons, including 11 on the ground, were killed; 170 were killed in the UTA explosion. The fact that some terrorist crimes, such as hostage-taking and attacks on diplomats, are already prohibited by UN conventions surely *strengthens* rather than weakens the case for adding international terrorist crimes to the ICC's remit; in any case, war crimes and genocide are also already dealt with in international conventions. The existence of international legislation in the form of conventions simply underlines the fact that these crimes are already viewed as crimes against the international rule of law in the eyes of most governments. It is worth adding that if the ICC had existed when the controversy over the indictment of two Libyan suspects in the Lockerbie case arose, the new court would have been the obvious body to deal with such a patently international crime against civil aviation passengers and crew.[12]

Other practical problems about the ICC project concern its relations with the UN Security Council and, in particular, with the United States and the other permanent members of the Council. Some have argued that each permanent member of the Security Council should have the power to veto an investigation by the ICC.

During the December 1997 meeting at the UN in New York to discuss the establishment of an ICC, the U.S. delegation argued that the court should not be permitted to investigate crimes committed in any conflict in which the Security Council is playing a peacekeeping role. Considering that the Security Council almost inevitably becomes involved in sending peacekeeping missions to most of the major conflicts, this requirement would virtually negate the value of the ICC.

Surely the vital requirement for the ICC is to ensure that its total independence from any and all of the major member states is established from the outset. If it is to have the credibility so vital to its role as an international court, it must be at liberty to examine any conflict referred to it by any concerned government or group of governments.

Of course it is the case that the ICC will depend on the goodwill and general support of the Security Council, and will need to look to Council to enforce its decisions. Singapore has proposed a sensible device for avoiding a head-on collision between Council and court: If the Security Council as a whole, including the five permanent members, voted to keep out of particular situation, the court would have to respect Council's wishes; but otherwise it would be free to investigate any case. Unfortunately, some of the key remaining issues of the ICC's relationship with the Security Council, with national governments and with national courts, could not be fully resolved in the June 1998 Rome conference on the ICC.

Terror as a Weapon in Ethnic Conflicts

All too frequently, sweeping generalizations about terrorism are made on the basis of a survey of a single historical phase or a single subspecies of this multifaceted phenomenon. Hence, just as many writers during the "dynamite decade" at the end of the nineteenth century in Europe equated terrorism with anarchism and nihilism, and those writing in the inter-war period naturally tended to focus on terrorism from the fascist and Nazi movements bidding to seize power in one European country after another, contemporary authors also tend to concentrate their attention on the types of terrorism they perceive as being the most significant threat to their own societies.

Accordingly, it is hardly surprising that most American analysts have focused primarily if not exclusively on international terrorist attacks, that is to say those terrorist events involving the citizens or jurisdictions of more than one country. This is the major terrorist threat to the United States and has remained so since the burgeoning of modern international terrorism in the late 1960s: Indeed, the United States has had the dubious privilege of being the most favored target of international terrorists throughout almost this entire period.[13] Yet it is important to remember that international incidents constitute only a tiny minority of the annual total of terror acts worldwide. The statistics on terrorism published in the U.S. Department of State's annual report, *Patterns of Global Terrorism*,[14] do not include the vast numbers of internal or domestic terrorist acts occurring within the borders of a single state against fellow citizens of the state concerned. Thus, for example, they do not cover the vast majority of attacks by groups such as the IRA, the Tamil Tigers, Sining Path (Sendero Luminoso), or the GIA in Algeria.

The narrow focus on international terrorist attacks gives a distorted picture of terrorist trends in another important respect: It inevitably emphasizes situations in which terrorist action is being taken in isolation from any wider form of struggle. Yet historically, the use of pure terror as a weapon is the exception rather than the rule. In the vast majority of cases through history and in the contemporary world, terrorism is used as part of a much broader repertoire of violent means, ranging from rural and urban guerilla to full-scale conventional warfare. This is not to say that the rich and powerful Western democracies are no longer having to contend with small terrorist groups and cells capable of posing threats to life and property. However, it is important not to exaggerate the significance of this aspect of terrorism when we are attempting to interpret the more complex relationship between terror and other forms of conflict in the wider world.

A major trend during the 1980s and 1990s has been an upsurge in the number and severity of ethnic and ethno-religious conflicts in which the use of mass terror against the designated "enemy" civilian population has become a standard weapon for forcing them to flee from their land and homes. Ninety-nine percent of significant armed conflicts in the world today are intra-state conflicts, the majority with an underlying ethnic or religious conflict at their root.[15] The causes of this upsurge in ethnic and religious civil wars are to be found not only in historical ethnic rivalries and hatreds but also in the structure of the post–Cold War international system. The collapse of the former communist empire in Eastern Europe and the Soviet Union simultaneously created new opportunities and security dilemmas for a large number of ethnic groups. The removal of the iron hand of centralized Communist Party dictatorship made them conscious of long-supported threats and rivalries from other national groups. Many Third World countries have been suffering from the consequences of ethnic and religious conflict ever since gaining independence from colonial rule—or at any rate for substantial periods of their existence as newly independent states, as in Sri Lanka, India, Pakistan, and Congo, for example.

The evidence suggests that the underlying causes of ethnic conflict include the strength of the ethnic group's identity and solidarity, availability of militant leaders capable of mobilizing a mass following, emotive appeals to history and historical myth, support from sponsor or allied states or groups, access to weapons, memories of recent attacks, atrocities or injustices alleged to have been inflicted by the "enemy" group, and bitter disputes over the control of land or the drawing of frontiers. As Barry Posen has pointed out,[16] the classic security dilemma operates just as strongly at the level of inter-ethnic conflict as it does at interstate level. When an ethnic group makes it apparent that it has significantly increased its security in the belief that this is a necessary defense against threat from other groups, neighboring groups tend to view this as a threat to their own security. This provokes them to take countermeasures that, paradoxically, are apt to make conflict between them more likely.

Far from seeing a strengthening of a "new international order" in the wake of the ending of the Cold War, we are seeing the spread of a new world disorder in which bitter ethnic and ethno-religious conflicts have become the characteristic mode of warfare from the Caucasus and the Balkans to South Asia and central Africa.[17]

Typically such wars are fought by armed militias, though they may get military assistance, weapons, or other resources from the regular troops of their allies. These wars are marked by extreme savagery toward the civilian population, frequently including the policy of "ethnic cleansing" or genocide to terrorize whole sectors of the population into fleeing from their homes; the use of massacre and mass rape as weapons; and total disregard of the international humanitarian laws of war. As we have seen in the conflicts in Chechnya and Bosnia, the taking of hostages, often on a mass scale, is also a feature of the use of terror in these savage ethnic conflicts.

By comparison with these eruptions of mass terror in the context of ethnic wars, long-standing campaigns by separatist terrorist groups—for example, ETA in Spain, the IRA in Northern Ireland, and the FLNC in Corsica—have been far less lethal and destructive.[18] The very fact that they have not succeeded in causing an escalation to full-scale civil war means that they do not constitute such a significant threat. Yet although these separatist terrorist movements have been conspicuously unsuccessful in delivering their strategic goals, they have succeeded in avoiding total defeat. This is largely because although they do not speak for anything more than a small minority of the group they claim to represent, they have a simple nationalist demand for national self-determination that has a resonance and emotional appeal to a core constituency of hard-line believers and that ensures a constant flow of new recruits, helpers, and cash to keep their campaign going.

On the other hand, democratic governments and societies facing violence from such groups can take some comfort in knowing that most members of these ethnic minorities within their jurisdiction have clearly shown their preference for democratic and peaceful ways of pursuing their political goals. A good illustration is the success of the autonomous regional government in the Basque region of Spain. It is worth remembering that some of the largest street demonstrations ever seen in postwar Western Europe have been by Basque citizens protesting against the continuing terrorist murders by ETA-militar, the fanatical Basque terrorist group.[19] Hence, although it may be impossible to persuade a residual hard core of irreconcilables to abandon the bomb and the gun, it is possible to ensure that the vast majority of the ethnic group they profess to speak for are fully won over to democratic means and feel they have a stake in the political system and the economy.

However, once ethnic terrorism has escalated to the level of full-scale civil war it is certain, based on the evidence of recent history, that it is going to be far more difficult to obtain a reduction or termination of the conflict.[20] It is true that an enormous amount of expertise is now available on ways of resolving protracted internal wars. The UN has had some impressive successes since the end of the Cold War—for example, in El Salvador, Nicaragua, and Mozambique—and partial successes, such as Cambodia.[21] But several factors make it particularly difficult for the UN to deploy an effective peacekeeping intervention to end ethnic civil wars. It is difficult, often well nigh impossible, to obtain the consent of the belligerents. Ethnic conflicts are often asymmetrical, and therefore the dominant belligerent will have no interest in securing a negotiated peace and will be unwilling to be deflected from its pursuit of all-out victory. In some cases the losers are forced to accept the reality that the victors have inflicted an irreversible defeat on them, the UN and voluntary relief agencies are allowed in for humanitarian reasons, and if a cease-fire is then negotiated it will inevitably tend to legitimate and entrench demographic changes imposed by the victors. Hence, as shown in the Balkans, the only forms of international intervention likely to succeed involve a genuine threat of force backed up by effective economic sanctions to deter or terminate a campaign of aggression and to enforce a cease-fire.

It is of course in the context of severe ethnic conflicts that the international community has greatest cause to invoke international tribunals, or better still the proposed International Criminal Court, to deal with those who commit crimes of genocide, crimes against humanity, and war crimes. It should be obvious that to be effective, an international criminal court must be—and must be seen to be—independent of all national governments and the UN Security Council. For example, consider the case of the Albanians massacred in Kosovo in late February 1998. It is widely believed that the massacre was carried out by members of the notorious Serb "anti-terrorist" unit, the SAJ, a 500-strong unit established at the behest of Mr. Milosevic and allegedly under the leadership of Frenki Simatovic, one of the most feared individuals in the Serb security apparat.[22] The power of an international court to investigate these crimes would be nullified if it depended on the prior approval of the Serb authorities, or if the investigation could simply be blocked by Russia, regarded by Serbs as a key friend and ally, in the UN Security Council. Kosovo is also a vivid illustration of the dangers of ethnic conflict spilling over into a wider international war. In a prescient study, Elez Biberaj drew attention to the growth of an organized resistance to the Serbs among the Albanian majority, with clear political aims and a united leadership.[23] Unfortunately, the warnings of intelligence experts and academic specialists were largely ignored until it was too late. And, as was widely predicted, the ensuing conflict did spill over into neighboring states and threaten their stability.

Because ethnic conflicts can so swiftly escalate into full-scale war, spilling over international frontiers, it is important for democratic governments and the wider international community to use preventive diplomacy and deterrence to stop this from happening, to contain and reduce the violence when such conflicts arise, and to promote cease-fires and peace agreements. The conflicts in Bosnia and Kosovo are dramatic illustrations of the cost in human lives and destruction when preventive diplomacy fails, and of the enormous difficulties involved in terminating this kind of conflict once it has taken hold.[24]

In the 1990s during the course of these tragic ethnic wars in which terror had been used as a weapon generally by both sides, we were dealing with *mass terror* causing death or serious injury to millions and forcing millions more to become external refugees or internally displaced persons. The sheer magnitude of the human costs involved in these eruptions of savage ethnic conflict is not fully comprehended by the citizens of relatively peaceful and prosperous western democracies.[25]

Yet by contrast the incidents of purely *international terrorism,* which arouse such concern in the United States, caused less than fifteen hundred deaths worldwide in the period 1991–96, and the annual total of such incidents is declining rapidly.[26] According to the RAND-St Andrews Chronology of International Terrorism figures, there were 350 incidents recorded in 1994, 278 in 1995, and 250 in 1996, the lowest annual total in 23 years.[27] There are, however, several interesting parallels between the trends in purely international terrorist incidents and the large-scale violence experienced in internal ethnic or ethno-religious wars. (This should hardly surprise us, because most of the groups carrying out international terrorist attacks are simultaneously involved in internal terrorist campaigns against their particular governmental "enemy" in their home country.) In both international and internal terrorism the most striking trend is that of increasing lethality. We have already noted this in respect to ethnic conflicts. It is also true of the terrorism motivated by religious extremism, for example, in Algeria and Kashmir. In the case of incidents of international terrorism it is striking that despite the dramatic fall in the number of recorded attacks, the numbers of fatalities have been growing dramatically. For example, the RAND-St Andrews statistics for 1996 record an annual death toll of 510, the fourth highest recorded since 1968.

A number of possible explanations have been put forward to account for this trend toward greater lethality. As government and private sector targets have "hardened" their security against terrorism, so the terrorist groups have sought out softer targets such as public buildings, squares, shopping centers, and public transport systems where larger numbers of the general public are likely to be killed or injured. Now that the public and the mass media have become to some extent desensitized by the sheer frequency of terrorist acts around the world, terrorist leaders and their followers may become convinced that only large-scale "spectacular" outrages will succeed in capturing the headlines and public attention. New generations of harder-line terrorists may have fewer compunctions about engaging in indiscriminate terrorist attacks, and may have convinced themselves that if they can shed enough blood it will force their opponents to give in to their demands. The development of terrorist tactics such as huge car and truck bombs in city centers and sabotage bombs aimed at blowing up jumbo jets in mid-air make these kinds of "spectacular" attack all too easily attainable for any group with access to sufficient quantities of explosives, bomb-making equipment, and expertise. It has also been argued that where the perpetrators are motivated by religious fanaticism this also contributes to the increased propensity for mass-lethality indiscriminate attacks, because a bomber who believes he is carrying out the will of God, or Allah, in waging a "Holy War" or "jihad" against an evil enemy is unlikely to be inhibited by the prospect of causing large-scale carnage. The religious fanatic bomber is also perhaps more susceptible to the idea of sacrificing his own life for the cause. Some would cite the Hezbollah truck bombers who attacked Western targets in Beirut in the early 1980s, or the Hamas suicide bombers who have attacked Israeli cities, in a deliberate effort to cause maximum civilian casualties. It is also noteworthy that the first sub-state group to have mounted nerve-gas attacks was a bizarre Japanese religious cult, Aum Shinrikyo, the organization that released sarin nerve gas in the Tokyo subway system, killing a dozen people and injuring 5,000.

Another key trend common to both international and internal terrorism is the emergence and consolidation of terrorist groups wholly or in part motivated by religious fanaticism. In the late 1970s all active international terrorist groups had secular goals and beliefs, a majority professing some variant of Marxism. By the end of the 1990s no less than a third of all currently active international terrorist groups were religiously motivated, the majority espousing Islamist beliefs.[28]

However, ethnic separatist groups have also continued to play a major role throughout the history of modern terrorism. According to the RAND-St Andrews statistics for 1996, no less than 37 percent of all international terrorist acts that could be definitely linked to an organization were committed by ethnic separatist groups.[29] This once again parallels the trends we can identify in internal terrorism, where ethnic separatism is still far and away the most frequent motivation behind terrorist actions.

An extremely important but frequently neglected trend in both internal and international terrorism is that almost all the experienced and firmly established terrorist groups, including those who confine their campaigns of violence within the borders of their own state, now operate increasingly sophisticated overseas infrastructures to ensure a constant supply of funds, to ensure weapons procurement, to gather intelligence of value to their organization, and to provide political and propaganda support. For example, the LTTE or Tamil Tigers organization has developed a formidable overseas support base of this nature.[30]

This trend, combined with the increasing use by terrorists of the Internet and other modern international communications systems, considerably complicates the task of monitoring and combating terrorist groups worldwide.

To sum up, the escalation of ethnic conflicts into savage warfare involving extensive use of the weapon of mass terror is the most striking feature of the patterns of terror worldwide in the late 1990s. Moreover, owing to the intractability of such conflicts and the international community's repeated failures to find effective ways of preventing or resolving them, this form of warfare and its concomitant mass violations of human rights are likely to spawn the major eruptions of terror violence well into the next century. The only real hope in the longer term is for the UN and other international institutions, in concert with the major powers, to develop the resources needed for effective preventive diplomacy, including earmarked UN forces capable of keeping the peace, to prevent such conflicts from breaking out and to find political and diplomatic solutions to inter-ethnic conflicts. To put it more simply, the UN Security Council and other major powers will need to act swiftly and decisively to establish the sinews of a new and just world order to counter the brutally divisive and destructive forces of disorder that threaten peace and stability in so many volatile regions. In a world in which ethnic and religious conflicts are escalating simultaneously with the proliferation of weapons of mass destruction, it is no longer unrealistic to urge that the pursuit of what the prescient but neglected Palme Commission termed the *Common Security*[31] of the international community be given the highest priority: It is not only realistic, it is vital to our survival. As a starting point, some of the extremely practical recommendations of Mr. Boutros Boutros-Ghali's *Agenda for Peace*[32] should be enacted by the UN Security Council. Member states should follow Britain's example in offering earmarked contingents of troops for UN tasks as required. Urgent consideration should also be given to the proposal that each member state should subscribe a percentage of its defense budget to preventive diplomacy tasks. This would be in the common interest of most UN members because it would avoid escalation into costly and destructive conflicts, which member states can ill afford.

Terror as a Weapon of Extreme Left Ideology

As made clear in an earlier chapter, most of the terrorist groups that emerged in the early 1970s professed some variant of Marxist ideology and saw themselves as part of a wider coalition of revolutionary "anti-imperialist" movements. This was true not only of the various Red Army or Fighting Communist organizations but also of the major "national liberation" groups using terror as a weapon. These groups included the PFLP and DFLP, ETA, and PKK, all of which aimed not only to establish independent statehood for their own ethnic group but also to ensure that it was run on revolutionary socialist lines.

The Red Army Faction emerged in West Germany in 1968 as an offshoot of the student protest movement, the Sozialistischer Deutscher Studentbund (SDS).[33] It was bitterly opposed to what it termed "American imperialism," for example condemning the U.S. role in Vietnam and the Middle East. Its leaders had an ideology closer to Maoism than to Marxism-Leninism, and viewed the West German state as "fascist." The group mounted bombing, shooting, and arson attacks on symbols of the U.S. presence in Germany as well as on government and judicial officials and business leaders. In the mid-1970s a new generation of better organized and more ruthless RAF terrorists emerged. However, following police success in bringing RAF terrorists to trial, and the failure of the 1997 Schleyer kidnap and Lufthansa hijack to force the West German authorities to release RAF leaders, the group began to wither. By the early 1990s, amid the collapse of communism, the discrediting of Marxist and Marxist-Leninist ideology, and the revelations of Stasi assistance to the RAF, the group gradually faded away. When the group issued a final communiqué announcing its formal disbandment, in April 1998, it came as no surprise.

The Italian Red Brigade, which emerged in 1969, had a similar ideology to the RAF. It regarded the Italian Communist Party as having sold out its revolutionary responsibilities, and believed it could win the support of factory workers and develop a wider revolutionary armed struggle against the Italian government. The Red Brigade movement was virtually defeated by 1982—as a result of a whole series of police arrests, trials and convictions—assisted by the *Pentiti* (repentant) terrorist legislation, which awarded generous remission of sentences to terrorists who collaborated with the criminal justice authorities in helping to bring fellow terrorists to justice.[34] By the early 1980s the BR were also badly split and demoralized.

The other Fighting Communist organizations in Western Europe[35] were even more short-lived and even less successful in winning political support and sympathizers among the extreme left. For example, Direct Action (AD) in France and the Fighting Communist Cells (CCC) in Belgium were soon eradicated by police action despite their rather grandiose efforts to ally themselves with the RAF in the mid-1980s to form a "Western European guerrilla" against "the hub of imperialist power, NATO." Far the most durable of these groups is the Revolutionary Organization 17 November in Greece, established in 1975 and taking its title from the date of the 1973 student uprising against the Greek military regime. The 17 November group remains bitterly opposed to the United States and to Greek membership of NATO and the European Union, as well as to members of the Greek political and business leadership. It remains very small, though it is probably linked to other extreme left Greek terrorist groups such as Revolutionary People's Struggle (ELA), and is of only marginal significance in Greek politics. However, it has succeeded in carrying out a long series of assassinations, using the same Colt .45 weapon and the same typewriter to produce its "communiqués." This is more of a commentary on the failure of the Greek authorities to take effective action than evidence of any real power or resources in the hands of the group.

A more bizarre case of a long-surviving Fighting Communist organization is the Japanese Red Army (JRA),[36] which emerged in 1970 and carried out a series of dramatic terrorist attacks abroad in the 1970s, including the 1972 massacre at Lod Airport, carried out on behalf of the PFLP, two hijackings of Japanese airliners, and attacks on the French Embassy at The Hague and the U.S. Embassy at Kuala Lumpur. Although the JRA is bitterly opposed to the Japanese government, since the early 1970s it has concentrated all its efforts on international activities that it claims are aimed at promoting world revolution. It is led by Fusako Shigenobu and is believed to have its base in the Bekaa Valley in Lebanon. It is believed that since the late 1980s the JRA has been operating under the title Anti-imperialist International Brigade (AIIB),[37] and that it has been attempting to establish cells in Asian cities such as Singapore and Manila. Despite these recent efforts, the group remains very small and of marginal significance in the wider terrorist picture.

Yet it would be a grave error to restrict our analysis of trends in terrorism by extreme left revolutionary groups to Europe and Japan.

It is, to say the least, somewhat premature to write the obituary of Marxist revolutionary movements in other parts of the world. In Latin America, for example, the insurgent and terrorist movements that continue to challenge the governments of the region are almost without exception ideologically of the extreme left. In Colombia the largest and best armed and trained group is the Revolutionary Armed Forces of Colombia (FARC), with an estimated 7,000 fighters and many more supporters, especially in the rural areas. Groups such as FARC and the National Liberation Army (ELN) are deeply involved in organized crime and racketeering on a very large scale in Colombia.[38] There is abundant evidence that ELN has been coercing coca and opium poppy cultivators to pay them protection money, and has been attacking the Colombian authorities' campaigns to destroy these crops. FARC has also been shown to be closely linked to drug traffickers and traffics in drugs. Both groups are also heavily involved in kidnaps for ransom, specializing in seizing the foreign employees of big corporations. This close tie to organized crime has led some analysts to dub them "degenerate guerrilla organizations." Nevertheless, these well-armed and relatively rich groups still profess to be pursuing revolutionary political goals, and the danger they pose to stability and the rule of law in a country like Colombia should not be underestimated. By spring 2000 the Colombian government had allowed FARC and ELN to have "designated zones" of 16,000 square miles and 1,800 square miles respectively. Government troops were not allowed to enter them. They were simply useful guerrila safe-havens. The government had allowed decadent guerrillas and their criminal gang allies to set up their own statelets within Colombia's internationally recognized borders, a major abdication of responsibility on the part of the lawful authorities.

It is also important to note that Sendero Luminoso (Shining Path), the largest and easily the most dangerous terrorist organization in Peru, espouses an extreme left revolutionary ideology.[39] Its founder, Abimael Guzman, believed he was following the true Maoist path. Despite the capture of Guzman by the authorities in 1992 the group continues with its campaign of particularly savage violence, including assassinations of local community leaders, officials, judges and other representatives of the Peruvian state, and indiscriminate bombings in the capital. It is estimated that the group has killed well over 30,000 people since 1980. The Tupac Amaru Movement (MRTA) poses a much less significant challenge to the Peruvian authorities than Sendero Luminoso. Even so, this smaller group—which has a more conventional Marxist-Leninist ideology and had almost been written off by the Peruvian government as a defeated organization—shocked the authorities in December 1996 by taking over the Japanese ambassador's residence in Lima during a diplomatic reception and seizing the estimated 600 guests as hostages. The resulting barricade and hostage situation was not resolved until four months later, when Peruvian soldiers stormed the Ambassador's residence and rescued the 72 remaining hostages. All MRTA hostage-takers were killed, together with one hostage and two soldiers. The tactics involved and the dilemmas of the siege situation for the Peruvian authorities are discussed in a later chapter. The key points to make here are that if we look at the terrorism scene in regions such as Latin America and South East Asia, it is certainly premature and downright dangerous to assume that the threat from Marxist, Marxist-Leninist, and Maoist groups has withered away.[40] These groups still have committed leaders and supporters. They claim that the collapse of Soviet communism was due to the revisionism and other major errors of Gorbachev and other communist leaders, and that they will avoid these errors and by following the correct path ultimately gain victory. Communist-inspired terrorism is, sadly, still very much alive in many areas of the Third World, and when we remind ourselves of the recent political history and current socioeconomic conditions prevailing in these regions, we should hardly be surprised by this.

Extreme Right Terrorism

The virtual eclipse of extreme left terrorism in Europe since the 1980s does not mean, however, that ideologically motivated terrorism has ended in this region. Ideologically driven groups have certainly been far less durable than those motivated by ethnic separatism. They are given to frequent splits and new organizational titles, and their fortunes change quite sharply under the impact of changes in the political, economic, and social environment and factors such as changing fashions in youth culture.

Since the ending of the Cold War there has been a worrying escalation of terrorism and other forms of political violence by ultra-right groups throughout Europe and the former Soviet Union as well as in the United States, where it presents the most significant domestic threat of politically motivated violence. In Europe in the 1990s the problem of the resurgence of extreme-right[41] violence has become a far more serious threat than ideologically motivated violence from the extreme left. In the mid-1990s the Bundesant für Verfassungsschutz (BfV)—(Federal Office for the Protection of the Constitution), reported the existence of 81 ultra-right extremist organizations, of which 27 were neo-Nazi. The BfV estimated that there were 42,100 members in these organizations, among them 6,200 extremists involved in violence, including skinhead gangs.[42] In Germany the widespread disillusion with mainstream political parties, the economic strains of reunification, high levels of unemployment, and the arrival of hundreds of thousands of newcomers has created a climate in which violent right-wing extremism thrives. In 1992 there were over 2,000 attacks by extreme right groups, causing 17 deaths and over 2,000 injuries, and between 1991 and 1993 the extreme-right groups killed 30 people.

In September 1993, Chancellor Kohl rather belatedly condemned the rise of these groups and their violent actions, and said they were as much of a threat to democratic society as extreme-left terror had been in the 1970s and early 1980s. A number of extreme-right groups were proscribed, and new special police units were set up to combat this type of crime. However, it is still possible for extreme groups to circumvent the ban on groups that threaten the constitutional order, under Article 9 of the German constitution. It is true that in 1994 there was a sharp decline in incidents of extreme-right violence, and there were no murders attributed to these groups in that year; but the danger of more crimes of extreme violence is still very real. For example, on 4 January 1998 at Magdeburg, a 23-year-old punk was brutally attacked by 11 neo-Nazi skinheads and nearly kicked to death. The attack occurred in the same home as the murder of another man by ultra-right extremists the previous year. And, despite the improved police measures, more arson attacks causing the deaths of immigrant families cannot be ruled out. One of the most horrifying terrorist incidents in Germany in recent years was the killing of three Turkish women and two young girls when their home was set ablaze in Solingen.

Extreme right-wing violence from skinhead and racist thugs has also been on the increase in many other parts of Europe, including Russia and the former Warsaw Pact countries.[43] Moreover, there has been a notable tendency for neo-Nazi groups—not only in Europe but also in America—to form links with similar groupings abroad, especially through the Internet.[44] For example, in Russia the extreme-right Liberal Democratic Party of Vladimir Zhirinovsky developed a close link with the German extreme-right party, Deutsche Volksunion, led by Gerhard Frey. Other active Russian ultra-right organizations include Russkoe Natsionalnoe Edintsvo (RNE)—(Russian National Unity), "Pamyat" (National Patriotic Front Remembrance), and the National Salvation Front, an extreme-right grouping. It is noteworthy that the closest foreign links of these Russian groups have been with the Serbian extreme nationalists, and especially with Radovan Karadzic, wanted for war crimes.

It is also worrying that extreme-right political parties in countries such as France, Italy, and Austria have considerably improved their electoral performance in the 1990s, and, as shown in the 1998 and 2002 elections in France, they may be able to exert a crucial influence on the overall balance of power between the major political parties. When Herr Haider's extreme-right Freedom Party joined a coalition government in Austria, concern was expressed by all major EU governments, and there were protests in Vienna.

However, it is in the United States where we find the extreme-right groupings that display the greatest potential for political violence and terrorism. The white-supremacist movement in the U.S. comprises dozens of extremist groups.[45] Many of these are linked to the so-called Christian Identity Movement, thus in fact combining religious extremism with the ultra-right-wing and racist beliefs. One authoritative source estimates that of the 25,000 estimated hard-core activists in the white-supremacist movement, roughly 14 percent are neo-Nazi skinheads, 5 percent are members of established neo-Nazi groupings, 20 percent are members of various factions of the Ku Klux Klan, and the remaining 60 percent belong to the various white-supremacist sects, such as the Phineas Priesthood—a clandestine group that takes its name from the Phineas legend in the Bible and is believed to have been involved in attacks on abortion clinics and their medical staffs—and the Aryan Nations.[46]

It should also be remembered that very small numbers of extremists can mount massively lethal terrorist attacks. The perpetrators of the bombing of the Alfred P. Murrah Federal Office Building in Oklahoma City in April 1995 were linked with one of the shadowy groupings within the American white supremacist movement. And in December the following year, six members of a white-supremacist group calling itself the Arizona Patriots were arrested and were later convicted on charges of conspiracy to bomb the Los Angeles Federal Building, an Inland Revenue Service office in Utah, and a synagogue in Phoenix. These groupings may be small, but they are well armed, and in some cases extremely dangerous. The success of the U.S. criminal justice authorities in securing convictions in these cases should not mislead us into assuming that the threat of further extreme-right terrorism has been overcome: On the contrary, it constitutes a huge problem for the U.S. counter-terrorism agencies because of the multiplicity of such groups; their access to firearms, explosives, and chemical and biological weaponry; and the law enforcement agencies' own lack of experience in combating a significant internal terrorist threat within U.S. borders.

Terror as a Weapon of Religious Fanaticism

Terror has been used as a weapon of religious persecution and religious warfare throughout history. One of the earliest recorded examples is the Sicarii (from the Greek *sikarioi*, "dagger men"), an extreme group of the Jewish Zealot sect.[47] They waged terrorism and assassination against the Roman occupation, 66–70 A.D., and against any Jews who cooperated with the Roman authorities. The Sicarii acquired their name from their practice of ambushing persons they classed as collaborators and murdering them with daggers. In 73 A.D. at Masada, they committed suicide rather than surrender the fortress to the Roman army.

The Assassin sect, a radical Shi'ite Ismaili brotherhood emerging at the end of the eleventh century, and from whose name the modern word *assassination* derives, was another prototypal terrorist movement.[48] They developed an explicit religious justification for killing those deemed to be "unrighteous" or "the servants of the unrighteous." There is some support in early Islamic doctrine for the principles of tyrannicide and just rebellion, and the Assassin sect reemphasized these doctrines, but we should also note that each act of murder was for the Assassin a *sacramental duty.* The weapon used was invariably a dagger. This made the capture of the Assassin all the more likely. Moreover there is evidence that sectaries willingly sacrificed their own lives. We are dealing here with a phenomenon that clearly invites comparison with a late twentieth-century terrorist phenomenon—the suicide bombers of Islamic Jihad and Hamas, who killed because they also believed themselves to be righteous, and because they believed that killing the unrighteous would guarantee their own salvation and assist in overthrowing a corrupt order.

One of the most notorious examples of terror as a weapon of religious persecution was the Spanish Inquisition, established by the Pope in the fifteenth century at the behest of the Spanish monarchy to combat heresy and apostasy, usury, and persons accused of sorcery and witchcraft. Torture and confiscation were the characteristic weapons of terror. Under Tomás de Torquemada, the first grand inquisitor, it is estimated that there were several thousand burnings at the stake, and 170,000 Jewish subjects who refused to be baptised were expelled from Spain.

As in earlier periods of history, religious fanaticism and terror are not the exclusive preserve of any single major religion. Christian identity cults and sects in the United States, preaching the hate propaganda of white supremacism and anti-Semitism and armed opposition to the federal government, are linked with the shadowy groups believed to have been involved in the Oklahoma bombing.[49] Nor should we forget the strand of religiously motivated terrorism in modern Jewish fundamentalism.[50] In 1984 the Israeli security forces managed to thwart a plot by Jewish extremists to bomb the Dome on the Rock, one of the holiest places in Islam. In February 1994 a Jewish extremist, Baruch Goldstein, a follower of Rabbi Kahane, massacred twenty-nine worshippers in a crowded mosque at Hebron. And in November 1995 Prime Minister Yitzhak Rabin was assassinated by a Jewish extremist who claimed to be carrying out God's orders.

It is extremely important to understand that terrorism is abhorred and condemned by the leaders of all the world's major religions. It is as absurd to equate mainstream Islamic religion with the terrorism committed by extremist groups acting in the name of Islamic beliefs, as it would be to blame the Christian religion for the actions of Torquemada or of the self-styled Phineas Priesthood in America. We must be vigilant in guarding against the prejudice, stereotyping, and intolerance that lead to anti-Semitism and Islamophobia. A clear manifestation of the latter in America was the way in which the U.S. mass media rushed to judgment over the Oklahoma bombing, immediately blaming the atrocity on an Islamic group—without any evidence. As a matter of historical record, the overwhelming majority of the victims of the terrorism committed by Islamist fanatics in the late twentieth century, for example in Algeria and Afghanistan, have been fellow Muslims.

The preceding caveats are vitally important if we are to place the trends in terrorism in the 1990s and into the next century in proper perspective. However, it is also extremely important not to underestimate the significance of the rise of groups of extreme Islamic fundamentalists, inspired—and in many cases actively encouraged—by the Islamic revolutionary regime in Iran, and ready to wage *jihad* (holy war) against pro-Western Arab regimes with the aim of setting up Islamic republics in their place.[51] As the examples of the GIA in Algeria and the Islamic Group in Egypt demonstrate, these groups are not confined to Shia populations. The primary targets of the groups' campaigns are the incumbent regimes and their military, police, and government officials, as well as the intellectuals who are identified with the regime.

As in the case of the ethnic conflicts described earlier in this chapter, terrorism is generally only one weapon in a wider struggle: others include propaganda; fighting elections (where this is permitted by the regime); and the development of a mass base of support by means of a wide range of welfare, medical, educational, and cultural activities under the fundamentalist movement's control. A key feature of all these groups is that they are bitterly opposed not only to the United States and Israel, but to all Western countries. Frequently they have widened their range of targets to attack Westerners within their countries, as with Hezbollah's seizure of Western hostages in Lebanon in the 1980s,[52] GIA murders of French and other foreign citizens in Algeria since 1993, and the 1997 Luxor massacre in which the Islamic group terrorists murdered 58 foreign tourists.

There is a further worrying implication of the trends in Islamic fundamentalist terrorism, one that has been stressed by my colleague, Bruce Hoffman,[53] and that concerns the modus operandi of fundamentalist groups' involvement in international terrorism. It appears highly likely that the group of Islamic fundamentalists responsible for blowing up the World Trade Center in New York in February 1993 was operating as a type of independent or freelance group, inspired and encouraged by their spiritual mentor, Sheikh Omar Abd-al-Rahman, and not controlled by a state sponsor or known major terrorist player. Such groups would pose a particular problem for the counterterrorism agencies of Western governments as they have no identifiable structure and previous track record. They would also be able to recruit fanatical members from their expatriate community in the host state with the great advantage of considerable local knowledge.

Some commentators claim that their challenge is beginning to recede.[54] However, during the mid-1990s a far more deadly covert Islamist terrorist organization was beginning to emerge: the Al Qaeda network. Founded by Osama bin Laden, Al Qaeda was responsible for the worst atrocity in the history of sub-state terrorism, the September 11 suicide hijacking attack in the towers of the World Trade Center, New York. The attacks on September 11 caused more civilian deaths in a single day than were caused by over a half-century of terrorism by Republicans and Loyalists in Northern Ireland.

Mass destruction or catastrophic terrorism on this scale had become a strategic threat not only to the United States but to the peace, security, and economic well-being of the entire international community. September 11 has brought us a step closer to terrorists using chemical, biological, radiological, or nuclear weapons. Captured documents and materials prove beyond a doubt that

Al Qaeda has been actively seeking means of acquiring such weapons. Who can seriously doubt that if they succeed, they will not hesitate to use them? In their obsession with the use of violence some millennialist groups have espoused a policy of terror,[55] but Al Qaeda goes much further. In Osama bin Laden's notorious 1996 Declaration of War Against America and his 1998 Fatwa, he goes to the lengths of calling on every Muslim, as a religious duty, to kill Americans, including civilians whenever and wherever the opportunity arises. A central aim of Osama bin Laden's network is to kill as many Americans as possible.

Moreover, Al Qaeda has demonstrated that you do not have to use chemical, biological, radiological, or nuclear weapons in order to cause mass destruction and carnage. They combined the well-tried and tested tactics of airliner hijacking and suicide attack in a coordinated assault. Future Al Qaeda attacks may again include acts of aviation terrorism. If FBI investigators are correct, Richard Reid, who tried to blow up an American Airlines plane using explosives hidden in his shoes, was linked to Al Qaeda. We need to be vigilant about the possibility of other attempts at suicide sabotage bombing of airliners. But Al Qaeda has shown it can use a variety of tactics and venues.

Although Osama bin Laden and his Al Qaeda network have tried to present themselves as fighting a jihad or holy war against America and its allies, and use religious language in an attempt to legitimize their terrorism, we should not overlook the fact that bin Laden's organization has a definite *political* agenda. They want to force the United States into withdrawing from Saudi Arabia and the Gulf region generally. They want to overthrow what they regard as collaborationist regimes in the Muslim world, which they accuse of betraying "true" Islam, and they want to unite all Muslims in a pan-Islamic Caliphate that would rule according to the principles of "true" Islam.

Al Qaeda is in many ways the prototype of what has been termed the "New Terrorism." The New Terrorism can be interpreted as both a *manifestation* of the globalization process and a *response* to globalization of the world economy and widely perceived U.S. hegemony. Unlike "traditional" terrorism the New Terrorism is more diffuse and amorphous, using an international network of loosely connected cells and support networks rather than the traditional hierarchical command and control structure of a group based in a country or region. Unlike traditional terrorism, it is no longer dependent on the sponsorship or funding of particular states or regimes: The New Terrorism typically employs sophisticated international support networks linking diasporas and sympathizers worldwide to raise funds; to procure weapons and explosives; and to recruit, train, and, when deemed necessary, to mount operations in foreign countries.

It would be a serious mistake to assume the New Terrorism groups have entirely displaced "traditional" terrorism. Even among the politico-religious groups there are many with traditional leadership structures and modus operandi. However, the New Terrorism of the kind represented by the Al Qaeda network is likely to prove extremely hard for the international community to eradicate, and is likely to inspire many offshoots and imitators.

Whatever the ultimate fate of Osama bin Laden, his terrorist network, or a successor organization under a different name, the New Terrorism is likely to continue to present a challenge to the United States and the international community for some time ahead.

State-Sponsored Terrorism

There are seven essential prerequisites for mounting terrorism. There must be some main *aim* or *motivation* among the perpetrators, even if it ultimately amounts to little more than an intense hatred of their perceived enemies or a desire for violent revenge against some alleged injustice. There must be *leaders* to instigate and direct the struggle. In any sustained and significant campaign, there will also need to be some degree of *organization,* some *training* in the special skills of terrorism, and *cash* that helps to buy *weapons and ammunition* and other essential needs. Finally, it is clearly vital for the terrorists to have *access to the target* country and the precise targets selected within that country. Of course, we know of numerous groups that possess considerable resources over and above those just listed. Some succeed in building up large numbers of supporters and sympathizers among the general population. Many obtain the substantial advantages of sponsorship by one or more states. In certain circumstances, terrorists can attain sanctuaries or safe bases beyond the reach of security forces or opposing factions, for example, in the remote terrain of the interior. But these are bonuses for the terrorists. We know that most of the terrorists operating in the contemporary international system do not have these advantages.

Exactly the same basic ingredients are required to mount a viable campaign of international terrorism. But unless the perpetrators restrict themselves to attacking foreign personnel and property within the terrorists' own country of origin, they will require significantly greater levels of organization, training, expertise, cash, and means of access to foreign states in order to wage a full international campaign.

The ending of the Cold War had the effect of dramatically reducing the number of states using terrorism as a weapon of foreign and domestic policy. The former Soviet Union and its Warsaw Pact communist satellite regimes in East Europe were extensively involved in assisting terrorist groups around the world on an opportunistic basis.[56]

In 2002, only five states still maintain and covertly employ the weapon of sponsoring international terrorism.[57] All of these are in the Middle East: Iran, Iraq, Syria, Sudan and Libya. Of these, Iran is far and away the most significant source of state-sponsored terrorism. The Iraqi regime is hobbled by the constraints imposed by the UN Security Council resolutions and has restricted itself to activities in the Kurdish area of Northern Iraq and the sponsorship of terrorism against Iran and targets in neighboring states. Syria provides a valuable safe haven for Hezbollah, for a number of radical Palestinian groups, and for the PKK. It also permits Iran to resupply its client Hezbollah with weapons and funds. But it also exercises some restraint over the activities of these groups, because Assad wants to retain the option of diplomatic negotiation with Israel for the return of the Golan Heights. Gadaffi, the Libyan dictator, is still providing training camps, safe haven, and cash and weapons for certain favored groups. He is also still using terrorism as a weapon against Libyan dissidents abroad. But since the U.S. bombing raid on Libya in April 1986, in the wake of the Berlin disco terrorist bomb, Gadaffi has fought to avoid direct confrontation with the United States. He has also been seeking to promote a more "respectable" image among the EU states, and wishes to improve economic relations with Europe. But his prospects of international rehabilitation will undoubtedly be affected by the verdict of the Pan Am Flight 103 trial at the Hague criminal court that charged two Libyans with the terrorist bombing of that airliner.

How significant is state-sponsored terrorism as a proportion of the international terrorism scene at this time? The overwhelming majority of terrorist acts of this kind are committed by sub-state groups that have their own infrastructures of support and resources. These groups still view terrorism as an effective weapon for attaining valuable tactical objectives. It is a relatively low-cost, low-risk, but potentially high-yield method of waging their struggles. Even if state sponsorship reduced dramatically as a result of action by the United States and the international community, terrorism would still remain the most ubiquitous form of politically motivated violence.

However, state-sponsored terrorism still poses particular dangers, which the community of law-abiding states would be foolish to ignore: (1) Where states use terrorism as a primary mode of clandestine warfare, there is a risk of inter-state conflict escalating from tit-for-tat retaliation to full-scale warfare, as has been seen in the Middle East;[58] (2) State-sponsored terrorism is potentially far more lethal and destructive because states can provide levels of firepower, funding, training, and intelligence far beyond the scope of sub-state groups, and they have the inestimable advantage of being able to provide safe havens and bases for planning and coordination;[59] (3) Terrorist groups, such as the IRA and Hezbollah, have been rendered infinitely more dangerous as a direct result of large-scale provision of weaponry by state sponsors (Libya and Iran respectively in the case of the IRA and Hezbollah); and (4) NATO and the G8 states have been deeply divided in their response to state sponsors of terrorism, and this weakens solidarity and effectiveness of cooperation against terrorism among the major states.

These dangers are well illustrated in the case of Iran, the leading state sponsor in the current terrorism scene. Iran's most important client terrorist movement is Hezbollah in Southern Lebanon, a movement which it helped to create and keeps well supplied with weapons and cash in addition to political and diplomatic support. Hezbollah attacks on Israeli and SLA forces and rocket attacks across Israel's northern border could easily become a catalyst for a fresh outbreak of war in the Middle East. Iran is also the leading inspiration and supporter state for most of the other major radical Islamic groups currently challenging the pro-Western regimes of the Middle East, in the Gulf, and in Egypt, Tunisia, and Algeria. It is encouraging radical Islamic tendencies in Turkey, the Balkans, and farther afield. The Iranian regime is also the leading rejectionist state, bitterly opposed to the Middle East peace process and taking a key role in backing a coalition of terrorist groups dedicated to derailing the process, including Hamas, Palestinian Islamic Jihad, and the PFLP-GC. Iran's client group, Hezbollah, is strongly suspected of involvement in the July 1994 bombing of the Argentine-Israel Mutual Association building in Buenos Aires, in which nearly 100 died: The most likely motivation for this and earlier attacks in Buenos Aires was bitter opposition to the Israeli-Palestinian peace process.

Iran has also used terrorism as a weapon against dissidents taking refuge abroad. For example, in December 1994 Iran was revealed as directly implicated in the plot to murder former Prime Minister Bakhtiar and his aide in Paris. One of the Iranians convicted received a life sentence and the other ten years' imprisonment. However, the most damning evidence of Iranian state-sponsored terrorism was the judgment in the German trial of those who murdered Kurdish dissidents in the Mykonos restaurant. The German court found that the Iranian regime at the highest level was involved in ordering the murders. Despite this, there have been no effective concerted sanctions against the Iranian regime by the EU states. Election of the moderate, Mohammad Khatami, to the position of President of Iran and the success of his supporters in elections for Iranian parliament certainly justifies the policy of constructive dialogue with Iran favored by EU states. But it must be remembered that hardline militants still control the state security system, the media, and other key institutions, and Khatami has been contending with constant political infighting with those bitterly opposed to any rapprochement with the West.

The Iranian regime also played the key part in encouraging its ally in Sudan, the National Islamic Front, to turn Sudan into a useful platform for training, safe haven, and assistance to a variety of extremist factions such as the Islamic Group, Hamas, Hezbollah, PIJ, and others. Egypt and Ethiopia have accused Sudan of complicity in the unsuccessful assassination attempt on President Hosni Mubarak in Addis Ababa in June 1995, carried out by Islamic Group terrorists.

Last but not least, the Iranian regime and militant religious leaders in Iran have continued to threaten the life of the British writer, Salman Rushdie, and all those involved in the publishing of his book *Satanic Verses*. This is based on a Fatwa by Ayatollah Khomeini calling for the death of Rushdie. In 1994 Iran's ambassador to Norway stated that it was every Muslim's duty to kill Salman Rushdie whenever and wherever they are able to do so. Recently Iran increased the bounty for the killing of Rushdie to $2.5 million.[60] These actions hardly suggest that Iran is abandoning the terrorist weapon!

Faced with these uncomfortable facts, the Western allies have been sadly divided and weak in their response. Germany and other EU states have clung to a policy of "critical dialogue" with Iran in the hope of changing the regime's mind, and of maintaining their markets and investments in Iran. America has sought tough measures, calling on its allies to support economic sanctions. It is surely desirable for NATO and G8 countries to adopt a more effective, concerted response if they are genuine in their opposition to terrorism. The election of President Khatami, a more liberal figure who has called for dialogue with the United States, is a hopeful sign, and provides a good reason for maintaining diplomatic contacts with the regime in Tehran. But in view of the fact that hard-liners are still in positions of real power and influence in Iran, any dialogue should be combined with firm collective international measures to demonstrate that continuing Iranian sponsorship of international terrorism will lead to Iran paying a heavy economic and political cost.

So far I have been discussing full-scale state sponsorship of terrorism, providing terrorist clients or agents with a whole range of support services ranging from diplomatic passports and intelligence to cash, weapons, and safe haven. But there are many other ways in which governments, including democratic governments, contribute general support for terrorism abroad without becoming sponsors, without having any control or influence over the terrorist groups that benefit from their policies, and without most of the public and the politicians realizing the implications of their governments' actions or failures to act.

At one end of the spectrum of support for terrorism is the policy of turning a blind eye to acts of state-sponsored terrorism in one's own territory. The refusal to take any effective action against the perpetrators is usually due to an overriding desire not to damage commercial interests or the belief that the terrorists can be bought off. A clear example of this was the French government's supine response to the murder of the former Iranian Prime Minister, Shapour Bakhtiar, in Paris in 1991 by an Iranian hit squad using diplomatic cover. Even though the French investigating judge had concluded that the murder was carried out on the direct orders of the Iranian regime, no proper action was taken. France continued to trade with Iran, and in 1993 France deported two suspects to Iran, both of whom were also wanted by Switzerland on charges of murder, thus violating both international law and French law.

Far more serious, however, are the allegations that surfaced in investigations by *Le Figaro* and by the French National Assembly "Information Committee" on Rwanda. It has been claimed that the two missiles which shot down the aircraft carrying the Presidents of Rwanda and Burundi were supplied by France, and that they originated from a stock of weapons confiscated by French forces in Iraq during Operation Desert Storm. The shooting down of the plane triggered the genocide in which an estimated 800,000 people were killed. Edouard Balladur, the former French Prime Minister in office at the time of the 1994 massacre of the Tutsis in Rwanda, has claimed that France was the only country "to take the initiative to do all it could" to stop the massacres. It is of course often claimed by arms manufacturers and arms dealers that it is not weapons that are to blame for conflict and violence, but the people who use them. Nevertheless it is surely difficult to deny that those who supply weapons to a regime or group that then uses them in a campaign of mass terror and genocide must share some responsibility for the ensuing catastrophe. The leading Western countries are major suppliers of conventional weapons to many volatile, conflict-ridden areas. It is these arms, and not weapons of mass destruction, that are killing so many innocent civilians in savage internal wars. Hence, despite embarrassing scandals such as the Iran-Contra arms for hostages affair and the UK's Scott Inquiry into the sale of British arms to Iraq, the flow of conventional arms, including sophisticated weapons, continues.[61]

It must also be recognized that although it is in modern dictatorships and authoritarian regimes that we find state terror being used routinely as an instrument of repression and political control, many democratic governments have been guilty of resorting to the methods of the dirty war and counter-terror in the name of combating terrorism. British security forces have been accused of engaging in a "shoot to kill" policy in Northern Ireland, for example, though it is noteworthy that John Stalker, appointed to inquire into these allegations and later removed from this task, has written that he found no evidence to prove the existence of any such policy. The Spanish Government is alleged to have been involved in the GAL, an assassination squad that hunted down and killed a number of ETA militants across the French border, though Prime Minister Felipe Gonzalez has strongly denied this.

It is also important to recognize that Western democracies have often been guilty of backing regimes and groups that have been involved in committing terrorist attacks on the civilian population. The most notable example is the role of the U.S. government in funding and assisting clients in Latin America during the Cold War—for example, the Somoza regime in Nicaragua and military dictatorship in Guatemala. U.S. policymakers repeatedly chose to turn a blind eye to the activities of right-wing and vigilante death squads, not because they approved of the gross human rights violations they committed but because they believed that military and financial support for their client regimes and groups was vital to preventing these Latin American countries from following the Cuban path and going over to the communist camp in the Cold War.

Interference in Central American countries during the Cold War in the name of protecting the region from communism led to some of the most shameful episodes in the history of U.S. foreign policy. The CIA arranged a coup in Guatemala in 1954, and then successive U.S. policymakers continued to give support to a regime that killed an estimated 100,000 of its own population. The dictatorships of Batista in Cuba, Trujillo in the Dominican Republic, and Somoza in Nicaragua all received substantial support from Washington during the Cold War. It has been estimated that approximately 100,000 people were killed in the conflicts in these countries during the Cold War. It was not until the 1980s that the U.S. government began to make U.S. financial assistance conditional on reforms in democratic practice and human rights. This important but long overdue policy change was introduced partly in response to the report of Henry Kissinger's 1983 National Bipartisan Commission on Central America, which accurately identified the massive economic and social problems of the region and recommended that the only way to prevent a communist revolution in the region was to introduce fundamental reforms to establish democracy and to protect human rights. The Kissinger Commission undoubtedly overestimated the threat of communism, but it was right to urge major reforms.

Some opponents of U.S. foreign policy, notably Noam Chomsky and his followers, have used the U.S. government's "disgraceful human rights record in policy towards Central America" to claim that the United States is the leading abuser of human rights and instigator of terrorism in the world. They are justified in attacking U.S. policy toward Central America, but their attempt to portray the United States as the main author of state terrorism in the world is patently absurd. Have they not heard of Stalin and the terrible crimes committed by his regime—and his successors in the former Soviet Union, in which millions of innocent citizens were killed or consigned to the Gulag Archipelago—or the Pol Pot regime, which slaughtered between 1 and 3 million of the population of Cambodia? It is the totalitarian regimes of Hitler, Stalin, and Stalin's successors that have been responsible for the overwhelming majority of acts of state terror in the twentieth century, not the world's leading democracy. The U.S. record may be far from perfect, but Chomsky and his supporters seem blissfully unaware that without U.S. global activism and the sacrifices of its soldiers, sailors, and airmen they would not be able to enjoy the freedom they are so ready to malign.

However, the most clear-cut and comprehensive evidence of a democratic government employing ruthless acts of counter-terror against terrorist opponents is provided by the case of Israel. Israeli governments have frequently used extrajudicial killing or assassination as a weapon of counter-terror. They believe that this is justified because the state of Israel has throughout most of its existence been forced to fight a war on all fronts against its Palestinian and other Arab opponents, including major terrorist campaigns.

However, just as terrorism as a weapon of insurgency often misfires, so the weapon of assassination as an instrument of counter-terror is frequently counterproductive. A vivid example was the bungled attempt in October 1997 by Mossad agents in Amman to assassinate Khaled Meshaal, a leading member of Hamas, by injecting poison into his ear. This attack infuriated King Hussein of Jordan and damaged Israel's relations with Jordan, one of its most valuable allies in the peace process.[62] It infuriated the Canadians because the Mossad agents were using false Canadian passports, and it further damaged the Israeli government's international reputation, already gravely damaged by the Netanyahu government's intransigence on the issues of the expansion of Jewish settlements and Israeli troop withdrawals from the West Bank. To soothe the anger of King Hussein, the Israeli government was forced to release Sheikh Yassin (the founder and spiritual mentor of Hamas) and 71 other Palestinians from prison. And as if this bungled foreign assassination operation wasn't enough, in February 1998 Mossad attempted, unsuccessfully, to assassinate two businessmen in Switzerland who were believed to be helping Hezbollah to obtain biological and chemical weapons.[63] According to a senior Mossad officer interviewed by *The Times,* the botched operation in Switzerland involved an attempt to use the powerful nerve agent Mossad agents had used previously in the failed operation in Jordan. The officer also stated that at least one of the Mossad team who had participated in the failed Amman assassination was among the team arrested in Switzerland.[64]

There is a widespread misconception that using terror to defeat terror will ultimately work. On the contrary, the evidence is that this policy is counter-productive. Instead of suppressing terrorism against Israel, these methods tend to reinvigorate the terrorist movements and gain them international sympathy. They have only tended to make it harder than ever to break the cycle of violence and sustain progress in the peace process.

Terrorism and Organized Crime

Terrorist activities such as murder, conspiracy to murder, kidnapping, and extortion are themselves obviously a form of serious organized crime, however much the perpetrators wish to see themselves as freedom fighters. Hence the various acts of terrorism almost invariably transgress the criminal law code of all civilized states. But most terrorist groups also get involved in organized crime for more mundane reasons: Unless they are lucky enough to be funded by a generous state-sponsored regime, they will resort to crimes of armed robbery, fraud, racketeering, and extortion in order to raise money to buy weapons, vehicles, and other resources necessary for their campaigns, and to generally sustain their organizations.

A common method of fund raising by terrorist organizations is the levying of revolutionary "taxes" among the businesses and families in the ethnic constituency of the terrorist group.[65] For example, ETA has long depended on a "revolutionary tax" among the Basque population. Nor should we be under any illusion about what happens to those who refuse to pay. There have been numerous cases of ETA "punishment" attacks on those who refuse to pay. A widely reported case of ETA's ruthless method of dealing with those who defy its writ was their murder of a businessman, Isdiro Usabiaga, in July 1996.[66] Señor Usabiaga had refused to pay the "revolutionary tax" despite having received death threats. ETA shot him in the back as he was returning home. Similarly savage treatment has been meted out by the IRA against individuals who challenged the Provisionals' control of the criminal network in the communities where they are entrenched. Sadly, there is no sign of these aspects of terrorist activity fading away. For instance, in Northern Ireland in April 1998, even after the Good Friday peace agreement, the terrorist groups were still engaging in punishment attacks, in one case knee-capping a 79-year-old man in the New Lodge area of Belfast.[67] When the armed organizations have become so habituated to committing these savage crimes, it is hard to imagine them ever transforming themselves into peaceable democratic organizations.

Just as there is nothing new about the depraved criminality of the terrorist organizations, so there is nothing remarkable in the continuing use of terror by traditional organized crime organizations such as the Mafia and the Triads. These gangs have routinely used lethal violence to instill fear in members of their own gangs and the communities in which they operate in order to suppress rivals and to deter anyone from informing on them to the authorities.

However, in the early 1990s organized criminal gangs in Italy and India dramatically increased the scale of threat posed to their respective societies and legal systems by adopting the tactic of large-scale urban bombing, long favored by the politically motivated terrorists.[68] The Italian Mafia blew up the motor convoy of Judge Giovanni Falcone, the leading judge in the fight against the Mafia,[69] on 23 May 1992. The huge bomb killed the judge, his wife, and three police bodyguards. There had been many previous Mafia assassinations, most notably the 1982 murder of General Dalla Chiesa, the civil governor of Palermo. As in the case of General Dalla Chiesa, the Mafia murdered Judge Falcone because they saw him as a threat to their whole criminal syndicate. It is known that the judge was on the brink of examining a list of secret Swiss bank accounts, some of which were believed to contain illegally held funds, and that they would have established the links between Italian politicians and businessmen to the Cosa Nostra. What was remarkable about the murder of Judge Falcone, however, was the method used: It was almost a carbon copy of the kind of bomb attack carried out in the past by Red Army terrorists; the typical method of assassination used by the Mafia in the past was shooting. The Mafia used the terrorist tactic again in July 1992, when they used a huge car bomb to blow up Judge Paolo Borsellino, the chief public prosecutor in Palermo who was in charge of coordinating anti-Mafia activity.[70] The judge's wife and three bodyguards were also killed in the explosion. The Italian prime minister at that time, Guiliano Amato, described the bombing as an "act of war against the state."

In the author's view these murders, like the Mafia's assassination of General Dalla Chiesa, were acts of pure terrorism. Their aim was not to promote any particular political ideology but to terrorize the state and its judicial and police institutions into abandoning their investigations and prosecutions of the Mafia. It is a sad fact that despite the courage and sacrifice of leading judges and police officials, the authorities' campaign against the terrorism of the Mafia has not met with the same success as the campaign against the Red Brigade in the late 1970s and early 1980s, and it is still hampered by corruption at many levels. The gravity of the continuing Mafia threat was underlined in July 1997 when Sicilian police seized a cache of Soviet-made heat-seeking rocket launchers, antitank grenades, detonators, and AK-47 assault rifles, which the police believe were to be used in an assassination attempt on a key figure.[71] According to Guide Le Forte, deputy prosecutor in Palermo, there has been a major revival in the activities of the Italian Mafia, now heavily involved in international drug dealing, arms smuggling, and money laundering. The Mafia is also believed to have subverted the *Pentito* programme (the use of reductions in sentences to reward Mafia criminals who collaborate with the authorities), and, according to *La Republica,* "many have used the *pentiti* for its own ends from the very beginning."[72]

The Italian Mafia is but one illustration that terrorist methods have become the stock in trade of international organized crime. According to U.S. experts, global organized crime is now at least a $400 billion-a-year business involving Colombian and Mexican drug cartels, the Russian "Mafiya" gangs, and heroin produced on a massive scale in Afghanistan, Pakistan, and the Golden Triangle (Burma, Laos, Thailand).

Leading experts on trends in global crime—such as the late Dr. Richard Clutterbuck and Professor Roy Godson—have long been warning that the battle against the alliance of powerful drug cartels and degenerate guerrilla organizations (FARC and ELN) would be lost unless drastic action was taken. Tragically, their advice was not heeded. In Professor Godson's view, Colombia is now "lost:" It is being torn apart by the faction wars between the drug barons, the paramilitaries, and the well-armed guerrilla forces of the "Revolutionary Armed Forces of Colombia" (FARC), which is itself creaming huge profits from drug trafficking, extortion, and kidnapping, and gaining an annual income estimated at 1 billion U.S. dollars. The Colombian Army is totally inadequate to the task of suppressing this lawlessness. Huge rural areas of the country are now totally ungovernable. As *The Economist* poignantly observed in a lead article:

> Caught terrorized in the middle are Colombia's rural people; extorted from, frightened or driven from their homes, kidnapped for ransom, "disappeared," murdered, at times massacred wholesale. And not all the victims are even adult. Which armed men do just what is, of course, disputed; conveniently but maybe rightly, the shadowy paramilitaries get much of the blame. But the results are plain, and horrible.[73]

Concluding Observations on Terrorism Trends

A close examination of trends in terrorism worldwide does not lead one to conclude that we now confront an entirely new phenomenon of "post-modern" terrorism in place of the "old" terrorist regimes and movements of the 1970s and 1980s. The regimes using terror against their own populations have been doing so for decades. The ending of the Cold War removed many state sponsors of terrorism from the scene at a stroke, but the currently active major state sponsors have been part of the international scene for between two and three decades. Most of the secular international terrorist movements active in the late 1990s were established in the 1970s, and most of those motivated by religion emerged in the 1980s. It is significant that only two of the active major terrorist groups listed in the U.S. State Department's *Patterns of Global Terrorism, 1996* were founded in the 1990s—the Armed Islamic Group (GIA) in Algeria and Harakat ul-Ansar (HUA) in Pakistan. All of these groups have known aims, organizational structures, leading activists, and various links with like-minded organizations and/or states.

It has been claimed that the post-modern terrorist groups do not claim responsibility for their attacks, but as Bruce Hoffman has argued,[74] this is by no means a new development. It is also claimed that the New Terrorism is more amorphous, more diffuse, and often planned and committed by "freelance" or "walk-on" terrorists. Here we must be very careful not to generalize about the terrorist scene on the basis of particular terrorist attacks, such as the first World Trade Center attack and the suicide airliner hijackings on September 11, which displayed some radical departures from the modus operandi more generally employed by terrorist organizations. If one looks at the world of domestic terrorist organizations, which still constitute the overwhelming majority of the world's terrorist groups, one is struck not only by their innate "conservatism" in choice of tactics, weaponry, and targeting but also by their ability to evolve and to adapt to changes in their environment and intensified efforts by governments to suppress them.

By far the most worrying and significant trend in terrorism worldwide is its growing lethality and tendency toward indiscriminate attacks in public places. Yet even when it comes to the terrorist group's choice of weaponry, it is by no means obvious or inevitable that they will decide to deploy weapons of mass destruction. There are factors that might impel terrorists toward use of weapons of mass destruction, but it is the New Terrorism and the groups motivated by religious fanaticism that are most likely to take this path. In the real world of terrorism, democratic governments and societies are going to have to deal with both old and new terrorist organizations, tactics, and weapons simultaneously; and we need to be aware of the continuities in terrorist developments as well as possible lessons from the past, which may help us to deal more effectively with such threats in the future.

Notes

1. Hannah Arendt, *The Origins of Totalitarianism*, 3rd ed. (London: Allen and Unwin, 1967).
2. See, for example, C. J. Friedrich and Z. Brzezinski, *Totalitarian Dictatorship and Autocracy* (New York: Pager, 1967).
3. Most notably the optimism of Francis Fukuyama, "The End of History," *The National Interest* 16 (Summer 1989):3–16; and Francis Fukuyama, *The End of History and the Last Man* (London: Hamish Hamilton, 1992).
4. For a valuable symposium on differing views on the impact of the ending of the Cold War on international relations, see Rich Fawn and Jeremy Larkins, ed., *International Society after the Cold War* (Basingstoke: Macmillan, 1996).
5. This point is emphasized by Timothy Gordon Ash in *We the People: The Revolution of '89* (Cambridge: Granta Books, 1990).

6. See Michael Sheridan, "Dissidents Wilt in 'Beijing Spring'," *Sunday Times* 26 April 1998:21.

7. See U.S. Department of State, *Country Report on Human Rights Practices for 1995* (Washington, D.C.: U.S. Government Printing Office, 1996).

8. See Alex P. Schmid and Albert J. Jongman, "Violent Conflicts and Human Rights Violations in the mid-1990's," *Terrorism and Political Violence* 9 (Autumn 1997):166–92.

9. Ibid.

10. This is a theme in Richard Falk, *The End of World Order* (New York: Holmes and Meier, 1983).

11. For a useful discussion of the problems confronting the ICC project, see "International Criminals Beware," *The Economist* (December 1997):6–12.

12. The two Libyans indicted for the Lockerbie bombing were handed over for trial at the Hague under Scots law but without a jury.

13. See the annual reports of the U.S. State Department, Coordinator for Counter-Terrorism, *Patterns of Global Terrorism*.

14. Ibid.

15. See Schmid and Jongmann, "Violent Conflicts."

16. Barry Posen, "The Security Dilemma and Ethnic Conflict," *Survival* 35 (No. 1, 1993):17–47.

17. For a useful brief survey of zones of conflict, see Richard Clutterbuck, *International Crisis and Conflict* (Basingstoke: Macmillan, 1993).

18. On ETA, see Fernando Reinares, "The Political Conditioning of Collective Violence," in *Research in Democracy and Society* 3 (JM Press, 1996):297–326; on the IRA, see Paul Wilkinson, *Republican Violence Re-appraised* (London: Research Institute for the Study of Conflict and Terrorism, 1991); and on the FLNC, see Peter Savigear, "Corsica 1975; Politics and Violence," *World Today* 31 (1975):462–68; for a perceptive and informed assessment. See also Edward Moxon-Browne, "Terrorism in France," in *The New Terrorism,* ed. William Gutteridge (London: Mansell, 1986):118–26.

19. For graphic reports of these demonstrations, see *The Times* and *Daily Telegraph* (15 July 1997).

20. Charles King, "Ending Civil Wars," IISS (Adelphi Paper 308, 1997) provides an excellent discussion of the problems involved.

21. For a useful comparative analysis of the successes and failures of recent PKOs, see Michael Wesley, *Bandanas and Blue Helmets,* unpublished Ph.D. thesis, University of St. Andrews, 1996; see also William J. Durch, ed., *The Evolution of UN Peacekeeping* (New York: St. Martin's, 1993); Thomas G. Weiss, ed., *The United Nations and Civil Wars* (Boulder, Colo.: Westview, 1993); and Michael Doyle, *UN Peacekeeping in Cambodia* (Boulder, Colo.: Lynne Reinner, 1995).

22. See Tom Walker, "Massacre by the Ethnic Cleansers: Feared Serb Unit Accused by Survivors," *The Times* (4 March 1998).

23. Elez Biberaj, Yugoslavia: a Continuing Crisis? *Conflict Studies* 225 (London: RISCT, 1989).

24. For very different interpretations, see Ed Vulliamy, "Bosnia: The Crime of Appeasement," *International Affairs* 74 (January 1998); and David Owen, *Balkan Odyssey* (London: Victor Gollancz, 1995).

25. One of the most thoughtful and lucid discussions of these conflicts is provided by Michael Ignatieff, *Blood and Belonging* (London: BBC Books, 1993).

26. For statistics on trends in international terrorism, see chronologies on international terrorism published annually in *Terrorism and Political Violence;* or for U.S. government statistics, see the Department of State's annual publication, *Patterns of Global Terrorism.*

27. See Bruce and Donna Hoffman, "Chronology of International Terrorism, 1996," *Terrorism and Political Violence* 10 (No. 3, 1998).

28. Ibid.

29. Ibid.

30. See Rohan Gunaratna, "Tamil Tiger Terror in Sri Lanka," in *Encyclopaedia of World Terrorism,* ed. Martha Crenshaw and John Pimlott (Armonk, N.Y.: Sharpe Reference, 1997):472–77.

31. See Olaf Palme et al., *Common Security: Report of the Palme Commission* (London: Pan Books).

32. Boutros Boutros-Ghali, *Agenda for Peace,* presented by UN Secretary General to the UN Security Council; see also Boutros Boutros-Ghali, "Challenges of Preventive Diplomacy: The Role of the UN and Its Secretary General," in *Preventive Diplomacy,* ed. Kevin Cahill (New York: Basic Books, 1996).

33. For an authoritative and perceptive account, see Jillian Becker, *Hitler's Children: The Story of the Baader-Meinhof Gang* (St. Albins: Granada, 1978).

34. See Donatella della Porta, *Social Movements, Political Violence and the State* (Cambridge: Cambridge University Press, 1995).

35. A valuable survey is provided by Yonah Alexander and Dennis A Pluchinsky, *Europe's Red Terrorists* (London: Frank Cass, 1992).

36. Bruce Hoffman, "Creatures of the Cold War: The JRA," *Jane's Intelligence Review* 9 (February 1992).

37. Ibid.

38. Richard Clutterbuck, *Terrorism in an Unstable World* (London: Routledge, 1994).

39. See Simon Strong, *Shining Path* (London: HarperCollins, 1992).

40. For example, those familiar with the recent history of the in Cambodia would not underestimate the capacity of a movement like the Khmer Rouge to survive; See David P. Chandler, *The Tragedy of Cambodian History, Politics, War and Revolution Since 1945* (New Haven: Yale University Press, 1991).

41. See Tore Bjorgo and Rob White, eds., *Racist Violence in Europe* (Basingstoke: Macmillan, 1993); and Paul Hainsworth, ed, *The Extreme Right in Europe and the USA* (London: Pinter, 1992).

42. See Bundesministerium des Innern, *Verfassungsschutzbericht, 1993* (Bonn:Bundesministerium des Innern, 1993).

43. Useful data on these trends can be found in the Institute for Jewish Policy Research, *Antisemitism: World Report 1996* (London: Institute of Jewish Policy Research, 1996).

44. Ibid.

45. See Jeffrey Kaplan, "Right-Wing Violence in North America," in *Terror from the Extreme Right,* ed. Tore Bjorgo (London: Frank Cass, 1995):44–95; and Michael Barkun, *Religion and the Racist Right* (Chapel Hill: University of North Carolina Press, 1994).

46. Barkun, *Religion and the Racist Right.*

47. See Walter Laqueur, *Terrorism* (London: Weidenfield & Nicolson, 1977).

48. Bernard Lewis, *The Assassins* (London: Al Saqi Books, 1979).

49. Anti-Defamation League of B'nai B'rith, *ADL Special Report: The Militia Movement in America* (New York: ADL 1995).

50. See Patrick Cockburn, "We Have Seen the Enemy and It Is US: The Assassination of Yitzhak Rabin Exposed the Deep Division within Iserali Society," *Independent* (26 December 1995).

51. See Ibrahim A. Karawan, *The Islamic Impasse* (London: IISS, Adelphi Paper 314).

52. See Mangus Ranstorp, "Radical Shi'ism in Lebanon," Ph.D. thesis, St. Andrews University, 1994.

53. See Bruce Hoffman, *Inside Terrorism* (London: Victor Gollancz, 1998).

54. For example, in *Islamist Impasse,* Karawan observes: "Islamists do not represent the force of the future in Arab politics. Their increased social presence has not translated into political power."

55. See Norman Cohn, *The Pursuit of the Millennium* (Oxford: Oxford University Press, 1970), and Yonina Talmon, "Millenarian Movements," *European Journal of Sociology* 7, (No. 2, 1966):159–200.

56. See Roberta Goren, *The Soviet Union and Terrorism,* ed. Jillian Becker (London: Allen & Unwin, 1984).

57. Iran, Iraq, Libya, Syria, and Sudan. Although Cuba and North Korea are still included in the State Department's list of state sponsors, I have not seen any firm evidence that they are still active.

58. For example, the Israeli invasion of Lebanon in 1982 was triggered by Abu Nidal group's assassination attempt against Mr. Shlomo Argov, Israel's ambassador in London.

59. On the key role of Gaddafi in supplying weapons to the Provisional IRA in the mid-1980s, see James Adams and Liam Clarke, "War without End," *Sunday Times,* (17 June 1990); and David McKittrick, "Voyage into the Business of Terror," *Independence* (12 January 1991). The importance of Iran's logistic support for Hezbollah is assessed in Magnus Ranstrop, *Hizb'allah in Lebanon* (Basingstoke: Macmillan, 1997).

60. In February 1997 the Iranian Revolutionary Guards issued a statement insisting that Mr. Rushdie should be murdered; the previous day, an Iranian religious foundation increased the bounty on his head to $2.5 million *The Times* (14 February 1997).

61. A timely report, with practical proposals for tackling proliferation, is Owen Green, *Tackling Light Weapons Proliferation* (London: Saferworld, April 1997).

62. See the report, "Victim of 'Hit' is Real Live Martyr for Bombers," an interview with Khaled Meshaal in *The Scotsman* (1 November 1997).

63. See Kevin Dowling and Christopher Walker, "Object of Bung Led Mission was Murdered, Says Mossad Agent," *The Times* (3 March 1998).

64. Ibid.

65. On terrorist fund raising generally, see James Adams, *The Financing of Terror* (New York: Simon & Schuster, 1986).

66. See Tunku Varadarajan, "ETA Kills Businessman Who Resisted Extortion," *The Times* (27 July 1996).

67. Children have also been targeted. In a paper to the British Psychological Society, 27 March 1998, Andrew Silke stressed that children and adolescents were often targets of Republican and Loyalists "punishment attacks." In a study of 477 punishment attacks that occurred over a 30-month period, Silke found 119 attacks

were directed against children or adolescents, and another 68 attacks involved children or adolescent witnesses. These facts should be more widely known.

68. See comments by the head of the Italian Parliamentary anti-Mafia commission after the Uffizi Gallery bombing, *Daily Telegraph* (29 May 1993); and the report, "Bombers Paid £111.00 for Bomb Attacks," *The Scotsman* (19 May 1993).

69. See *The Guardian,* 25 May 1992, and commentary by Ed Vulliamy, "The Man Who Got Too Close," *The Guardian* (26 May 1992).

70. See report, "Mafia Blows up Judge," *The Guardian* (20 July 1992).

71. See "Mafia Arsenal Sized by Police in Sicily Raid," *The Times* (23 July 1997).

72. This worrying trend is emphasised by Richard Owen, "Fugitive Godfather Leading Mafia Revival," *The Times* (20 October 1997).

73. *The Economist* (16–22 August 1977):13.

74. Bruce Hoffman, "Why Terrorists Don't Claim Credit," *Terrorism and Political Violence* 9 (Spring 1997):2–3.

Chapter 10

THE PSYCHO-POLITICAL SOURCES
OF TERRORISM

RICHARD E. RUBENSTEIN

Explaining Terrorist Motivation

Thankfully, the search for the "terrorist mind" is now all but abandoned. As Walter Laqueur pointed out twenty-five years ago, the task is quixotic, seeing that among those engaging in political violence there exist so many varieties of terrorist organization and behavior, sociocultural and political contexts for conflict, and diverse personality types.[1] In a useful review of attempts to "psychologize" the subject, Walter Reich notes "the habit, unfortunately endemic in so many areas of psychological discourse, of having a single idea and applying it to everything," and remarks, "Even the briefest review of the history of terrorism reveals how varied and complex a phenomenon it is, and therefore how futile it is to attribute simple, global, and general psychological characteristics to all terrorists and all terrorisms."[2] Reich's comment leaves open the question whether some more complex, less-global psychological analysis might not illuminate aspects of terrorist behavior, but the recent research does not seem to have produced significant breakthroughs. Most efforts to explain terrorist thinking and behavior on the basis of psychological theories still seem overly general and of uncertain applicability.

For example, Jerrold M. Post's suggestion, derived from Heinz Kohut's work, that terrorists' alleged tendencies toward psychic "externalization" and "splitting" are a result of "narcissistic wounds"[3] seems plausible in some cases but implausible in others, and gives little indication of the circumstances in which it may be more or less applicable. Jeffrey Ian Ross identifies "five etiological factors of terrorism" that appear in the psychological literature (development of facilitating traits, frustration-aggression or narcissism-aggression, associational drives, learning opportunities, and cost-benefit calculations), and calls for their testing and integration in a single model. But the utility of these theories individually is questionable, it is not clear how they are to be tested, and as Ross himself admits, it is difficult to integrate theories that have "fundamentally different logics."[4] Vamik Volkan's interesting notion of the "chosen trauma" has more point, since it is an adaptation of depth-psychological theory that attempts to explain aspects of ethnic warfare (including ethnic terrorism).[5] The "chosen trauma" helps us understand, for example, why, for many Muslims, Western intervention in the Middle East reopens the wound of the Crusades. But even here, the theory is correlated with a general type of conflict rather than a specific historical dynamic, with the result that the linkage between psychodynamics and sociopolitical change remains undeveloped.

Faced with these difficulties, many scholars attempting to understand the motives of terrorist actors have turned to situational theories that derive behaviors from contextual rather than personality-driven factors.[6] Several studies, including one of my own, suggest that, while there may be no terrorist personality, one can describe certain "terrorist situations," and on that basis discover strategic motives that seem to animate many terrorist fighters of different types.[7] We know, for example, that much modern terrorism involves attempts by relatively small groups with arguable claims of mass representation to vindicate those claims by resorting to exemplary violent action. One common situation involves the political isolation of morally ambitious young adults, who, while seriously alienated from the state or its ruling class, find themselves unable to mobilize mass support of the sort necessary to foment a popular revolt or wage a large-scale war. Under these circumstances, various "triggers" may impel relatively small numbers of activists to take the burden of struggle on their own shoulders, and to attempt through terrorist action to generate the conditions necessary for mass struggle. In this situation, the motives that frequently generate terrorist violence include the following:

- To publicize the activists' cause, provide evidence of its supporters' intensity, and force both enemies and potential allies to take it seriously;
- To awaken the masses, who have been bribed or coerced into silence, by performing acts of "heroic," sacrificial violence that will inspire imitation;
- To expose the state, which hides behind norms of legality and democracy, as a brutal and oppressive force requiring violent opposition or overthrow;
- To mobilize and activate neutrals or passive sympathizers by catching them in the "crossfire" between the state and the terrorist fighters;
- To eliminate or incapacitate leaders or organizations that might otherwise be effective opponents of the terrorists' cause, and
- To make territory ungovernable, or governable only at an unacceptable cost, thereby forcing the withdrawal of foreign occupiers or a change of regime.

These goals may be more or less realistically attainable, but unless they are utterly divorced from reality, terrorist actions in their pursuit can be thought of as strategically rational or instrumental. Of course, one may consider terrorist thinking morally obtuse or deformed by bad ideas, but it makes little sense to attribute most terrorist acts to some sort of psychopathology or expressive "acting out." Terrorism's strategic rationality is most evident where the activists' motives are most modest and least speculative; for example, in cases in which conservative nationalists seek to foment disorder for the sake of expelling a foreign occupier or convincing a population exhausted by inconclusive civil struggles that order must be restored at any cost.[8] But even where the terrorists are social revolutionaries (those whom Marx scornfully labeled "alchemists of revolution"),[9] their activities are ordinarily conducted with the same mixture of zeal, anger, vengefulness, and strategic calculation that one may observe among the volunteer soldiers of a regular army. Clearly, the expressive features of terrorist violence cannot be ignored any more than can the expressive features of "conventional" warfare, but there is little reason to consider terrorist violence exceptionally or uniquely expressive, except, perhaps, in cases of "lost cause" terrorism, where individuals or small groups whose forces have clearly been defeated commit acts of violence in a spirit of pure defiance or revenge, in order to salvage their honor.[10]

After September 11: The Expressivist Comeback

Since the mid-1980s, scholars have identified additional instrumental motives for terrorism, or have analyzed terrorist praxis creatively from the standpoint of other perspectives: for example, organizational behavior,[11] religious ideology,[12] and cultural narrative.[13] But the scholarly atmosphere, reflective of the general atmosphere in the United States, was inevitably affected by the terrorist attacks of September 11, 2001, on the World Trade Center in New York City and the Pentagon in Arlington, Virginia. Almost immediately, one began to hear explanations of the terrorists' motives emphasizing their expressive (if not entirely pathological) nature. The popular form of this sentiment produced statements like, "These terrorist fanatics have no motives except to kill Americans," but the expressivist revival was not limited to television talk shows. On November 5, 2001, several participants in a professorial symposium held at the Harvard Law School adopted a slightly more sophisticated version of the same approach.

A key to this discussion was the attempt to distinguish "mass or catastrophic terrorism" from "ordinary or traditional terrorism." Assuming the existence of this distinction, Ashton Carter of the Kennedy School of Government at Harvard University argued that "the motivation for mass terror is a vengeful or messianic one, rather than a politically purposeful one." "When we talk about mass terrorism," he asserted, "we may be dealing with truly fringe motivations that it's very difficult even to understand, let alone to deter, or to bargain with."[14] Eva Bellin, a Middle East specialist, agreed that "the aims of these terrorist networks are much more expressive than programmatic."[15] And Jessica Stern, resident terrorism expert at Harvard's Kennedy School, asserted that "Osama bin Laden's objectives are really expressive, not instrumental" for the following reasons: (1) catastrophic attacks will not achieve the attackers' objectives; (2) "groups that are expressing anger can continuously change their mission statement;" and (3) expressive terrorism "enables cynical leaders to attract youth who feel humiliated, culturally or personally."[16]

This attempt to distinguish catastrophic from traditional terrorism was very odd. No doubt, the attacks of September 11 were unusually destructive, but that destruction was made possible by the same technology that has made warfare in general more destructive since the advent of highly explosive substances, jet aircraft, and other technological advances. (In fact, the September attacks have been described as a form of technological jujitsu in which civilian airliners were transformed by hijackers into cruise missiles.) The question begged by the Harvard discussants is what technique has to do with motivation. Does terrorism become more expressive as the destructiveness of its weaponry and the number of its victims increase? This makes little sense. Although "catastrophic" violence by terrorists or the state may be related to ideology—racist or nationalist ideology, for example, may designate all the members of another race or nation an "enemy"—the lone assassin's motives are surely no more instrumental than the truck bomber's. Moreover, the distinction between these alleged types of terrorism becomes faint, indeed, when one considers that nineteenth-century anarchists threw bombs into crowded European cafes, that Italian neofascists of the 1980s attempted to kill as many people as possible in bombings like that of the Bologna railway station, and that U.S. "militiaman" Timothy McVeigh obliterated the Murrah Federal Center in Oklahoma City in 1995 using trucks packed with explosives similar to those employed a decade earlier in the bombing of the American army headquarters in Beirut by Shi'ite fighters.

Each of these instances of destructive terrorism involved a mix of instrumental and expressive motives. According to Mark Juergensmeyer, even the 1995 sarin gas attack mounted by the Aum Shinryko sect in the Tokyo subway system was "the product of rational thought."[17] Juergensmeyer suggests that actions of this sort may be "more symbolic than strategic"—a point that will concern us in a moment—but they clearly escape the Kennedy School professors' definition of catastrophic terrorist acts as objectiveless expressions of anger. Acts of war generally, whether committed as part of terrorist campaigns or organized interstate wars, tend to combine instrumental goals with expressive motives like anger, fear, and the desire for revenge. That the destructiveness of an act tells us nothing about its "ratio" of instrumentality to expressiveness becomes clear the moment one imagines the crew of a B-52 bomber dropping "daisy cutter" bombs—the most destructive ordnance short of nuclear weapons—on targets selected by satellites from 30,000 feet at the command of an electronic voice. Nor, despite the pervasive stereotype of the religious "fanatic," is there any demonstrable relationship between the I/E ratio and a violent act's religious motivation. Religious action may be carefully calculated to achieve some instrumental goal, while secular fighters who give their lives for a popular cause are called, not martyrs, but heroes.

It seems, in fact, that the tendency to explain a terrorist's motivation by recourse to expressivist concepts is directly proportional to the degree to which the analyst herself is reacting expressively to the terrorist's act. Or, to put it more simply, "Anger in, anger out." Throughout the history of political violence, one observes a tendency on the part of those under attack to characterize their attackers in terms that deprive the latter's actions of rationality, comprehensibility, and political significance, and that therefore justify a wholly punitive response.[18]

The reactions of American analysts to the first major terrorist attack on their homeland are clearly no exception. Assertions that the targets selected by the September 11 attackers are randomly selected or strategically insignificant will not bear scrutiny. Like Al Qaeda's previous targets (the Khobar Towers apartment in Daharan, Saudi Arabia; the U.S.S. *Cole* in Yemen; and, very likely, the U.S. forces intervening in Djibouti), the Pentagon and the World Trade Center were, respectively, key military and infrastructural facilities of the type customarily targeted by forces engaged in war. Similarly, it makes little sense to say that these attacks must be considered strategically irrational because they will not achieve the terrorists' objectives. On the contrary, they delivered a very costly blow to the U.S. economy, publicized the extreme Islamists' cause, polarized public opinion in the Islamic world, and provoked an intensely violent reaction by the United States—all instrumental goals of the terrorists, whether or not their achievement ultimately proves beneficial to or destructive of their cause. Finally, the idea that Osama bin Laden's political demands are a mere "cover" for psychopathological hatred may well be attributable to the analyst's own fear and hatred. Osama bin Laden's demands for the removal of U.S. troops from Saudi Arabia, termination of hostilities against Iraq, and an end to American support for the Israeli occupation of Palestine represent a coherent political position that is shared by many Muslims and non-Muslims who do not approve of his neo-Wahabist theology or his terrorist tactics.

There may be a general rule of conflict psychology to the effect that parties to conflict, especially when under direct attack, tend to consider their adversary's behavior purely expressive, while those less embroiled in the conflict perceive the parties' behavior on both sides as primarily instrumental, with an admixture of expressive motivation. Following the Japanese Empire's air attack on Pearl Harbor in 1941, and for a long time thereafter, Americans characterized this action as an eruption of pure evil motivated by cruelty, hatred, vengefulness, deviousness, and power-lust. Like the attacks of September 11, 2001, the surprise and sheer destructiveness of that assault in a nation that had not experienced a direct attack since the War of 1812 made it virtually impossible to think of their assailants as rational human beings. There was little inclination to consider the 1941 attack as strategically rational, although disabling the American Pacific Fleet was a step clearly mandated by military necessity once the decision to go to war had been reached by the Japanese General Staff. And there was even less inclination to consider it a response to an escalating series of hostile political, economic, and military moves made by each side over a period of years, much less to inquire into the underlying conditions that had generated the conflict in the first place. In fact, those who dared raise such issues, even if strongly opposed to Japanese imperialism and militarism, were immediately branded disloyal "apologists" for Japan.[19]

This may be one of the most pernicious effects of treating an adversary's behavior as purely expressive. One cannot talk rationally with people motivated solely by uncontrollable rage, a craving for revenge, or the dictates of a lunatic ideology. Therefore, as Harvard's Ashton Carter glibly asserts of the September 11 attackers, their demands (conceived of nominalistically as mere words) must be seen as nonbargainable. But if the adversary's words and actions have no political meaning, the conflict itself is rendered meaningless. It appears to be *uncaused* in any historical sense. In this perception of uncaused conflict lies the real significance of U.S. President George W. Bush's reiteration of the adjective *evil* to describe the Al Qaeda fighters and a growing list of movements and governments hostile to the United States. Evil, in the Augustinian sense in which Bush uses the word, is uncaused, except to the extent that we are Adam's heirs. It is the result of a misuse of human beings' free will that persists existentially (like Satan himself) regardless of particular historical circumstances. Adopting this perspective makes it useless to inquire into the socioeconomic or geopolitical factors that make terrorism seem an attractive or even a necessary activity to hundreds of thousands of young militants around the world. This is why Ashton Carter's reference to "truly fringe motives that it's very difficult even to understand" seems to me both ill considered and dangerous—for without identifying the underlying causes of a conflict, one cannot begin to resolve it.

Terrorism and the Psychology of Anti-Imperialism

Ultimately, neither the instrumentalist nor expressivist approaches succeed in capturing the complexity and particularity of terrorist thinking and behavior. If expressivism deprives terrorist activity of political meaning, instrumentalism deprives it of "soul" by ignoring its emotional basis and picturing it as a matter of purely rational choice. As a result, certain important aspects of terrorism—for example, the passion with which relatively privileged young people may identify with oppressed groups, or the willingness of some fighters to commit suicidal acts in pursuit of a distant goal—remain mysterious. Indeed, while instrumentalism credits the subject of analysis with strategic rationality, its overall tendency (as in the case of other theories reflecting a "mind-body split") is to *objectify* the subject, and thus to dehumanize her or him. The instrumentalist and expressivist approaches are so much opposites, in any case, as correlatives, and there is a point at which they both render the subject of analysis an utterly incomprehensible Other. From the instrumentalist perspective, this happens when one assumes that the terrorists are acting rationally, but within the parameters of a worldview that is entirely separate from and alien to that of the analyst. If the rational actor is entirely Other in his or her worldview, the effect, in terms of communicating with that person and understanding the conflict that embroils him, is exactly the same as if he or she were acting purely irrationally.

    In one effort to bridge the gap between these deficient approaches, Mark Juergensmeyer argues persuasively that some acts of terrorism are "performative acts" with high symbolic content that aim through their dramatic impact to change people's perceptions of the world.[20] In his view, religious terrorism, in particular, adheres to the symbolic "script" of cosmic warfare—a struggle that links current political issues with a timeless battle between the forces of Good and Evil. "What makes religious violence particularly savage and relentless," he maintains, "is that its perpetrators have placed such religious images of divine struggle—cosmic war—in the service of worldly political battles."[21] This provides a useful jumping-off point for further exploration of the subject, although one must begin with a few qualifications and caveats.

First, it is not clear that religious violence is "particularly" savage and relentless. The most violent struggles in history have been those fought under the aegis of secular ideology by modern nation-states. Second, many of the features often considered peculiar to religious terrorism also characterize certain forms of secular struggle. Suicidal acts of violence, for example, were performed by Russian Social-Revolutionary fighters like Kaliayev and by communist terrorists during the Chinese Revolution, and have become something of a specialty among Tamil independence fighters in contemporary Sri Lanka.[22] One might argue, of course, that self-martyrdom in the faith that one's cause will ultimately triumph is a "religious" act whether or not done in the name of an organized religion, but this rather begs the question of the relationship of terrorist violence to preexisting religious scripts. Similarly, while there may well be some connection between the terrorist's willingness to take many lives and the idea that highly destructive acts are necessary in cosmic warfare, one can observe the same link operating secularly in the case of "conventional" interstate war. The belief of the Allies in World War II that they were fighting for the soul of humanity as well as for global hegemony clearly had something to do with their unconditional surrender demands and their willingness to annihilate undefended Axis cities like Dresden, Hiroshima, and Nagasaki in support of this "cosmic" goal.

Third, there is the danger mentioned earlier (which Juergensmeyer, to his credit, largely avoids) that picturing the terrorists as rational actors wholly in the grip of an alien worldview will make it impossible to communicate with them and to understand the roots of their struggle. How can one talk to cosmic warriors, much less frame a method of resolving conflicts with them? One way to escape this dehumanizing trap is to bring into clearer focus the socioeconomic and geopolitical factors that incline people to accept a violence-justifying interpretation of some broader, more flexible and complex religious tradition. These worldly factors not only generate the kind of anger and desperation that may lead people in the direction of violent action, they also constitute the data that ideologies seek to explain and transform. A second way forward is to identify some of the key psychological states or syndromes that correlate with both the sociopolitical context of the conflict and with its religious dimension. This sort of situation-specific theorizing may help researchers avoid the over-general psychologizing that I criticized in the first part of this chapter.

Consider the current conflict between extreme Islamist groups like Al Qaeda and the American government. The sociopolitical context of this conflict involves factors both internal and external to the Islamic world, but one set of causes and conditions, at least, clearly derives from what has variously been termed imperialism, neocolonialism, modernization, or, in Benjamin Barber's phrase, "McWorld":[23] the rapid and pervasive spread of Western (especially American) political, economic, military, and cultural influence around the globe since the end of World War II, culminating at the end of the Cold War in America's emergence as the world's sole superpower. This vast expansion of American power has been perceived by many groups abroad, particularly in volatile, resource-rich regions subject to U.S. economic and military intervention, as an "invasion" that undermines local and regional autonomy, divides and conquers peoples, generates massive political corruption, disrupts long-established patterns of social interaction, and exposes local communities to a barrage of physical and cultural imports that challenge traditional religious values and threaten people's core identities.

It is important to understand that this invasion is not merely cultural or symbolic. As the history of terrorism demonstrates, small group violence is most often a physically violent response to physical violence.[24] The event that, above all others, generated Osama bin Laden's turn toward anti-American terrorism was the U.S. war against Iraq in 1990–1991 and subsequent punitive sanctions against that country, which not only devastated the Iraqi nation but also established a massive U.S. military presence in Saudi Arabia and the Gulf states. At the same time, as Barber and others have pointed out, the spread of Western cultural influence in non-Western lands has also been welcomed, in some respects, by certain groups in the receiving nations.[25] Particularly among younger, more urbanized people there may be intense interest in Coca-Cola®, freedom of expression, Beverly Hills fashions, gender equality, Internet pornography, parliamentary democracy, gangsta rap, religious pluralism, TV satellite dishes, and the whole panoply of American and European lifestyles and politico-cultural values. Yet the desire for these goods can be intensely ambivalent and guilt-producing, since they threaten traditional identities, patterns of social order, and belief systems. This may have been the case even among the Al Qaeda operatives living in Florida, who reportedly imbibed alcohol and visited strip bars in what may have been a wholly or partly conscious attempt to heighten their ambivalence toward America prior to going into battle.

The two faces of imperialism are therefore intimidation and temptation—a combination that, I would contend, has been a potent source of religious terrorism throughout history. One example that seems particularly apposite is the Jewish revolt against the Seleucid Greeks in the second century, B.C.E.—the Maccabean revolt that eventually expelled the forces of Antiochus II from Judea and created the Hasmonean kingdom. The context for this rebellion was the military and political domination of the Jewish state by the Seleucid Greeks, a domination that carried in its wake increasing cultural penetration of the Jewish community by the culturally sophisticated, politically advanced, and economically expansive Greek Empire. Alexander the Great's heirs controlled an invincible military machine. At the same time, their worldly, tolerant, permissive culture was admired and welcomed by key elements of the Jewish ruling class, who went so far as to educate their children in the Greek style and to adopt themselves to Greek customs and lifestyles.[26] Their behavior was seen as a political and a cultural betrayal by more "fundamentalist" elements of the community interested, simultaneously, in communal political autonomy and religious purity.

The result was one of history's first recorded acts of religious terrorism. When a Greek official and his Jewish collaborator visited the hill town of Modin near Jerusalem for the purpose of conducting a civic ceremony, they were stabbed to death by Mattathias, father of Judah the Maccabee, who called upon faithful Jews to rebel and to follow him into the hills. Antiochus made the mistake of trying to smash this uprising with conventional forces, and after six years of grueling guerrilla warfare the Greeks withdrew, permitting the Jews to establish the Hasmonean kingdom. This dynasty was still nominally in power two centuries later, when an even more violent rebellion began against Judea's Roman overlords. In the first and second centuries C.E., groups of Jewish militants known as the Sicarii (dagger-wielders) and Zealots participated in intense, organized terrorist activity, in each case followed by a popular rebellion against the immensely superior military power of the Romans. These anti-Greek and anti-Roman revolts provide us with the first clear examples of politico-religious martyrdom and suicidal resistance to imperialist power. They ought to be studied with special care today.

From the viewpoint of understanding recent episodes of religious terrorism, one important feature of these rebellions is that the rebels perceived imperialist domination not just as oppression, but also as *desecration;* and they responded violently not only for the sake of national liberation but for the sake of collective and self-*purification*. Similarly, Osama bin Laden and his followers, very likely supported passively by many other Muslims in the Persian Gulf region, saw the positioning of U.S. military forces on Saudi Arabia's "sacred soil" as a desecration. This was partly a matter of religious belief or ideology, given Arabia's special status in Islamic history as the birthplace of the faith and in current Islamic observance as the holy place to which one returns on pilgrimage. But it also involves a more modern ideological and emotional inclination to view the soil of one's nation as sacred, and unwanted touchings of it as taboo. The French Revolutionaries assaulted by foreign intervenors gave us the notion of "la Patrie," the Fatherland; the Russians worshipped their Motherland, picturing the Napoleonic invasion of 1812 as a rape; and the Americans are now displaying similar convictions in terming their nation under attack a Homeland. In the waking dream that we call ideology, the soil of the nation is its body, and it is a forbidden body, like the bodies of one's parents or one's siblings, whose violation is considered taboo whether one is a conservative Muslim or a liberal secularist.

What is crucial here, in my view, is the convergence of political interests, religious values, and emotional states in response to the new drive for influence in the Persian Gulf and Central Asia by the American superpower. This convergence may also be observed on the individual level, where desecration takes the internalized form of yielding to temptation, and where harboring forbidden desires can produce a desperate longing for self-purification. Modern capitalist hegemony, which is far more transformative in its socioeconomic and cultural impact than classical imperialism, sustains itself by involving subject populations in a variety of complicities.[27] For example, those in nations subject to imperialist hegemony may participate actively in the armed forces, the government, the business community, or other sectors of society effectively dominated by outsiders, effectively "Westernizing" themselves for the sake of power, income, social status, or enjoyment. Or, they may become socially inactive, unable or unwilling to participate in the imperialist project, but deterred from organizing oppositional movements by intimidation, disorientation, and self-doubt. Finally, they may participate marginally but significantly in the foreign-dominated economy and culture, for example, by consuming cultural imports, providing low-wage labor, "hustling" on the margins of the economy, or (more and more frequently), relying on foreign or government assistance in the absence of remunerative and dignified jobs.

In all of these cases, complicity in a system dominated by outsiders which oppresses one's own people and alters one's own culture can produce intense feelings of shame and guilt, demanding expiation. This seems to be the case especially where it is not simply a matter of being imposed upon, but, at least in part, of welcoming the imposition. Religious systems are particularly well positioned to recognize and express these feelings, since they emphasize the element of free choice in decision making and offer believers ritualized and nonritualized methods of self-purification. In the case of Islamist groups like Al Qaeda, the number of well-educated, reasonably prosperous, technically proficient fighters with some experience of the world is notable. One can hypothesize (subject to confirmation by other data) that some of them, at least, felt besmirched by willing complicity in the alien system and viewed martyrdom as the ultimate act of self-purification. It is important to note, however, that the geopolitical situation, not religious beliefs per se, generates such feelings and needs. Irreligious rebels like the Cuban Fidelistas have demonstrated a similar passion for self-purification. One recalls that Fidel Castro's first act on assuming power was to close the country's mafia-operated casinos and whorehouses, and to promise Cubans that they would no longer be tempted to engage in such degrading occupations.

Mark Gopin has argued that the traditions of the world religions provide believers with a wide array of peacemaking and warmaking alternatives.[28] One cannot understand religious terrorism simply by analyzing the sources and structures of belief, since the factors that influence believers to adopt this or that interpretation of sacred texts and traditions lie outside as well as inside these religious worldviews. The analysis most urgently needed, in my view, is one that explores the effects of capitalism's global expansion on the mental and emotional lives of peoples "targeted" for hegemonic control either as collaborators or consumers. This may help us to understand how such targets make use of whatever political and cultural materials they can mobilize to resist intolerable impositions and to restore their self-respect.

Notes

1. Walter Laqueur, *Terrorism* (Boston: Little Brown, 1977):120.
2. Walter Reich, "Understanding Terrorist Behavior: The Limits and Opportunities of Psychological Inquiry," in Reich, ed., *Origins of Terrorism: Psychologies, Ideologies, Theologies, States of Mind* (Cambridge: Cambridge University Press, 1990):262–63.
3. "Terrorist Psycho-Logic: Terrorist Behavior as a Product of Psychological Forces," in Reich, ed., 1990, 27. See also John W. Cayton, "Terrorism and the Psychology of the Self," in *Perspectives on Terrorism*, ed. Freeman and Alexander (Wilmington: Delaware Scholarly Resources, 1983); Richard M. Pearlstein, *The Mind of the Political Terrorist* (Wilmington: Delaware Scholarly Resources, 1991); Jerrold Post, "Current Understanding of Terrorist Motivation and Psychology: Implications for a Differentiated Antiterrorist Policy," *Terrorism* 13 (No. 1, 1990):65–71.
4. Jeffrey Ian Ross, "Beyond the Conceptualization of Terrorism: A Psychological-Structural Model of the Causes of This Activity," in *Collective Violence: Harmful Behavior in Groups and Government*, ed. Summers and Markusen (New York: Rowman and Littlefield, 1999):182, 189 n. 13. Essentially the same conclusion is reached by the authors of the recent report of the Federal Research Division of the Library of Congress, "The Sociology and Psychology of Terrorism: Who Becomes a Terrorist and Why?" (September 1999):16–19.
5. Vamik Volkan, *Bloodlines: From Ethnic Pride to Ethnic Terrorism* (Boulder, Colo.: Westview Press, 1999).
6. See the general discussion by Daniel Druckman, "Situations," in *Conflict: From Analysis to Intervention*, ed. Druckman, Cheldelin, and Fast (London: Continuum, 2002).
7. Richard E. Rubenstein, *Alchemists of Revolution: Terrorism in the Modern World* (New York: Basic Books, 1987). See also Bruce Hoffman, *Inside Terrorism* (New York; Columbia University Press, 1999).
8. See the discussion of Ku Klux Klan terrorism in the post–Civil War South in Rubenstein, *Alchemists of Revolution*.
9. Karl Marx and Friedrich Engels, *Collected Works*, Vol. 10 (New York: International Publishers, 1975):318.
10. The classic example of "lost cause" terrorism is John Wilkes Booth's assassination of Abraham Lincoln.
11. Martha Crenshaw, "Theories of Terrorism: Instrumental and Organizational Approaches," in *Inside Terrorist Organizations*, ed. David C. Rapoport (London: Frank Cass, 2001):13–31.
12. Mark Juergensmeyer, *Terror in the Mind of God* (Berkeley: University of California Press, 2000).
13. Khachig Tololyan, "Cultural Narrative and the Motivation of the Terrorist," in Rapoport, *Inside Terrorist Organizations* 217–33.
14. "Understanding Terrorism," in *Harvard Magazine* (January–February 2002):38.
15. Ibid., 46.
16. Ibid., 48–49.
17. Juergensmeyer, *Terror in the Mind of God*, 124.
18. See Richard E. Rubenstein, *Rebels in Eden* (Boston: Little Brown, 1970):8–13.

19. John W. Burton, former head of the Australian Foreign Office and a founder of the field of conflict analysis and resolution, has frequently made this point in conversations and lectures.

20. Juergensmeyer, *Terror in the Mind of God,* 124.

21. Ibid., 146.

22. On Kaliayev, see the description of Russian S-R terrorism in Richard E. Rubenstein, *Comrade Valentine: The Story of Azef the Spy* (New York: Harcourt, Brace, 1994), esp. 128–31. On China, see the descriptions of the terrorist Ch'en in Andre Malraux' novel, *Man's Fate* (New York: Vintage, 1990), esp. 188–95.

23. Benjamin R. Barber, *Jihad vs. McWorld* (New York: Ballantine Books, 1995).

24. See Walter Laqueur, *A History of Terrorism* (New Brunswick: Transaction Books, 2001).

25. Barber, *Jihad vs. McWorld* 17–20, *passim.*

26. See Paul Johnson, *History of the Jews,* 97–108.

27. These issues are thoughtfully discussed in Albert Memmi, *The Colonizer and the Colonized* (Boston: Beacon, 1991) and Franz Fanon and Jean-Paul Sartre, *Black Skin, White Masks* (New York: Grove, 1991).

28. Marc Gopin, *From Eden to Armaggedon: The Future of World Religions, Violence, and Peacemaking* (Oxford: Oxford University Press, 2000).

Chapter 11

POSTMODERN TERRORISM

WALTER LAQUEUR

New Rules for an Old Game

As the nineteenth century ended, it seemed no one was safe from terrorist attack. In 1894 an Italian anarchist assassinated French President Sadi Carnot. In 1897 anarchists fatally stabbed Empress Elizabeth of Austria and killed Antonio Cánovas, the Spanish prime minister. In 1900 Umberto I, the Italian king, fell in yet another anarchist attack; in 1901 an American anarchist killed William McKinley, president of the United States. Terrorism became the leading preoccupation of politicians, police chiefs, journalists, and writers from Dostoevsky to Henry James. If in the year 1900 the leaders of the main industrial powers had assembled, most of them would have insisted on giving terrorism top priority on their agenda, as President Clinton did at the Group of Seven meeting after the June bombing of the U.S. military compound in Dhahran, Saudi Arabia.

From this perspective the recent upsurge of terrorist activity is not particularly threatening. According to the State Department's annual report on the subject, more people died [in 2001] in incidents of international terrorism (3,547) than the year before (409). Such figures, however, are almost meaningless, because of both the incidents they disregard and those they count. Current definitions of terrorism fail to capture the magnitude of the problem worldwide.

Terrorism has been defined as the substate application of violence or threatened violence intended to sow panic in a society, to weaken or even overthrow the incumbents, and to bring about political change. It shades on occasion into guerrilla warfare (although unlike guerrillas, terrorists are unable or unwilling to take or hold territory) and even a substitute for war between states. In its long history terrorism has appeared in many guises; today society faces not one terrorism but many terrorisms.

Since 1900, terrorists' motivation, strategy, and weapons have changed to some extent. The anarchists and the left-wing terrorist groups that succeeded them, down through the Red Armies that operated in Germany, Italy, and Japan in the 1970s, have vanished; if anything, the initiative has passed to the extreme right. Most international and domestic terrorism these days, however, is neither left nor right, but ethnic-separatist in inspiration. Ethnic terrorists have more staying power than ideologically motivated ones, since they draw on a large reservoir of public support.

The greatest change in recent decades is that terrorism is by no means militants' only strategy. The many-branched Muslim Brotherhood, the Palestinian Hamas, the Irish Republican Army (IRA), the Kurdish extremists in Turkey and

Iraq, the Tamil Tigers of Sri Lanka, the Basque Homeland and Liberty (ETA) movement in Spain, and many other groups that have sprung up in this century have had political as well as terrorist wings from the beginning. The political arm provides social services and education, runs businesses, and contests elections while the "military wing" engages in ambushes and assassinations. Such division of labor has advantages: the political leadership can publicly disassociate itself when the terrorists commit a particularly outrageous act or something goes wrong. The claimed lack of control can be quite real because the armed wing tends to become independent; the men and women with the guns and bombs often lose sight of the movement's wider aims and may end up doing more harm than good.

Terrorist operations have also changed somewhat. Airline hijackings have become rare, since hijacked planes cannot stay in the air forever and few countries today are willing to let them land, thereby incurring the stigma of openly supporting terrorism. Terrorists, too, saw diminishing returns on hijackings. The trend now seems to be away from attacking specific targets like the other side's officials and toward more indiscriminate killing. Furthermore, the dividing line between urban terrorism and other tactics has become less distinct, while the line between politically motivated terrorism and the operation of national and international crime syndicates is often impossible for outsiders to discern in the former Soviet Union, Latin America, and other parts of the world. But there is one fundamental difference between international crime and terrorism: mafias have no interest in overthrowing the government and decisively weakening society; in fact, they have a vested interest in a prosperous economy.

Misapprehensions, not only semantic, surround the various forms of political violence. A terrorist is not a guerrilla, strictly speaking. There are no longer any guerrillas engaging in Maoist-style liberation of territories that become the base of a counter-society and a regular army fighting the central government—except perhaps in remote places like Afghanistan, the Philippines, and Sri Lanka. The term "guerrilla" has had a long life partly because terrorists prefer the label, for its more positive connotations. It also persists because governments and media in other countries do not wish to offend terrorists by calling them terrorists. The French and British press would not dream of referring to their countries' native terrorists by any other name but call terrorists in other nations militants, activists, national liberation fighters, or even "gun persons."

The belief has gained ground that terrorist missions by volunteers bent on committing suicide constitute a radical new departure, dangerous because they are impossible to prevent. But that is a myth, like the many others in which terrorism has always been shrouded. The bomber willing and indeed eager to blow himself up has appeared in all eras and cultural traditions, espousing politics ranging from the leftism of the Baader-Meinhof Gang in 1970s Germany to rightist extremism. When the Japanese military wanted kamikaze pilots at the end of World War II, thousands of volunteers rushed to offer themselves. The young Arab bombers on Jerusalem buses looking to be rewarded by the virgins in Paradise are a link in an old chain.

State-sponsored terrorism has not disappeared. Terrorists can no longer count on the Soviet Union and its Eastern European allies, but some Middle Eastern and North African countries still provide support. Tehran and Tripoli, however, are less eager to argue that they have a divine right to engage in terrorist operations outside their borders; the 1986 U.S. air strike against Libya and the various boycotts against Libya and Iran had an effect. No government today boasts about surrogate warfare it instigates and backs.

On the other hand, Sudan, without fanfare, has become for terrorists what the Barbary Coast was for pirates of another age: a safe haven. Politically isolated and presiding over a disastrous economy, the military government in Khartoum, backed by Muslim leaders, believes that no one wants to become involved in Sudan and thus it can get away with lending support to terrorists from many nations. Such confidence is justified so long as terrorism is only a nuisance. But if it becomes more than that, the rules of the game change, and both terrorists and their protectors come under great pressure.

Opportunities in Terrorism

History shows that terrorism more often than not has little political impact, and that when it has an effect it is often the opposite of the one desired. Terrorism in the 1980s and 1990s was no exception. The 1991 assassination of Rajaiv Gandhi as he campaigned to retake the prime ministership neither hastened nor inhibited the decline of India's Congress Party. Hamas' and Hezbollah's stepped-up terrorism in Israel undoubtedly influenced the outcome of Israeli elections in 1996, but while it achieved its immediate objective of setting back the peace process on which Palestine Authority President Yasir Arafat has gambled his future, was a hard-line Likud government really in these groups' interests? On the other side, Yagal Amir, the right-wing orthodox Jewish student who assassinated Prime Minister Yitzhak Rabin [in 1995] because he disapproved of the peace agreement with the Palestinians, might well have helped elect Rabin's dovish second-in-command, Shimon Peres, to a full term had the Muslim terrorists not made Israeli security an issue again.

Terrorists caused disruption and destabilization in other parts of the world, such as Sri Lanka, where economic decline has accompanied the war between the government and the Tamil Tigers. But in Israel and in Spain, where Basque extremists have been staging attacks for decades, terrorism has had no effect on the economy. Even in Algeria, where terrorism has exacted the highest toll in human lives, Muslim extremists have made little headway since 1992–1993, when many predicted the demise of the unpopular military regime.

Some argue that terrorism must be effective because certain terrorist leaders have become president or prime minister of their country. In those cases, however, the terrorists had first forsworn violence and adjusted to the political process. Finally, the common wisdom holds that terrorism can spark a war or, at least, prevent peace. That is true, but only where there is much inflammable material: as in Sarajevo in 1914, [or] in the Middle East and elsewhere today. Nor can one ever say with certainty that the conflagration would not have occurred sooner or later in any case.

Nevertheless, terrorism's prospects, often overrated by the media, the public, and some politicians, are improving as its destructive potential increases. This has to do both with the rise of groups and individuals that practice or might take up terrorism and with the weapons available to them. The past few decades have witnessed the birth of dozens of aggressive movements espousing varieties of nationalism, religious fundamentalism, fascism, and apocalyptic millenarianism, from Hindu nationalists in India to neofascists in Europe and the developing world to the Branch Davidian cult of Waco, Texas. The earlier fascists believed in military aggression and engaged in a huge military buildup, but such a strategy has become too expensive even for superpowers. Now, mail-order catalogs tempt militants with readily available, far cheaper, unconventional as well as conventional weapons—the poor man's nuclear bomb, Iranian President Ali Akbar Hashemi Rafsanjani called them.

In addition to nuclear arms, the weapons of mass destruction include biological agents and man-made chemical compounds that attack the nervous system, skin, or blood. Governments have engaged in the production of chemical weapons for almost a century and in the production of nuclear and biological weapons for many decades, during which time proliferation has been continuous and access ever easier. The means of delivery—ballistic missiles, cruise missiles, and aerosols—have also become far more effective. While in the past missiles were deployed only in wars between states, recently they have played a role in civil wars in Afghanistan and Yemen. Use by terrorist groups would be but one step further.

Until the 1970s most observers believed that stolen nuclear material constituted the greatest threat in the escalation of terrorist weapons, but many now think the danger could lie elsewhere. An April 1996 U.S. Defense Department report says that "most terrorist groups do not have the financial and technical resources to acquire nuclear weapons but could gather materials to make radiological dispersion devices and some biological and chemical agents." Some groups have state sponsors that possess or can obtain weapons of the latter three types. Terrorist groups themselves have investigated the use of poisons since the nineteenth century. The Aum Shinrikyo cult staged a poison gas attack in March 1995 in the Tokyo subway; exposure to the nerve gas sarin killed 10 people and injured 5,000. Other more amateurish attempts in the United States and abroad to experiment with chemical substance and biological agents for use in terrorism have involved the toxin that cause botulism, the poisonous protein rycin (twice), sarin (twice), bubonic plague bacteria, typhoid bacteria, hydrogen cyanide, vx (another nerve gas), and possibly the Ebola virus.

To Use or Not to Use?

If terrorists have used chemical weapons only once and nuclear material never, to some extent the reasons are technical. The scientific literature is replete with the technical problems inherent in the production, manufacture, storage, and delivery of each of the three classes of unconventional weapons.

The manufacture of nuclear weapons is not that simple, nor is delivery to their target. Nuclear material, of which a limited supply exists, is monitored by the U.N.-affiliated International Atomic Energy Agency. Only governments can legally procure it, so that even in this age of proliferation investigators could trace those abetting nuclear terrorists without great difficulty. Monitoring can overlook a more primitive nuclear weapon: nonfissile but radioactive nuclear material. Iranian agents in Turkey, Kazakhstan, and elsewhere are known to have tried to buy such material originating in the former Soviet Union.

Chemical agents are much easier to produce or obtain but not so easy to keep safely in stable condition, and their dispersal depends largely on climatic factors. The terrorists behind [the 1995] attack in Tokyo chose a convenient target where crowds of people gather, but their sarin was apparently dilute. The biological agents are far and away the most dangerous: they could kill hundreds of thousands where chemicals might kill only thousands. They are relatively easy to procure, but storage and dispersal are even trickier than for nerve gases. The risk of contamination for the people handling them is high, and many of the most lethal bacteria and spores do not survive well outside the laboratory. Aum Shinrikyo reportedly released anthrax bacteria—among the most toxic agents known—on two occasions from a building in Tokyo without harming anyone.

Given the technical difficulties, terrorists are probably less likely to use nuclear devices than chemical weapons, and least likely to attempt to use biological weapons. But difficulties could be overcome, and the choice of unconventional weapons will in the end come down to the specialties of the terrorists and their access to deadly substances.

The political arguments for shunning unconventional weapons are equally weighty. The risk of detection and subsequent severe retaliation or punishment is great, and while this may not deter terrorists it may put off their sponsors and suppliers. Terrorists eager to use weapons of mass destruction may alienate at least some supporters, not so much because the dissenters hate the enemy less or have greater moral qualms but because they think the use of such violence counterproductive. Unconventional weapon strikes could render whole regions uninhabitable for long periods. Use of biological arms poses the additional risk of an uncontrollable epidemic. And while terrorism seems to be tending toward more indiscriminate killing and mayhem, terrorists may draw the line at weapons of superviolence likely to harm both foes and large numbers of relatives and friends—say, Kurds in Turkey, Tamils in Sri Lanka, or Arabs in Israel.

Furthermore, traditional terrorism rests on the heroic gesture, on the willingness to sacrifice one's own life as proof of one's idealism. Obviously there is not much heroism in spreading botulism or anthrax. Since most terrorist groups are as interested in publicity as in violence, and as publicity for a mass poisoning or nuclear bombing would be far more unfavorable than for a focused conventional attack, only terrorists who do not care about publicity will even consider the applications of unconventional weapons.

Broadly speaking, terrorists will not engage in overkill if their traditional weapons—the submachine gun and the conventional bomb—are sufficient to continue the struggle and achieve their aims. But the decision to use terrorist violence is not always a rational one; if it were, there would be much less terrorism, since terrorist activity seldom achieves its aims. What if, after years of armed struggle and the loss of many of their militants, terrorist groups see no progress? Despair could lead to giving up the armed struggle, or to suicide. But it might also lead to a last desperate attempt to defeat the hated enemy by arms not tried before. As one of Racine's heroes said of himself, their "only hope lies in their despair."

Apocalypse Soon

Terrorist groups traditionally contain strong quasi-religious, fanatical elements, for only total certainty of belief (or total moral relativism) provides justification for taking lives. That element was strong among the prerevolutionary Russian terrorists and the Romanian fascists of the Iron Guard in the 1930s, as it is among today's Tamil Tigers. Fanatical Muslims consider the killing of the enemies of God a religious commandment, and believe that the secularists at home as well as the State of Israel will be annihilated because it is Allah's will. Aum Shinrikyo doctrine held that murder could help both victim and murderer to salvation. Sectarian fanaticism has surged during the past decade, and in general, the smaller the group, the more fanatical.

As humankind [starts the third] millennium of the Christian era, apocalyptic movements are on the rise. The belief in the impending end of the world is probably as old as history, but for reasons not entirely clear, sects and movements preaching the end of the world gain influence toward the end of a century, and all the more at the close of a millennium. Most of the preachers of doom do not advocate violence, and some even herald a renaissance, the birth of a new kind of man and woman. Others, however, believe that the sooner the reign of the Antichrist is established, the sooner this corrupt world will be destroyed and the new heaven and earth foreseen by St. John in the Book of Revelation, Nostradamus, and a host of other prophets will be realized.

Extreme millenarians would like to give history a push, helping create world-ending havoc replete with universal war, famine, pestilence, and other scourges. It is possible that members of certain Christian and Jewish sects that believe in Armageddon or Gog and Magog or the Muslims and Buddhists who harbor related extreme beliefs could attempt to play out a doomsday scenario. A small group of Israeli extremists, for instance, firmly believes that blowing up Temple Mount in Jerusalem would bring about a final (religious) war and the beginning of redemption with the coming of the Kingdom of God. The visions of Shoko Asahara, the charismatic leader of Aum Shinrikyo, grew increasingly apocalyptic, and David Koresh proclaimed the Last Day's arrival in the Branch Davidians' 1994 confrontation with Bureau of Alcohol, Tobacco, and Firearms agents.

Those who subscribe to such beliefs number in the hundreds of thousands and perhaps millions. They have their own subcultures, produce books and CDs by the thousands, and build temples and communities of whose existence most of their contemporaries are unaware. They have substantial financial means at their disposal. Although the more extreme apocalyptic groups are potentially terrorist, intelligence services have generally overlooked their activities; hence the shock over the subway attack in Tokyo and Rabin's assassination, to name but two recent events.

Apocalyptic elements crop up in contemporary intellectual fashions and extremist politics as well. For instance, extreme environmentalists, particularly the so-called restoration ecologists, believe that environmental disasters will destroy civilization as we know it—no loss, in their view—and regard the vast majority of human beings as expendable. From such beliefs and values it is not a large step to engaging in acts of terrorism to expedite the process. If the eradication of smallpox upset ecosystems, why not restore the balance by bringing back the virus? The motto of *Chaos International,* one of many journals in this field, is a quotation from Hassan I Sabbah, the master of the Assassins, a medieval sect whose members killed Crusaders and others in a "religious" ecstasy; everything is permitted, the master says. The premodern world and postmodernism meet at this point.

Future Shock

Scanning the contemporary scene, one encounters a bewildering multiplicity of terrorist and potentially terrorist groups and sects. The practitioners of terrorism as we have known it to this point were nationalists and anarchists, extremists of the left and the right. But the new age has brought new inspiration for the users of violence along with the old.

In the past, terrorism was almost always the province of groups of militants that had the backing of political forces like the Irish and Russian social revolutionary movements of 1900. In the future, terrorists will be individuals or like-minded people working in very small groups, on the pattern of the technology-hating Unabomber, who apparently worked alone sending out parcel bombs over two decades, or the perpetrators of the 1995 bombing of the federal building in Oklahoma City. An individual may possess the technical competence to steal, buy, or manufacture the weapons he or she needs for a terrorist purpose; he or she may or may not require help from one or two others in delivering these weapons to the designated target. The ideologies such individuals and mini-groups espouse are likely to be even more aberrant than those of larger groups. And terrorists working alone or in very small groups will be more difficult to detect unless they make a major mistake or are discovered by accident.

Thus at one end of the scale, the lone terrorist has appeared, and at the other, state-sponsored terrorism is quietly flourishing in these days when wars of aggression have become too expensive and too risky. As the [twenty-first century unfolds], terrorism is becoming the substitute for the great wars of the 1800s and early 1900s.

Proliferation of the weapons of mass destruction does not mean that most terrorist groups are likely to use them in the foreseeable future, but some almost certainly will, in spite of all the reasons militating against it. Governments, however ruthless, ambitious, and ideologically extreme, will be reluctant to pass on unconventional weapons to terrorist groups over which they cannot have full control; the governments may be tempted to use such arms themselves in a first strike, but it is more probable that they would employ them in blackmail than in actual warfare. Individuals and small groups, however, will not be bound by the constraints that hold back even the most reckless government.

Society has also become vulnerable to a new kind of terrorism, in which the destructive power of both the individual terrorist and terrorism as a tactic are infinitely greater. Earlier terrorists could kill kings or high officials, but others only too eager to inherit their mantle quickly stepped in. The advanced societies of today are more dependent every day on the electronic storage, retrieval, analysis, and transmission of information. Defense, the police, banking, trade, transportation, scientific work, and a large percentage of the government's and private sector's transactions are on-line. That exposes enormous vital areas of national life to mischief or sabotage by any computer hacker, and concerted sabotage could render a country unable to function. Hence the growing speculation about infoterrorism and cyberwarfare.

An unnamed U.S. intelligence official has boasted that with $1 billion and 20 capable hackers, he could shut down America. What he could achieve, a terrorist could too. There is little secrecy in the wired society, and protective measures have proved of limited value—teenage hackers have penetrated highly secret systems in every field. The possibilities for creating chaos are almost unlimited even now, and vulnerability will almost certainly increase. Terrorists' targets will change: why assassinate a politician or indiscriminately kill people when an attack on electronic switching will produce far more dramatic and lasting results? The switch at the Culpeper, Virginia, headquarters of the Federal Reserve's electronic network, which handles all federal funds and transactions, would be an obvious place to hit. If the new terrorism directs its energies toward information warfare, its destructive power will be exponentially greater than any it wielded in the past—greater even than it would be with biological and chemical weapons.

Still, the vulnerability of states and societies will be of less interest to terrorists than to ordinary criminals and organized crime, disgruntled employees of big corporations, and, of course, spies and hostile governments. Electronic thieves, whether engaged in credit card fraud or industrial espionage, are part of the system, using it rather than destroying it; its destruction would cost them their livelihood. Politically motivated terrorist groups, above all separatists bent on establishing states of their own, have limited aims. The Kurdish Workers Party, the IRA, the Basque ETA, and the Tamil Tigers want to weaken their enemies and compel them to make far-reaching concessions, but they cannot realistically hope to destroy them. It is also possible, however, that terrorist groups on the verge of defeat or acting on apocalyptic visions may not hesitate to apply all destructive means at their disposal.

All that leads well beyond terrorism as we have known it. New definitions and new terms may have to be developed for new realities, and intelligence services and policy makers must learn to discern the significant differences among terrorists' motivations, approaches, and aims. The Bible says that when the Old Testament hero Samson brought down the temple, burying himself along with the Philistines in the ruins, "the dead which he slew at his death were more than he slew in his life." The Samsons of a society have been relatively few in all ages. But with the new technologies and the changed nature of the world in which they operate, a handful of angry Samsons and disciples of apocalypse would suffice to cause havoc. Chances are that of 100 attempts at terrorist superviolence, 99 would fail. But as [9/11 showed], the single successful one could claim many more victims, do more material damage, and unleash far greater panic than anything the world has yet experienced.

Chapter 12

WHY IS AMERICA THE PRIMARY TARGET? TERRORISM AS GLOBALIZED CIVIL WAR

MARTHA CRENSHAW

The magnitude of the September 11 assaults on the World Trade Center and the Pentagon was unprecedented in the history of terrorism. The method of attack represented a novel combination of the familiar tactics of aircraft hijackings, which began in 1968, and suicide bombings, which developed in the 1980s. The four simultaneous hijackings required much more complicated and long-term planning and organization than had previous terrorist actions. Subsequent investigations revealed the existence of a vast and complex transnational conspiracy behind the hijackings.

The September 11 attacks are also the culmination of a pattern of anti-American terrorism on the international level. Since the late 1960s the United States has been a preferred target, the victim of approximately one-third of all international terrorist attacks over the past thirty years. In most instances Americans and American interests were attractive to the practitioners of terrorism because of United States support for unpopular local governments or regional enemies. This terrorism can thus be interpreted as a form of *compellence:* the use or threat of violence to compel the United States to withdraw from its external commitments. Terrorism should be seen as a strategic reaction to American power in the context of globalized civil war. Extremist religious beliefs play a role in motivating terrorism, but they also display an instrumental logic.

Making the United States the Target

The development of international terrorism as it came to characterize the second half of the twentieth century was initially associated with left-wing social revolution. Beginning in 1965, the war in Vietnam legitimized anti-Americanism and equated hostility to the United States with anti-imperialism and national liberation around the world. Independent terrorist campaigns also emerged simultaneously in Latin America, the Middle East, and Europe as a result of localized conflicts and issues. These converging waves of terrorism shared an important feature that distinguished them from earlier violence. Primarily, the attacks involved the seizure of hostages to make political demands on governments. They also involved attacks on diplomats and on civil aviation, a newly available and convenient target.

In Central and South America, kidnappings and assassinations of American and other Western diplomats broke the taboo of diplomatic immunity. Revolutionary organizations, typically inspired by the Cuban example, wanted to demonstrate American complicity in perpetuating the military dictatorships they sought to overthrow. Their belief was that if the dependence of authoritarian regimes on superior outside power could either be revealed to the world or brought to an end, revolution could succeed. Unable to mobilize the countryside, their strategic emphasis shifted from rural insurgency to "urban guerrilla" warfare. Violent revolutionary campaigns flared briefly but were suppressed, often with extreme brutality, in the late 1960s and 1970s.

In the Middle East, the stunning Arab defeat in the 1967 Arab-Israeli war and the Israeli occupation of the West Bank and the Gaza Strip aroused a Palestinian national consciousness. To the newly established Palestine Liberation Organization (PLO) under the leadership of Yasir Arafat, the unmistakable lesson was that neither conventional war nor reliance on sympathetic Arab states could help the Palestinian cause. In 1968 the Popular Front for the Liberation of Palestine (PFLP), a minority faction of the PLO, initiated the practice of hijackings by seizing an Israeli El Al airliner. The PFLP claimed that the airplane was a legitimate military target because El Al had been used to transport Israeli troops in 1967.

The strategy quickly expanded to include the airlines of any country dealing with Israel—including the United States, which was fast becoming Israel's chief ally and weapons supplier. In 1970 the PFLP accomplished a feat that before September 2001 was considered, according to analyst Peter St. John, the "most dramatic multiple hijack in history." A TWA plane from Frankfurt, a Swissair flight from Zurich, and an El Al flight from New York were hijacked to Jordan on September 6. At the same time, a Pan Am plane was hijacked to Cairo. Two days later, a British plane was also hijacked. Four of the planes were destroyed. Fortunately, the hundreds of passengers were eventually released unharmed.

Terrorism generated by the conflict between Israel and the Palestinians escalated to include not only hijackings that ended without loss of life but also lethal attacks on diplomats, takeovers of embassies or other prominent public buildings ("barricade and hostage" incidents), bombings of aircraft, and armed attacks on passengers at airports. Most terrorist incidents were attributable to the more radical and Marxist-oriented Palestinian factions, which also attacked conservative Arab regimes. (As in Latin America, these regimes were doubly vulnerable as local elites and as American allies.) These secular extremist groups aimed for revolution throughout the Arab world, not just the liberation of Palestine.

Also as in Latin America, Middle Eastern terrorism involved attacks on diplomatic targets, notably in the March 1973 Khartoum incident in Sudan. Two American diplomats and a Belgian diplomat were killed by the Palestinian Black

September organization, which had seized the Saudi Arabian embassy during a diplomatic reception. The American rejection of the hostage-takers' demands marked the first implementation of the recently adopted no-concessions policy. Subsequent terrorist attacks killed American passengers at the Rome and Athens airports in August and December. In 1974 a TWA plane en route from Tel Aviv to New York crashed as a result of an on-board explosion, for which the Arab Nationalist Youth for the Liberation of Palestine took credit. In 1976 PFLP militants assassinated the American ambassador to Lebanon, along with the embassy's economic counselor.

Membership in NATO as well as the Vietnam war enhanced the attractiveness of American targets in Western Europe, where two related developments stimulated terrorism. First, indigenous left-revolutionary movements rose from social protest movements in West Germany and Italy. Their roots were primarily in student disaffection, framed in terms of anti-imperialism and sympathy for the Third World. Second, although the social and political roots of these organizations were domestic rather than international, they were inspired and assisted by the spillover of Palestinian terrorism to the European scene. This spillover effect was demonstrated most shockingly with the Black September attack on Israeli athletes at the 1972 Munich Olympics, during which 11 Israeli athletes were killed. Combined operations between German and Palestinian groups became reasonably common in the 1970s, as did cooperation between Palestinians and the Japanese Red Army.

Furthermore, West European revolutionaries, lacking popular support, saw their mission not only as overthrowing oppressive regimes at home but as assisting Third World revolutionary movements, protesting American involvement in the Vietnam war, and revealing that NATO's European members were merely fascist puppets of American hegemonic ambitions. The American military presence was thus anathema, leading to bombings of military bases (especially air force bases in Germany), assassination attempts, and kidnappings (for example, of General James Dozier in Italy in 1980). Terrorism in Western Europe declined through the 1980s as governments became more efficient at countering the problem and as the social movements from which the terrorist groups recruited subsided.

Enter the State—and Religion

In the 1980s, terrorism did not end but shifted course. Persistent state involvement, or "sponsorship," of terrorism, especially by Libya and Iran, marked this period. The decade saw the advent of what is thought of as religious terrorism, driven by the success of the Iran's Islamic revolution in 1979 and Iran's intervention in the Lebanese civil war on the side of Lebanon's Shia community in the 1980s. The war between Iran and Iraq that began in September 1980 exacerbated tensions between Iran and the West, since most Western states sided with Iraq. Libya supported anti-American terrorism for reasons that remain obscure beyond a generic anti-imperialism without religious connotations.

The administration of President Ronald Reagan immediately adopted a "proactive" stance toward terrorism. The Iran hostage crisis had been a major turning point for the United States and a painful personal defeat for the previous president, Jimmy Carter. The crisis had a profound impact for several reasons: the Iranian government's public assumption of responsibility for seizing and holding American diplomats; the seriousness of the violation of international laws and norms; and the apparent success of state terrorism. The failed military mission to rescue the embassy hostages was an added blow to American prestige. The Reagan administration was determined to respond vigorously to the next challenge.

The hostage crisis reverberated beyond the immediate Iranian context not only because of the lessons learned by the United States but also because Iran was determined to spread the Islamic revolution to surrounding Arab countries with Shi'ite populations: from Lebanon and Iraq to American allies such as Kuwait. Iranian ambitions thus threatened the stability of a region that was and is economically and strategically vital to United States interests. Although Iran explained its actions in terms of religious principles, the original reason for the seizure of the American embassy in Tehran was not new. It was a reaction to American support for the shah's autocratic regime and not only that, for the shah himself, whose admission to the United States for medical treatment precipitated the embassy takeover.

These new dimensions of terrorism—open and deliberate state involvement and religious justification—heightened American anxiety. The civil war in Lebanon brought matters to a head. When Israel invaded Lebanon in 1982 in a bid to end PLO attacks on Israel's border, the stage was set for American intervention in a benign effort to negotiate the PLO's withdrawal from Lebanon to Tunisia. After successfully overseeing the PLO's departure, United States forces withdrew. But the massacre of Palestinian civilians at the Sabra and Shatila refugee camps in Beirut by Israel's Lebanese allies brought the United States back into the conflict as a would-be peacekeeper on both a local and a regional scale. Hoping to recapture the success of the 1978 Camp David accords between Israel and Egypt, the United States expanded its mission to include resolution of the conflict between Israel, Lebanon, the PLO, and Syria. American efforts to rebuild a Lebanese state had the unintended consequence of convincing Shi'ite militants in Lebanon, supported by Iran, that the United States was acting as Israel's key ally and also backing the more immediate enemy, conservative Christian Lebanese factions. The most militant of Shi'ite organizations was Hezbollah, whose guerrilla arm inaugurated the tactic of massive truck or vehicle bombs. Some of these attacks were so-called suicide bombings—terrorist acts that require the death of the bomber to succeed. The American embassy in Lebanon was bombed twice, once in April 1983, with a loss of 86 lives, and again when a van exploded in front of the United States embassy annex, killing 2 American military officers and 12 Lebanese in 1984. In 1983 the American embassy in Kuwait was also bombed. Most traumatically, in October 1983 a Hezbollah suicide bomber killed 214 marines in an attack on the American

Marine barracks at the Beirut airport. Early the next year, United States forces withdrew from Lebanon. Whatever the reason for the decision, Hezbollah proudly regarded it as a victory.

Retreat from Lebanon did not end terrorism, which continued with a spate of kidnappings and assassinations of Westerners. Since military targets were now scarce, Hezbollah turned to civilians, including journalists and educators at the American University of Beirut, as well as officials. Kidnappings began in 1982, with the abduction of David Dodge, acting president of the American University of Beirut. Iran apparently instigated the kidnapping to pressure the United States to obtain the release of four Iranian embassy employees who had been kidnapped by Christian Lebanese militia. In 1984 Dodge's successor, Malcolm Kerr, was assassinated. More kidnappings of Americans, as well as other Westerners, followed in sequence. In addition to Iran's interests, Hezbollah leaders objected to Kuwait's arrest of a number of suspected terrorists with links to Lebanon. Hezbollah hoped to use the United States hostages to ensure that Kuwait release or at least proceed leniently with the prisoners, several of whom were linked by family relationships to Hezbollah leaders. William Buckley, the CIA station chief in Lebanon, was abducted at this time, probably due to Iran's interest in halting aid to Iraq. He died in captivity. The kidnapping of American journalist Terry Anderson in 1985 may have been a reaction to the United States veto of a UN resolution condemning Israel's occupation of southern Lebanon.

In June 1985, just as Israel relinquished most of the territory it had held in Lebanon, Hezbollah militants hijacked TWA Flight 847 to Beirut and murdered an American Navy diver on board. The militants demanded the release of over 700 Shi'ite prisoners in Israeli jails, most of them Lebanese. The demand was also linked to two other kidnappings of Americans. After two weeks of crisis, accompanied by massive publicity, a deal was successfully brokered. The hostages were then released unharmed.

In October 1985 Palestinian radicals affiliated with the PLO hijacked an Italian cruise ship, the *Achille Lauro,* and killed an American passenger, Leon Klinghoffer. The group also demanded the release of prisoners held in Israel. The United States military forced an Egyptian plane carrying the hijackers to land in Italy, where they were arrested.

Libya's militant adventurism added to the explosive mix of terrorism in the 1980s. Libyan leader Muammar Qaddafi had embarked on an anti-Western campaign that included supporting terrorism by extremist Palestinian factions as well as financing and arming practically any group that caused trouble for the West, such as the Irish Republican Army. In December 1985 the Abu Nidal organization, a radical Palestinian group and a Libyan client, attacked El Al and TWA passengers at the Rome and Vienna airports.

In 1986 Libyan-sponsored terrorism (specifically the bombing of Berlin's La Belle discotheque, which killed an American soldier) as well as provocative naval maneuvers in the Gulf of Sidra provoked the United States to respond with air power for the first time. The American bombing of Tripoli apparently led Libya to seek revenge by organizing the mid-air bombing of Pan Am Flight 103 over Lockerbie, Scotland, in December 1988. The bombing killed 259 passengers, 189 of whom were American. That act was eventually traced directly to agents of the Libyan state, whom British and American authorities indicted in 1991. The imposition of sanctions against Libya by the United Nations in 1992 and 1993 appeared finally to subdue Libyan-sponsored terrorism. However, when a special Scottish court in the Netherlands convicted a Libyan official of the crime in 2001, the Libyan government was defiant.

A "New" Terrorism

The 1990s were not supposed to be an era of terrorism. The Persian Gulf war had ended in 1991 with the defeat of the Iraqi invasion of Kuwait, an outcome that seemed to presage a geopolitical realignment in the Middle East that could bring a stable peace. The remaining hostages in Lebanon were released in 1991. The Cold War had ended that year also, and with it the generalized sense of insecurity caused by the nuclear stalemate between the two superpowers. The 1993 Oslo accords signaled the beginning of a peace process between Israelis and Palestinians.

When it came to office in 1993, President Bill Clinton's administration minimized the threat of terrorism, defining it as one of a number of transnational or border-crossing threats such as the proliferation of weapons of mass destruction, environmental disasters, crime, and epidemics of disease. Instead of peace and security, however, by mid-decade the United States felt threatened by the prospect of a "new" terrorism that would be decentralized, fanatical, and inclined to mass casualty attacks that included the use of weapons of mass destruction. The 1993 bombing of the World Trade Center and the 1995 Oklahoma City bombing made terrorist attacks on American soil a tragic reality. A 1995 sarin gas attack on the Tokyo subway system by the Aum Shinrikyo religious sect suggested new vulnerabilities and new terrorist methods. There were also bombings of military installations in Saudi Arabia in 1995 and 1996, two American embassies in East Africa in 1998, and a United States destroyer in Yemen in October, 2000. In 2001 the new Bush administration had barely had time to set its agenda before the nation's worst fears were realized in the devastating terrorist attacks on the World Trade Center and the Pentagon. In October a series of suspicious anthrax infections gave a concrete shape to the new specter of bioterrorism.

Many sources of the terrorism of the 1990s can be traced to specific events associated with the Persian Gulf war and the Soviet invasion of Afghanistan in December 1979. The postwar sanctions against Iraq and the military enforcement of the no-fly zones in Iraq (the prohibition on Iraqi military aircraft in most of the northern and southern parts of the country) perpetuated that conflict and mobilized anti-American sentiment. American support for the Afghan resistance to the Soviet Union in the 1980s, followed by neglect as the country collapsed into chaos, mobilized the resistance (called the mujahideen) and may have permitted the Taliban to seize power in 1996.

Islamic militants from around the world gained experience fighting the Soviet Union in Afghanistan and then returned to their homes, where radical organizations proliferated. Some, unwanted at home due to their militance, settled abroad. After the Soviet withdrawal from Afghanistan in 1989, the establishment of training camps in Afghanistan by Saudi-born terrorist Osama bin Laden and his Al Qaeda organization provided an ongoing arena for the socialization of Islamic radicals from across the world.

Yet much is familiar about the current manifestation of anti-American terrorism. Although often justified in terms of religious principle, its roots lie in American support for regimes with embittered domestic oppositions who appeal to Islamic values and have formed transnational ties and allegiances. Militant Islamist movements could not have emerged in the absence of social and political conditions that leave many Muslims desperate and aggrieved. As close American allies, Egypt and Saudi Arabia are critical cases in point. Algeria is a third strand (the United States supports the Algerian government but is not a mainstay of the regime).

For many of the militants now engaged in Al Qaeda, opposition to authority at home, whether peaceful or violent, was ineffective. Local regimes countered dissent with severe repression. As a result, radical frustrations apparently were transferred to the United States as a symbol of both oppression and arrogance. As a free and affluent society, America is a target-rich environment, and one where sensational attacks elicit gratifying media attention. Portraying the United States as an immoral enemy justifies terrorism to the audiences of the dispossessed, especially young men without life prospects whose only education is religious. These various strands have been knitted together in the transnational conspiracy that is Al Qaeda. One cannot understand Al Qaeda without understanding the domestic politics of Egypt and Saudi Arabia, or now much of the Muslim world.

First, the American alliance with Egypt, a reward for making peace with Israel, made the United States a target of radical Islamic groups seeking the overthrow of President Hosni Mubarak's regime (in 1981 President Anwar Sadat paid with his life for signing the Camp David accords). In the 1990s, Egyptian politics apparently spilled onto American soil. In October 1995 a blind Egyptian cleric, Umar Abd al-Rahman, along with nine others, was convicted of the February 1993 bombing of the World Trade Center, which killed 6 people and injured more than 1,000. Planning to bomb other New York landmarks, including the Lincoln and Holland Tunnels and the United Nations building, was also part of the charges. Rahman was the spiritual leader of the al-Gamaa al-Islamiyya (IG), an extremist Sunni Muslim group active in Egypt since the late 1970s. Its aim was to overthrow the government and replace it with an Islamic state. The group was involved in several attempts to assassinate President Mubarak, including a June 1995 attempt in Ethiopia, after which the suspects were believed to have fled to the Sudan. In 1996 the IG and a companion radical group, Islamic Jihad, first began to operate extensively outside Egypt.

Another more mysterious figure behind the 1993 World Trade Center bombing was Ramzi Yousef. In 1995 he was arrested in Pakistan and extradited to the United States. In 1998 he was sentenced to life in prison with solitary confinement for his role in the World Trade Center bombing and for his plan to blow up other New York landmarks. He was also convicted in 1996 for his role in a conspiracy based in Manila, which planned to bomb several American airliners over the Pacific in 1995. Yousef's closing statement referred in rambling fashion to the atomic bomb dropped on Japan, the fire bombing of Tokyo, the war in Vietnam, the embargoes imposed on Iraq and Cuba, United States support for Israel, and opposition to the Palestinian peace process. Religion was not a dominant theme, although the judge said that Yousef claimed to be an Islamic militant.

The Egyptian connection also shows up in the Al Qaeda leadership. Ayman al-Zawahiri, a key associate of Osama bin Laden, is the founder of Egyptian Islamic Jihad. He apparently joined Al Qaeda in 1998. Similarly, Muhammad Atef, Al Qaeda's military commander, is Egyptian, as are at least four other advisers to bin Laden. All were placed on the joint FBI-State Department most wanted list in October 2001. In Egypt, factions associated with IG and Islamic Jihad were also responsible for deadly attacks on tourists in Egypt in 1997. Egyptian Islamic Jihad's alliance with Al Qaeda can be interpreted as an outcome of the group's inability to continue its terrorist activities within Egypt.

The Saudi Conundrum

The problem in Saudi Arabia is more complicated. Here, as in Egypt, American support for a repressive regime as well as its continued military presence after the Persian Gulf war drew the wrath of domestic dissidents, who used Islam to oppose the conservative Saudi monarchy. However, the Saudi government itself bases its legitimacy on a strict and puritanical version of Islam, and it has encouraged and supported fundamentalist religious doctrine. Until September 11 it was one of the few governments that recognized the Taliban. The government and officially sanctioned charities fund the *madrassas* (religious schools) in Pakistan that educate the constituencies of young Muslim men from which Al Qaeda recruits, for example. Of the 19 hijackers on September 11, the United States government has concluded that 15 were Saudi nationals.

In 1995 five Americans were killed in the bombing of a Saudi National Guard office in Riyadh used by United States military trainers. Three of the four religious militants who confessed and were subsequently executed had fought in Afghanistan, Bosnia, and Chechnya. In 1996 a truck-bomb attack on Khobar Towers, an American military housing complex in Saudi Arabia, killed 19 United States military personnel, wounded 372 other United States citizens, and injured more than 200 non-Americans. The facility housed almost 3,000 military personnel responsible for enforcing the no-fly zone in Iraq.

Iran was suspected of involvement by assisting a group called Saudi Hezbollah, an offshoot of the Lebanese Hezbollah. Syria also was thought to have helped with the preparations. Although four members of the group were subsequently placed on the terrorist most wanted list, the United States could not acquire sufficient evidence to justify retaliation against Iran. Shortly before the Khobar Towers bombing, Secretary of State Warren Christopher had publicly condemned Iran for encouraging and financing terrorism designed to disrupt the Middle East peace process, specifically suicide bombings in Israel by Palestinian Islamic Jihad and Hamas, the major Palestinian militant Islamic fundamentalist group. FBI investigators complained of lack of cooperation from the Saudis.

In June 2001 United States courts indicted 13 members of Saudi Hezbollah plus 1 Lebanese (11 of the accused are in prison in Saudi Arabia, where they will be tried). The plot had taken about three years, and its purpose was apparently to support Iran in driving the United States from the Persian Gulf region. No mention of Iran was made in the United States indictment, however, and Iran denies involvement.

Osama bin Laden came to the attention of American officials during investigations into the 1993 World Trade Center bombing, although whether he played an active role in that attack is unclear. bin Laden's history as wealthy financier of the resistance to the Soviet Union in Afghanistan is now well known. Returning to Saudi Arabia after the Soviet withdrawal—which must have been seen as a major victory—bin Laden turned to violence against Saudi and American interests. Saudi Arabia expelled him to Sudan in 1991, where he flourished with the support of Sudan's radical Islamist regime. However, Sudan in turn expelled him at the insistence of the United States. He retreated to Afghanistan in 1996, on the eve of the Taliban's seizure of power.

In 1997, from his hidden bases in the caves of Afghanistan, bin Laden gave an interview to CNN in which he declared a jihad against the United States. He had issued earlier calls to arms but now used American television media to communicate his message. He claimed that jihad was a response to United States support for Israel, America's military presence in Saudi Arabia, and America's "aggressive intervention against Muslims in the whole world." In 1998 he joined with Egyptian Islamic Jihad to establish an "International Front for Islamic Holy War against the Jews and Crusaders." The front called for attacks on American targets across the globe, both civil and military, to force an American withdrawal from Saudi Arabia and to end the Israeli occupation of Jerusalem. It focused on the plight of the Iraqi people, but not the Palestinian cause. This appeal was ambitiously presented as a *fatwa*, or religious edict, which all Muslims were called on to obey.

In 1996 the United States had already initiated a grand jury investigation into bin Laden's activities, and the CIA began to target and "disrupt" his network. By the spring United States agencies were specifically monitoring his activities in Nairobi, Kenya. In March 1998 the State Department issued a worldwide alert drawing attention to a threat against American military and civilians following the February fatwa. A sealed indictment in June 1998 led to the arrest of 21 of Osama bin Laden's associates during the summer. It charged the group with attacks on United States and UN troops in Somalia in 1993 and with leading a terrorist conspiracy in concert with Sudan, Iraq, and Iran. Press reports later indicated that the United States was also considering a raid into Afghanistan to arrest bin Laden, as a result of a 1998 presidential finding that authorized covert operations, including blocking bin Laden's financial assets and exercising close surveillance.

Despite this awareness and these actions, the August 1998 bombings of the American embassies in Kenya and Tanzania came as a surprise. The Nairobi bombing killed 12 Americans, 32 other United States employees, and more than 200 Kenyans. Thousands were injured. In Dar es Salaam, Tanzania, 11 people were killed and 85 injured. No Americans died. In form, the attacks resembled the bombings of the United States embassy in Beirut in 1983 and 1984, but the message was not that the United States should withdraw from Kenya and Tanzania. The intent instead appeared to be to issue a general warning of a terrorist campaign. In tactical terms, what distinguished the attacks and alarmed American authorities was that two embassies in different countries were bombed simultaneously, which indicated a highly organized conspiracy.

The Clinton administration responded immediately with cruise missile attacks on Al Qaeda training camps in Afghanistan and on a pharmaceuticals plant in the Sudan. (The latter was suspected of manufacturing precursor chemicals for weapons use and was believed to have connections to bin Laden's business enterprises as well as to the Sudanese regime.) The decision to use military force was controversial. In particular, critics disputed the link between the pharmaceuticals plant, chemical precursors, and bin Laden. The retaliatory attacks may have been a signal of American resolve, but they inflicted no serious damage on Al Qaeda's capabilities. They may also have cost the United States the moral high ground. Rather than stressing that most of the victims of the bombings were African, the United States was seen to be bombing Muslim countries.

A second avenue of response was a strengthened law enforcement effort. United States authorities quickly apprehended four of the men who planned and executed the East Africa bombings. All four were convicted (and in October 2001 they were sentenced to life in prison). The group included a Saudi, a Tanzanian, a Jordanian, and an American who was born in Lebanon. Two were charged with direct participation; the other two were found guilty of participation in the broader conspiracy. The lengthy trial in New York revealed many details of the operations of the Al Qaeda network, which appeared less like a cult of religious zealots than a far-reaching and profitable business enterprise. bin Laden was said to control a global banking network as well as agricultural, construction, transportation, and investment companies in Sudan. bin Laden was also said to have developed his hostility to the United States as a result of the 1993 intervention in Somalia. According to witness testimony (from Jamal Ahmed al-Fadl, a former bin Laden associate who had been cooperating with the United States since 1996), Al Qaeda was divided over whether to retaliate after the arrest of Sheik Rahman in 1993.

The Egyptian members wanted to avenge his arrest, but others objected that innocent people would be killed. Some of the Egyptian members then left the organization.

The Taliban continued to reject the American demand to surrender bin Laden, which was first made in 1998. This persistent refusal resulted in the imposition of United Nations sanctions and the isolation of the Taliban regime.

The next public manifestation of Al Qaeda's terrorist activity came in December 1999, when a series of "millennium plots" was foiled. One involved an Algerian, Ahmed Ressam, who entered the United States from Canada to bomb the Los Angeles airport. His fortuitous arrest showed that Al Qaeda cells were operating in Canada and that the Algerian Armed Islamic Group (GIA) was involved. The plot was also linked to Al Qaeda cells in Britain. Eventually four Algerians were charged in the plot and brought to trial in June and July 2001.

Training in Afghanistan was a common theme in their experience. Ahmed Ressam described a decentralized organizational structure. Militants were trained by the organization, but then given funds and substantial autonomy in selecting targets. He also testified that Sheik Rahman had issued orders to kill Americans. (Another thwarted millennium plot involved attacks on tourists in Jordan and Israel. Jordan arrested a number of suspects.)

The link between Al Qaeda and the GIA was a product of Algeria's bloody civil war in the 1990s. When the Islamic Salvation Front was poised to win Algeria's national elections in December 1991, the Algerian government canceled the results. The GIA emerged as the most extreme of the opposition movements. In 1994 members of the GIA hijacked a plane to Marseilles and threatened to fly it into the Eiffel Tower before they were killed by French security forces. As elsewhere, many Algerian militants had fought in Afghanistan in the 1980s.

In October 2000 Al Qaeda struck again. Although conclusive proof is lacking, the United States is certain that bin Laden's followers organized the suicide bombing of the United States destroyer *Cole* while it was refueling in Yemen. The death toll was 17 Navy personnel. The bombers were apparently Yemenis, but Osama bin Laden was suspected of backing them. The mastermind was thought to be a Saudi of Yemeni origin, living in the United Arab Emirates. As in Saudi Arabia, the FBI encountered difficulties in getting Yemeni authorities to cooperate in the investigation.

The Scope Broadens

The attacks of September 11 fit a pattern but also marked a dramatic escalation of violence. Subsequent investigations into the hijackings also revealed the astonishing scope of the transnational conspiracy involved. The hijackers included Egyptian, Saudi, and Lebanese citizens. The apparent leaders came from a cell headquartered at a technical university in Hamburg, Germany. Arrests in other countries such as Spain, Britain, Germany, and France targeted Kuwaiti, French, Algerian, Yemeni, Moroccan, Libyan, Syrian, and Tunisian activists, among others. One group was apparently organizing a parallel plot to attack the American embassy in Paris. The organizers were mostly Al Qaeda second-generation Algerians in France. The European branch of the conspiracy was said to revolve around two groups, the Egyptian Takfir wal Hijra (known in Europe as Vanguards of the Conquest or the New Jihad Group), led by Al Qaeda lieutenant Ayman al-Zawahiri, and the Algerian Salafist Group for Preaching and Combat. The Salafists are thought to work with bin Laden but to maintain an independent leadership (in 1998 the Salafist Group broke from the GIA and apparently formed an alliance with Al Qaeda).

The reasoning behind the September 11 attacks was expressed primarily in a statement from Osama bin Laden broadcast in Qatar on October 7, and to a lesser degree in subsequent pronouncements from Al Qaeda leaders. Such statements show a keen appreciation of different audiences and constituencies and are attuned to sensitivities to specific grievances. Typically, bin Laden did not claim direct credit for the actions but praised those responsible as a "group of vanguard Muslims." The statement referred specifically to eighty years of humiliation of Islam. It thus apparently dated the period of humiliation to 1921, the dissolution of the Ottoman Empire, and the establishment of Britain's Palestine Mandate that provided for a Jewish homeland. Specific references to Palestine and Iraq were made, as well as more vague allegations that countries that believe in Islam had been turned against bin Laden by the United States. bin Laden cited United States retaliation against Afghanistan in 1998 as another grievance. Echoing Ramzi Yousef, he also condemned the United States bombing of Japan in 1945. This comparison may be an attempt to provide moral justification for causing large numbers of civilian casualties.

The anthrax incidents in October 2001 have not been conclusively linked to Al Qaeda operatives. Previously, the only terrorist attacks using chemical and biological weapons occurred in Japan, most notably with the subway sarin gas attack in 1995 by the Aum Shinrikyo cult. Since then the American government had undertaken a range of efforts to protect American cities and prepare for terrorist-caused disaster ("consequence management"). "Bioterrorism" was seen as the most likely manifestation of the threat. Even if the anthrax scare is not linked to international terrorism, it will increase fears that such attacks are likely.

The Preposterous Idea

The United States has been susceptible to international terrorism primarily because of its engagement on the world scene and its choice of allies. Extremist groups in countries around the world have targeted United States interests in an effort to achieve radical political change at home. The United States military presence, whether in assisting local regimes or in peacemaking exercises, attracted terrorism, but so too did diplomatic and cultural institutions.

In the 1990s, a determined leadership, drawing its inspiration from an extreme version of Islam, took advantage of permissive political conditions and ample financial resources to construct a transnational terrorist coalition with deadly ambitions. To Americans, the idea that the United States could be compelled by terrorism to abandon its interests in the Middle East is preposterous; to the leaders and followers of Al Qaeda there is precedent in Lebanon and Somalia. In a war of attrition, superior motivation is often the key to the successful compellence of an adversary, and terrorism is a way of demonstrating their determination and power. When civil war is expanded to the international system, vulnerability may be the inevitable accompaniment to the exercise of power. Although the response must deal with the immediate threat and the actors who are behind it, it must also deal with the long term. Future American foreign policy must consider the risk of terrorism as a central factor in calculating interests and strategies.

Chapter 13

IS THE NEW GLOBAL TERRORISM A CLASH OF CIVILIZATIONS? EVALUATING TERRORISM'S MULTIPLE SOURCES

LLEWELLYN D. HOWELL

In the fraught time after September 11, 2001, there remains the need to use reason in order to attempt to understand the origins of the terrorist attacks on the World Trade Center and the Pentagon, to in turn be able to respond to them meaningfully. We need to impose a paradigm, a structure, on the picture of the world that we have so that we can determine causality, and then select an appropriate response to that cause. As in carpentry, we need to use a wrench to turn a bolt, a hammer to pound a nail. We need the proper tool for each task. In medicine, the sequence is theory, diagnosis, prescription. Theory determines what we see, diagnosis defines the problem, prescription specifies the tool. If any theory at all has been applied in pursuit of the September 11 terrorists, it is the wrong one. The tools we have used so far are not fully adequate to the task at hand. The U.S. response to the attacks—whether in the form of bunker busters or bank busters—has been a treatment of symptoms, with the underlying cause as yet unaddressed.

The pursuit of Al Qaeda and the Taliban in Afghanistan and elsewhere clearly has had benefits in delaying the impact of terrorists on American and Western society, but there are many more terrorists in the making. What is to be done about them?

Terrorism: Uncivil War

It's a new world with many milestones passed at the onset of a new millennium. Among the most critical is the conduct of war. Terrorism, although by no means a new phenomenon, has come to the fore. Warhead delivery systems and "star wars" have taken a back seat. War, this unique human character flaw, began with sticks and stones, grew to an exploding powder stage, escalated to the air, then to space, and fell again to Earth in the form of body bombs. But while stick war reached only a few doorsteps, terrorist war is stepping across every hearth in every corner of the globe.

What is terrorism, anyway? It's not difficult to define, actually. Terrorism is war conducted outside the construct of nation-states. More than simple destructiveness, it is an act of violence intended to have a far wider effect than mere destruction of physical objects or the killing of human beings, military or civilian. As its name implies, among the desired effects is the creation of fear and all its associated side effects. Fear destroys will; the loss of will undermines determination and interest in progress; and that, in turn, suppresses opposition.

The major changes in the conduct of war haven't been linked with particular numbers of years, whether millennia or centuries, although they have been accelerating. Firing from cover was a monumental change in tactic for Western armies that arose in the mid-eighteenth century following encounters with savages in the colonies. Armored ships and vehicles entered the war picture a century later in the American Civil War. In the mid-twentieth century, atomic weapons intruded on the primitiveness of human fighting by initiating the use of mass destruction in international conduct.

Now, however, the fast pace of technological change, an increasing level of knowledge in every imaginable party and group, easy access across borders made more porous for the purpose of international trade and investment, and a rapidly increasing global population combine to shift not only the tactics and strategies but also the very nature of war itself. The weapons of choice have now become fueled civilian aircraft, nuclear contamination, backpack bombs, computer viruses, biological viruses, and chemicals. Military units are no longer divisions and battalions but are instead teams of two, or four, or ten. Terrorism is the next and highest stage of war in a globalizing system.

Formerly, armies were needed not only to wield the weapons of war but also to occupy the land of the enemy, like the Germans occupied much of Europe for a time or the Japanese occupied China and Korea. Modern war doesn't involve occupation. Americans will never occupy China or Russia or Afghanistan, and no one will occupy America. The United States couldn't occupy Vietnam, and NATO forces couldn't really occupy Kosovo—even with a mostly friendly and appreciative population. An army of occupiers is no longer the name of the game. The game is now the dramatic explosion or chemical attack that generates fear and destroys economic functions. The objective is no longer to kill or capture or bring down a government but instead is to undermine, cause panic, destabilize, hinder, or simply get revenge.

The shift to terrorism as the means of conducting war poses a dramatic problem for which nation-states are still unprepared. The key issue is defense. A war by a country's armed forces can be responded to by another country's armed forces. There is a matching of military power measured in men, weapons, and technology. How is an act of terror to be matched? More importantly, how is it to be prevented? The best defense, until September 11, seemed to be the errors and clumsiness of the terrorists themselves.

The origins of conventional war were always in governments. In the Twenty-First century, however, even individuals can wage war but the most frequent use has been by small groups, whose power is multiplied exponentially by the change in the nature of weapons. But their power also lies in the lack of a defense against them. Armies, no matter how well trained or equipped, can't search every truck, car, and individual crossing the border into the United States, let alone cordon off vast stretches of border that are open and untended.

Most critical, on the defensive side, is that modern states cannot apply the old aphorism that "the best defense is a good offense." The enemy of the state could be any one of five billion individuals. The nationality, sex, color, or religion of the enemy can never be consistently known, although Muslims, Arabs, the unshaven, and others are profiled, and were even before September 11.

Governments sometimes directly support terrorists but often they do not, out of concern that the weapons of terrorism could be turned on them. Given the wide and increasing availability of the weapons of terrorism, the critical variable in defense is determining *intent*. The key ingredients in Timothy McVeigh's bombing of the federal building in Oklahoma were low-tech ammonium nitrate and a rental truck. These are the weapons of modern war. What made them weapons was what was in Timothy McVeigh's mind. The U.S.S. *Cole* was heavily damaged and nearly sunk, and 17 Americans were killed by two men in a small boat who seemed friendly until the moment of impact. What were their beliefs that allowed them to sacrifice their lives? What was in the minds of the 19 hijackers who flew fuel-laden planes into buildings in New York and Washington?

There has been greatly increased attention in the United States to defense against terrorism over the two decades since the American embassy was seized in Tehran. Training in counter-terrorism by government agencies and even businesses has expanded greatly in recent years. Counter-terrorism measures (U.S. defense) include the sensitive acts of infiltration, electronic surveillance, interception of mail and phone calls, and the sharing of information among intelligence services about the characteristics and behaviors of profiled individuals and groups.

The trends in the impact of terrorism have not been heartening. A study in the *Journal of Conflict Resolution* (June 2000) by Walter Enders and Todd Sandler showed convincingly that although the numbers of terrorist incidents had declined, those that were still occurring were even more deadly. Each incident is now much more likely to result in death or injury than those of the 1980s, more than making up for the decline in occurrences. The attacks of September 11 fit perfectly into this profile.

The authors also noted that there had been a dramatic shift from politically based acts to religious-based terrorism. The origins of this war are not found in easily identified governments and nation-states but reside instead in group ideologies, cult beliefs, and religious dogma, they said. Targets of terrorists, sometimes shifting away from defended facilities and secure installations, have become office buildings, monuments, market places, and transportation facilities. The objective in this altered form of modern war is not conquest or change of government. It is terror aimed at destabilization in some instances or simple religious merit on behalf of a cause in many others.

The question of the nature of a defense for a new form of war for a new century is critical in the response to the new impetus of global terrorism. Should the focus of a defense strategy and budget be on conventional war-fighting power, antiballistic missile capability, electronic warfare in space, or on detecting intent and capability of groups and individuals who focus on killing of the innocent, instilling fear, and creating chaos? The forces of economy and familiarity drive governmental strategies toward technology and raw power, while the real threat and vulnerability lie in the hearts and minds of men. If theory tells us that this is the problem, what is the tool that we must use to get at hearts and minds?

How about a "War" against "Terrorism"?

The 1993 bombings of the U.S. embassies and their surroundings in Kenya and Tanzania were not new events for Americans, nor were they the most proximate instances of terrorism that we had encountered at the time. The surprise for all was the rapid and extralegal response by the United States. For the first time, the United States had entered into the ongoing war constituted by terrorism on the same grounds as employed by the terrorists.

The missile responses against terrorist-linked facilities in Sudan and Afghanistan were thought of by many as somehow "uncivilized." There was no warning. These acts of war were undertaken without submitting them to the formal American processes of warmaking. Sovereign territory was invaded without regard to consideration of the sovereigns involved.

The transition was very much like that made in the American colonial period, when the conduct of war shifted from men in bright uniforms standing in straight lines firing at one another in coordinated volleys to the use of ambushes, camouflage, and firing from protective cover. That full transition began in fighting between colonizers and Indians and wasn't complete until after the Civil War. The full conversion to terrorist tactics by the United States was evident in the first days of the 2001 attack on Afghanistan. Infiltration, disguise, and deception are now common tactics of U.S. ground forces, as they must be in face-to-face fighting with terrorist adherents. The old rules of war have fallen by the wayside.

Few ordinary citizens appreciate the extent to which war has been conducted according to rules. Historian Frederick H. Hartmann noted that while war planning and conduct was dominated by the "big three" considerations—finances, strategy, and deployment and tactics, he notes that law and rules have played a critical role. In his *The Relations of Nations,* Hartmann cites the *United States Rules of Land Warfare of 1914,* which states in Article 10 that "the object of war is to bring about the complete submission of the enemy as soon as possible by means of regulated violence." Regulated violence? It's difficult to think of war as being such, but it is. As a general rule, some weapons have been used and some not. Civilians have been treated differently than soldiers. Soldiers were to be taken prisoner when possible and not summarily killed.

The rules of war have been undergoing a process of degradation since World War II. Especially as conducted war has shifted from being conflicts between nations to being conflicts within nations and between ethnic, racial, cultural, and religious groups, the enforcers of the rules of war—national governments and international organizations—have been powerless to intervene. The rules have fallen one by one. The debate following the U.S. and allied capture of fighters in Afghanistan about what constitutes a "POW" (prisoner of war) and where the Geneva Convention applies is reflective of the decline— and of the debate over applicability—of the traditional rules of war.

Weapons with field testing (or actual use) include chemical and biological agents. Civilian women have recently been the explicit targets of rape and sexual molestation with the clear intent of destruction of cultures and their will to fight on. Captured soldiers are subject to mass execution and burial in unmarked graves, lost forever to families and societies. Terrorism is only the downward linear extension of such conduct, away from the civilizing controls of nation-states. It is indeed a degradation as relations among human beings deteriorate in an inexorable regression toward the primitive.

Military historians often note the argument of General Karl von Clausewitz, who in his 1911 three-volume *On War* contended that "war is . . . a continuation of policy by other means. It is not merely a political act, but a real political instrument, a continuation of political intercourse, a conduct of political intercourse by other means." It is just as easy—or perhaps easier—to argue the opposite, as Thomas Hobbes did more than four centuries ago, that the primitive and natural state of man is violence. Government and the rule of law are the civilizing veneer, the more "developed" state of man. In this line of thinking, war is not a "continuation of political intercourse" but is rather a *falling back from political acts to acts of base violence*. The use of terrorism is, in this line of thinking, a further diminution of human choice to even rawer instincts. Politics, we should have understood, is a continuation of war by other means. As terrorism engulfs us, we wish for politics again.

Why Terrorism?

Why is this happening? Why now? Fear—and the threat from which it is derived—like the influence of alcohol, causes inhibitions to fall away and the most primitive instincts of human beings come forth. In the conflagration of September 11 and the conflicts that have followed, what is the threat that has stimulated the spiraling cycle of terrorism and violence?

Four factors in the nature of human life seem to offer themselves most prominently to explain the expansion of terrorism: (1) increasing population; (2) increasing disparities in wealth and benefits; (3) the expansion of religious extremism; and (4) increased technology and access to it. The first three are related to the perception of threat, the fourth to its implementation.

Despite arguments that the Earth can handle even larger populations, this is not apparent to most humans who find their available space diminishing.

A logical, linear progression of thought explains the perception: more people, less space per person, more interactions, more opportunities for conflict, more conflict, more preparation for conflict. Robert Frost observed that "good fences make good neighbors," but as populations have grown, sufficient numbers of fences have become impossible to build. The intrusion of too many neighbors competing for a limited number of resources has produced anxiety that leads to striking out, sometimes in the form of terrorist activity.

Another important function derived from population growth is a mathematical opportunity outcome. It takes only one person to carry a bomb into a crowded dance hall or four to commandeer an aircraft. The more people there are in the world, the more likely it is that there will be one or four willing to do it. The larger the population, therefore, the greater the opportunity for the occurrence of terrorism.

Partly because of growing populations but also because of differences in cultures and capabilities, there is an ever-widening disparity between the developed and less developed worlds, and increasing disparities even within societies—like the United States. The rich are getting richer and the poor, poorer. While it may be possible to reverse this trend, growing populations and resistance from the "haves" (however it is argued) have exacerbated the problem. With the classical "demonstration effect" from development economics magnified by access to television and the Internet, disparities and awareness of them will continue to grow. Whatever the have-nots might or might not deserve, some of them are likely to strike out in the face of that disparity, hoping to obtain the gold at the end of the rainbow. They have little to lose and maybe much to gain in their version of the "hereafter."

Many argue that religious adherence is important in human life. While this may be so, it is also the case that such adherence can become excessive. It perhaps does so more often under circumstances of deprivation and loss of hope. If rapid population growth depletes resources relatively, and the economic system is one that has left many impoverished without hope, fundamentalist, extremist, and radical religion offers an opportunity for escape.

Fundamentalist religion has become a much more common recourse in the late twentieth century. Andrew Sullivan, writing in the *New York Times Magazine* (October 7, 2001), chronicles the linkages between physical and psychological deprivation and the search for salvation in successful battle against the infidels or in an eternal afterlife. Fundamentalism and terrorism seem to have become joined at the hip. As Enders and Sandler noted, fundamentalism is the organizing influence behind most terrorism today. This includes fundamentalist radicals among Muslims and Christians, Hindus and Jews, Buddhists and Animists. As the ranks of radical fundamentalists grow, the numbers of terrorists *will* increase, simply as a function of population growth on a planet with limited space and resources.

There are thus a growing number of potential terrorist agents, with a growing number of perceived threats, with greater unhappiness about the distribution of wealth and health, with increasing theological justification for acting in a violent manner. Add to this mix greater knowledge of the means of destruction. Technology has added not only the means of learning how but also the means of movement on a global basis such that terrorists can strike anywhere. In our country. In our town. In our workplace.

How should the United States have responded to the attacks of September 11? How do Americans protect themselves against terrorists? It isn't by killing a few of them, although that might be a temporary deterrence for those who remain. It isn't by stooping to the lowest common denominator in tactical violence. Ultimately it has to be by addressing the sources of terrorism rather than just the symptoms represented by the few agents that can be captured or killed. The sources lie in the human condition, not in the attributes of the few.

In the Hearts and Minds of Terrorists

Broad categories of theories and diagnoses about the sources of the attacks were dispersed in the news analyses in the aftermath of the September 11 attacks. The theories range from the simple to the complex and are often intermingled. One is the sentiment that the attacks were an act of "evil." By ascribing the deeds to the existence of evil in the world, we also incapacitate ourselves since this explanation requires calling upon a deity or religious resources to expunge the source of the problem. Prayer is a primary recourse.

Another theory posits that the terrorists are "nihilists" out to destroy all of humanity. Like anarchists, whose acts are in themselves the objectives, nihilism can be responded to only by eliminating the true believers or by convincing them one by one to replace their belief systems.

Some have argued that the attacks were "criminal." The individuals who carried them out were societal deviants motivated by base instincts, limited intelligence, or an inability to perform even near the mainstream of human society. If the actions are criminal, they are perpetual and can only be policed, not eliminated. There will always be a fringe to society, and nonconforming acts will always be represented in the actions of that fringe, requiring perpetual police and a police state.

Many have suggested that these were the actions of primitives, undertaken by the "uncivilized" against the "civilized." The act was so heinous, one U.S. official said, that "maybe even some of those in the uncivilized world now realize that they are on the wrong side." The "barbarian" paradigm has the virtue of making the world into a simple "us versus them." It provides targets and justification for immediate response and serves the purpose of a paradigm. If the problem is that there are people somewhere who are uncivilized, the solution is to civilize them or, in the short term, eliminate them, by capturing, imprisoning, or killing them to remove the threat of future cataclysms.

This explanation, though, removes the rallying motivation of war. War isn't waged against the ignorant or the primitive. It isn't waged against hooligans, even highly successful ones. It is waged against entities and enemies. Entities like nation-states or civilizations. And war, President Bush has declared, it is. So if it's war, where is the paradigmatic explanation that involves an entity?

In a 1993 *Foreign Affairs* article titled "The Clash of Civilizations?", Harvard's Samuel P. Huntington initiated a debate about the best paradigm to replace the Cold War construct that had explained so much in international affairs in the forty years after the Berlin wall. He cited Thomas Kuhn's classic text, *The Structure of Scientific Revolutions*, in arguing that what is the best explanation is the most useful explanation.

Huntington's hypothesis is that "the fundamental source of conflict in this new world [of the twenty-first century] will not be primarily ideological or primarily economic. The great divisions among humankind and the dominating source of conflict will be cultural. . . . The clash of civilizations will dominate global politics. . . . Conflict between civilizations will supplant ideological and other forms of conflict as the dominant global form of conflict."

Huntington's thesis about the nature of human conflict was met with considerable opposition. The argument, in the minds of some, is a formalizing of racism, a legitimizing of the use of religion and ethnicity in the intentional division of human society. To others it was an overestimation of the power of culture or missed the subtleties of cultural accommodation. For many more it is simply that this is not the way they want the world to be. In the days since the September 11 attacks, almost all references in intellectual discourse to "the clash of civilizations" have been of denial and dismissal—especially from those on the left in international society.

But the frequency of reference indicates that the thesis has struck a chord. A great many want to use the phrase because it seems to be a popular and immediate solution. Some have embraced it emotionally. The Italian Prime Minister, Silvio Berlusconi, both identified the terrorist question as being one of civilizations clashing and "praised Western civilization today as superior to that of the Islamic world" (*New York Times*, 27 September 2001, A8).

The dissenters are still the clear majority. They don't want the theory that defines how we look at the problem to be culturally based. But arguments against the clash of civilizations thesis miss a critical point. It is not whether we are choosing to wage a war on Islam or any civilization, but rather, are they waging war on us as a civilization? Engaging Huntington's hypothesis, we have to answer two questions. How do the terrorists define themselves? And were the terrorist attacks a clash with the American government, the American military, or American culture?

At least some element in these terrorists' definition of themselves has to do with religious beliefs. We have to assume that all saw a continuation of themselves beyond the deadly impact of the jetliners that they controlled. From what was written by them and from materials they were reading, we also have to assume that an interpretation of Islam was the source of their beliefs, their values, their culture, their civilization.

The strikes at Wall Street and the military establishment, it has been argued, were strikes at symbols of American culture, at the financial system that supports it, at the American way of life. The Taliban employed this paradigm themselves in arguing that a responding U.S. attack on Afghanistan would be an attack on all of Islam, a response of one civilization to another. Many Americans, especially including the president of the United States, have responded in religious terms. They call upon "God" continuously, to bless America, to receive those killed by the terrorists, to aid our side in achieving victory over the enemy. This is our God, not theirs—a different one.

Especially in the early days after the attacks in New York and Virginia, there were some references to a "crusade" against terrorists, including from high-level American officials. There is really no such thing as "inadvertent." The clash of civilizations is in their minds, as well.

Some sense of goodness in many of us wants to deny that races and linked cultures are at the origin of this war. "But if not a clash of civilizations, then what?" Huntington countered his critics with this same challenge. If this was evil, how do we respond to evil? If nihilism, what then? How do we deal meaningfully with the uncivilized, the primitive? Can we hate them?

Thomas Kuhn's notion that the appropriate theory is the most useful theory has to be considered here. And we need to be very careful in applying any of the alternatives. If evil, or nihilism, or criminality, or primitiveness are argued to be the underlying causal factor for the acts of September 11, and the reason for the deaths of thousands of noncombatants, Americans leave themselves open to accusations of similar barbarism or criminality in U.S. bombings of Vietnam and Germany and Japan, especially in the use of atomic weapons in the latter case. Was there a difference between what was in the minds of the terrorists when they died for a cause, and what was in the minds of the pilots who bombed Hanoi or Dresden or Nagasaki? And if so, was it more than just "my civilization is better than your civilization?"

If the problem is that there are gaps between civilizations, the ultimate solution (and not just a treatment of the symptom) is to find ways in which differences can be accommodated or reduced. In rebutting Huntington at the origin of the 1993 debate, Johns Hopkins University scholar Fouad Ajami argued that the process of accommodation between civilizations is already underway, fed by the drive for the economic rewards that the West has generated and demonstrated to the rest. "In making itself over the centuries, the West helped make the others as well," he notes.

Ironically, Ajami inadvertently posits that there *has been and is* a clash between civilizations, although a nonviolent one, and that the West is winning. An implication is that the clash of civilizations can be pursued without war, and that the best way to reduce the lines of conflict is for the West to absorb immigrants, to educate the world, to feed its poor—just what we have already been doing.

These acts of terrorism were undertaken by an organization on behalf of a culture, of what they see as a civilization. Cultures are defined by religions and are pressed forth by the true believers, the fundamentalists. In dealing with terrorism, as with any medical problem, we need to see the symptoms and treat them. But the underlying cause of those symptoms is what is really at issue for the "long term" that we have been hearing so much about since September 11. Huntington's paradigm may not satisfy the demand for a perfect explanation of those underlying causes, but, like Churchill's democracy, it's better than all the others in telling us why this happened, what to do about it, and how to live with ourselves in a very long future. In the West we want to continue to be a civilization of enlightenment and reason, not vindictive angels of war. Cultures can change. But how?

Can Pluralism Be Accepting of Those Who Hate Pluralism? No!

Thomas Friedman has suggested on a number of recent occasions in his *New York Times* columns that what was lacking in the Taliban—and by extension in conservative Islam—was any sense of pluralism. Pluralism is the underlying principle that represents the blooming of a thousand flowers in any domestic society but also in a globalized society. Pluralism is the pride in one's culture as distinct from the blending and compromising of integration and assimilation. It is the live-and-let-live concept that has made the United States the home to so many contradictory ways of life, so much dissention, so much conflict and rivalry, so much inventiveness, so much freedom. Its antithesis is the notion that there is right and wrong, with a need to force on some an understanding of what is right.

Pluralist thought is so prevalent in intellectual America that it has become a mantra, reflecting the right of *every* culture not only to exist, but to hold every facet of its construction sacred and thereby permanent. Pluralism was the put-down to the integrationists who had carried the early and hard years of the civil rights movement in America. Multiculturalism, rather than "melting pot," has come, in America, to be the underlying, politically correct version of how cultures and subcultures deal with each other. Every species has to survive.

Globally, pluralism is the underpinning of expanding tribalism and subdivision. It is the right of every ethnic group to have a government, of every government to have territory, of every territory to have a defense. Territorial defense, of course, means conflict and fighting and war. And there we are. Ultimately, pluralism means war on a planet where nearly every culture is expanding its population. And yet, Friedman and others have also suggested that mainstream Islam can and must "modernize." While modernizing in these references implies an acceptance of pluralism—and the right of differing cultures, thought, and political beliefs to coexist, it also contradicts pluralist thought. To suggest modernizing is to suggest a change in a culture.

By proposing that a culture modernize, one suggests that the way the culture is now is wrong, that they need to change in a direction that is more broadly acceptable. Or maybe more acceptable to a more dominant culture? Isn't this integration? Assimilation? What have all these terms come to mean, and how are they affected by events in September 2001? Who is to decide what "modernization" means to Muslims or Wahhabis or the Taliban or Mormons?

Rather than perpetually puzzling over this conundrum, though, let's think about how this fits post–September 11 realities, both domestic and global. Within the United States, Americans long ago decided that some religions and cultures needed to have limits to their practices. The culture of the rural South had to give up slavery. Mormons had to give up the idea of polygamy (although some sects still abide by this practice). Some Native American and other cultures have been legally prohibited from using hallucinogenic drugs in their religious practices. The "illegal" practices were all regarded as those that caused some damage in the larger American society, and the cultures that practiced them were told to change or face the consequences.

Globalization has effectively created a single larger culture. Immigrants are flooding many societies, from the United States to Australia to the Middle East to Malaysia. National borders mean less and less, even outside the European Union. Are there global standards, universal human rights? Many waited until after the September 11 attacks to jump on the bandwagon of women's rights in Afghanistan. The subjugation of women by the Taliban justified, in the minds of many, the elimination of Taliban governance, apart from the question of terrorism. Can other Islamic cultures continue to practice such subjugation, or can they be told by the larger human society that they must change, that they must modernize? What about female circumcision in many African cultures? What about slavery, which is still practiced widely? Can't we, shouldn't we, force them to change too?

Taken question by question, as in the matter of female subjugation, many of the elites in the global culture have come to argue that, at minimum, there are limits to pluralism, that integration and assimilation in the form of modernization (this is what we call the new global culture) are necessary. And some cultures are wrong and therefore have to change.

It can be argued, then, that some cultures have faults, that they are "wrong" in some aspect of what is required in global human society. For the good of the larger society, those cultures can be forced to change their practices, to eliminate a part of themselves. What we have established in Afghanistan is that one culture can use armies and massive destruction against another to force it to change, in part because it wasn't sufficiently pluralistic, but also in part because there is a larger culture that has to control its subcultures in order for the systemic body to continue to exist.

From here it is easy to argue that cultures with practices unacceptable on a universal human rights level should be allowed to perish altogether, not just be offered an opportunity to adapt. Another internal contradiction of pluralism is that every culture, every set of religious beliefs, every tribal redoubt will exist for all time. Some can't, and shouldn't. We need to face the fact that not every "primitive" culture can modernize and still be the same culture. Those educated to be architects and engineers won't have the time for hunting and gathering as central activities of life. Social Darwinists would argue that, in at least some cases, cultures will sink of their own weight—and should be allowed to.

The next step, though, is the most difficult one. What if a culture resists all efforts to make it be more pluralistic or more modern? Does the larger society have the right to eliminate the lesser culture entirely? A case can be made that a culture that will not leave behind its practices of slavery should be destroyed, just as the United States is effectively eliminating Taliban society and attacking the culture of fundamentalist Islam. There has been widespread approval for this effort, both in the West and elsewhere. But won't this just be Western "jihad"?

So, in the end, we'll become them. We'll fight fire with fire. Head to head, civilizations will fight each other until one is destroyed. This is the course we are embarked on now. Fouad Ajami has the only real alternative solution. It is not a pluralist solution. It is absorption and integration. One society must absorb the other, or both must give on some critical values. Anthropologist Geert Hofstede, along with many others, argues that values are set in the young (before age ten). Here is where they must be changed, within families or within schools. Here is the solution. How do we get into the schools of Afghanistan and other societies? Here is where George W. Bush was at least partly right. It is not the Special Forces, it is the Peace Corps. This is the new paradigm, the new construct that we must use in order to meaningfully address the underlying causes of terrorism. Now American civilization simply needs to face up to putting its resources into the proper tool.

Chapter 14

THE RELIGIOUS ROOTS OF CONTEMPORARY TERRORISM

MARK JUERGENSMEYER

Perhaps nothing demonstrated so vividly the shocking return of religion to public affairs than the horrific images of the September 11, 2001, aerial assaults on the World Trade Center and the Pentagon. As the twin towers crumbled in a cloud of dust and the identities and motives of the perpetrators began to emerge, the initial question of why anyone would do such a thing turned to an even more perplexing query: Why would anyone want to do such a thing in the name of God?

This is a question that has arisen frequently in the post–Cold War world. The Al Qaeda network has not been alone in the religious assault on the secular state. In the last fifteen years religion seems to have been connected with violence everywhere—from the World Trade Center bombings to suicide attacks in Israel and Palestine; assassinations in India, Israel, Egypt, and Algeria; nerve gas in the Tokyo subways; abortion clinic killings in Florida; and the bombing of Oklahoma City's federal building. What unites these disparate acts of violence is their perpetrators' hatred of the global reach of the modern secular state, and the image of warfare that gives meaning to their sporadic acts of violence.

What is odd about this war is not only the difficulty in defining it and the non-state, transnational character of its forces, but also the motivation of the opposition that has been attributed to religion. The tradition of secular politics from the time of the Enlightenment has comfortably ignored religion, marginalized its role in public life, and frequently co-opted it for its own civil religion of public religiosity. No one in the secular world could have predicted that the first confrontations of the twenty-first century would involve, of all things, religion—secularism's old, long-banished foe.

Religious activists are puzzling anomalies in the secular world. Most religious people and their organizations are either firmly supportive of the secular state or quiescently uninterested in it. Osama bin Laden's Al Qaeda network, like most of the new religious activists, comprises a small group at the extreme end of a hostile subculture that itself is a small minority within the larger world of their religious cultures. Osama bin Laden is no more representative of Islam than Timothy McVeigh is of Christianity, or Japan's Shoko Asahara is of Buddhism.

Still one cannot deny that the ideals and ideas of activists like bin Laden are authentically and thoroughly religious and could conceivably become popular among their religious compatriots. The authority of religion has given bin Laden's cadres the moral legitimacy of employing violence in their assault on the very symbol of global economic power. It has also provided the metaphor of cosmic war, an image of spiritual struggle that every religion has within its repository of symbols—the fight between good and bad, truth and evil. In this sense, then, the attack on the World Trade Center was very religious. It was meant to be catastrophic, an act of biblical proportions.

What is striking about religious terrorism is that it has no obvious military purpose—it is almost exclusively symbolic. These are acts meant for television: for the news-format channels around the world and especially for al Jazeera, the Qatar-based television station that has such influence among the politicized elements of the Islamic world. The extraordinary assault on the World Trade Center, then, was a kind of perverse performance of power meant to ennoble the perpetrators' view of the world and to draw the television audience into their view of global war.

The September 11, 2001, attacks on the World Trade Center and the Pentagon—although unusual in their scale—are remarkably similar to many other acts of religious terrorism around the world. In my comparative study of religious terrorism I found a strikingly similar pattern.[1] In each case, concepts of cosmic war are accompanied by strong claims of moral justification and enduring absolutism that transforms worldly struggles into sacred battles. It is not so much that religion has become politicized, but that politics have become religionized. Worldly struggles have been lifted onto the high proscenium of sacred battle.

This is what makes religious terrorism so difficult to combat. Its enemies have become satanized: One cannot negotiate with them or easily compromise. The rewards for those who fight for the cause are trans-temporal, and the time lines of their struggles are vast. Most social and political struggles have looked for conclusions within the lifetimes of their participants. But religious struggles have taken generations to succeed. The leaders of Hamas have claimed that they can persevere even in the face of Israel's overwhelming military superiority. "Palestine was occupied before, for two hundred years," the political head of Hamas reminded me in an interview at his home in Khan Yunis in Gaza. He assured me that he and his Palestinian comrades "can wait again—at least that long."[2]

In some cases religious activists have been prepared to wait for eons—and some struggles have not been expected to be completed in human history. They must await their fulfillment in some trans-temporal realm. There has been no need, therefore, to compromise one's goals in a struggle that has been waged in divine time and with heaven's rewards. No need, also, to contend with society's laws and limitations when one has been obeying a higher authority. In spiritualizing violence, therefore, religion has given terrorism a remarkable power.

Ironically, the reverse is also true: Terrorism has given religion power as well. Although sporadic acts of terrorism do not lead to the establishment of new religious states, they make the political potency of religious ideology impossible to ignore. Along with empowering individuals and movements, therefore, violence has empowered religion—it has given religious organizations and ideas a public attention and importance that they have not enjoyed for many years. In modern American and Europe, it has given religion a prominence in public life that it has not held since before the Enlightenment over two centuries ago.

Empowering Religion

Although each of the violent religious movements that have emerged around the world has its own distinctive culture and history, I have found that they have several things in common regarding their attitudes towards religion in society. First, they reject the compromises with liberal values and secular institutions that most mainstream religion has made, be it Christian, Muslim, Jewish, Hindu, Sikh, or Buddhist. Second, radical religious movements refuse to observe the boundaries that secular society has set around religion—keeping it private rather than allowing it to intrude into public spaces. And third, these movements try to create a new form of religiosity that rejects what they regard as weak modern substitutes for the more vibrant and demanding forms of religion that they imagine to be essential to their religion's origins.

One of the men accused of bombing the World Trade Center in 1993 told me in a prison interview that the critical moment in his religious life came when he realized that he could not compromise his Islamic integrity with the easy vices offered by modern society. The convicted terrorist, Mahmud Abouhalima, claimed that the early part of his life was spent running away from himself. Although involved in radical Egyptian Islamic movements since his college years in Alexandria, he felt there was no place where he could settle down. He told me that the low point came when he was in Germany, trying to live the way that he imagined Europeans and Americans carried on: a life in which the superficial comforts of sex and inebriates masked an internal emptiness and despair. Abouhalima said his return to Islam as the center of his life carried with it a renewed sense of obligation to make Islamic society truly Islamic—to "struggle against oppression and injustice" wherever it existed. What was now constant, Abouhalima said, was his family and his faith. Islam was both "a rock and a pillar of mercy."[3] But it was not the Islam of liberal, modern Muslims; they, he felt, had compromised the tough and disciplined life the faith demanded.

In Abouhalima's case, he wanted his religion to be hard, not soft like the humiliating, mind-numbing comforts of secular modernity. Activists such as Abouhalima—and Osama bin Laden—have imagined themselves to be defenders of ancient faiths. But in fact they have created new forms of religiosity: like many present-day religious leaders they have used the language of traditional religion in order to build bulwarks around aspects of modernity that have threatened them, and to suggest ways out of the mindless humiliation of modern life. It was vital to their image of religion, however, that it be perceived as ancient.

The need for religion—a "hard" religion, as Abouhalima called it—was a response to the soft treachery they had observed in the new societies around them. The modern secular world that Abouhalima and the others inhabited was a dangerous, chaotic, and violent sea for which religion was an anchor in a harbor of calm. At some deep and almost transcendent level of their consciousnesses, they sensed their lives slipping out of control; and they felt both responsible for the disarray and a victim of it. To be abandoned by religion in such a world would mean a loss of their own individual locations and identities. In fashioning a "traditional religion" of their own making they exposed their concerns not so much with their religious, ethnic, or national communities, but with their own personal, perilous selves.

Assaults on Secularism

These intimate concerns have been prompted by the perceived failures of public institutions. As Pierre Bourdieu has observed, social structures never have a disembodied reality; they are always negotiated by individuals in their own strategies for maintaining self-identity and success in life. Such institutions are legitimized by the "symbolic capital" they accrue through the collective trust of many individuals.[4] When that symbolic capital is devalued, when political and religious institutions undergo what the German social philosopher, Jurgen Habermas, has called a "crisis of legitimacy," this devaluation of authority is experienced not only as a political problem but as an intensely personal one, as a loss of agency.[5]

This sense of a personal loss of power in the face of chaotic political and religious authorities is common, and I believe critical, to Osama bin Laden's Al Qaeda group and most other movements for Christian, Muslim, Jewish, Sikh, Buddhist, and Hindu nationalism around the world. The syndrome begins with the perception that the public world has gone awry, and the suspicion that behind this social confusion lies a great spiritual and moral conflict, a cosmic battle between the forces of order and chaos, good and evil. Such a conflict is understandably violent, a violence that is often felt by the victimized activist as powerlessness, either individually or in association with others of his gender, race or ethnicity. The government—already delegitimized—is perceived to be in league with the forces of chaos and evil.

One of the reasons secular government is easily labeled as the enemy of religion is that to some degree it is. By its nature, the secular state is opposed to the idea that religion should have a role in public life. From the time that modern secular nationalism emerged in the eighteenth century as a product of the European Enlightenment's political values, it did so with a distinctly antireligious, or at least anticlerical, posture. The ideas of John Locke about the origins of a civil community, and the "social contract" theories of Jean Jacques Rousseau, required very little commitment to religious belief. Although they allowed for a divine order that made the rights of humans possible, their ideas had the effect of taking religion—at least Church religion—out of public life. At the time, religious "enemies of the Enlightenment"—as the historian, Darrin McMahon, described them in a fascinating book on the religious roots of the far right—protested religion's public demise.[6] But their views were submerged in a wave of approval for a new view of social order in which secular nationalism was thought to be virtually a natural law, universally applicable and morally right.

Post-Enlightenment modernity proclaimed the death of religion. Modernity signaled not only the demise of the Church's institutional authority and clerical control but also the loosening of religion's ideological and intellectual grip on society. Scientific reasoning and the moral claims of the secular social contract replaced theology and the Church as the bases for truth and social identity. The result of religion's devaluation has been "a general crisis of religious belief," as Bourdieu has put it.[7]

In countering this disintegration, resurgent religious activists have proclaimed the death of secularism. They have dismissed the efforts of secular culture and its forms of nationalism to replace religion. They have challenged the notion that secular society and the modern nation-state are able to provide the moral fiber that unites national communities, or give it the ideological strength to sustain states buffeted by ethical, economic, and military failures. Their message has been easy to believe and has been widely received because the failures of the secular state have been so real.

Antiglobalism

The moral leadership of the secular state was increasingly challenged in the last decade of the twentieth century, following the breakup of the Cold War and the rise of a global economy. The Cold War provided contesting models of moral politics—communism and democracy—that were replaced with a global market that weakened national sovereignty and was conspicuously devoid of political ideals. The global economy became controlled by transnational businesses accountable to no single governmental authority and with no clear ideological or moral standards of behavior. But while both Christian and Enlightenment values were left behind, transnational commerce did transport aspects of westernerized popular culture to the rest of the world. American and European music, videos, and films were beamed across national boundaries, where they threatened to obliterate local and traditional forms of artistic expression.

Added to this social confusion were convulsive shifts in political power that followed the breakup of the Soviet Union and the collapse of Asian economies at the end of the twentieth century. The public sense of insecurity that came in the wake of these cataclysmic global changes was felt not only in the societies of those nations that were economically devastated by them—especially countries in the former Soviet Union—but also in economically stronger industrialized societies. The United States, for example; saw a remarkable degree of disaffection with its political leaders and witnessed the rise of right-wing religious movements that fed on the public's perception of the inherent immorality of government.

Is the rise of religious terrorism related to these global changes? We know that some groups associated with violence in industrialized societies have had an antimodernist political agenda. At the extreme end of this religious rejection in the United States were members of the American antiabortion group, Defensive Action; the Christian militia and Christian Identity movement; and isolated groups such as the Branch Davidian sect in Waco, Texas. Similar attitudes towards secular government emerged in Israel—the religious nationalist ideology of the Kach party was an extreme example—and as the Aum Shinrikyo movement has demonstrated, in Japan. Like the United States, contentious groups within these countries were disillusioned about the ability of secular leaders to guide their countries' destinies. They identified government as the enemy.

The global shifts that have given rise to antimodernist movements have also affected less-developed nations. India's Jawaharlal Nehru, Egypt's Gamal Abdel Nasser, and Iran's Riza Shah Pahlavi once were committed to creating versions of America—or a kind of cross between America and the Soviet Union—in their own countries. But new generations of leaders no longer believed in the Westernized visions of Nehru, Nasser, or the shah. Rather, they were eager to complete the process of decolonization and build new, indigenous nationalisms.

When activists in Algeria who demonstrated against the crackdown against the Islamic Salvation Front in 1991 proclaimed that they were continuing the war of liberation against French colonialism, they had the ideological rather than political reach of European influence in mind. Religious activists such as the Algerian leaders, the Ayatullah Khomeini in Iran, Sheik Ahmed Yassin in Palestine, Sayyid Qutb and his disciple, Sheik Omar Abdul Rahman in Egypt, L.K. Advani in India, and Sant Jarnail Singh Bhindranwale in India's Punjab have asserted the legitimacy of a postcolonial national identity based on traditional culture.[8]

The result of this disaffection with the values of the modern West has been what I have earlier described as a "loss of faith" in the ideological form of that culture, secular nationalism.[9] Although a few years ago it would have been a startling notion, the idea has now become virtually commonplace that secular nationalism—the idea that the nation is rooted in a secular compact rather than religious or ethnic identity—is in crisis. In many parts of the world it is seen as an alien cultural construction, one closely linked with what has been called "the project of modernity."[10] In such cases, religious alternatives to secular ideologies have had extraordinary appeal.

This uncertainty about what constitutes a valid basis for national identity is a political form of postmodernism. In Iran it has resulted in the rejection of a modern Western political regime and the creation of a successful religious state. Increasingly, even secular scholars in the West have recognized that religious ideologies might offer an alternative to modernity in the political sphere.[11] Yet, what lies beyond modernity is not necessarily a new form of political order, religious or not. In nations formerly under Soviet control, for example, the specter of the future beyond the socialist form of modernity has been one of cultural anarchism.

The Al Qaeda network associated with Osama bin Laden takes religious violence to yet another level. The implicit attacks on global economic and political systems that are leveled by religious nationalists from Algeria to Indonesia are made explicit: America is the enemy. Moreover, it is a war waged not on a national plane but a transnational one. Their agenda is not for any specific form of religious nation-state but an inchoate vision of a global rule of religious law. Rather than religious nationalists, transnational activists like bin Laden are guerilla antiglobalists.

Postmodern Terror

bin Laden and his vicious acts have a credibility in some quarters of the world because of the uncertainties of this moment in global history. The fear that there will be a spiritual as well as a political collapse at modernity's center has, in many parts of the world, led to terror. Both violence and religion have appeared at times when authority is in question, since they are both ways of challenging and replacing authority. One gains its power from force and the other from its claims to ultimate order. The combination of the two in acts of religious terrorism has been a potent assertion indeed.

Regardless of whether the perpetrators consciously intend them to be political acts, all public acts of violence have political consequences. Insofar as they have been attempts to reshape the public order, they have been examples of what Jose Casanova has called the increasing "deprivatization" of religion.[12] In various parts of the world where attempts have been made by defenders of religion to reclaim the center of public attention and authority, religious terrorism is often the violent face of these attempts.

The postmodern religious rebels such as those who rally to the side of Osama bin Laden have therefore been neither anomalies nor anachronisms. From Algeria to Idaho, their small but potent groups of violent activists have represented masses of potential supporters, and they have exemplified currents of thinking and cultures of commitment that have risen to counter the prevailing modernism—the ideology of individualism and skepticism—that in the past three centuries emerged from the European Enlightenment and spread throughout the world. They have come to hate secular governments with an almost transcendent passion. They have dreamed of revolutionary changes that would establish a godly social order in the rubble of what the citizens of most secular societies have regarded as modern, egalitarian democracies. Their enemies have seemed to most people to be both benign and banal—such symbols of prosperity and authority as the World Trade Center.

The logic of this kind of militant religiosity has therefore been difficult for many people to comprehend. Yet its challenge has been profound, for it has contained a fundamental critique of the world's post-Enlightenment secular culture and politics.

Acts of religious terrorism have thus been attempts to purchase public recognition of the legitimacy of its view of the world at war with the currency of violence. Since religious authority can provide a ready-made replacement for secular leadership, it is no surprise that when secular authority has been deemed to be morally insufficient, the challenges to their legitimacy and the attempts to gain support for their rivals have been based in religion. When the proponents of religion have asserted their claims to be the moral force under-girding public order, they sometimes have done so with the kind of power that a confused society can graphically recognize—the force of terror.

What the perpetrators of such acts of terror expect, and indeed welcome, is a response as vicious as the acts themselves. By goading secular authorities in responding to terror with terror, they hope to accomplish two things—to make the monster that they have claimed that the secular enemy is, and to bring to surface the great war that they had told their potential supporters was hidden but real. When the American missiles began to fall in Afghanistan on October 2, less than three weeks after the September 11 attacks, the Al Qaeda forces must initially have been exhilarated, for the war they had anticipated for so long had finally arrived. Its outcome, however, likely gave them less satisfaction: Their bases were routed, their leadership demolished, and the Muslim world did not rise up in support in the numbers and enthusiasm they had expected. Yet the time line of religious warfare is long, and the remnant forces of Al Qaeda most likely still yearn for the final confrontation. They are assured that the glorious victory will ultimately be achieved, for they are certain that it is, after all, God's war, not theirs.

Notes

1. Mark Juergensmeyer, *Terror in the Mind of God: The Global Rise of Religious Violence*. Excerpts from this book have been utilized for this chapter.
2. Author's interview with Dr. Abdul Aziz Rantisi, co-founder and political leader of Hamas; Khan Yunis, Gaza, March 1, 1998.
3. Interview with Abouhalima, September 30, 1997.
4. Pierre Bourdieu, *Language and Symbolic Power*, (Cambridge, Mass.: Harvard University Press, 1993):72–76. See also his *Outline of a Theory of Practice,* trans. Richard Nice (Cambridge: Cambridge University Press, 1977):171–83.
5. Jurgen Habermas, *Legitimation Crisis,* trans. Thomas McCarthy, (Boston: Beacon Press, 1975).
6. Darrin McMahon, *Enemies of the Enlightenment: The French Counter-Enlightenment and the Making of Modernity* (New York: Oxford University Press, 2001).
7. Bourdieu, *Language and Symbolic Power,* 116.

8. For a forceful statement of this thesis, see Partha Chatterjee, *The Nation and Its Fragments: Colonial and Postcolonial Histories* (Princeton: Princeton University Press, 1993).

9. Juergensmeyer, *The New Cold War?* (Berkeley, Calif.: University of California Press, 1993):11–25.

10. Jurgen Habermas, "Modernity—An Incomplete Project," reprinted in *Interpretive Social Science: A Second Look*, ed. Paul Rabinow and William M. Sullivan (Berkeley: University of California Press, 1987):148.

11. See, for instance, Roger Friedland, "When God Walks in History: The Institutional Politics of Religious Nationalism," in *International Sociology* 14 (September 1999):301–319.

12. Jose Casanova, *Public Religions in the Modern World* (Chicago: University of Chicago Press, 1994):211.

Chapter 15

THE ROOTS OF MUSLIM RAGE

BERNARD LEWIS

. . . Islam is one of the world's great religions. . . . Islam has brought comfort and peace of mind to countless millions of men and women. It has given dignity and meaning to drab and impoverished lives. It has taught people of different races to live in brotherhood and people of different creeds to live side by side in reasonable tolerance. It inspired a great civilization in which others besides Muslims lived creative and useful lives and which, by its achievement, enriched the whole world. But Islam, like other religions, has also known periods when it inspired in some of its followers a mood of hatred and violence. It is [the West's] misfortune that part, though by no means all or even most, of the Muslim world is now going through such a period, and that much, though again not all, of that hatred is directed against [it].

We should not exaggerate the dimensions of the problem. The Muslim world is far from unanimous in its rejection of the West, nor have the Muslim regions of the Third World been the most passionate and the most extreme in their hostility. . . . But there is a Libya, an Iran, and a Lebanon, and a surge of hatred that distresses, alarms, and above all baffles Americans.

At times this hatred goes beyond hostility to specific interests or actions or policies or even countries and becomes a rejection of Western civilization as such, not only what it does but what it is, and the principles and values that it practices and professes. These are indeed seen as innately evil, and those who promote or accept them as the "enemies of God."

This phrase, which recurs so frequently in the language of the Iranian leadership, in both their judicial proceedings and their political pronouncements, must seem very strange to the modern outsider, whether religious or secular. The idea that God has enemies, and needs human help in order to identify and dispose of them, is a little difficult to assimilate. It is not, however, all that alien. The concept of the enemies of God is familiar in preclassical and classical antiquity, and in both the Old and New Testaments, as well as in the Koran. A particularly relevant version of the idea occurs in the dualist religions of ancient Iran, whose cosmogony assumed not one but two supreme powers. The Zoroastrian devil, unlike the Christian or Muslim or Jewish devil, is not one of God's creatures performing some of God's more mysterious tasks but an independent power, a supreme force of evil engaged in a cosmic struggle against God. This belief influenced a number of Christian, Muslim, and Jewish sects, through Manichaeism and other routes. The almost forgotten religion of the Manichees has given its name to the perception of problems as a stark and simple conflict between matching forces of pure good and pure evil.

The Koran is of course strictly monotheistic, and recognizes one God, one universal power only. There is a struggle in human hearts between good and evil, between God's commandments and the tempter, but this is seen as a struggle ordained by God, with its outcome preordained by God, serving as a test of mankind, and not, as in some of the old dualist religions, a struggle in which mankind has a crucial part to play in bringing about the victory of good over evil. Despite this monotheism, Islam, like Judaism and Christianity, was at various stages influenced, especially in Iran, by the dualist idea of a cosmic clash of good and evil, light and darkness, order and chaos, truth and falsehood, God and the Adversary, variously known as devil, Iblis, Satan, and by other names.

The Rise of the House of Unbelief

In Islam the struggle of good and evil very soon acquired political and even military dimensions. Muhammad, it will be recalled, was not only a prophet and a teacher, like the founders of other religions; he was also the head of a polity and of a community, a ruler and a soldier. Hence his struggle involved a state and its armed forces. If the fighters in the war for Islam, the holy war "in the path of God," are fighting for God, it follows that their opponents are fighting against God. And since God is in principle the sovereign, the supreme head of the Islamic state—and the Prophet and, after the Prophet, the caliphs are his vicegerents—then God as sovereign commands the army. The army is God's army and the enemy is God's enemy. The duty of God's soldiers is to dispatch God's enemies as quickly as possible to the place where God will chastise them—that is to say, the afterlife.

Clearly related to this is the basic division of mankind as perceived in Islam. Most, probably all, human societies have a way of distinguishing between themselves and others: insider and outsider, in-group and out-group, kinsman or neighbor and foreigner. These definitions not only define the outsider but also, and perhaps more particularly, help to define and illustrate our perception of ourselves.

In the classical Islamic view, to which many Muslims are beginning to return, the world and all mankind are divided into two: the House of Islam, where the Muslim law and faith prevail, and the rest, known as the House of Unbelief or the House of War, which it is the duty of Muslims ultimately to bring to Islam. But the greater part of the world is still outside Islam, and even inside the Islamic lands, according to the view of the Muslim radicals, the faith of Islam has been undermined and the law of Islam has been abrogated. The obligation of holy war therefore begins at home and continues abroad, against the same infidel enemy.

Like every other civilization known to human history, the Muslim world in its heyday saw itself as the center of truth and enlightenment, surrounded by infidel barbarians whom it would in due course enlighten and civilize. But between the different groups of barbarians there was a crucial difference. The barbarians to the east and the south were polytheists and idolaters, offering no serious threat and no competition at all to Islam. In the north and west, in contrast, Muslims from an early date recognized a genuine rival—a competing world religion, a distinctive civilization inspired by that religion, and an empire that, though much smaller than theirs, was no less ambitious in its claims and aspirations. This was the entity known to itself and others as Christendom, a term that was long almost identical with Europe.

The struggle between these rival systems has now lasted for some fourteen centuries. It began with the advent of Islam, in the seventh century, and has continued virtually to the present day. It has consisted of a long series of attacks and counterattacks, jihads and crusades, conquests and reconquests. For the first thousand years Islam was advancing, Christendom in retreat and under threat. The new faith conquered the old Christian lands of the Levant and North Africa, and invaded Europe, ruling for a while in Sicily, Spain, Portugal, and even parts of France. The attempt by the Crusaders to recover the lost lands of Christendom in the east was held and thrown back, and even the Muslims' loss of southwestern Europe to the Reconquista was amply compensated by the Islamic advance into southeastern Europe, which twice reached as far as Vienna. For the past three hundred years, since the failure of the second Turkish siege of Vienna in 1683 and the rise of the European colonial empires in Asia and Africa, Islam has been on the defensive, and the Christian and post-Christian civilization of Europe and her daughters has brought the whole world, including Islam, within its orbit.

For a long time now there has been a rising tide of rebellion against this Western paramountcy, and a desire to reassert Muslim values and restore Muslim greatness. The Muslim has suffered successive stages of defeat. The first was his loss of domination in the world, to the advancing power of Russia and the West. The second was the undermining of his authority in his own country, through an invasion of foreign ideas and laws and ways of life and sometimes even foreign rulers or settlers, and the enfranchisement of native non-Muslim elements. The third—the last straw—was the challenge to his mastery in his own house, from emancipated women and rebellious children. It was too much to endure, and the outbreak of rage against these alien, infidel, and incomprehensible forces that had subverted his dominance, disrupted his society, and finally violated the sanctuary of his home was inevitable. It was also natural that this rage should be directed primarily against the millennial enemy and should draw its strength from ancient beliefs and loyalties. . . .

[During the 1980s the Islamic leaders of this] widespread and widening religious revival sought out and identified their enemies as the enemies of God, and gave them "a local habitation and a name" in the Western Hemisphere. Suddenly, or so it seemed, America had become the archenemy, the incarnation of evil, the diabolic opponent of all that is good, and specifically, for Muslims, of Islam. Why?

Some Familiar Accusations

. . . If we [focus on] the specific, there is no lack of individual policies and actions, pursued and taken by individual Western governments, that have aroused the passionate anger of Middle Eastern and other Islamic peoples. Yet all too often, when these policies are abandoned and the problems resolved, there is only a local and temporary alleviation. The French have left Algeria, the British have left Egypt, the Western oil companies have left their oil wells, the westernizing Shah has left Iran—yet the generalized resentment of the fundamentalists and other extremists against the West and its friends remains and grows and is not appeased.

The cause most frequently adduced for anti-American feeling among Muslims today is American support for Israel. This support is certainly a factor of importance, increasing with nearness and involvement. But here again there are some oddities, difficult to explain in terms of a single, simple cause. In the early days of the foundation of Israel, while the United States maintained a certain distance, the Soviet Union granted immediate *de jure* recognition and support, and arms sent from a Soviet satellite, Czechoslovakia, saved the infant state of Israel from defeat and death in its first weeks of life. Yet there seems to have been no great ill will toward the Soviets for these policies, and no corresponding good will toward the United States. In 1956 it was the United States that intervened, forcefully and decisively, to secure the withdrawal of Israeli, British, and French forces from Egypt—yet in the late 1950s and 1960s it was to the Soviets, not America, that the rulers of Egypt, Syria, Iraq, and other states turned for arms; it was with the Soviet bloc that they formed bonds of solidarity at the United Nations and in the world generally. More recently, the rulers of the Islamic Republic of Iran have offered the most principled and uncompromising denunciation of Israel and Zionism. Yet even these leaders, before as well as after the death of Ayatollah Ruhollah Khomeini, when they decided for reasons of their own to enter into a dialogue of sorts, found it easier to talk to Jerusalem than to Washington. At the same time, Western hostages in Lebanon, many of them devoted to Arab causes and some of them converts to Islam, are seen and treated by their captors as limbs of the Great Satan.

Another explanation, more often heard from Muslim dissidents, attributes anti-American feeling to American support for hated regimes, seen as reactionary by radicals, as impious by conservatives, as corrupt and tyrannical by both. This accusation has some plausibility, and could help to explain why an essentially inner-directed, often anti-nationalist movement should turn against a foreign power. But it does not suffice, especially since support for such regimes has been limited both in extent and—as the Shah discovered—in effectiveness.

Clearly, something deeper is involved than these specific grievances, numerous and important as they may be—something deeper that turns every disagreement into a problem and makes every problem insoluble.

This revulsion against America, more generally against the West, is by no means limited to the Muslim world; nor have Muslims, with the exception of the Iranian mullahs and their disciples elsewhere, experienced and exhibited the more virulent forms of this feeling. The mood of disillusionment and hostility has affected many other parts of the world, and has even reached some elements in the United States. It is from these last, speaking for themselves and claiming to speak for the oppressed peoples of the Third World, that the most widely publicized explanations—and justifications—of this rejection of Western civilization and its values have of late been heard.

The accusations are familiar. We of the West are accused of sexism, racism, and imperialism, institutionalized in patriarchy and slavery, tyranny and exploitation. To these charges, and to others as heinous, we have no option but to plead guilty—not as Americans, nor yet as Westerners, but simply as human beings, as members of the human race. In none of these sins are we the only sinners, and in some of them we are very far from being the worst. The treatment of women in the Western world, and more generally in Christendom, has always been unequal and often oppressive, but even at its worst it was rather better than the rule of polygamy and concubinage that has otherwise been the almost universal lot of womankind on this planet.

Is racism, then, the main grievance? Certainly the word figures prominently in publicity addressed to Western, Eastern European, and some Third World audiences. It figures less prominently in what is written and published for home consumption, and has become a generalized and meaningless term of abuse—rather like "fascism," which is nowadays imputed to opponents even by spokesmen for one-party, nationalist dictatorships of various complexions and shirt colors.

Slavery is today universally denounced as an offense against humanity, but within living memory it has been practiced and even defended as a necessary institution, established and regulated by divine law. The peculiarity of the peculiar institution, as Americans once called it, lay not in its existence but in its abolition. Westerners were the first to break the consensus of acceptance and to outlaw slavery, first at home, then in the other territories they controlled, and finally wherever in the world they were able to exercise power or influence—in a word, by means of imperialism.

Is imperialism, then, the grievance? Some Western powers, and in a sense Western civilization as a whole, have certainly been guilty of imperialism, but are we really to believe that in the expansion of Western Europe there was a quality of moral delinquency lacking in such earlier, relatively innocent expansions as those of the Arabs or the Mongols or the Ottomans, or in more recent expansions such as that which brought the rulers of Muscovy to the Baltic, the Black Sea, the Caspian, the Hindu Kush, and the Pacific Ocean? In having practiced sexism, racism, and imperialism, the West was merely following the common practice of mankind through the millennia of recorded history. Where it is distinct from all other civilizations is in having recognized, named, and tried, not entirely without success, to remedy these historic diseases. And that is surely a matter for congratulation, not condemnation. We do not hold Western medical science in general, or Dr. Parkinson and Dr. Alzheimer in particular, responsible for the diseases they diagnosed and to which they gave their names.

Of all these offenses the one that is most widely, frequently, and vehemently denounced is undoubtedly imperialism—sometimes just Western, sometimes Eastern (that is, Soviet) and Western alike. But the way this term is used in the literature of Islamic fundamentalists often suggests that it may not carry quite the same meaning for them as for its Western critics. In many of these writings the term "imperialist" is given a distinctly religious significance, being used in association, and sometimes interchangeably, with "missionary," and denoting a form of attack that includes the Crusades as well as the modern colonial empires. One also sometimes gets the impression that the offense of imperialism is not—as for Western critics—the domination by one people over another but rather the allocation of roles in this relationship. What is truly evil and unacceptable is the domination of infidels over true believers. For true believers to rule misbelievers is proper and natural, since this provides for the maintenance of the holy law, and gives the misbelievers both the opportunity and the incentive to embrace the true faith. But for misbelievers to rule over true believers is blasphemous and unnatural, since it leads to the corruption of religion and morality in society, and to the flouting or even the abrogation of God's law. . . . Fundamentalist leaders [see] in Western civilization the greatest challenge to the way of life that they wish to retain or restore for their people.

A Clash of Civilizations

The origins of secularism in the West may be found in two circumstances—in early Christian teachings and, still more, experience, which created two institutions, Church and State; and in later Christian conflicts, which drove the two apart. Muslims, too, had their religious disagreements, but there was nothing remotely approaching the ferocity of the Christian struggles between Protestants and Catholics, which devastated Christian Europe in the sixteenth and seventeenth centuries and finally drove Christians in desperation to evolve a doctrine of the separation of religion from the state. Only by depriving religious institutions of coercive power, it seemed, could Christendom restrain the murderous intolerance and persecution that Christians had visited on followers of other religions and, most of all, on those who professed other forms of their own. Muslims experienced no such need and evolved no such doctrine. There was no need for secularism in Islam. . . .

At first the Muslim response to Western civilization was one of admiration and emulation—an immense respect for the achievements of the West, and a desire to imitate and adopt them. . . . In our own time this mood of admiration and emulation has, among many Muslims, given way to one of hostility and rejection. In part this mood is surely due to a feeling of humiliation—a growing awareness, among the heirs of an old, proud, and long dominant civilization, of having been overtaken, overborne, and overwhelmed by those whom they regarded as their inferiors. In part this mood is due to events in the Western world itself. . . . For vast numbers of Middle Easterners, Western-style economic methods brought poverty, Western-style political institutions brought tyranny, even Western-style warfare brought defeat. It is hardly surprising that so many were willing to listen to voices telling them that the old Islamic ways were best and that their only salvation was to throw aside the pagan innovations of the reformers and return to the True Path that God had prescribed for his people.

Ultimately, the struggle of the fundamentalists is against two enemies, secularism and modernism. The war against secularism is conscious and explicit, and there is by now a whole literature denouncing secularism as an evil neo-pagan force in the modern world and attributing it variously to the Jews, the West, and the United States. The war against modernity is for the most part neither conscious nor explicit, and is directed against the whole process of change that has taken place in the Islamic world in the past century or more and has transformed the political, economic, social, and even cultural structures of Muslim countries. Islamic fundamentalism has given an aim and a form to the otherwise aimless and formless resentment and anger of the Muslim masses at the forces that have devalued their traditional values and loyalties and, in the final analysis, robbed them of their beliefs, their aspirations, their dignity, and to an increasing extent even their livelihood.

There is something in the religious culture of Islam which inspired, in even the humblest peasant or peddler, a dignity and a courtesy toward others never exceeded and rarely equalled in other civilizations. And yet, in moments of upheaval and disruption, when the deeper passions are stirred, this dignity and courtesy toward others can give way to an explosive mixture of rage and hatred which impels even the government of an ancient and civilized country—even the spokesman of a great spiritual and ethical religion—to espouse kidnapping and assassination, and try to find, in the life of their Prophet, approval and indeed precedent for such actions.

The instinct of the masses is not false in locating the ultimate source of these cataclysmic changes in the West and in attributing the disruption of their old way of life to the impact of Western domination, Western influence, or Western precept and example. And since the United States is the legitimate heir of European civilization and the recognized and unchallenged leader of the West, the United States has inherited the resulting grievances and become the focus for the pent-up hate and anger. Two examples may suffice. In November of 1979 an angry mob attacked and burned the U.S. Embassy in Islamabad, Pakistan. The stated cause of the crowd's anger was the seizure of the Great Mosque in Mecca by a group of Muslim dissidents—an event in which there was no American involvement whatsoever. Almost ten years later, in February of 1989, again in Islamabad, the USIS center was attacked by angry crowds, this time to protest the publication of Salman Rushdie's *Satanic*

Verses. Rushdie is a British citizen of Indian birth, and his book had been published five months previously in England. But what provoked the mob's anger, and also the Ayatollah Khomeini's subsequent pronouncement of a death sentence on the author, was the publication of the book in the United States.

It should by now be clear that we are facing a mood and a movement far transcending the level of issues and policies and the governments that pursue them. This is no less than a clash of civilizations—the perhaps irrational but surely historic reaction of an ancient rival against our Judeo-Christian heritage, our secular present, and the worldwide expansion of both. It is crucially important that we on our side should not be provoked into an equally historic but also equally irrational reaction against that rival. . . .

Chapter 16

TERRORISM IN DEMOCRACIES: WHEN IT OCCURS, WHY IT FAILS[1]

TED ROBERT GURR

In the wake of the September 11 terrorist attacks, much speculation arose over the causes of this catastrophic new form of global terror as the world struggled to find answers to the challenge of reducing the probability that the future would be haunted by subsequent acts of international terrorism. My thesis is that the campaigns of domestic political terrorists in democratic societies almost invariably emerge out of larger conflicts, and that they reflect, in however distorted a form, the political beliefs and aspirations of a larger segment of society. Recognition of the changing nature of the relationship between violent activists and their community of support is essential to understanding the onset, persistence, and methods of bringing the frequency and lethality of terrorist activities under control. The test of the twenty-first century will be understanding the origins of terrorist movements as well as discovering how and why they decline. This thesis implies, among other things, that analysis of the ideologies and psychological traits of violent activists and of the sociodynamics of terrorist groups is incomplete unless we understand their reciprocal relations with larger publics. Implications of the argument for the success and failure of campaigns of international terrorism are discussed in the conclusion.

Two problems are examined in the light of this thesis. The first consists of the circumstances under which the political culture of communal and political minorities comes to provide a supportive climate of belief within which terrorism emerges and persists. The second consists of the processes by which these supportive climates erode—which they usually do. The general arguments are derived from conflict theory and from the observation of the dynamics of groups that have used terrorism in Western societies. Evidence from some specific episodes is cited in support of the arguments, but it is suggestive, not decisive. The purpose here is to set up plausible theoretical arguments that can and should be examined in future studies.

The theoretical arguments are specific to democratic societies, that is, to societies in which (1) there is organized expression of contending political views and (2) office holding and policy depend directly or indirectly on elections. Terrorist campaigns in authoritarian societies also require supportive climates of opinion, but police-state tactics ordinarily preclude any organized expression of oppositional opinion, especially its violent manifestations. The leaders of most authoritarian states have more latitude than elected officials in whether and how they respond to discontent and disorder. They are less concerned than democratic leaders with maintaining a politically acceptable balance between suppressing violence and accommodating or deterring those who support the purposes but not the tactics of terrorists.

The Political Context of Terrorism's Onset

The general proposition is that violent activism in democracies requires a climate of acceptance of unconventional means of political action among a support group. The support group is any social segment—a communal group, faction, political tendency, or class—whose members seek a particular kind of political change. There are two main routes by which (some of the members of) such groups come to accept extreme means: radicalization and reaction.

Radicalization refers to a process in which the group has been mobilized in pursuit of a social or political objective but has failed to make enough progress toward the objective to satisfy all activists. Some become discouraged, while others intensify their efforts, lose patience with conventional means of political action, and look for tactics that will have greater impact. This is the kind of situation in which modeling or "Imitative" behavior occurs. Impatience and frustration provide an expressive motivation (anger) and rationalistic grounds (dramatic episodes of violence elsewhere) that make it likely that some activists will decide to experiment with terror tactics. The choice is made, and justified, as a means to the original ends of radical reform, group autonomy, or whatever. And the dynamics of the process are such that the terrorists believe that they enjoy the support of some larger community in revolt.

Two North American terrorist groups of the 1960s and 1970s provide evidence of the process of radicalization and its bases of community support. The *Front de Liberātiōn du Québec* (FLQ) had its origins in the separatist sentiment that become widespread among French-speaking Canadians in the late 1950s and early 1960s. Disaffection with the policies of governments then in power in Québec and Ottawa was particularly intense in the growing class of young, urban Québecois men in skilled and technical occupations and in the teaching and liberal professions. The first important separatist organizations were founded in 1960. The FLQ was established by dissatisfied members of these groups, twenty-four of whom met in November 1962 to develop more radical but nonviolent forms of action for the cause of independence. In February 1963 three members of this group in turn rejected nonviolence and formed the FLQ.

The violent actions of the FLQ occurred in two distinct waves, one of them beginning in 1963, the second in 1968. Initially, adherents of the FLQ bombed military targets; then they extended their campaign to government buildings, the economic infrastructure, and targets that symbolized the FLQ's support of striking workers. Before the conclusion of the FLQ campaign in 1972 (for reasons examined later), people acting in its name carried out 169 actions resulting in eight deaths. The strength of separatist sentiment, of which the FLQ's campaigns were an extreme manifestation, is evident from the electoral success of the separatist *Parti Quebécois* (PQ), which won 23 percent of the provincial vote in the first election it contested, in December 1970.

The Weather Underground, the second case examined here, was the lineal descendent of the Students for a Democratic Society (SDS), which was founded in 1959 as an alliance of students, blacks (who soon left), and peace groups intent on influencing the politics of the Democratic party. Radicalized by the Vietnam War and the failure of mass political action to alter U.S. policy, the SDS split in 1969 into various factions, one of which was the Weathermen, later named the Weather Underground, then the Weather People. Its leadership, the Weather Bureau, attempted mass revolutionary action in the streets of Chicago in October 1969. They judged the strategy a failure in the face of overwhelming police response and went underground. The membership was purged and the remainder, perhaps fifty in all, organized communes called "focals" to carry out urban guerrilla warfare. A four-year campaign followed, during which there were nineteen dramatic bombings aimed at corporate offices, New York City police headquarters, the Capitol, and the Pentagon.

The psycho-politics of the New Left during the 1960s has been described as a crisis of legitimacy. The essential point is that the New Left was a mass movement that led, and fed upon, growing public opposition to U.S. involvement in Vietnam. Between 1965 and 1970, more than 3 million people were estimated to have taken part in antiwar demonstrations in the United States. By 1968–1969 more than half of the respondents to public opinion polls expressed verbal opposition to the war. Only a handful of the New Left were alienated enough to embrace revolutionary strategies, but many of them agreed with the objectives, if not the tactics, of the militant Weather People, and some provided active support for them. Testimony to the effectiveness of that support network is the fact that no Weather People were arrested during the early 1970s or after the voluntary cessation of their bombing campaign in 1975—except for those who chose, years later, to emerge from the underground.

Reaction is an analytically distinct process in which members of a regional, communal, or political group resort to terrorism in response to threatening social change or intervention by authorities. Whereas *radicalization* characterizes groups with future-oriented objectives, *reaction* occurs in defense of a group's threatened rights and status. Right-wing terrorism often is reactive in this sense, for example, the terrorism practiced by the Ku Klux Klan. The first Klan was established by Confederate veterans in 1867 who, along with like-minded groups, carried out a four-year campaign of coercion, threats, and terroristic violence against the supporters and agents of the Reconstruction state governments, which the North had imposed on the defeated South. They acted on behalf of, and generally with the active support of, white southerners. Moreover, many of their goals were achieved when state governments were restored to white southern control in the early 1870s and blacks were effectively disenfranchised.

The resurgence of terrorism by southern white supremacists after 1957 was a traditional response to new pressures from civil rights workers and the federal government. Acts of terror such as the bombing of black churches and assassinations of NAACP leaders peaked in the early 1960s when civil rights marches and voter-registration campaigns were at their peak, but in this instance terrorism failed to reverse change. Although both these episodes of reactionary terrorism enjoyed support among many rural and small-town southerners, the violent white supremacists of the 1960s could not count on the backing of the southern political elite or the urban middle and professional classes.

The question is whether there are analogues to reactionary, Klan-style terrorism in other democratic societies. One feature that distinguishes the process of reactionary terror is the fact that deadly violence is usually an early response to perceived threat rather than the culmination of a long process of radicalization. A related feature is the existence of a tradition of violent resistance in the affected community, which is more or less quickly activated by externally imposed change. An example of this is a small Canadian religious sect of Russian origin, the Sons of Freedom Doukhobors, who live in British Columbia. The Freedomites, as they are known, hold religiously conservative views, reject materialism, and oppose government regulation and public education. During episodes of purification and renunciation they have perpetrated waves of reactive terrorism against commercial and government buildings and against other Doukhobors; more than 120 such terrorist actions were carried out in the early 1960s.

Terrorist actions on behalf of regional minorities—such as the German-speakers of the Alto Adige in northern Italy during the early 1960s, and Basques and Corsicans from the 1960s to the present—also have some reactive characteristics. The militants claim to act in defense of a larger community whose integrity and well-being are at risk. One does not have to accept such claims at face value to recognize that these communally based terrorists, by invoking traditions of group autonomy, often elicit some community support because of latent resentment of ancient injustices and modern inequalities. The terrorism of some right-wing political groups in continental democracies has reactive characteristics as well. Neo-Nazis in Germany are marginal people with little or no prospects for political influence by conventional means. The processes of delegitimation and radicalization presumably evolve within small groups of believers, perhaps under the influence of old fighters who have never accepted the postwar political settlement. Their ideas are not tested in the democratic political arena because they reject its validity from the outset. When such groups do enter political combat, they tend to begin with violent means because they do not think other means are worth using. Something similar has happened among some small, right-wing extremist groups in the United States, such as the Aryan Nations. But most of the terrorist activities of these kinds of right-wing groups in contemporary Europe and North America have been short-lived, because they had little public support for their purposes even at the outset. In this respect they are different from the communally based terrorists identified earlier, who generally can count on some sympathetic support.

The terrorist insurgency of Catholics in Northern Ireland provides a final example, one that combines elements of radicalization and reaction. The fundamental issues that divide Catholic from Protestant need not be repeated here. What began in 1967–1969 was a process of radicalization among Northern Irish Catholics who, taking their cues from events in the United States, initiated a civil rights campaign. Ultraloyalist Protestants responded with coercion and violence, which provided an opening for intervention by the Irish Republican Army (IRA) on behalf of threatened Catholics. Military intervention by the British government, and the 1972 killing of Derry civil rights marchers, confirmed for many Northern Irish Catholics the justice of resistance by all means against the loyalists and the British. Opinion polls throughout the years of violence have shown majorities among Northern Irish Catholics favoring union with the Republic of Ireland, while the militant Sinn Fein—closely associated with the Provisional IRA (PIRA)—still commanded 35 percent of the Catholic vote in the early 1980s. But Catholics' ideological commitment to the Irish Republican cause gradually eroded was replaced by a war-weary acceptance of reconciliation and reformism within the political structure established by the Good Friday Accords of 1998.

The Political Psychology of Terrorism's Decline

The decline of public support for terrorism in Northern Ireland introduces the second topic, which is to specify the processes and conditions that undermine acceptance of violent political action by the terrorists' community of support. Most terrorist organizations have finite life spans, and their actions, plotted over time, represent one or a series of "waves" with distinctive phases of increase and decline. The life spans of groups using terrorist strategies have been studied by Martha Crenshaw. She identified 31 such groups that were active in Europe and North American democracies between the 1950s and 1980s. Twenty of those groups ceased to exist after an average of 6.5 years of activity. The most durable of the ongoing campaigns have been carried out on behalf of communal minorities like the Basques and the contending religious factions of Northern Ireland. ETA has used terror on behalf of autonomy for Spanish Basques almost continuously since 1959, and five terrorist organizations in Northern Ireland have been active from the 1960s and 1970s.[2]

Most of the major terrorist campaigns that began in Western societies in the 1960s and 1970s have ended. The issues that animated them may again lead to terrorism by militants using new names, though. Ethnic grievances and demands for autonomy are particularly likely to resurface in this way. Nonetheless domestic terrorism has been generally declining in most Western societies. Some quantitative documentation about particular movements illustrates this phenomenon:

Canada. Terrorist actions by Québec terrorists began in 1963 (twenty events), reached their highest level in 1968 (thirty-eight events), then declined to two in 1972 and, with the exception of a single bombing in 1980, have not recurred.

United States. Terrorism by the revolutionary left in the United States began with the 1970–1974 campaign of the Weather Underground. Five successor organizations, using a dozen different names, carried out bombings in the name of revolutionary causes into the mid-1980s, but with ever-fewer members and diminishing public attention. Federal Bureau of Investigation data show a decline in the number of incidents of political terrorism in the United States of all kinds from an average of 119 per year in 1975–1977 to twelve per year in the mid-1980s and three per year in the 1990s.

Puerto Rico. Puerto Rican nationalists on that island dependency have been responsible for the most deadly of contemporary terrorist campaigns based in North America. Since their first violent acts in 1950 they have been active sporadically on the island and the U.S. mainland. Major campaigns, which reached their peak in 1974–1977, ended in 1980 on the mainland with a series of arrests but continued for several more years in Puerto Rico. After a lull of several years, terrorism resumed on the island in 1986, but at a low level. For example there were five bombings in Puerto Rico in 1990, another two in 1991, and three in 1998.

Italy. Terrorist events of all kinds in Italy, most of them the work of the Red Brigades, numbered less than 400 per year in 1969–1970, peaked at more than 2,000 actions annually in 1978–1979, then declined to less than 100 per year in the mid-1980s.

Northern Ireland. In this, the most enduring and deadly of all contemporary terrorist campaigns in Western democracies, 2,532 people—nationalists, loyalists, security forces, and passers-by—died between January 1969 and the end of 1986. Yet the trend was unmistakably downward. In 1971–1973 the annual death toll averaged 300; in 1977–1979 the average was 97; in 1984–1986 it was 61.

The literature on terrorism is preoccupied with its causes and says little about the general circumstances responsible for such declines. Insofar as the question is addressed at all, it is assumed that movements decline as a result of some combination of security countermeasures and failure to achieve publicity or larger political objectives. I doubt that these answers are sufficient. They certainly seem inadequate to explain, for example, why revolutionary terrorism repeatedly reemerged in the Federal Republic of Germany from the 1960s to the 1980s despite its lack of achievements, many arrests, and intensive security measures; or why elements of the IRA continued a deadly campaign for three decades, even after a political settlement; or, for that matter, why ETA persists in a campaign, now more than forty years long, despite the achievement by Spanish Basques of a substantial measure of regional autonomy.

I propose to examine the conditions and events likely to undermine the larger basis of group support which, I have argued, is essential to sustain terrorist activities. The erosion of political support is not an immediate cause of decline in terrorist campaigns but an underlying one, and conditions the effects of almost all public policies directed at terrorism. Three general kinds of processes contribute to the erosion of support—backlash, reform, and deterrence.

Backlash is a widely observed phenomenon in the analysis of conflict processes. Acts of disruption and violence that are intended to attract favorable attention from a relevant public often have the opposite effect. Backlash was evident in the German public's hardening attitudes toward "revolutionary" acts by the Baader-Meinhof group and its main successor, the Red Army Faction, during the 1970s. But general public antagonism and its counterpart, support for strong countermeasures, were not fatal—evidently because a significant residue of sympathy for revolutionary action remained on the German left. A significant number of leftists with university backgrounds continued to be concentrated in some cities; their radical commitments and preferences for collective action provided a community of support for more violent militants—and may do so in the future.

Backlash within the group that initially supported the terrorists' cause is even more devastating to the militants than backlash among the larger public. If and when active support dries up, the group finds it increasingly difficult to attract new recruits, to get material resources, to find refuge among reliable sympathizers, or to avoid informants. Dramatic acts of violence directed against victims thought to be innocent are particularly likely to provide backlash. Sympathy and support also may be reduced through propaganda campaigns by public officials and the media that aim at discrediting terrorists' causes and their supposed allies. Support also can be undercut by counterterror strategies that raise the costs for ordinary citizens of tolerating the terrorists' presence.

The decline of support for the FLQ and the revolutionary left in the United States are illustrative. The decline of the FLQ in the early 1970s can be attributed directly to the successive kidnappings (by two separate FLQ cells) of James Cross, the British trade commissioner in Montreal, on 5 October 1970, and Pierre Laporte, the Québec minister of labor and immigration, five days later. The Ottawa government promptly proclaimed the War Measures Act, equivalent to a declaration of martial law, whereupon Laporte was killed and left in the trunk of an abandoned car. On 4 December, Cross's abductors traded his life for safe conduct to Cuba. Major labor unions in Québec formed a common front to denounce the FLQ, and the general public also seemed overwhelmingly in support of the emergency powers and the presence of the army in Québec. Almost simultaneously, in December 1970, the separatist *Parti Québecois* (PQ) came in second in the provincial election. Its *Manifesto,* issued a year later, proclaimed the need for struggle for national independence but also condemned political violence as "humanly immoral and politically pointless." In the Québec case it is evident that backlash did not discredit separatism as an objective; it discredited the FLQ and the use of terrorism as a means to greater autonomy.

The New Left in the United States, some members of which were revolutionaries and some reformers, never agreed on strategy. Many who advocated revolutionary objectives during the late 1960s thought revolution could be pursued nonviolently, whereas the handful who plotted strategies of violence sought conscientiously to avoid killing people. Nonetheless, a series of deadly episodes discredited revolutionary terrorism for virtually all the New Left. On 6 March 1970, before the Weather Underground planted its first bomb, three of its members died in accidental explosions that wrecked their bomb factory in a Greenwich Village townhouse. The next death also was accidental. Dr. Robert Fassnacht, a mathematics researcher at the University of Wisconsin, died on 24 August because he happened to be working late at the U.S. Army-supported Mathematics Research Center, where a bomb was set off by a freelance radical, Karleton Lewis Armstrong. These deaths reportedly led to considerable soul-searching among militants and persuaded some activists to give up more violent kinds of activism.

The Weather Underground itself avoided risking lives after the townhouse explosion, but the Symbionese Liberation Army (SLA) had no such compunctions. In 1973–1974 the SLA enjoyed a brief but spectacular career based on the exploits of its dozen members, white radicals of middle-class origin who had joined with black ex-convicts. The SLA echoed, almost parodied, the revolutionary rhetoric of the 1960s by advocating the "unity in love" of all oppressed people, redistribution of capital, dismantling of the prison system, and so forth. But the SLA's first revolutionary action was the 1973 murder of Oakland's black superintendent of schools, Marcus Foster, because he had cooperated with police in planning a school identity card system. This action was followed in early 1974 by the kidnapping and conversion of Patty Hearst, and in May of that year by the fiery shootout in Los Angeles in which six SLA members died.

Shortly before the SLA's fatal denouement, *Ramparts* magazine, a journal of the New Left, wrote what seems in retrospect an epitaph for revolutionary action in the United States. It attributed the emergence of the SLA "to the collapse of the organized left at the end of the 1960s, and its continuing failure to regroup itself and survive." The SLA itself was criticized as a "self-appointed vigilante group" and its murder of Marcus Foster condemned as an act of "desperate violence."[3] Although a few violent acts of would-be revolutionaries continued until the mid-1980s, there is little doubt that by 1974 events had helped discredit both revolutionary objectives and violent means for virtually the entire left.

Revulsion against deadly violence is not a sufficient explanation for the decline of militancy on the American left. Just as revolutionaries lost the support of the New Left, the larger political movement was itself eroding as a consequence of widespread changes in political attitudes. A larger cycle of political change was underway, one that Arthur Schlesinger Jr. characterized as a shift from "public purpose" to "private interest."[4] The 1960s were a time when public purposes prevailed, a time of rapid political change induced by pressures from below but also encouraged by the commitment of national leaders to social change. I suspect that during such periods of rapid political change more and more activists become convinced that all political ends are possible, and that any means can be used in the pursuit of those ends. The general public's reaction to the rhetoric, disorder, and violence of this era crystallized in the 1968 election of Richard Nixon as president. In the years that followed, Americans became increasingly preoccupied with the pursuit of private interests. The "me generation" of the 1970s and 1980s was widely opposed to radical social change and sharply resented groups making extreme demands or using disruptive or violent tactics. In short, the immediate backlash against revolutionary rhetoric and action was part of a larger swing in public sentiment away from sympathy with any kind of radical purpose or campaign.

Reform also is likely to undermine support for terrorists in democratic societies. I use *reform* as a shorthand term for government policies and actions that meet some of the grievances of the groups on which terrorists rely for support, as well as for policies that open up alternative means to the attainment of group goals. Such reforms are unlikely to dissuade people who have already been recruited and socialized into isolated cells of militant true believers. There is ample evidence that exit from such cells of people committed to violent activism is psychologically very difficult as well as personally dangerous. Moreover, achievement of limited or tactical successes is more likely to increase the "utilities" they attribute to terrorism (in rational-choice terminology) and to reinforce their disposition to choose violence in the future (in terms of learning theory).

Political leaders rarely acknowledge the validity of terrorists' demands or negotiate directly with them. The risks of doing so are too great: Negotiation would add to the stature of terrorist groups and provide an incentive for them to escalate violence as a bargaining tactic. The main aim—and effect—of the process of reform is to undermine the political basis of support for the terrorist group. Once it becomes evident to an aggrieved minority that dominant groups are prepared to accommodate some of their demands, most are likely to conclude that terrorism is a less attractive strategy. For potential recruits, the relative utilities of terrorism may no longer compensate for its personal costs and risks. It becomes apparent to the nonmilitant majority that there are less costly ways of achieving moderate but more certain gains for the group. For those who share the cause advocated by terrorists but reject their tactics, the continued operation of terrorists now becomes an active threat to the process of accommodation. Thus, groups that once supported terrorists may become politically mobilized against terrorists and actively assist police in identifying them.

Richard E. Rubenstein has argued, based on comparative studies, that reform is not enough to discourage young intellectuals from terrorism. They will resort to extreme means unless convinced that there are opportunities for radical political change by nonviolent means. This may be a correct assessment for the most ideologically committed people, but it overlooks the fact that reformist strategies are likely to erode the basis of political support that is essential for any sustained and significant terrorist action.[5] The tension between these two political processes may account for the desperate and seemingly irrational escalation of terrorism that sometimes accompanies or follows the introduction of reforms.

A prima facie case can be made that reforms contributed to the decline of violent separatism in Canada. The province of Québec gained substantial autonomy from the federal government and increased control over its own economy during the 1960s and 1970s. Although these gains were not nearly enough to satisfy the militants' demands for independence, the rise of the *Parti Québecois* offered a more promising alternative to FLQ terrorism, especially after the party won seven seats and second ranking in the December 1970 provincial elections. In 1971 and later, a number of activists left the FLQ and joined the PQ in decisions that seemed to be justified by the PQ's victory in the 1976 provincial elections. The electoral victory showed that the pursuit of independence did not require acts of terrorism but could take place within the framework of democracy and majority rule. The irony of nonviolent separatism was that the *Québecois* majority in 1980 rejected the PQ's referendum on "sovereignty association," a watered-down form of autonomy. In other words, public support for the independence sought by the FLQ was not there—in fact, public support had been eroded by the gains made toward political and economic autonomy for Québec and by fears about the economic consequences of complete independence.

Reforms also were relevant to the subsidence of revolutionary terrorism in the United States. Two immediate and personal reasons for militant opposition to the government disappeared with the end of the draft in 1972 and with the simultaneous signing of a peace treaty by the United States and the two Vietnamese regimes, which paved the way for American troop withdrawals. Many former antiwar activists joined the forces of reform within the Democratic party, which, operating under revised rules, succeeded in nominating a liberal peace candidate, George McGovern, for the presidency in 1972. Some activists kept their ideological commitment to the revolutionary transformation of America, but their support among college and university youth had largely vanished.

Puerto Rican nationalism was the other major issue responsible for terrorism in the United States during the 1970s, and, as noted earlier, it also declined—but not because of any major concessions to the *Independentistas* or, so far as I can judge, because of backlash in Puerto Rico. An appreciable minority of Puerto Ricans continue to support independence, and the long-term decline in Puerto Rican terrorism is more likely explained by police and FBI actions than by the dissipation of political support. This setting and issue is most likely to give rise to future campaigns of domestic terrorism in the United States.

Deterrence is the third factor that can alter the psychology of support for terrorism. Deterrence can rarely be observed directly—only its presumed causes and inferred consequences. Deterrence is assumed to increase when terrorists are imprisoned or killed, their targets hardened, tough laws against terrorism enacted, and anti-terrorist squads and tactics put in place. When terrorists defect and the incidence of violent acts tapers off in the aftermath of such events, security officials and many analysts assume that the anti-terrorist policies were responsible. Observers of terrorism in Italy suggest that legal changes—specifically the introduction in 1979 and 1983 of flexible judicial instruments that made it easier for militants to leave terrorist cells without fear of criminal penalties—contributed to the decline in Red Brigade terrorism.

My argument is that deterrent policies are effective to the extent that they reinforce, and are reinforced by, other changes in the bases of support for terrorism among wider sectors of the population. This means that the effects of both backlash and reform must be considered. If the community that once tolerated or supported terrorism has already begun to reject it because of revulsion against violence and expectations of peaceful change, deterrence will enhance the process. But if support for the cause and tactics of terrorism is still substantial, the likely effect of apprehension and killings of terrorists, or tough new anti-terrorist policies, will be to intensify resentment among the support group. Whether and how they act on that resentment depends on how high the costs and risks seem to be: If resentment is high and widespread, the risks posed by security policies must appear very high in order for them to have a deterrent effect. Moreover, deterrent effects under such circumstances are likely to be transient. Potential terrorists have demonstrated that they will bide their time and start new campaigns when security relaxes. I suspect that these kinds of processes were responsible for the periodic resurgence of left-wing and neo-Nazi terrorism in Germany and of nationalist terrorism among Puerto Ricans and other communal separatists. The communities of support, small though they are, have objectives that are beyond the reach of any generally acceptable reforms, and they tolerate the use of violence on behalf of those objectives. Hence security countermeasures have only temporary effects.

The Canadian and U.S. cases provide some suggestive evidence about the effects of deterrence. The arrest and conviction of twenty FLQ members in the aftermath of the Cross and Laporte kidnappings, and the detention of more than five hundred others, did not prevent a new wave of FLQ bombings and holdups, which began in March 1971 and lasted through the autumn. Hard-core activists were not deterred until a series of arrests in late 1971 and throughout 1972, aided by informants, put a decisive end to their actions. This fact leads to two inferences: first, that militants who escaped initial arrest were not deterred until actually apprehended; and second, that the declining political support enjoyed by the FLQ made it easier for police to gather intelligence about the cells and to penetrate them with informers.

Revolutionary terrorism by the two most active American groups of the 1970s, the Weather Underground and the New World Liberation Front, was never effectively countered by the authorities. Both groups voluntarily suspended campaigns of violence, in 1974 and 1978, respectively, without arrests of their members. The most that can be said about deterrence is that the Weather People were afflicted by paranoia about being penetrated or detected by the FBI and police. Their leaders' obsession with security had corrosive effects on morale and inhibited revolutionary actions. Smaller groups of revolutionary terrorists who operated during the 1970s and 1980s, including some activists from the organizations mentioned, were broken by the arrest (or, in the case of the SLA, the killings) of all of their key members. As in the Canadian case, the supposition is that the New Left's rejection of revolutionary adventurism had much to do with the fact that these groups remained small, achieved little support, and were vulnerable to detection.

To summarize, counter-terrorist policies in democracies, whether they emphasize traditional law enforcement techniques or, as in Italy, incentives to defect, are most effective when they coincide with larger shifts in the climate of political opinion away from support for, or sympathy with, terrorist causes and tactics. Law enforcement strategies may reinforce the erosion in support for radical action; they cannot create it.

Conclusions

The arguments of this chapter have substantial implications for the analysis of the onset and decline of domestic terrorism. The understanding of the process that leads to episodes of terrorism in Western democracies requires an analysis of the political circumstances that create the political beliefs that encourage extremists. The explanation of the "exit from terrorism," a phrase used by Franco Ferracuti, requires a parallel analysis. Rational-choice explanations for why active terrorists give up armed struggle are not enough. We need to understand why ordinary people and activists stop giving credence and support to the ideological justifications and tactics of terrorism. And to understand this we have to examine the ways in which backlash, reform, and deterrence alter the psychological environment within which terrorists operate.

Backlash is crucial. Just as revolutionaries hope or expect that government repression will increase support for their cause, ill-conceived acts of terrorism can and do extend and solidify public antagonism toward the terrorists and, by extension, undermine the credibility of their objectives. One can argue that in democracies, where most groups have ample opportunities for seeking redress of grievances, almost any widely publicized act of terror will have such a backlash effect. In the instance of the revolutionary Left in the United States, the judgment is that deadly violence, especially the death of a mathematician in a bombing at the University of Wisconsin, also was critical in undermining support for the movement among its radical sympathizers. In Europe, terrorist campaigns in Germany, Italy, France, Spain, and Northern Ireland have been accompanied by increased general support for strong countermeasures by the state. Support for terrorists' objectives remains only among distinctive minorities—a few Catholics in Northern Ireland and some militant Basques in Spain.

Equally important is the public response to issues that provide activists with their rationale for opposing the regime. "Redress of grievances" is unlikely to change the views or actions of committed revolutionaries or terrorists, but it is likely to dry up the bases of their social and political support. Large-scale public efforts to reduce racial inequalities did contribute to the decline of racial violence in the United States. Reform and the rise of a legitimate separatist party in Québec eliminated the rationale for continued violence by the FLQ.

A rational-choice perspective on public support for terrorism emphasizes the extent to which various publics think that their interests are served by terrorists. The line of analysis developed here zeros in instead on group and community norms. Terrorist violence in democratic societies offends most people and undermines not only support for the groups using it but also their purposes. In these circumstances there will be no "third generation" of militants, terrorists will find fewer sympathizers among whom to take shelter, and security agencies will find it much easier to find informants and entice defectors. Therefore, most terrorist campaigns in democratic societies contain the seeds of their own demise. The exceptions are based on distinctive communal and political minorities with unsatisfied, and often unsatisfiable, goals of fundamental change.

This analysis has implications for the future of international terrorism of the kind directed against the United States by Al Qaeda—a campaign that began with the February 1993 bombing of the World Trade Center, long before the events of September 11, 2001. International terror campaigns require a base of communal support—somewhere. Al Qaeda needs Islamic communities that share its fundamental vision to provide recruits and money, and sympathetic governments or religious bodies to provide shelter and logistical support. Despite the toppling of the Taliban regime in Afghanistan, these conditions persist in parts of the Islamic world. But they do not exist in the United States or most other Western democracies. Muslim and Arab peoples have migrated to the West in search of alternatives to the poverty, intolerance, political instability, and repression of their countries of origin. A few recent immigrants are sympathetic to the fundamentalist Islamic vision, but most Muslims in the West reject it. They may give monetary and political support to Palestinian nationalism, but not to Islamist attacks on the United States. By and large they reject and fear such attacks because anti-Western violence in the name of Islam is a threat to their own status and security in Western societies. It has been possible for Islamist militants to live undetected for a few months or years in Islamic communities in Western societies, as the Al Qaeda hijackers did in Germany and the United States. No longer. They now attract the suspicious scrutiny of Muslim neighbors as well as closer attention from security personnel.

The lack of community support in the United States for militant Islam has been reinforced by public backlash among Muslims and non-Muslims alike, which makes counter-terror strategies easier to carry out. The risk of terrorist attacks from overseas is still present but substantially diminished. The people and institutions at greatest future risk are those closest to the terrorist support bases in the Islamic world—terrorists will strike at enemies they can reach. This includes U.S. civilians and military personnel in countries like Saudi Arabia, Pakistan, and Indonesia as well as the governments and officials of Islamic countries that are seen to be allied with the West. The short-run strategy is heightened security and better intelligence work in these regions. The best long-run strategy probably is the use of development, educational, and participatory strategies to restrain corruption and open up alternatives for future generations in the most isolated and impoverished corners of the Islamic world.

Notes

1. This is a revised version of a chapter that first appeared in Walter Reich, ed., *Origins of Terrorism: Psychologies, Ideologies, Theologies, States of Mind* (New York: Cambridge University Press for the Woodrow Wilson International Center for Scholars, 1990), 86–102. For more detailed discussion of the evidence and arguments see Ted Robert Gurr, "Political Terrorism in the United States: Historical Antecedents and Contemporary Trends," in Michael Stohl, ed., *The Politics of Terrorism,* 3rd edition (New York: Marcel Dekker, 1987), 549–78; and Jeffrey Ian Ross and Ted Robert Gurr, "Why Terrorism Subsides: A Comparative Study of Terrorism in Canada and the United States," *Comparative Politics* 21 (July 1989): 405–26.

2. My calculations from information provided in Martha Crenshaw, "How Terrorism Ends," paper presented at the Annual Meetings of the American Political Science Association, Chicago:3–6 September 1987.

3. "The Symbionese Liberation Army: Terrorism and the Left," *Ramparts* 12 (May 1974):21ff.

4. Arthur Schlesinger Jr., *The Cycles of American History* (Boston: Houghton Mifflin, 1986), chap. 2.

5. Richard E. Rubenstein, *Alchemists of Revolution: Terrorism in the Modern World* (New York: Basic Books, 1987).

The Control of the New Global Terrorism

●

Chapter 17

◆

THE AFTERMATH OF 9/11 AND THE SEARCH FOR LIMITS: IN DEFENSE OF JUST WAR THINKING

RICHARD A. FALK

America and Americans on September 11th experienced the full horror of one of the greatest displays of *grotesque cunning* in human history. Its essence consisted in transforming the benign everyday technology of commercial jet aircraft into malignant weapons of mass destruction to be deliberately directed at civilian targets. Americans on this day abruptly discovered the vulnerability of their heartland in a manner that is more heartrending than the collective trauma associated with the Japanese attack on Pearl Harbor. But the new vulnerability is radically different and far more threatening. It involves the comprehensive vulnerability of this society to the very technology that accounts for its incredible prosperity and unprecedented global dominance. This technological vulnerability is pervasive, giving prospective terrorists a seemingly unlimited array of soft targets from which to choose so as to inflict severe harm.

To protect ourselves fully as a country against this range of potential threats that could be mounted by those of fanatical persuasion is a mission impossible. The very attempt to reach such a goal would turn America quickly into a prison state of militarist persuasion. Ensuing months have given rise to huge budgetary commitments to homeland security, to the intelligence serves, and to the Pentagon, as well as to raised concerns about infringements on basic liberties.

And yet who could blame the government for doing what it can in the coming months to reassure a frightened citizenry and to the extent possible to prevent future attacks? The steps seem designed to make it more difficult to repeat the operations that produced the World Trade Center/Pentagon tragedy, but it seems highly unlikely that a terrorist machine intelligent enough to pull off this gruesome operation would suddenly become so stupid as to attempt the same kind of thing soon again. If subsequent megaterrorist attacks are repeated, they will undoubtedly seek quite different points of vulnerability and likely rely on different methods of attack.

The atrocity of September 11th must be understood as the work of dark genius, a penetrating tactical insight that could endanger our future in fundamental respects that we are only beginning to apprehend. This breakthrough in terrorist tactics occurred in three mutually reinforcing dimensions: (1) the shift from extremely violent acts, with a symbolic intent to shock more than to kill, to onslaughts intended to make the enemy's society into a bloody battlefield, in this instance, both symbolically (capitalism and militarism) and substantively (massive human carnage and economic dislocation); (2) the use of primitive capabilities by the perpetrators to appropriate complex modern technology that can then be instantly transformed into weaponry of mass destruction through the mere act of seizure and delivery; (3) the availability of competent militants willing to commit suicide so as to be able to carry out such crimes against humanity. Such a lethal, and essentially novel, combination of elements poses an unprecedented challenge to civic order and democratic liberties of even the most powerful sovereign state. It is truly a declaration of war mounted at a great distance from the lower depths.

It is important to appreciate this transformative shift in the nature of the terrorist challenge both *conceptually* and *tactically*. Without comprehending these shifts, it will not be possible to fashion a response that is either effective or legitimate, and both are needed. It remains obscure on the terrorist side of Al Qaeda whether a *strategic* plan of any coherence accompanied this tactical escalation. It increasingly appears that the tactical brilliance of this megaterrorist operation will soon be widely understood as a strategic blunder of colossal proportions. It would seem that the main beneficiaries of the attack in the near future are also the principal enemies of the perpetrators. And the principal victims seem to be the forces most closely associated with Al Qaeda. Both the United States globally and Israel regionally emerge from this disaster with greatly strengthened geopolitical hands. Did the sense of hatred and fanaticism of the tactical masterminds induce this seeming strategic blindness? There is no indication that the forces behind the attack on 9/11 were acting on any basis beyond their vengeful intent. There have been some rather far-fetched speculations that the attack on the United States was mainly designed to provoke a retaliation against an Islamic country, which would have the further effect of unifying Islam for the sake of waging *jihad* against the United States.

What emerges is the overwhelming impression that the attack was an act of war, and that it would produce a reaction based on self-defense, and that a war would result. Such an assessment raises several pivotal questions: What kind of war? Against whom? With what goals and what limits? It is, above all, a war unlike all past international wars. It is a major war without an enemy state to blame and defeat; it is a war that cannot be won by relying primarily on military solutions. Indeed, it is a war in which the pursuit of the traditional military goal of "victory" is almost certain to intensify the challenge and spread the violence. This interpretation of the response challenge does not question the propriety of the effort to identify and punish the perpetrators, and to cut their links to supportive governmental powers. The war fever produced by an unholy alliance of government and media should not let us forget that the attacks of 9/11 were massive crimes against humanity in a technical legal sense, and those guilty of their commission should be punished to the extent possible. Having acknowledged this legitimate right of response is by no means equivalent to an endorsement of a defensive war, and certainly not a mandate to unleash unlimited force. Indeed, an overreaction may be what the terrorists were somehow seeking to provoke so as to mobilize popular resentment against the United States on a global scale. The United States needed to act effectively, but within the legitimating framework of accepted moral and legal restraints.

First of all, there should have been the elementary due process of identifying convincingly the perpetrators, and their backers. Secondly, there should have been to the extent possible a maximal effort to obtain authorization for any use of force in a specific form through the procedures of the United Nations Security Council. Unlike the Gulf War model, the collective character of the undertaking should be integral at the operational level, and not serve merely as window dressing for unilateralism. Thirdly, any use of force should be consistent with international law and with the just war tradition governing the use of force—that is, *discriminating* between military and civilian targets, *proportionate* to the challenge, and *necessary* to achieve a military objective, avoiding *superfluous* suffering. If retaliatory action fails to abide by these guidelines, with due allowance for flexibility depending on the circumstances, then it will be seen by most others as replicating the fundamental evil of terrorism. It will be seen as violence directed against those who are innocent and against civilian society. And fourthly, the political and moral justifications for the use of force should be accompanied by the concerted and energetic protection of those resident in American society who share an ethnic and religious identity with the targets of retaliatory violence.

Counseling such guidelines does not overcome a dilemma that has become more obvious as time passes: Something must be done, but there is nothing to do. What should be done if no targets can be found that are consistent with the guidelines of law and morality? We must assume that the terrorist network has anticipated retaliation even before the attack, and has taken whatever steps it can to "disappear" from the planet, to render itself invisible. The test then is whether our leaders have the forbearance to refrain from uses of forces that are directed toward those who are innocent in these circumstances, and whether our citizenry has the patience to indulge and accept such forbearance. It cannot be too much stressed that the only way to win this "war" (if war it is) against terrorism is by manifesting a respect for the innocence of civilian life, and to reinforce that respect by a credible commitment to the global promotion of social justice.

The Bush Administration came to Washington with a resolve to conduct a more unilateralist foreign policy that abandoned the sorts of humanitarian pretenses that led to significant American-led involvements in sub-Saharan Africa and the Balkans during the 1990s. The main idea seemed to be to move away from a kind of liberal geopolitics and downsize the American international role by limiting overseas military action to the domain of strategic interests and to uphold such interests by a primary reliance on its own independent capabilities. Behind such thinking was the view that the United States did not need the sort of help that it required during the Cold War, and at the same time it should not shoulder the humanitarian burdens of concern for matters that were remote from its direct interests. Combined with its enthusiasm for missile defense and weapons in space, such a repositioning of U.S. foreign policy was supposed to be an adjustment to the new realities of the post–Cold War world. Contrary to many commentaries, such a repositioning was not an embrace of isolationism, but represented a revised version of internationalism based on a blend of unilateralism and militarism.

In the early months of the Bush presidency this altered foreign policy was mainly expressed by repudiating a series of important, widely supported multilateral treaty frameworks, including the Kyoto Protocol dealing with global warming, the ABM Treaty dealing with the militarization of space, and the Biological Weapons Convention Protocol dealing with implementing the prohibition on developing biological weaponry. Allies of the United States were stunned by such actions, which seemed to reject the need for international cooperation to address global problems of a deeply threatening nature.

And then came 9/11, and an immediate realization in Washington that the overwhelming priority of its foreign policy now rested upon soliciting precisely the sort of cooperative international framework it had worked so hard to throw into the nearest garbage bin. Whether such a realization goes deeper than a mobilization of support for global war only time will tell. Unlike the Gulf War or Kosovo War, which were rapidly carried to their completion by military means, a struggle against global terrorism even in its narrowest sense would require the most intense forms of intergovernmental cooperation ever experienced in the history of international relations. Hopefully, the diplomacy needed to receive this cooperation might set some useful restraining limits on the current American impulse to use force excessively and irresponsibly.

A root question underlying the American response is how it deals with the United Nations. There is reportedly a debate within the Bush Administration between those hardliners who believe that the United States should claim control over the response by invoking the international law doctrine of "the inherent right of self-defense" and those who are more diplomatically inclined and favor seeking a mandate from the Security Council to act in collective self-defense. Among the initiatives being discussed in the search for meaningful responses is the establishment through UN authority of a special tribunal entrusted with the prosecution of those indicted for the crime of international terrorism, possibly commencing with the apprehension and trial of Osama bin Laden. Such reliance on the rule of law would be a major step in seeking to make the struggle against terrorism enjoy the genuine support of the entire organized international community.

It needs to be understood that the huge challenge posed by the attacks can be met effectively only by establishing the greatest possible distance between the perpetrators and those who are acting on behalf of their victims. And what is the content of this distance? An unconditional respect for the sacredness of life, and the dignity of the human person. One of the undoubted difficulties in the weeks and months ahead will be to satisfy the bloodthirst that has accompanied the mobilization of America for war while satisfying the rest of the world that it is acting in a manner that displays respect for civilian innocence and human solidarity. A slightly related problem, but with deeper implications, is to avoid seeming to exempt state violence from moral and legal limitations, while insisting that such limitations apply to the civic violence of the terrorists. Such double standards will damage the indispensable effort to draw a credible distinction between the criminality of the attack and the legitimacy of the retaliation.

There are contradictory ways to address the atrocities of 9/11: The prevailing mood is to invoke the metaphor of cancer, and to preach military surgery of a complex and globe-girdling character that needs to be elevated to the status of a world war, and bears comparison with World War I and II; the alternative, which I believe is far more accurate as diagnosis and cure, is to rely on the metaphor of an iceberg. The attack on America was the tip of an iceberg, the submerged portions being the mass of humanity that is not sharing in the fruits of modernity, but finds itself under the heel of American economic, military, cultural, and diplomatic power. To eliminate the visible tip of the iceberg of discontent and resentment may bring us a momentary catharsis, but it will at best create an illusion of "victory." What needs to be done is to extend a commitment to the sacredness of life to the entire human family, in effect, joining in a collective effort to achieve what might be called "humane globalization"—although such deeper causes of 9/11 cannot be addressed until the immediate threat posed by the existence of Al Qaeda is addressed.

Against such a background of considerations, recourse to war against Afghanistan seemed legally and morally justified, provided it was conducted in accordance with the law of war, and especially, that a credible effort was made to spare Afghan civilians. The American approach would seem to have set a better precedent if more of an effort had been made to achieve satisfactory results through diplomacy, and if a greater effort had been made to avoid civilian casualty by so disciplining the use of military force. At the same time, the Taliban was an illegitimate regime oppressive to its own people in a brutal manner, and a considerable effort was made to minimize Afghan civilian casualties so long as American military personnel were not put at higher risk. We should demand more of those who claim to be fighting a just war, but the outcome did validate the undertaking, weakening Al Qaeda and superseding the Taliban with a new governing process that seems likely to improve the life circumstances of most of the Afghan population.

The Israel/Palestine conflict, its concreteness and persistence, is part of this new global reality. All sides acknowledge relevance, but the contradictory narratives deform our understanding in serious respects. Israel itself has seized the occasion to drop any pretense of sensitivity to international criticism and calls for restraint in its occupation of the Palestinian Territories. Israeli spokespersons have been active in spreading the word that now America and the world should appreciate what sorts of adversaries Israel has faced for decades, and should learn from Israel's efforts to control and destroy its terrorist enemies. Those supporting Palestinian rights in contrast argue that the sorts of violence generated by Israeli oppression and refusal to uphold international law and human rights gives rise to a politics of desperation that includes savage attacks on Israeli civilian society. They argue that giving a suppressed people the choice between terrorism and surrender is abusive, as well as dangerous.

On the deepest levels, the high-tech dominance achieved by American power, so vividly expressed in the pride associated with "zero casualties" in the 1999 NATO war over Kosovo, is giving to the peoples of the world a similar kind of choice between poverty and subjugation and vindictive violence. The post–Afghanistan War plans being advanced in Washington at the present time are grounds for discouragement and concern. These plans, as articulated by President Bush in the 2002 State of the Union Address, seemed determined to extend the war well beyond Afghanistan, and not just war in a metaphorical sense. The reference to "an axis of evil" consisting of Iran, Iraq, and North Korea by its language recalled both the axis powers of World War II and Ronald Reagan's famous reference to the Soviet Union as "the evil empire." Beyond the inflammatory language was the substantive arrogance of challenging the fundamental sovereignty of countries that had no confirmed connection with the events of 9/11 or were in any way aligned with Al Qaeda. The justification for war against Afghanistan rested on such linkage and alignment. In fact, objectively considered, these three countries, which are indeed subject to criticism on human rights and other grounds, pose no security threat to the United States. If anything, such states even before being warned by President Bush were more threatened (by the United States) than threatening to it.

Is our civil society robust enough to deliver a critical message in some influential way? We cannot know at this point; but we must try, especially if we value the benefits of discussion and debate as integral to the health of democracy. Such an imperative seems particularly urgent because of the absence of moral and political imagination (with the partial exception of the Secretary of State, Colin Powell) at leadership levels in the U.S. government. There have been some terrible days of grieving for what has been lost, with scant indication of how beyond the military mode we might all become better able to cope with this catastrophe. We should make the life of critics too easy by placing all of the blame for the deficiencies of response on George W. Bush and his Republican cohorts. The Democratic Party and its leaders have shown little willingness or capacity to think any differently about what has occurred and what to do about it. Mainstream TV has apparently seen its role as a war-mobilizing and patrioteering mechanism, with neither interest nor capacity to include alternative voices and interpretations. The same tired icons of the establishment were awakened once more to do the journeyman work of constructing a national consensus in favor of all-out war, a recipe for spreading chaos around the world and bringing discredit to ourselves. Critical voices were not even heard, much less heeded.

We are continuing to flirt with a global inter-civilizational war without battlefields and borders, a war initially focused on the enigmatic and elusive solitary figure of Osama bin Laden stalking remote, mountainous Afghanistan while masterminding a holy war against a mighty superpower. To the extent that this portrayal is accurate it underscores a dramatic subversion of world order based on the relations among sovereign, territorial states. But it also suggests that the idea of national security in a world of states is becoming obsolete, and that the only viable security is what is being increasingly called these days "human security." Yet, the news has not reached Washington, or for that matter, the other capitals of the world. There is still present the conviction that missile defense shields, space weaponry, and antiterrorist grand coalitions can keep the barbarians at bay. In fact, this conviction has turned into a frenzy in the aftermath of 9/11, giving us continuing reason to fear the response almost as much as the initial, traumatizing provocations and the danger of their recurrence. As the sun slowly sets on a world of states, the sun of its militarism appears ready to burn more brightly than ever!

Chapter 18

JUST WAR THEORY: RESPONDING MORALLY TO GLOBAL TERRORISM

JAMES TURNER JOHNSON

On September 11, 2001, almost 3,000 people died when three hijacked airliners loaded with jet fuel crashed into the World Trade Center towers and the Pentagon and a fourth plane crashed in western Pennsylvania after passengers attempted to overcome the hijackers. In all four cases the deliberate intent was to take American lives on American soil—in the words of a *fatwa,* or religious ruling, authored by Osama bin Laden and four associates in 1998 that may be taken as the manifesto for these attacks, "to kill the Americans and their allies . . . in any country in which it is possible to do it."[1] It is important to note that the effort by Osama bin Laden and his associates to ground such attacks in Islamic tradition has since been condemned by mainstream Muslim authorities. Part of their purpose was to protect Islamic tradition from distortion and co-optation for private purposes, but part reflects a deep truth shared by the moral traditions of both Islam and the West—that it is wrong directly and intentionally to attack the innocent.

Terrorism In Moral Perspective

What was centrally wrong, in moral terms, about the attacks of September 11 may be put this way: The people who died and were wounded there, the people who died and were wounded by their efforts at rescue, all the other people who have suffered harm as a result of the attacks *had done nothing to deserve what happened to them.* This is the essential moral difference between unjustified killing and killing that can be morally justified (or more broadly, between unjustified and justified uses of force). It is essential to emphasize that the combatant–noncombatant distinction is not the same as the military–civilian distinction. In peacetime both military and civilians are, in moral terms, noncombatants. Likewise, in war some civilians may perform as combatants, while some people in the military (e.g., chaplains, medical personnel) are noncombatants because of their function.

What justifies the killing of soldiers in wartime is that killing someone who directly and intentionally threatens another human life by his or her own actions is fundamentally different, in moral terms, from killing someone who does not pose such a threat. While pacifists may reject all killing for whatever reason as unjustified, nonpacifist moral tradition accepts the possibility of war as justified because of the threat posed to the innocent. The difference between acting as an agent of this threat and not doing so is the root of the distinction made in moral thinking about war and in international law between combatants and noncombatants. However regrettable it may be, it is morally justified and lawful to kill combatants in wartime; it is never morally justified or legal to kill noncombatants in wartime or to kill anyone in a political dispute outside of war, because when there is no state of war, all are by definition noncombatants.

What was wrong, then, at the most fundamental level in the attacks of September 11 was that in a time of peace these attacks aimed directly at the deaths of people who were simply going about their ordinary lives, who were not themselves engaged in a threat against the lives of others. This was as true of the uniformed military personnel targeted in the attack on the Pentagon as well as the civilians there, in the World Trade Center towers, and on all four hijacked planes. What was morally wrong in the September 11 attacks is also a characteristic of the phenomenon of terrorism in general—it deliberately chooses noncombatants as its targets.

Related to this is a second basic problem with the September 11 attacks and much terrorism in general—a generalized animosity toward a whole group of people and their way of life that is taken as justifying violence. While Osama bin Laden and his associates identified several specific United States policies as the basis for violent response, they moved seamlessly to hold responsible all Americans and American culture generally for those specific policies. In their 1998 *fatwa* and in statements made after the September 11 attacks they represented America and the West as engaged in a war of humiliation and annihilation against Muslims, justifying a similar war of annihilation by them and all Muslims back toward all Americans, allies of America, and Western culture generally. Thinking in this way is morally wrong for two reasons. First, it deliberately denies the essential moral difference between combatants and noncombatants in a military struggle, which was just discussed; second, it exhibits what Augustine called an "implacable animosity" toward an entire culture—an unreasoned hatred that cannot be satisfied except by the annihilation of the designated enemy.

Taken together, these two characteristics of the September 11 attacks and of the phenomenon of terrorism more broadly show why noncombatants are intentionally the targets of choice. First, they are defined as guilty simply by being members of the hated society; second, they are "soft" targets, easier to attack with the limited means available to terrorists; third, a successful deadly attack on ordinary people in a society, people going about their everyday lives, implicitly reveals the impotence of their government, which failed to protect them, and undermines the assumptions that make everyday life in that society what it is. So for terrorism it is not simply that the combatant–noncombatant distinction is erased; perversely, it is kept in a certain way, as the most innocent, ordinary people are made the targets of choice. Thus terrorism reverses the moral priorities of killing in war: It deliberately chooses to kill the innocent rather than seeking to avoid harm to them.

A third deep-rooted moral problem with the September 11 attacks was their source. There is a fundamental moral difference between uses of violence to protect a political community by those responsible for the well-being of that community and the use of violence by any individual or group for other reasons. The September 11 attacks were launched by members of Al Qaeda, an organization constituted for the purpose of terror, with planning, direction, and support from the leaders of the organization itself. In moral and legal terms, such an organization has no standing to use violence in pursuit of its ends. It is essentially a criminal organization, a mafia—self-constituted, responsible to no political community, acting on behalf of its own ends. Whatever the high moral goods claimed as justifying their actions, the people who planned, directed, supported, and carried out those actions had no moral right to do so.

Terrorism, in short, is deeply evil. The threat it poses touches values essential to private life and life in community, including not just our own national community but the order of international society as a whole. The response to it, accordingly, must be correspondingly deeply rooted in the reaffirmation of those values it threatens and in the commitment to protect them and their embodiment in the institutions of personal and common life. That is, the response has to be one that includes not only military, diplomatic, economic, intelligence, and police efforts; it also has to include a moral analysis aimed at reaffirming the values threatened and criticizing and rejecting the terrorist rationales. Accordingly, it has to be cross-cultural, since the threat posed by the new global terrorism touches every major culture on the globe. In the context of American society this moral analysis has to begin with a reorientation of U.S. public moral discourse on the rights and wrongs of the use of force.

Terrorism and American Moral Discourse: The Need to Rethink the Moral Status of the Use of Force

Prior to the September 11 attacks, very little attention was given to the problem of terrorism in American moral discourse on the use of armed force and the problem of war. Rather, the moral debate tracked and responded to the kinds of conflicts in which the United States was involved or was perceived as likely to be involved. Thus in the context of the 1960s, when Paul Ramsey's work (*War and the Christian Conscience* and *The Just War*)[2] revived interest in the idea of just war as a focus for moral reflection on war, the central concern was with nuclear weapons, deterrence, and the possibility of nuclear war. That same concern dominated the debates of the 1980s, when books like Jonathan Schell's *The Fate of the Earth* held up a vision of the aftermath of nuclear war as a "republic of insects and grasses"[3] and the United States Catholic bishops' 1983 pastoral letter *The Challenge of Peace* laid down a "presumption against war" as the first step in a moral argument that rejected all use of nuclear weapons and only temporarily accepted possession of such weapons as a deterrent.[4] In between these two periods of focus on nuclear weapons lay, of course, the Vietnam War, which provided the central focus of moral discourse related to war in the 1970s. Part of the enduring value of Michael Walzer's *Just and Unjust Wars* was that it had a broader compass, advancing its moral analysis and argument by means of historical examples ranging from classical Athens to World War II—though it also had significant focus on the Vietnam War and the problems of nuclear weapons.[5]

As the examples of Ramsey, Walzer, and the U.S. Catholic bishops demonstrate, this period from the early 1960s to the end of the 1980s and the end of the era of the Cold War was marked in moral debate by the introduction, consolidation, and increasing use of the idea of just war as the focus for analysis and argument. There was also, however, running through this same period a strong stream of pacifist opposition to war. Three broad forms of this opposition can be distinguished. First there was the pacifism of total rejection of all war, based either in religious conviction or in personal philosophical rationales. Second was a form of rejection of war based on the judgment that contemporary war is inherently indiscriminate and disproportionate in its destructiveness. This kind of argument—sometimes focused only on the destructive potential of nuclear weapons but at other times made more broadly in terms of the destructiveness of the wars of the twentieth century—has been variously called modern-war pacifism, nuclear pacifism, and just war pacifism; it used the just war categories of discrimination and proportionality to carry on what Ramsey in various places termed a *bellum contra bellum justum*, a "war against just war" in favor of a pacifist rejection of all contemporary warfare as immoral. Finally, there was the form of opposition to war that focused on the perceived immorality of the state and its policies. First coalescing as a form of moral opposition to the American involvement in Vietnam, this kind of pacifism nurtured a suspicion of government, of the military, and of the idea of national interest as a justification for the use of armed force.

What one finds on examining the moral debates of this roughly thirty-year period is that even as the language of the just war categories has become more dominant in these debates, the assumptions of the latter two forms of pacifism have persisted and shaped a significant moral opposition to the use of armed force by the state for reasons based in the national interest. The case of the moral debate over the Gulf War provides a striking example of both these tendencies. On the one hand, in justifying the American use of armed force in that conflict, the first President Bush used language that closely tracked the traditional just war categories; and the actual application of that force, first in Operation Desert Shield and then in Desert Storm, fit the requirements of those categories perhaps as well as any military operation could do so in real terms. It also was a casebook application of the requirements of international law for the resort to armed force, and conduct in the use of that force (see James Johnson and George Weigel, *Just War and the Gulf War*).[6] The use of precision-guided munitions for the first time in combat made possible a level of discrimination in attacks against military targets never before reached; this also lowered the level of collateral damage significantly and changed the calculus of proportionality relative to results achieved versus total damage done. When the ground war began, it took place in areas where there was effectively no noncombatant population, either because of the nature of the terrain or because, as in the case of Kuwait City and its environs, the Iraqis had driven the noncombatants out.

Yet the moral discourse from this conflict reveals much opposition to the American resort to armed force in the first place and to the manner of use of that force in the conflict.[7] Arguments against the resort to force called in question the United States motives (the "no blood for oil" argument), accused the United States of having contributed to the crisis by its earlier support of Iraq (the "dirty hands" argument), held out the specter of an escalating conflict that would engulf the region and perhaps the world and would involve the use of weapons of mass destruction (the disproportionality argument), and favored an extended search for nonviolent options (the last resort argument). Once the air war began, criticism was directed against the bombing of dual-use (military–civilian) facilities like the electric power network and bridges; late in Desert Storm the attacks on retreating Iraqi Republican Guard elements on the Basra Road were castigated as indiscriminate (because these elements were no longer organized as a fighting force) and disproportionate (because the air attacks were unopposed); after the war the total destruction caused, including the deliberate torching of the Kuwaiti oil fields by the retreating Iraqis, was laid at the feet of the American decision to use armed force. We see here the marks of all the broad forms of opposition to armed force identified earlier—refusal to acknowledge that resort to force is ever justified; the expectation that any use of force will inevitably escalate to all-out war; the ready identification of all uses of force as indiscriminate and disproportionate; a deep-rooted suspicion of motives of national interest as inherently tainting any possible just cause; a suspicion of government rationales as deceptive and immoral.

In all of this the growing phenomenon of terror was generally ignored in civilian moral discourse, though in military contexts there was a significant effort to stimulate moral discussion in the 1980s, first in response to the truck bombing of the Marine barracks at Beirut airport and later in connection with the larger phenomenon of low-intensity conflict. But aside from the work of the people involved in this effort there was another line of moral discourse critical not of terrorist activity itself, nor of the people behind it, but of the U.S. policy that had led to the Marine presence in Lebanon and of U.S. uses of military force in response to low-intensity threats in Latin America and elsewhere. This was, indeed, a pattern throughout this period—if terrorism did not affect the United States directly, it was ignored in the moral literature on war; if it did do so in any way, such as in the case of the Marine barracks bombing, the United States support of the Contras in Nicaragua, or the use of military forces in the war on the drug trade, the fact of terror became an occasion for moral criticism of United States policy, the administration, and the U.S. military.

During the 1990s after the Gulf War and up to the September 11 attacks, something of a sea change began to appear in American moral discourse on war as erstwhile opponents of use of military force joined with others closer to the just war mainstream to argue for the interventionary use of military force in response to human rights abuses and complex humanitarian emergencies caused by civil war. Some of the old suspicion over the use of force remained, however. Two examples will illustrate the persistence of such suspicion. In 1993 the U.S. Catholic bishops issued a new statement on the use of armed force; though it represented intervention as a "duty" in the face of egregious violations of human rights, it distinguished between such uses of military force and "war" for purposes of national interest, about which the bishops continued to have serious reservations. In 1998 the General Assembly of the United Presbyterian Church formally adopted a resolution, titled "Just Peacemaking and the Call for International Intervention for Humanitarian Rescue," in which it strongly supported the idea of using military force for humanitarian intervention, yet cautioned that in no case should humanitarian purpose "cloak" the pursuit of national interest.

I suggest that the terror attacks of September 11 have decisively changed the balance in American moral discourse about the use of military force and, at a deeper level, about the purpose of government in relation to the public good. While a small amount of moral criticism was advanced early after the attacks, sounding the old themes that the attacks somehow resulted from flawed U.S. policies toward Israel and the Arab world, the presence of U.S. military forces in the Middle East, and American dependence on oil, this line of moral discourse never became the mainstream. Rather, a near unanamity quickly emerged and has persisted on the justifiedness of an American military response, on the moral obligation of the Bush Administration to undertake such a response and on its competence to do so, and on the general obligation of the government to undertake measures aimed at increasing homeland security, apprehending potential terrorist actors, and interdicting terrorist activity throughout the world. There has been no criticism of the place of national interest in justifying these measures as they have developed, and no second-guessing of the use of military force in the campaign in Afghanistan (in sharp contrast to the cases of Somalia, Bosnia, and Kosovo). In the September 11 attacks terrorism came home to America, and one result has been a significant refocusing of moral attitudes toward the government, its purposes, and the role of military force in the pursuit of those purposes.

Responding Morally to a Terrorist Attack

How to think morally about the response to acts of terror? The answer is not, in principle, different for this and for other forms of attacks against the public good and the order that supports it. The essentials of the answer were put succinctly over seven centuries ago by Thomas Aquinas in his "On War."[8] What is necessary for a war to be just, he argued, are sovereign authority, a just cause, and a right intention, including both avoidance of wrong intentions and the aim of achieving peace. At the time he was writing, Aquinas was not yet the authority that he has since become, but his pithy treatment of the question of war in moral terms serves in his own historical context as a window on a cultural consensus that already had coalesced around its central elements, the moral requirements he cited. This consensus drew heavily on the work of Augustine some eight hundred years earlier, and through him, on the Hebraic and the classical Roman and Greek traditions—the deepest roots of Western civilization. In short, Aquinas's formulation reflects a fundamental and deep-seated moral valuation of the use of armed force in relation to the ideals of public life. The just war tradition, which is the term we use today to refer to the concrete expression of that valuation by means of definite moral requirements for the just use of armed force, thus tells us important things about who we are as moral beings and what we should—indeed, must—do in the face of injustice.

Much recent just war reasoning differs from that of Aquinas—and I think wrongly—in two important ways. First, it has typically placed the requirement of just cause first, over that of sovereign authority (usually rendered in recent terms as "right" or "competent" authority); second, it has tended to focus on the prudential requirements of last resort, that the use of force be expected to cause more good than harm, and that it have a reasonable hope of success. These three prudential requirements did not appear in Aquinas's listing of the necessities for a just war. What is to be made of these differences? How do they bear on the question of a moral response to the terror attacks of September 11 and the general phenomenon of terrorism?

Aquinas, following Augustine, began by requiring sovereign authority for two basic reasons. First, this concept made a moral distinction between use of force by public authority for the public good and uses by private persons for private ends. In medieval terms, this distinction was put as that between *bellum* and *duellum*. This was an important distinction in a cultural context in which every knight could claim to have the right to use the sword on his own judgment and in which banditry was widespread. What Aquinas said reflected the work of more than a century of canonical thought and political efforts to deal with such endemic violence—similar in important ways to contemporary terrorism—by restricting the right of resort to armed force to the highest temporal authorities, those with no superior able to adjudicate their differences. At the same time, this work emphasized the responsibility of those in sovereign authority to ensure justice, both in their domains and in their relations with other sovereigns. This was a concern deeply rooted in classical political thought, and it has continued at the center of Western political theory: The reason for the existence of the political community is to serve the good of those within it and to serve the general order within which all political communities exist and on which they depend—those in political authority have as their fundamental responsibility to ensure these goods against harm. Understood within this frame, Aquinas's placing the requirement of sovereign authority first in his listing of the requirements for a just war was not simply accidental; it followed from an understanding of the nature of the political order in itself.

Thinking of the requirement of sovereign authority first emphasizes that protecting the political community and the order within which it exists is what government is ultimately for. The sovereign authority thus has responsibility to weigh and make judgment on the presence of just cause and to initiate action not marked by a wrong intention and aimed at the achievement of peace. Much recent just war thinking, typified by the two statements of the U.S. Catholic bishops cited earlier, has placed the question of just cause first, as if it can be determined in the abstract, so that response by a "competent" authority simply follows this determination. Yet who can rightly determine the existence of a just cause for the use of armed force on behalf of the political community? Should it be moralists, who by their profession focus on problems of moral analysis and judgment? This seems to be the implication of subordinating the authority to use force to the determination of just cause. Yet there is a basic problem with this line of reasoning: Moralists—indeed, anyone other than the person or persons in the position of sovereign authority—do not have responsibility for the common welfare or, indeed, for the institutional system of order in which the values they seek to determine are preserved. Nor do they have the wherewithal to act to serve these goods. They have a role in the moral determination whether to resort to force, but it is a supportive, advisory one. The ultimate determination belongs to the sovereign authority, who bears the responsibility for the common good and has command of the resources able to serve it.

The idea of just cause itself, in classic just war terms, requires one or more of three purposes—defense against an attack already made or in progress, recovery of something wrongly taken, and punishment of evil. By the terms of the United Nations Charter, only self-defense—by an individual state or a collectivity of states—against "armed attack" is allowed. Though the international law requirement seems on the face of it more restrictive, in practice the idea of defense has expanded to include the ideas found in the just war formulation as well as the idea of retaliation even when it can serve no defensive purpose, as in a nuclear second strike. The British use of military force in the Falklands War was justified in international law as a defensive reaction to an ongoing "armed attack" by Argentine forces; yet since Argentina had already occupied and claimed the islands, the British use of military force was clearly also an effort to retake them for Britain. Similarly, in the case of the Gulf War, the international law justification for use of force against Iraq was collective defense against an ongoing "armed attack," the occupation of Kuwait. Yet since Iraq had announced its annexation of Kuwait, this military response was clearly also an effort to retake it and restore the Kuwaiti government. At the same time, the direction of the force used also clearly sought to punish Iraqi leader Saddam Hussein for initiating the aggression and his elite forces, the Republican Guards, for their role in the takeover. So the older moral formulation of the idea of just cause still has force, though in international law this formulation is buried in an expanded notion of what counts as defense.

A terrorist attack initiated and carried out by a non-state actor is not the same as an "armed attack" initiated and carried out by a state, but in just war terms this is a distinction without a difference, because in either case the common welfare of the political community that has been attacked is under assault, and the governing authority of that community has the responsibility to act to defend it, to recover anything wrongly taken in the attack, and to punish those responsible and their supporters. So in just war terms there is no doubt that the attacks of September 11 constitute just cause for a response up to and including the use of United States military force.

Yet there are still other moral tests, tests that the sovereign authority has the responsibility to apply and satisfy. Of those identified in Aquinas's listing, two remain—the avoidance of wrong intention in the sense of those motivations first rejected by Augustine, the desire to dominate, a lust for power, an implacable animosity, cruelty in seeking vengeance, and so on; and the aim of achieving peace. If it were true, as Osama bin Laden in 1998 claimed, that the United States is engaged in a war against Islam, "occupying the lands of Islam in the holiest of places, the Arabian Peninsula, plundering its riches, dictating to its rulers, humiliating its people, terrorizing its neighbors, and turning its bases in the Peninsula into a spearhead through which to fight the neighboring Muslim peoples,"[9] in short, if the United States were in fact engaged in a war of imperial domination based in an implacable animosity toward Muslims and toward Islam, then this would constitute wrong intention, and action motivated in this way would be unjust. Yet the reverse is in fact true: The United States presence in Saudi Arabia and the Gulf states is defensive, not offensive; this presence, as well as the continuing economic and military pressure on Iraq, is the direct result of responding to Iraq's aggression in 1990–1991; the use of military force and other measures since the September 11 attacks have been clearly purposed as a response to those attacks and the threat of others, not an attack on Islam.

Is any credence at all to be given to the argument of bin Laden and his supporters? One must grant that there is a fundamental cultural gap between his perspective and that of the United States and of Western culture generally. bin Laden has repeatedly characterized America and the West as "crusaders" supporting "Zionists," while (as noted) appealing to the Islamic tradition of defensive *jihad* to justify killing "the Americans and their allies—civilian and military" as "an individual duty for every Muslim who can do it in any country in which it is possible to do it."[10] This is an explicitly religious way of casting the conflict and the motivations on each side. The roots of bin Laden's argument lie in a view of the world first defined by Muslim jurists in the period from the late eighth through early tenth centuries, according to which the world is divided into two spheres, the territory of Islam (*dar al-islam*) and the territory of war (*dar al-harb*). All conflict comes from the territory of war; all peace is found in the territory of Islam. This latter territory is at peace because it is ruled in accordance with God's law by a ruler who has inherited the dual mantle of political and religious leadership from the Prophet Mohammad. Thus any attack on the territory of Islam is, by definition, aimed against it not just as a political entity but also against the religion of Islam. This conception of the inherent relation between religion and politics is also turned outward to describe the territory of war. bin Laden's characterization of the West in terms of religiously defined animosity—"crusaders" supporting "Zionists"—reflects this worldview. On it there simply is no possibility of a state founded on secular values taken to be universal, no possibility of a state acting out of concern for the welfare of its own citizens as defined in the terms of constitutionally granted rights and a deeper respect for human rights, a state in which religious freedom guarantees the existence of a pluralistic religious culture. By contrast with this worldview, however, war for religion has been explicitly ruled out in Western conceptions of politics since the Peace of Westphalia, and the idea of a separation between the sphere of faith and that of temporal order goes back much earlier; it is found, as I suggest earlier, in the basic just war understanding of the rights and responsibilities of sovereignty, including the right and responsibility to use force on behalf of the common welfare. By this latter measure it is bin Laden and his supporters who manifest implacable animosity toward America and the West, who desire to dominate it, who seek to inflict harm against it simply because it is there.

Thinking of these competing worldviews suggests why the achievement of peace in the war against terrorism will require much more than success in the use of coercive force. To suppress terror and establish an order of life in which innocent people do not become the targets of violence aimed at some larger goal is a necessary priority, but there also needs to be another kind of struggle, a multifaceted one aimed at establishing a worldview in which difference does not translate to hostility. Here a major part of the problem is to be found in the world of Islam itself, where religious reflection and political theory need to reopen understanding of the experience and thought of the Muslim past so as to enunciate an understanding of world on such terms as just described as authentically Islamic. For the simple fact is that Muslim states have never constituted a single politico-religious dar al-islam; such states have lived in peace with non-Muslim neighbors for extended periods; and today Muslims live with religious and cultural freedom in all kinds of states (indeed, with more room for the diversity inherent in Islam than has been allowed in states like Afghanistan under the Taliban, theocratic Iran, or Wahhabi-dominated Saudi Arabia). The United States and other Western societies can take the lead in establishing and enforcing a world order in which terrorism is unambiguously criminalized and rooted out, but the problem of the use of Islamic tradition to rationalize and justify terrorism is a problem that needs to be addressed and resolved by Muslims themselves.

Three prudential concerns—that use of force be a last resort, that it be expected not to create more harm than good, and that it have a reasonable prospect of success—have figured prominently in some recent just war thinking, again notably that of the United States Catholic bishops. The bishops have taken the position that their tradition includes a primal "presumption against war," which the various *jus ad bellum* tests must overcome for a use of force to be justified. Neither the idea of such a "presumption" nor the three prudential tests were part of the listing of what is necessary for a just war found in Aquinas and other formative just war thought. There the moral conception of the use of force is strikingly different: Force may be used for good as well as ill, and the just war idea spells out what is necessary for it to be used as a tool for good.

It may, of course, be understood that, while the three prudential criteria just mentioned were not among the necessities for a just war as recognized in formative just war theory, they may be counted among the considerations one in sovereign authority must take into account after deciding, on the basis of the criteria of just cause, right intention, and the aim of peace, that use of force in a given case is morally justified. That is, the prudential criteria have a secondary role—given that a use of force in the case at hand is justified, is it prudent to use such force at the moment. I take it that the Catholic bishops and others who have followed their line of thinking—including some who are not interested in the full range of just war reasoning at all but use the just war criteria to oppose use of force—are saying something different—that resort to force is not morally justified unless these prudential criteria are unambiguously satisfied. The problem is that the prudential tests are interpreted in such a way that unambiguous satisfaction is essentially impossible to achieve. The criterion of last resort is understood as meaning that all measures short of force must have been tried and found to fail before force is justified, when as a prudential criterion for moral decision it properly means that the moral agent considers whether nonforceful means are likely to reach the justified end or not; and if not, then only force remains. The criterion of no greater harm than good has been habitually interpreted by reference to a view of modern warfare that represents it as inherently so destructive that, in the terms of Pope John XXIII in *Pacem in Terris*, it can no longer serve justice, when in fact the face of warfare has decisively changed as a result of precision-guided weaponry, able to strike an intended target without great collateral damage. The criterion of reasonable hope of success has been interpreted eschatologically, so that the peace sought is the ultimate peace with justice of the City of God, not the relative peace possible in the actual world. So there is a place for use of these prudential criteria in the decision whether to use force, but they need to be used properly, in a way that reflects their secondary role in the moral decision whether to resort to force and accepts the possibility for using force in the service of good—not in a leading role and not as a way to bolster a presumption that the use of force is always prima facie wrong.

In the response to terrorism, a strong case can be made for a wide range of types of action, of which the use of military force is only one. The reason is that terrorism is a multifaceted phenomenon, and terrorist acts cross many of the lines we habitually draw in contemporary life. It makes sense most of the time to draw distinctions between police work and military action, between domestic surveillance and espionage, between uses of force (whether domestic or foreign) and other measures including economic and diplomatic ones. But the phenomenon of terrorism runs across these ordinary distinctions, so that in some ways it is a police problem and in others a military one; in some ways a domestic problem and others a foreign one; in some ways a problem to be addressed by economic means, in others by diplomatic means, in others by military means. Accordingly, the usual just war calculations of proportionality, last resort, and reasonable hope of success are made more complex, but by no means impossible. The moral agent simply has to think in a multivariate way, seeking to maximize the good and minimize the harm of chosen paths of action overall, while using different means to address different aspects of the problem. This is in no way inconsistent with the basic moral perspective of just war thinking—that the sovereign authority has the responsibility to act on behalf of the political community to protect it from danger and remove threats to its common life and the individuals who make it up, including threats to the values that define the community and knit it together.

In my judgment, a moral response to the terrorist attacks of September 11 and the continuing threat posed by the authors of those attacks justifies a robust but finely tuned military response like the one directed against Al Qaeda and the Taliban in Afghanistan, and more broadly they justify use of military force against other targets as appropriate in the future. Yet the actual use of military force in the future needs to be determined morally through a review of the full range of concerns laid out in the *jus ad bellum*. There is also no doubt in my mind that those attacks and the continuing threat justify the range of nonmilitary responses we have seen. But in it all, the aim of those in political authority must remain the protection and defense of the American political community, the values on which it is based, and the larger framework of values and institutions that constitute the international order. The responsibility to do this at once confers the authority to act and sets limits on what may be done, for a just response must finally respect who we are as a people and the values we hold, both those specific to our own political community and those shared with others within the international order.

Once the decision has been made that the use of force is morally the right choice, the focus shifts to how that force is in fact used. In recent just war thinking this matter, traditionally called the *jus in bello,* is typically treated, following the example of Paul Ramsey, in terms of two moral principles—discrimination and proportionality of means. Discrimination means avoidance of direct, intentional harm to noncombatants. It may be derived deontologically, as it was for Ramsey, or teleologically, as it is for utilitarian philosophers who use this term, but in either case the result is the moral obligation not directly and intentionally to harm noncombatants. Proportionality of means, by contrast, is an inherently teleological idea, following from a prudential calculation of the least destructive means available to carry out an attack on a justified target.

Both these principles are problematic in practice. The problem with the use of the principle of discrimination is that even if one postulates that it is never morally right to attack noncombatants directly and intentionally, it is still necessary to say who the noncombatants are; the idea of discrimination in itself does not do this. Thus the contemporary use of the principle of discrimination opens itself to fuzziness, disagreement, and confusion as to just who counts as a noncombatant. Is everyone in a modern society in some sense a combatant because of the integrated nature of modern societies? Are all citizens in a democracy combatants if they concur in their government's use of force? Are soldiers who are not actively fighting but have not laid down their weapons and surrendered to be counted as noncombatants, as some moralists argued about the Iraqi Republican Guards on the Basra Road in the last stages of the Gulf War? All these kinds of reasoning can be found in the literature. The principle of discrimination turns out to be not so distinct after all, and to have importantly variant meanings.

The principle of proportionality of means has different, but equally bothersome, problems. Most important, there is widespread variation in how to apply it. Sometimes the measure seems to focus on outputs, at other times on inputs. Sometimes it seems simply to refer to a high level of destructiveness, not measured against the ends achieved but against the moralist's personal idea of what counts as disproportionate force. This can lead to an utterly wrong judgment as to appropriate level of force, as when the use of overwhelming force is decried as disproportionate even if, as is usually the case, using such a level of force is the best way to lower the level of casualties. Sometimes proportionality of means is conflated with the *jus ad bellum* idea of overall proportionality of the choice to use force, a conflation that leads to serious confusion when applied to the decision what to do in a given case. Sometimes this principle is used to argue that the risk to both sides in combat should be relatively equal, as in the criticism of the bombing campaign against Serbia over Kosovo for being carried out from a height that made the pilots unreachable by antiaircraft fire and missiles. All these are, to my mind, wrong ways of using the idea of proportionality of means. There is a proper use of this principle, a use in accord with its fundamental meaning that requires measuring the means used against the results to be achieved, so that the most moral form of force is that which achieves the justified object at the cost of the least destruction. But even here there is disagreement among moralists as to whether to count only harm to the enemy or also harm to one's own forces. In sum, the principle of proportionality is even more problematical, in practice, than the principle of discrimination.

Fortunately there are alternatives to the use of these two principles, and these alternatives are in fact truer reflections of just war tradition than are these principles. The ideas of discrimination and proportionality of means do not appear anywhere in just war thought prior to Ramsey; they are his invention. What one finds running through earlier just war tradition is something much more closely mirrored in the positive international law on armed conflicts— definition of noncombatant immunity by the identification of classes of people who normally, because of personal characteristics or social function, take no part in war and thus should not have war directed at them, and efforts to ban certain specific kinds of weapons as contributing to indiscriminate or more destructive warfare. Similar ideas are also found in other cultural traditions; thus to focus on them provides a link with those traditions that is less direct if one seeks to work from the principles of discrimination and proportionality.

So far as protection of noncombatant immunity is concerned, beginning with the classes of persons who deserve such protection because their personal condition (age, physical or mental illness, gender) or social function (essentially all persons in civilian occupations who do the same job whether their nation is at war or not) is to start where the principle of discrimination must go if it is to be anything more than an abstract idea. However one gets to this point, the important thing is the principle of justice: The people in these classes do nothing to deserve to be attacked, and thus they should not be. They are simply going about their normal lives as best they can, and even if their society is at war, this should not make them targets. Understanding this reveals what is most heinous about terrorism. It inverts the places of combatants and noncombatants relative to the use of force, so that it is noncombatants who are explicitly targeted by terrorist acts. Moral conduct in the use of force, by contrast, requires respecting the natural immunity of such persons, except when in individual cases they engage in activities that make them combatants—like women who serve in combat roles in the military, for example, or like child soldiers in some contemporary civil wars. Such people are not noncombatants despite belonging to traditionally defined classes of noncombatants, but recognizing them as combatants because of their activity in carrying on war does not destroy the immunity of other women and children who do not do so. These exceptions do not diminish the general rule; because they are exceptions, they make the general rule more important to observe.

As for means in combat, working from limits or bans on the use of particular weapons does not lead to the confusions and differences of interpretation encountered in moralists' efforts to apply the principle of proportionality. Arguably, the restraints imposed by limits or bans on particular weapons may not be restrictive enough for some readings of the requirements of the moral principle of proportionality. The reason is that not all weapons that are often criticized as causing disproportionate damage are limited or banned in international agreements or in national policy or law. Examples of such weapons include antipersonnel mines and cluster bombs, which have also been criticized as indiscriminate. Yet used with care, targeted directly on combatants who could not be reached otherwise except by more destructive means, such weapons as these may actually be morally the weapons of choice. From all accounts, this is how such weapons have been used by American forces in Afghanistan.

As I suggested earlier on, a significant current in American moral discourse on war continues to be driven by assumptions about war shaped by the images of high-altitude carpet bombing and the possibility of the use of nuclear weapons in contemporary warfare. Some early criticism of the American military buildup directed against Al Qaeda and the Taliban incorporated such assumptions. But it is time for just war thinkers to recognize that American military capabilities today are very different from those of World War II and the strategic nuclear debates. The difference is at root technological, but dramatically improved technology has been reflected in new tactics. Precision-guided munitions directed to their targets by laser illumination or by GPS units incorporated into them have dramatically changed targeting expectations. One of the reasons in the past for developing targeting strategies aimed at large areas was that smaller targets could not be hit with any accuracy. This was also one important reason for increasing the yield of nuclear warheads to the multi-megaton range. If one could expect no more than to hit within several hundred yards of a hardened target, then the weapon's destructive power had to be increased so as to deal with that fact. PGM capabilities have altered these expectations—these can hit within tens, not hundreds, of yards of the center of their targets, which for practical purposes means bullseye capability. Use of such munitions more exclusively, made possible by inexpensive retrofitting of formerly "dumb" bombs, has been a feature of the Afghanistan campaign. This leads to two important tactical changes. First, the number and size of warheads necessary for a decisive strike against a particular target has sharply diminished. With this has come also a radical diminution in collateral damage, the sort of harm that in traditional just war thinking had to be dealt with by reference to the rule of double effect as unintended but undesired. The second tactical change is that close combat support of ground forces is possible even from high-flying, relatively invulnerable platforms, including B-52s, bombers that were previously known best for their carpet-bombing capability.

Moral reflection and discourse on war needs to take account of these dramatic changes. The simple truth is that the new technologies of warfare make honoring the moral requirements of the just war *jus in bello* much easier and more straightforward, and the new tactics reflecting these technologies carry this possibility into practice. The war on terrorism should make maximum use of these new technologies and tactics.

Conclusion

The gist of what I have been arguing can be put simply, in terms of several propositions. First, terrorism is a distinctive phenomenon that disregards or inverts fundamental moral values, and thus challenges not only the persons and societies directly targeted by terrorist activity, but also those fundamental moral values themselves, and thus through them all personal and social life. Accordingly, terrorism is deeply evil. Second, as a result the response to terrorism must include moral reflection and discourse as well as other means. While this response should take place in every culture, in the American context this requires close attention to the idea of just war and its context in a moral conception of the political community. This in turn means rethinking and backing away from certain tendencies in American moral thought on war, tendencies rooted in a misreading of the purposes of the political community, the right to use force in pursuit of those purposes, and the nature of modern warfare. Whatever one may say about the justifiability of those tendencies in the historical contexts where they first appeared, they have wrongly skewed moral thinking about the use of force by the political community, and they need to be left behind. Third, in military terms the American response to the attacks of September 11 has thus far satisfied the moral criteria of just war tradition. Indeed, I have argued that reasoning from those criteria obligated such a response. The means used have shown that we are in a new day as regards conduct in the use of armed force, so that the moral distinction between the justified use of such force and terrorist acts is drawn the more sharply. At this point we do not know where the struggle against terrorism may lead, but the moral direction laid out in just war tradition, including the conception of the responsibilities of the political community assumed there, provide lasting guidance for this struggle.

Notes

1. Osama bin Laden, et al., "Jihad Against Jews and Crusaders: World Islamic Front Statement," 23 February 1998. Available at http://www.library.cornell.edu/colldev/mideast/wif.htm.
2. Paul Ramsey, *War and the Christian Conscience* (Durham, N.C.: Duke University Press, 1961); and *The Just War* (New York: Scribners, 1968).
3. Jonathan Schell, *The Fate of the Earth* (New York: Alfred Knopf, 1982).
4. National Conference of Catholic Bishops, *The Challenge of Peace* (Washington, D.C.: United States Catholic Conference, 1983).
5. Michael Walzer, *Just and Unjust Wars* (New York: Basic Books, 1977).
6. James Turner Johnson, and George Weigel, *Just War and the Gulf War* (Washington, D.C.: Ethics and Public Policy Center, 1991).
7. Johnson and Weigel, *Just War.* Part Three.
8. *Summa Theologica* II/II, Q. 40, Al.
9. bin Laden, "Jihad."
10. bin Laden, "Jihad." John F. Burns, "bin Laden Stirs Struggle on Meaning of Jihad," *The New York Times,* (2002)1,15.

Chapter 19

STRATEGIC INTELLIGENCE: THE WEAKEST LINK IN THE WAR AGAINST WORLD TERRORISM

LOCH K. JOHNSON

As the world's preeminent military and economic power, the United States has long stood out as a lightning rod in the storm of terrorism that has arisen from the Middle East since the mid-1980s. It suffered major assaults in 1983 against its armed forces, diplomats, and citizens in Lebanon, the World Trade Center in New York City in 1993, Saudi Arabia in 1996, Kenya and Tanzania in 1998, and Yemen in 2000. Yet, despite these earlier tragedies, the terrorist attacks of September 11, 2001, directed against the World Trade Center as well as the Pentagon in Arlington, Virginia, caught the United States completely by surprise, in the worst intelligence failure of its history. This chapter examines the intelligence deficiencies that resulted in the deaths of almost three thousand people during that dark hour, and explores how the nations of the world might collectively strengthen their intelligence shields in a common defense against further acts of terrorism.

America's Troubled Intelligence Agencies

America's secret agencies have been on the ropes since the end of the Cold War, battered by one failure after another that has led critics like Senator Daniel P. Moynihan to call for abolition of the Central Intelligence Agency (CIA) and a fundamental restructuring of the entire "intelligence community." In the aftermath of the bombing of the U.S.S. *Cole* in the Yemeni port of Aden in 2000 and the death of seventeen Navy personnel, former Secretary of the Navy John Lehman criticized "the obscene failure of intelligence" to anticipate the attack. He dismissed America's intelligence efforts as "a $30 billion jobs program that takes the most wondrous products of space and electronic technology and turns them into useless mush." Lehman's lament echoed an earlier call by Senator Moynihan, appalled by the inability of the intelligence agencies to forecast the fall of the Soviet Union in 1991, for a prompt burial of the CIA and reliance instead on the Department of State for information about foreign affairs.

Intelligence critics have had plenty of ammunition since the end of the Cold War. Policy makers in Washington, D.C., claimed that in 1990 they were never provided adequate warning of Iraq's surprise invasion into neighboring

Kuwait. Subsequently, during the war to repel Iraqi forces known as Operation Desert Storm, the CIA and U.S. military intelligence proved unable to assassinate Iraq's leader Saddam Hussein, because they could not find him. Nor could they locate the prominent warlord Mohammed Farah Aidid during America's intervention into Somalia in 1993. On top of these failures came the shocking discovery in 1994 that a decade earlier Soviet intelligence had managed to recruit a mole, Aldrich H. "Rick" Ames, burrowed deeply in the heart of the CIA's Operations Directorate, who revealed hundreds of operations to his masters in Moscow. It also came to light at this time that during the Cold War all of the CIA's agents in Cuba and East Germany had been discovered by Soviet intelligence and turned back against the United States. Another blow fell in 1995 with the revelation that, in direct violation of congressional guidelines, the CIA had failed to report to legislative overseers its close ties with an army colonel in Guatemala, Julio Roberto Alpirez, suspected of playing a role in two murders (including the death of an American citizen's spouse).

In 1998, the CIA raised further doubts about its credibility by never resolving the confusion over whether a Sudanese factory, bombed by the United States, had really been producing chemical weapons (as the Agency claimed) or merely common household medicines. Also in 1998, the CIA could not pinpoint the whereabouts of terrorist leader Osama Bin Laden in Afghanistan, with U.S. warships in the Arabian Sea launching multimillion-dollar cruise missiles at what proved to be empty tents in the desert south of Kabul near the Pakistani border. Then, in 1999, the Cox Report disclosed the possibility that nuclear weapons secrets had been stolen by a Chinese intelligence asset inside the Los Alamos Nuclear Laboratory. Subsequent reporting by the *Washington Post* in 2000 indicated that four years prior to the Cox Report the CIA had acquired 13,000 technical documents from a Chinese defector that pointed to the theft of U.S. nuclear secrets, yet the agency had never gotten around to translating the documents into English.

Of even greater immediate embarrassment to the CIA, in 1999 one of its analysts provided bombing coordinates for NATO that mistakenly designated a building in Belgrade as a local arms depot rather than the Chinese embassy, leading to the death or injury of several Chinese diplomats in an air attack against the Yugoslav city. That same year, the agency erroneously dismissed the prospect of a nuclear weapons test by the government of India, even though statements about the impending test were commonplace among politicians during the country's national elections that preceded the test.

The flaws in America's intelligence establishment run deeper than even this unhappy litany of recent failures suggests. In a time of accelerated technological advances around the world, the United States and its allies face serious challenges ahead in trying to maintain an information advantage over terrorists and renegade states. The current edge enjoyed by the liberal democracies in satellite photography ("imagery") is rapidly eroding. In 1999, the private U.S. company Space Imaging launched a surveillance satellite named *Ikonos II* that yields photographs almost as detailed as the American government's most secret satellite photography, pictures of almost any part of the planet for sale to anyone with cash or a credit card. Within a few years, Iraq and other pariah nations will be able to manufacture home-grown spy satellites or acquire commercially available substitutes (the Rent-a-Satellite option) that will provide them with their own capacity for battlefield transparency—a huge advantage for the United States during the Persian Gulf War against the largely blind Iraqi force and during its war against the Taliban regime in Afghanistan in 2001 and 2002.

The advantages in signals intelligence are in decline as well. The listening satellites of America's National Security Agency (NSA), for example, are designed to capture analog communications from out of the air. The world, though, is rapidly switching to digital cell phones, along with underground and undersea fiber-optic modes of transmission—glass conduits ("pipe lights") that rely on light waves instead of electrons to carry information. These new forms of communication are much harder to tap, leaving the NSA with a sky full of increasingly irrelevant satellites.

Furthermore, the NSA has traditionally depended on its skills at decoding to gain access to foreign diplomatic communications, but nations and terrorist groups are growing more clever at encrypting their messages with complex, computer-based technologies that can stymie even the most experienced NSA cryptologists. Under pressure from the U.S. software industry and the Department of Commerce, the Clinton administration decided in 1999 to allow the export of advanced American software that encrypts electronic communications, making it more difficult for the NSA and the Federal Bureau of Investigation (FBI) to decipher the communications of foreign powers that might intend harm to the United States. Responding to market pressures of its own, the European Union is on the verge of removing its restrictions on the sale of encryption software by European companies.

America's intelligence community suffers as well from an excessive redundancy built into its collection systems, with satellites, airplanes, and unmanned aerial vehicles (UAVs) often staring down at the same targets. Moreover, many of the satellites are gold-plated Cadillac de Ville models, with all the latest accessories. For certain missions, as in the broad coverage of a battlefield, they are valuable; but for many others, they could be replaced with less expensive, smaller satellites—serviceable Chevies. (The smaller the satellite the less expense involved in positioning it in space, since launch costs are linear with weight). The U-2 *Dragon Lady* piloted aircraft and the RQ-4A *Global Hawk* and *Predator* UAVs are also far less costly than the large, elaborate satellites and much more effective in locating foes in places like Afghanistan, Kosovo, and the Korean peninsula.

One of the most important responsibilities of the U.S. intelligence agencies is to warn Americans and their allies about terrorist efforts to acquire weapons of mass destruction, an extraordinarily difficult mission. The case of the suspected chemical weapons plant in Sudan is illustrative. In 1998 at a pharmaceutical factory near Khartoum, CIA sensing devices sniffed out what seemed to be the chemical Empta, a precursor for the production of the deadly nerve agent VX.

The intelligence community had already collected signals intelligence and agent reports that linked the factory in the past with the terrorist bin Laden and his Al Qaeda organization. Putting two and two together, analysts estimated with a high degree of confidence that the factory was manufacturing chemical weapons. Following a U.S. cruise missile attack against the facility, the Sudanese government denounced the United States and claimed that it had gone to war against an aspirin factory. The CIA stuck with its original assessment, but did acknowledge that detective work of this kind is difficult and imprecise. "The turning of a few valves can mean the difference between a pharmaceutical company and a chemical or biological plant," said the Agency's leading proliferation specialist.

In the case of the Indian nuclear test—after the failure to warn of the attacks against the World Trade Center and the Pentagon in 2001, the next most egregious U.S. intelligence breakdown since the end of Cold War—America's intelligence agencies were well aware that the Indians intended to accelerate their nuclear program. After all, this is what top-level party officials had been saying publicly throughout the Indian election season. Even the average tourist wandering around India in the spring of 1998 and listening to the local media would have concluded that a resumption of the program was likely. What surprised the intelligence agencies was how fast the test had taken place. It was "a good kick in the ass for us," admits a senior CIA official. In part the miscalculation was a result of what a CIA inquiry into the matter (led by retired Admiral David Jeremiah) referred to as "mirror imaging." Agency analysts assumed that Indian politicians were just like their American counterparts— both made a good many campaign promises, few of which were ever kept. To win votes for boldness, Indian politicians in the victorious party (the BJP) had promised a nuclear test; now that the election hoopla was over, surely they would back away from this rash position. Such was the thinking at the CIA.

Further clouding accurate analysis by CIA analysts were successful efforts by officials in India to evade America's spy satellites. The Indians knew exactly when the satellite cameras would be passing over the nuclear testing facility near Pokharan in the Rajasthan Desert and, in synchrony with these flights (every three days), scientists camouflaged their preparations. Ironically, U.S. officials had explicitly informed the Indian government about the timing of U.S. satellite coverage for South Asia in hopes of impressing upon them the futility of trying to conceal test activity. Even without this unintended assistance, though, the Indians could have figured out the cycles for themselves; even amateur astronomers can track the orbits of spy satellites.

Moreover, the Indians had become adroit at deception, both technical and political. On the technical side, the ground cables normally moved into place for a nuclear test were nowhere to be seen in U.S. satellite photographs of the site. The Indians had devised less visible ignition techniques. The Indians also stepped up activities at their far-removed missile testing site in an attempt to draw the attention of spy cameras away from the nuclear testing site. On the political side, Indian officials expanded their coordinated deception operation by misleading American and other international diplomats about the impending nuclear test, offering assurances that it was simply not going to happen.

Finally, a dearth of reliable intelligence agents ("assets") contributed to the CIA's blindness. During the Cold War, South Asia received limited attention from the U.S. intelligence agencies, compared to their concentration on the Soviet Union and its surrogates; therefore, building up an espionage ring in this region after the fall of communism still had a long way to go at the time of the Indian tests. These excuses notwithstanding, American citizens may have wondered with a reasonable sense of indignation—not to say outrage—why their well-funded intelligence community proved ignorant of what was going on inside the largest democracy and one of the most open countries in the world.

Far more difficult than keeping an eye on India is the challenge of gaining access to intelligence on reclusive terrorist organizations and renegade states like Iraq, Iran, Libya, and North Korea—dangerous, isolated, and unpredictable adversaries known to leave footprints of fire. It is difficult as well to keep track of companies engaged in commercial transactions that aid and abet the spread of weaponry, like the German corporations that secretly assisted the Iraqi weapons buildup and the construction of the large chemical weapons plant at Rabta in Libya.

Strengthening America's Intelligence Capabilities

Intelligence, the means by which nations acquire and assess information apt to protect their citizens from harm, is a process that has several phases, from planning, collection, and processing to analysis and dissemination—what intelligence professionals refer to as the "intelligence cycle." If peaceful nations are to be successful in thwarting future terrorist operations against their territories, they will have to undertake extensive reforms to correct the weaknesses in each of these steps.

PLANNING

The planning phase involves deciding which nations and groups abroad (and at home) warrant intelligence surveillance. At the beginning of every new administration in Washington, D.C., White House officials work with the Director of Central Intelligence (the DCI, who heads America's thirteen secret agencies) to prepare a "threat assessment"—a priority listing of most dangerous perils faced by the United States, arrayed from the highest targets like the Taliban forces in Afghanistan through currently less worrisome places like Cuba. These officials then determine how much money from the intelligence budget will be spent tracking the activities of each target.

This planning stage is critical; unless a target is taken seriously in the initial setting of priorities in Washington, D.C., it is unlikely to receive much attention by those with responsibilities for collecting information in the field. During the Cold War, the United States concentrated mainly on gathering intelligence about the Soviet Union and other communist powers, neglecting lesser targets like Afghanistan and the rest of South Asia (where Americans found themselves surprised by the hostility displayed toward them by the Taliban regime in Afghanistan, and were taken aback as well as by the Indian nuclear test). Terrorism has risen steadily on the list of intelligence priorities since the end of the Cold War, but until September 11 it remained just one of several demands on the resources of the U.S. intelligence agencies, including North Korea, Iraq, Iran, China, and Russia (whose massive nuclear arsenal has kept the attention of Washington officials).

Now terrorism holds a position of preeminence on Washington, D.C.'s threat list, resulting in a greater focus of U.S. worldwide intelligence resources on Osama bin Laden and his Al Qaeda network.

COLLECTION

The collection phase became skewed as well during the Cold War, in a manner that has further harmed America's counter-terrorist preparedness. Understandably awed by the technological capabilities of satellites and reconnaissance airplanes (U-2s, SR-21s, or UAVs), officials poured most of the intelligence budget into surveillance machines capable of photographing Soviet tanks and missile silos and eavesdropping on telephone conversations in communist capitals. Human spy networks became the neglected stepchild of intelligence.

Machines certainly have their place in America's spy defenses. They played an important role in Afghanistan in 2001 and 2002, as satellites hovered over its mountains taking photographs and UAVs swooped into its valleys in search of Al Qaeda terrorists and their Taliban accomplices. But machines cannot peer inside caves or see through the canvas tents or the roofed mud huts where terrorists gather to plan their lethal operations. A secret agent in the enemy's camp is necessary to acquire this kind of information—the only kind of information likely to give the peaceful societies advance warning of future attacks. Human intelligence ("humint") remains the key to protecting the United States and its allies against terrorist attacks.

Humint networks take time to develop, though, and only recently has the DCI launched a major recruitment drive to hire Americans into the CIA with language skills and knowledge about Afghanistan and other parts of the world largely ignored by the United States. Intelligence officers with these skills are needed to recruit local agents overseas who do the actual snooping for the CIA.

The September attacks will accelerate these efforts, although finding American citizens who speak pasto, Arab, and Farsi and want to work for the intelligence agencies–operating overseas in less than luxurious (and sometimes dangerous) conditions at a modest government salary–may prove difficult.

PROCESSING

When the director of the NSA (which collects electronic information for the United States from around the world) was asked recently what his major problems were, he replied, "I have three: processing, processing, and processing."

In this third phase, information is converted from "raw" intelligence—that is, in its original language (perhaps Farsi), in the form of a secret code, or in the obscure details of satellite photographs—into plain English. The chief difficulty is the sheer volume of information that pours into the secret agencies, especially from machines around the globe. A former intelligence manager recalls that he often felt like a fire hose was being held to his mouth. Hundreds of photographs from satellites stream back to the United States each day, along with thousands of untranslated telephone intercepts.

The task of sorting through this flood tide to determine what is important and what is routine has sometimes failed to produce key information in a timely manner. The CIA could use some help from the computer whizzes in Seattle and the Silicon Valley on how to manage information flows more expeditiously. It has begun to move in this direction with the recent creation of a nonprofit venture-capital firm called In-Q-Tel, located in Silicon Valley and meant to rub shoulders with information technology experts in the area.

ANALYSIS

Once information is processed, it must be studied for insights into the intentions of our adversaries. This fourth step, called analysis, lies at the heart of the intelligence process. If the CIA is unable to provide reliable insights into what all the information means, all the preceding stages are for nought. It is one thing to discover that a group of terrorists have convened in Kuala Lumpur, but what policy makers really want to know is why the meeting took place. What are the specific implications for the security of the United States and its antiterrorism partners?

Good analysis depends upon assembling the best brains possible to evaluate global events and conditions, drawing upon a blend of public knowledge and secrets purloined from adversaries. In the United States, the chief problem once again is recruiting into the intelligence service well-educated Americans who have deep knowledge about the politics, economics, culture, and military affairs of places like Afghanistan and Sudan.

The CIA and the other secret agencies have been scrambling to redirect their resources from the communist world to the forgotten world, but—like the establishment of new humint spy rings—hiring and training outstanding analysts takes time.

DISSEMINATION

Finally, intelligence must be disseminated to those who make decisions in a nation's government. This may seem simple enough, but it is a phase rife with opportunities for error. The information must have five essential characteristics for it to be useful—relevance, timeliness, accuracy, breadth, and purity.

Relevance is essential. If intelligence fails to help put out the fires that have flared up in the policy maker's in-box, it will be ignored. Incisive reports on political elections in Poland have their place, but in the United States what the White House wants above all is knowledge about the progress of the ongoing political and military campaigns in Afghanistan. Often intelligence is out of sync with the main issues before policy makers, because analysts become too wedded to their own research interests (the state of the Mongolian People's Army, for example) at the expense of other topics currently more pressing to decision makers. The White House declaration of war against Al Qaeda, the Taliban, and global terrorism in 2001 will help focus the work of the intelligence agencies—or their top managers will be out of a job.

Timeliness is equally vital. The worst acronym an analyst can see scrawled across his intelligence report is OBE—"overtaken by events." Reports on the whereabouts of terrorists are especially perishable, as we discovered in 1999 when the United States fired cruise missiles at bin Laden's encampment in the Zhawar Kili region of Afghanistan's Paktia Province, only to learn that he had departed hours earlier.

Similarly, the accuracy of information is critical. One of the worst intelligence embarrassments for the United States came in 1999 when the CIA misidentified the Chinese Embassy in Belgrade as a weapons depot, leading to a NATO bombing of the building and the death of Chinese diplomats.

Intelligence must be comprehensive as well, drawn from all of a nation's intelligence agencies and coordinated into a meaningful whole—what intelligence officers refer to as "all-source" intelligence. The United States has been plagued by the vexing problem of institutional fragmentation within its so-called intelligence "community" (a misnomer if there ever was one). Its thirteen secret agencies often act more like separate medieval fiefdoms than a cluster of organizations all trying to provide the president with the best possible information from around the world. One of the most important needed reforms of intelligence is to elevate the statute and authority of the DCI so that he (or she) can truly harness all of the secret agencies. As things stand now, the DCI has neither budgetary nor appointment powers over the NSA and other agencies. As a result, the "all-source" goal dreamed of by President Harry S Truman when he created a *Central* Intelligence Agency remains unfulfilled.

Intelligence must also be free of political spin. An analyst is expected to assess the facts in a dispassionate manner. Usually intelligence officers maintain this ethos, but occasionally in the United States they succumb to White House pressure for "intelligence to please"—data that support the president's political agenda rather than reflect the often unpleasant reality that an administration's policy has failed.

Much can go wrong with intelligence—and has. If it is to function properly in the new war against terrorism, the planning phase must identify the correct targets and direct adequate resources against them; collection must be riveted on tracking the terrorists and must employ the right mix of machines and human spies (especially the latter). Processing must move faster and with greater skill in discriminating the wheat from the chaff. Analysts must possess a deeper understanding of foreign countries that harbor terrorist cells, as well as a better comprehension of what makes the terrorists tick. And, at the end of the pipeline, intelligence officers must redouble their efforts to provide policy makers with information that is pertinent, on time, reliable, all-source, and unbiased. Policymakers must also have the courage to hear the truth rather than brush it aside, as President Lyndon B. Johnson did with intelligence reports that brought him bad news about the war in Vietnam.

That's a tall order for the United States, in light of its extensive global interests and responsibilities. Places like Rwanda and Somalia can seem all-important one day and not the next. New "flavors of the month" pop up and demand attention. At least with terrorism, though, Americans have become painfully aware that this threat has reached a more virulent form and is going to take a long, patient effort to subdue. This is not a flavor of the month, but rather a new global war against a particularly insidious ghost-like enemy who operates in secret and must be hunted down with a stronger reliance on America's secret agencies than any other war has required. Just as the Pentagon has geared up to fight this war using a range of weapons, troops, and tactics, so must the intelligence agencies move to improve their capabilities for more focused planning, collection, processing, analysis, and dissemination of information on the terrorist target.

Americans and their friends abroad must brace themselves for further mistakes, though, since all nations will continue to have only imperfect information about the activities of adversaries and thugs around the world. The liberal democracies have learned how cunning their enemies can be and the many hiding places they have. Still, the United States has the world's largest and most effective intelligence agencies in history. They have patiently tracked down and captured Carlos the Jackal in Sudan, the ringleader of the World Trade Center bombing in 1993, the two Libyan intelligence officers convicted in the bombing of Pan Am 103, the leaders of the Shining Path in Peru, and the Pakistani (Mir Aimal Kansi) who murdered two CIA officers near the Agency's Headquarters in 1993. In due time and with the assistance of allied intelligence services, they will find those who masterminded the horrible murders in September of 2001.

The Latest and Most Urgent Wake Up Call

The coalition of countries aligned in the global war against global terrorism have much work to do, however, to improve their intelligence defenses. If one good thing can come out of the national tragedy of September 11, it may be an awakening to the necessity for intelligence reform in the United States and allied nations. Officials in Washington, D.C. are still operating under the antiquated National Security Act of 1947. Fresh initiatives are necessary to combat the stealthy enemies faced by the civilized world in the post-communist era. In the United States, the place to begin is with consolidation of the intelligence agencies under the control of a stronger DCI, held accountable to congressional oversight committees. A DCI with the proper authority can in turn support the new Office of Homeland Defense with the kind of relevant, timely, accurate, all-source, unbiased intelligence on terrorists that were so badly needed before the attacks against New York City and Washington, D.C.

The United States and its allies must also accelerate the hiring of new intelligence officers. A generational wave of retirements has left the CIA with an insufficient number of case officers abroad to recruit foreign agents, especially in places where the United States has never had much of a presence (as in South Asia). In the years from 1993–1997, the CIA's Operations Directorate shrank by seven hundred positions. Personnel losses have been deepest in Africa, with an attempt to make up for the deficiencies by using "fly aways," that is, case officers sent over for a short time. This approach has proved ineffective, however, because the officers are in place too short a time to develop productive contacts.

Even if this agent problem were solved, the U.S. intelligence community faces another, equally serious human deficiency—analytic brain power. From 1993–1997, fully one thousand analysts retired from the CIA alone—a one-third reduction, back to 1977 levels. By the year 2005, the current DCI George J. Tenet anticipates that up to 40 percent of the workforce at the CIA will have served for five years or less. As a result, the secret agencies lack enough talented interpreters of information to make sense of the data that flood their offices. On the eve of the Persian Gulf War, the Defense Intelligence Agency had only two analysts assigned to study intelligence on Iraq. Across the board of the various intelligence methods, America's analytic depth is uncomfortably shallow. Imagery analysis in particular has suffered from inadequate attention. The hundreds of photographs a day that return to the United States from surveillance satellites have overwhelmed interpreters. A senior congressional staffer with responsibilities for intelligence oversight has complained that "less than half of the pictures taken by our satellites ever get looked at by human eyes," or, for that matter, "by any sort of mechanized device or computerized device detecting change."

To remedy the staff deficiencies, America's intelligence agencies are currently undertaking their largest recruitment effort since the 1950s. According to a CIA official, the ideal profile for a new recruit is an "Arabic-speaking second generation American living in Detroit." Assuming these ideal rookies can be found and persuaded to join the CIA, they must be thoroughly trained before they are sent overseas. Then it can take several years for them to mature into effective case officers with a productive stable of foreign assets. "We need to recruit talent, grow it, and nurture it," emphasizes another senior CIA official, who points to a further difficulty: "And this means paying and promoting area experts in a way that is competitive with the private sector." This is not an easy task, when today's government salaries are substantially below what smart young people can draw in the business world.

The shallowness of the CIA's spy networks abroad is further weakened by the agency's shortsighted rotation policy of stationing officers for only a year or two in a foreign country before sending them somewhere else. One recent CIA case officer in Latin America served in Argentina, the Dominican

Republic, Bolivia, Venezuela, and Peru all in a single ten-year period—not a pattern conducive to developing expertise and strong relationships with potential agents in any one country. Sometimes senior officers are rewarded with the top CIA position in a foreign country (the job of Chief of Station or COS) without even having expertise in its language and culture. In contrast, during the Cold War KGB officer Geli Dnyeprovsky spent the thirteen years from 1965 to 1978 largely in New York City and became a mastermind of Soviet recruiting operations at the United Nations. Another Soviet agent, Colonel Rudolf Abel, remained underground for years in the United States before finally being caught.

Most of the CIA's case officers are placed undercover in U.S. embassies overseas. An alternative is to conceal them in positions outside the embassy— say, as international travel agents, computer software salespeople, or even bartenders—in what the CIA calls "non-official cover" (yielding the acronym NOC, pronounced "knock"). By day, NOCs carry out normal jobs; by night, they don cloak and dagger. While most intelligence services around the world use a NOC system, the CIA has relied more on official embassy cover. Setting up shop inside an embassy is far easier and less expensive for the CIA (even if the diplomats in the Department of State frown on having spies in their buildings overseas). Moreover, being part of the diplomatic world is far more hospitable for CIA case officers—a lifestyle that is comparatively safe, familiar, and enjoyable, with opportunities for collegial associations with compatriots and fellow intelligence officers. In contrast, the NOC faces a considerably more isolated, demanding, and dangerous existence, combining a daytime "cover" job with a stressful evening of espionage, with fewer opportunities to associate with Americans and—if one is caught in an act of lèse-majesté—no diplomatic immunity.

Reliance on embassy cover for case officers has made it much easier for the counterintelligence services of hostile nations (not to mention terrorist groups) to spot CIA officers in foreign capitals and, over the years, this transparency has cost the lives of several intelligence officers. In addition, according to a close observer, intelligence officers end up recruiting mainly "drunken foreign diplomats at embassy parties." The CIA also continues to cling to the wrong career incentives for its case officers. Top management relies on a reward system that leans toward counting the number of assets case officers have recruited, rather than assessing the quality of information provided by each asset (an analogue of the propensity to count the number of articles published by young scholars in lieu of trying to evaluate their significance during the promotion and tenure decisions of academe).

Analysts, the CIA's country or regional experts, have their own problems of detachment from the nations they are assigned to study and understand. They seldom venture overseas for any length of time, tethered to their desks at headquarters in Langley, Virginia, and reliant on the public literature and secret cable traffic from case officers to keep them informed. It is obviously important for analysts to be close at hand in Washington throughout most of their careers, preparing reports for policy makers and answering their questions. But they also need to travel abroad more frequently to the places that are the subject of their reports and, from time to time, to spend longer sabbaticals overseas (in those locales where Americans can live)—or else lose touch with their areas of expertise and end up passing on to policymakers out-of-date interpretations.

THE CHALLENGE OF SUPERWEAPONS

Most prominent on the list of U.S. intelligence targets today is not a country, but a threat that cuts across national boundaries—the spread of nuclear, biological, and chemical (so-called NBC) weapons. "The threat of an all-out nuclear war once drove our intelligence systems," remarks a senior official in the Department of Defense; "now it's proliferation, with the threat of a single nuke going off somewhere in the next decade. We're trying to prevent this from happening and intelligence is important." At the beginning of the Clinton administration, U.S. intelligence discovered a scheme in which criminal elements in Kazakhstan intended to steal highly enriched uranium and sell it to Iran. After being alerted by the State Department, the government in Alma-Ata managed to foil the plot and arrest the thieves. Intelligence was indispensable, too, in verifying assurances from three former Soviet republics that possessed nuclear warheads at the end of the Cold War (Belarus, Kazakhstan, and Ukraine) that they were in fact giving up these weapons, leaving only Russia so armed in that part of the world. These newly independent nations kept their promise, thanks in part to watchful Western eyes as well as the inducement of large investments by the United States and its allies in their economic development.

Of special concern is the threat of biological warfare (BW). Biological weapons, employing such agents and toxins as anthrax bacteria, botulinum toxin, smallpox virus, tularemia, cholera, and plague bacillus, are cheaper to produce than nuclear weapons (costing millions rather than billions of dollars). Moreover, they are easier to conceal and can cause a greater number of casualties, although their dissemination is vulnerable to winds and other weather conditions. For delivery, a terrorist could even use a crude system of aerosol sprayers attached to an aircraft, a boat, a truck, or simply a portable device strapped into a backpack.

By weight, biological warfare materials are hundreds of thousands of times more potent than the most toxic chemical warfare (CW) agents, such as the sarin gas used ineffectually by Aum Shinrikyo in the Tokyo subway system. If the terrorist knows how to disseminate the agent or toxin, BW provides ground coverage that is far more expansive than any other weapons—including nuclear. Existing BW agents can also be modified by genetic engineering, making the materials still more pathogenic or infectious. Even benign microorganisms can be converted into pathogenic or toxin-producing BW agents by inserting genetic material into them from harmful species. "With recombinant DNA technology, for example," notes an unclassified intelligence report, "it is possible to produce new organisms, exploit variations on organisms, or induce organisms to respond in new ways, such as producing synthetic bioregulators or chemical toxins."

Intelligence for a New Age

Given the long list of potential dangers in the world, clearly the United States and its allies must have strong intelligence shields; just as certain, too, is the imperative that the secret agencies in the antiterrorist nations embrace fundamental reform or become irrelevant. They need improved technology, smaller (and less expensive) surveillance satellites, a greater use of U-2s and UAVs, more NOCs in the streets of foreign capitals, additional analysts at home, and greater integration in all the phases of intelligence—from the gathering and analysis of information to its timely dissemination to policymakers.

In the United States, the clandestine services are in trouble. The authority of their leader, the DCI, is weak and, as a consequence, the intelligence "community" lacks organizational unity. Its global network of spies has crumbled due to a generational wave of retirements and a fascination among intelligence managers for expensive satellites that has diverted their attention from the recruitment of foreign human assets. Remarkably, despite these handicaps, the CIA and its companion agencies have been able to provide top officials with reliable and timely information on many important world developments—a testimony to the talent of the men and women who serve as intelligence officers. But they need help if America's "first line of defense" (former President George Bush's definition of intelligence) hopes to avoid the fate of another famous line of defense, the Maginot.

More money is not the answer; the U.S. intelligence agencies are bloated as it is. The solution lies in a shift of priorities toward a better balance between civilian and military intelligence, between hardware and the recruitment of agents, between embassy and non-official cover, and between the gathering of information and the even harder job of providing insights into what it means. These goals can be achieved. The intelligence agencies have already begun to take some modest steps in the right direction, with more attention to the recruitment of a new generation of case officers at the CIA and efforts to revamp the NSA's antiquated eavesdropping technology.

The secret agencies and the legislative oversight committees that deal with intelligence have also made advances in refining their delicate relationship. The objective is to find the proper balance between maintaining a robust security against foreign threats, on the one hand, and the preservation of civil liberties at home, on the other hand. The intelligence agencies must not be hobbled, but at the same time they must be subject to checks and balances just like the rest of the government. The CIA and Congress have come to a better understanding recently about the especially vexing gray area of ethical standards related to the recruitment and handling of especially odious foreign agents (like Col. Alpirez). As DCI John Deutch once put it, the CIA from time to time will be "drawn into relationships with people of questionable character." Nuns and boy scouts are not known to have access to state secrets, nor do they belong to terrorist cells; the CIA must recruit individuals, often highly unsavory individuals, who do. Yet many Americans recoil at the notion of the United States working hand in hand with profoundly disreputable characters, perhaps murderers—even if the alliance may benefit America's interests.

Responding to this sense of idealism, Deutch promised the public that there would be limits to the CIA's recruitment practices. He ordered his general counsel to work with legislators to determine what the intelligence community should do about agents who "may have violated human rights or U.S. law." The CIA is now on notice: Keep the congressional oversight committees informed of the activities of its foreign assets that are particularly questionable. In this way, legislators and intelligence managers together can weigh the advantages of continuing the relationship with the spy, as set against the need to honor and protect moral principles important to the United States in its conduct of world affairs. When it comes to infiltrating terrorist cells like Al Qaeda, though, the DCI is likely to continue to approve any possible recruitment that can provide advance warning of further lethal attacks against the United States and its allies.

This spirit of cooperation between the secret agencies and overseers in Congress is a vital part of raising the performance level of U.S. intelligence. But the more sweeping changes necessary to redress its profound weaknesses will require the close attention of the one person who can truly reform the hidden side of government—the president. Left to its own devices, the intelligence bureaucracy will tinker with changes only at the margins, and America's secret agencies will continue their drift toward obsolescence.

What better time than now for correcting the information inadequacies that allowed the devastating attacks against the American homeland? Will President George W. Bush take the time and display the determination to bring about the necessary reforms in the United States, as well as improve intelligence sharing among all the antiterrorist nations? The events of September 11 give him and his counterparts in the free world no other choice.

Chapter 20

Bringing International Law to Bear on the Control of the New Terrorism in the Global Age[1]

David Held

On Sunday, 23 September 2001, the novelist Barbara Kingsolver wrote in the *Los Angeles Times*:

> It's the worst thing that's happened, but only this week. Two years ago, an earthquake in Turkey killed 17,000 people in a day, babies and mothers and businessmen. . . . The November before that, a hurricane hit Honduras and Nicaragua and killed even more. . . . Which end of the world shall we talk about? Sixty years ago, Japanese airplanes bombed Navy boys who were sleeping on ships in gentle Pacific waters. Three and a half years later, American planes bombed a plaza in Japan where men and women were going to work, where schoolchildren were playing, and more humans died at once than anyone thought possible. Seventy thousand in a minute. Imagine. . . .
>
> There are no worst days, it seems. Ten years ago, early on a January morning, bombs rained down from the sky and caused great buildings in the city of Baghdad to fall down—hotels, hospitals, palaces, buildings with mothers and soldiers inside—and here in the place I want to love best, I had to watch people cheering about it. In Baghdad, survivors shook their fists at the sky and said the word "evil." When many lives are lost all at once, people gather together and say words like "heinous" and "honor" and "revenge.". . . . They raise up their compatriots' lives to a sacred place—we do this, all of us who are human—thinking our own citizens to be more worthy of grief and less willingly risked than lives on other soil.

This is an unsettling and challenging passage. When I first read it, I felt angered and unsympathetic to its call to think systematically about September 11 in the context of other disasters, acts of aggression, and wars. A few days later I found it helpful to connect its sentiments to my own strong cosmopolitan orientations.

Immanual Kant wrote over two hundred years ago that we are "unavoidably side by side." A violent challenge to law and justice in one place has consequences for many other places and can be experienced everywhere. While he dwelt on these matters and their implications at length, Kant could not have known how profound and immediate his concerns would become.

Since Kant, our mutual interconnectedness and vulnerability have grown rapidly. We no longer live, if we ever did, in a world of discrete national communities. Instead, we live in a world of what I like to call "overlapping communities of fate" where the trajectories of countries are heavily enmeshed with each other. In our world, it is not only the violent exception that links people together across borders; the very nature of everyday problems and processes joins people in multiple ways. From the movement of ideas and cultural artifacts to the fundamental issues raised by genetic engineering, from the conditions of financial stability to environmental degradation, the fate and fortunes of each of us are thoroughly intertwined.

The story of our increasingly global order—"globalization"—is not a singular one. Globalization is not a one-dimensional phenomena. For example, there has been an expansion of global markets that has altered the political terrain, increasing exit options for capital of all kinds and putting pressure on polities everywhere. But the story of globalization is not just economic; it is also one of growing aspirations for international law and justice. From the United Nations system to the European Union, from changes to the laws of war to the entrenchment of human rights, from the emergence of international environmental regimes to the foundation of the International Criminal Court, another narrative is being told—a narrative that seeks to reframe human activity and entrench it in law, rights, and responsibilities. In the first section of this chapter, I reflect on this second narrative and highlight some of its strengths and limitations. Once this background is sketched, elements of the legal and political context of September 11 can be better grasped.

Reframing Human Activity: International Law, Rights, and Responsibilities

The process of the gradual delimitation of political power, and the increasing significance of international law and justice, can be illustrated by reflecting on a strand in international legal thinking that has overturned the exclusive position of the state in international law, and buttressed the role of the individual—in relation to, and with responsibility for—systematic violence against others.

In the first instance, by recognizing the legal status of conscientious objection, many states—particularly Western states (I shall return to the significance of this later)—have acknowledged there are clear occasions when an individual has a moral obligation beyond that of his or her obligation as a citizen of a state. The refusal to serve in national armies triggers a claim to a "higher moral court" of rights and duties. Such claims are exemplified as well in the changing legal position of those who are willing to go to war. The recognition in international law of the offenses of war crimes, genocide, and crimes against humanity makes clear that acquiescence to the commands of national leaders will not be considered sufficient grounds for absolving individual guilt in these cases. A turning point in this regard was the judgment of the International Tribunal at Nuremberg (and the parallel tribunal in Tokyo). The Tribunal laid down, for the first time in history, that when *international rules* that protect basic humanitarian values are in conflict with *state laws*, every individual must transgress the state laws (except where there is no room for "moral choice;" that is, when a gun is being held to someone's head. Modern international law has generally endorsed the position taken by the Tribunal, and has affirmed its rejection of the defense of obedience to superior orders in matters of responsibility for crimes against peace and humanity. As one commentator has noted, "since the Nuremberg Trials, it has been acknowledged that war criminals cannot relieve themselves of criminal responsibility by citing official position or superior orders. Even obedience to explicit national legislation provides no protection against international law."[2]

The most notable recent extension of the application of the Nuremberg principles has been the establishment of the war crimes tribunals for the former Yugoslavia (established by the UN Security Council in 1993) and for Rwanda (set up in 1994). The Yugoslav tribunal has issued indictments against people from all three ethnic groups in Bosnia, and is investigating crimes in Kosovo, although it has encountered serious difficulty in obtaining custody of the key people accused. (Significantly, of course, ex-President Slobodan Milosevic was arrested and in 2001 brought before The Hague war crimes tribunal.) Neither the tribunal for Rwanda nor the Yugoslav tribunal have had the ability to detain and try more than a fraction of those engaged in atrocities. But both have taken important steps toward implementing the law governing war crimes, thereby reducing the credibility gap between the promises of such law, on the one hand, and the weakness of its application, on the other.

Most recently, the proposals put forward for the establishment of a permanent International Criminal Court are designed to help close this gap in the longer term. Several major hurdles remain to its successful entrenchment, including the continuing opposition from the United States (which fears its soldiers will be the target of politically motivated prosecutions) and dependency upon individual state consent for its effectiveness. However, the courts formal establishment in June 2002 (over U.S. opposition) marks another significant step away from the classic regime of state sovereignty—sovereignty, that is, as effective power—toward the firm entrenchment of the "liberal regime of international sovereignty" as I refer to it—sovereignty shaped and delimited by new broader frameworks of governance and law.[3]

The ground now being staked out in international legal agreements suggests something of particular importance—that the containment of armed aggression and abuses of power can only be achieved through both the control of warfare and the prevention of the abuse of human rights. For it is only too apparent that many forms of violence perpetrated against individuals, and many forms of abuse of power, do not take place during declared acts of war. In fact, it can be argued that the distinctions between war and peace, and between aggression and repression, are eroded by changing patterns of violence.[4] The kinds of violence witnessed in Bosnia and Kosovo highlight the role of paramilitaries and of organized crime, and the use of parts of national armies that may no longer be under the direct control of a state. What these kinds of violence signal is that there is a very fine line between explicit formal crimes committed during acts of national war, and major attacks on the welfare and physical integrity of citizens in situations that may not involve a declaration of war by states. While many of the new forms of warfare do not fall directly under the classic rules of war, they are massive violations of international human rights. Accordingly, the rules of war and human rights law can be seen as two complementary forms of international rules that aim to circumscribe the proper form, scope, and use of coercive power. For all the limitations of its enforcement, these are significant changes. When taken together, they amount to the rejection of the doctrine of legitimate power as effective control and to its replacement by international rules that entrench basic humanitarian values as the criteria for legitimate government.

How do the 9/11 terrorist attacks on the World Trade Center and the Pentagon fit into this pattern of legal change? A wide variety of legal instruments, dating back to the 1963 *Convention on Offences and Certain Other Acts Committed on Board Aircraft,* enable the international community to take action against terrorism and bring those responsible to justice. If the persons responsible for the September 11 attacks can be apprehended, they could face prosecution in virtually any country that obtains custody of them. In particular, the widely ratified 1970 Hague *Convention for the Suppression of Unlawful Seizure of Aircraft* makes the hijacking of aircraft an international criminal offense. The offense is regarded as extraditable under any extradition treaty in force between contracting states, and it applies to accomplices as well as hijackers. In addition, the use of hijacked aircraft as lethal weapons can be interpreted as a crime against humanity under international law (although there is some legal argument about this). Frederic Kirgis has noted that the statute of the International Criminal Court "defines a crime against humanity as any of several listed acts 'when committed as part of a widespread or systematic attack directed against any civilian population'. . . ." The acts include murder and "other inhumane acts of a similar character intentionally causing great suffering, or serious injury to body or to mental or physical health?"[5]

Changes in the law of war, human rights law, and in other legal domains have placed individuals, governments, and nongovernmental organizations under new systems of legal regulation—regulation that, in principle, recasts the legal significance of state boundaries. The regime of liberal international sovereignty entrenches powers and constraints, and rights and duties in international law that—albeit ultimately formulated by states—go beyond the traditional conception of the proper scope and boundaries of states, and can come into conflict, and sometimes contradiction, with national laws. Within this framework, states may forfeit claims to sovereignty, and individuals their right to sovereign protection, if they violate the standards and values embedded in the liberal international order; and such violations no longer become a matter of morality alone. Rather, they become a breach of a legal code, a breach that may call forth the means to challenge, prosecute, and rectify it. To this end, a bridge is created between morality and law where, at best, only stepping stones existed before in the era of classic sovereignty. These are transformative changes that alter the form and content of politics, nationally, regionally and globally. They signify the enlarging normative reach, extending scope, and growing institutionalization of international legal rules and practices—the beginnings of a "universal constitutional order" in which the state is no longer the only layer of legal competence to which people have transferred public powers.

In short, boundaries between states are of decreasing legal and moral significance. States are no longer regarded as discrete political worlds. International standards breach boundaries in numerous ways. Within Europe, the *European Convention for the Protection of Human Rights and Fundamental Freedoms* and the European Union create new institutions and layers of law and governance that have divided political authority. Any assumption that sovereignty is an indivisible, illimitable, exclusive, and perpetual form of public power—entrenched within an individual state—is now defunct. Within the wider international community, rules governing war, weapon systems, terrorism, human rights and the environment, among other areas, have transformed and delimited the order of states, embedding national polities in new forms and layers of accountability and governance (from particular regimes such as the *Nuclear Non-Proliferation Treaty* to wider frameworks of regulation laid down by the UN charter and a host of specialized agencies). Accordingly, the boundaries between states, nations, and societies can no longer claim the deep legal and moral significance they once had; they can be judged, along with the communities they embody, by general, if not universal, standards. That is to say, they can be scrutinized and appraised in relation to standards that, in principle, apply to each person, each individual, who is held to be equally worthy of concern and respect. At the same time, shared membership in a political community, or spatial proximity, is not regarded as a sufficient source of moral privilege.

The political and legal transformations of the last fifty years have gone some way toward circumscribing and delimiting political power on a regional and global basis. Several major difficulties remain, nonetheless, at the core of the liberal international regime of sovereignty which create tensions, if not faultlines, at its center. I shall dwell on just one aspect of these here.

Serious deficiencies can, of course, be documented in the implementation and enforcement of democratic and human rights, and of international law more generally. Despite the development and consolidation of the regime of liberal international sovereignty, massive inequalities of power and economic resource continue to grow. There is an accelerating gap between rich and poor states as well as between peoples in the global economy. The human rights agenda often has a hollow ring. The development of regional trade and investment blocs, particularly the Triad (NAFTA, the EU, and Japan), has concentrated economic transactions within and between these areas. The Triad accounts for two-thirds to three-quarters of world economic activity, with shifting patterns of resources across each region. However, one further element of inequality is particularly apparent: A significant proportion of the world's population remains marginal to these networks.

Does this growing gulf in the life circumstances and life chances of the world's population highlight intrinsic limits to the liberal international order, or should this disparity be traced to other phenomena—the particularization of nation-states or the inequalities of regions with their own distinctive cultural, religious, and political problems? The latter phenomena are contributors to the disparity between the universal claims of the human rights regime and its often tragically limited impact. But a key cause of the gulf lies, in my judgment, elsewhere—in the tangential impact of the liberal international order on the regulation of economic power and market mechanisms. The focus of the liberal international order is on the curtailment of the abuse of political power, not economic power. It has few, if any, systematic means to address sources of power other than the political. Its conceptual resources and leading ideas do not suggest or push toward the pursuit of self-determination and autonomy in the economic domain; they do not seek the entrenchment of democratic rights and obligations outside the sphere of the political. Hence, it is hardly a surprise that liberal democracy and flourishing economic inequalities exist side by side.

Thus, the complex and differentiated narratives of globalization point in stark and often contradictory directions. On the one side, there is the dominant tendency of economic globalization over the last three decades toward a pattern set by the deregulatory, neoliberal model; an increase in the exit options of corporate and finance capital relative to labor and the state, and an increase in the volatility of market responses, which has exacerbated a growing sense of political uncertainty and risk; and the marked polarization of global relative economic inequalities (as well as serious doubt as to whether there has been a trickle-down effect to the world's poorest at all). On the other side, there is the significant entrenchment of cosmopolitan values concerning the equal dignity and worth of all human beings; the reconnection of international law and morality; the establishment of regional and global systems of governance; and growing recognition that the public good—whether conceived as financial stability, environmental protection, or global egalitarianism—requires coordinated multilateral action if it is to be achieved in the long term.

The 11th of September—War and Justice

If the September 11 terrorist attack was not a defining moment in human history, it certainly was for today's generations. The terrorist violence was an atrocity of extraordinary proportions. It was a crime against America and against humanity; a massive breach of many of the core codes of international law; and an attack on the fundamental principles of freedom, democracy, justice, and humanity itself; that is, those principles which affirm the sanctity of life, the importance of self-determination, and the advantages of equal rights and liberty.

These principles are not just Western principles. Elements of them had their origins in the early modern period in the West, but their validity extends much further than this. For these principles are the basis of a fair, humane, and decent society—of whatever religion or cultural tradition. There is no nation without a woman who yearns for equal rights, no society without a man who denies the need for deference, and no developing country without a person who does not wish for the minimum means of subsistence so that they may go about their everyday lives. The principles of freedom, democracy, and justice are the basis for articulating and entrenching the equal liberty of all human beings, wherever they were born or brought up. They are the basis of underwriting the liberty of others, not of obliterating it. Their concern is with the irreducible moral status of each and every person—the acknowledgement of which links directly to the possibility of self-determination and the capacity to make independent choices.

The intensity of the range of responses to the atrocities of September 11 is fully understandable. There cannot be many people in the world who did not experience shock, revulsion, horror, anger, and a desire for vengeance, as the Kingsolver passage acknowledges. This emotional range is perfectly natural within the context of the immediate events. But it cannot be the basis for a more considered and wise response. The founding principles of civilized society dictate that we do not overgeneralize our response from one moment and one set of events; that we do not jump to conclusions based on concerns that emerge in one particular country at one moment; and that we do not rewrite and rework international law and governance arrangements from one place—in other words, that we do not think and act overhastily and take the law into our hands. Clearly, the fight against terror must be put on a new footing. Terrorists must be brought to heel, and those who protect and nurture them must be brought to account. Zero tolerance is fully justified in these circumstances. Terrorism does negate our most elementary and cherished principles and values. But any defensible, justifiable, and sustainable response to the September 11 atrocity must be consistent with our founding principles and the aspirations of international society for security, law, and the impartial administration of justice—aspirations painfully articulated after the Holocaust and the Second World War—and embedded, albeit imperfectly, in regional and global law and the institutions of global governance. If the means deployed to fight terrorism contradict these principles and achievements, then the emotion of the moment might be satisfied, but our mutual vulnerability will be deepened.

War and bombing were and are one option. President Bush described the attacks of September 11, and the U.S.-led coalition response, as a "new kind of war," and indeed the September 11 attacks can be viewed as a more dramatic version of patterns of violence witnessed during the last decade, in the wars in the Balkans, the Middle East, and Africa. These wars are quite different from, for example, the Second World War. They are wars that are difficult to end and difficult to contain, where, typically, there have been no clear victories and many defeats for those who champion the sanctity of human life, human rights, and human welfare. Much can be learned from these experiences that is relevant to the situation now unfolding.

The contours of these "new wars" are distinctive in many respects because the range of social and political groups involved no longer fit the pattern of a classical interstate war; the type of violence deployed by the terrorist aggressors is no longer carried out by the agents of a state (although states, or parts of states, may have a supporting role); violence is dispersed, fragmented, and directed against citizens; and political aims are combined with the deliberate commission of atrocities that are a massive violation of human rights. Such a war is not typically triggered by a state interest, but by religious identity, zeal, and fanaticism. The aim is not to acquire territory, as was the case in "old wars," but to gain political power through generating fear and hatred. War itself becomes a form of political mobilization in which the pursuit of violence promotes extremist causes.

In Western security policy, there is a dangerous gulf between the dominant thinking about security based on "old wars"—like the Second World War and the Cold War—and the reality in the field. The so-called revolution in military affairs, the development of "smart" weaponry to fight wars at long distance, and the proposals for the National Missile Defense program were all predicated on outdated assumptions about the nature of war—the idea that it is possible to protect territory from attacks by outsiders. The language of President Bush, with its emphasis on the defense of America and of dividing the world between those "who are with us or against us," tends to reproduce the illusion, drawn from the experience of World War II, that this is a war between simply "good" states led by the United States and "bad" states. Such an approach is regrettable and, potentially, very dangerous.

Today, a clear-cut military victory is very difficult to achieve because the advantages of supposed superior technology have been eroded in many contexts. As the Russians discovered in Afghanistan and Chechnya, the Americans in Vietnam, and the Israelis in the current period, conquering people and territory by military means has become an increasingly problematic form of warfare. These military campaigns have all been lost or suffered serious and continuous setbacks because of the stubborn refusal of movements for independence or autonomy to be suppressed; by the refusal to meet the deployment of the conventional means of interstate warfare with similar forces that play by the same set of rules; and by the constantly shifting use of irregular or guerrilla forces that sporadically but steadily inflict major casualties on states (whose domestic populations become increasingly anxious and weary). And the risks of using high-tech weapon systems, carpet bombing, and other very destructive means of interstate warfare are very high, to say the least.

The risks of concentrating military action against states like Afghanistan are the risks of ratcheting up fear and hatred, of actually creating a "new war" between the West and Islam, a war that is not only between states but within every community in the West as well as in the Middle East. No doubt, the terrorists always hoped for air strikes, which would rally more supporters to their cause. No doubt they are now actively hoping for a global division between those states who side with America and those who do not. The fanatical Islamic networks that were probably responsible for the attacks have groups and cells in many places, including Britain and the United States. The effect of the U.S.-led war might very well be to expand the networks of fanatics—who may gain access to even more horrendous weapons, to increase racist and xenophobic feelings of all kinds, and to increase repressive powers everywhere, justified in the name of fighting terrorism.

An alternative approach existed, and might even be salvaged in some respects—although the longer the bombing goes on, and the longer the forces of the United States and its allies have to remain in place to secure foreign lands, the less optimistic one can be. An alternative approach is one that counters the strategy of "fear and hate." What is needed is a movement for global, not American, justice and legitimacy, aimed at establishing and extending the rule of law in place of war and at fostering understanding between communities in place of terror. Such a movement must press upon governments and international institutions the importance of three things.

First, there must be a commitment to the rule of law, not the prosecution of war. Civilians of all faiths and nationalities need protection, wherever they live, and terrorists must be captured and brought before an international criminal court, which could be either permanent or modelled on the Nuremberg or Yugoslav war crimes tribunals. The terrorists must be treated as criminals, and not glamorized as military adversaries. This does not preclude internationally sanctioned military action under the auspices of the United Nations, both to arrest suspects and to dismantle terrorist networks—not at all. But such action should always be understood as a robust form of policing, above all as a way of protecting civilians and bringing criminals to trial. Moreover, this type of action must scrupulously preserve both the laws of war and human rights law. Imran Khan put a similar point forcefully when in 2001 he wrote:

> The only way to deal with global terrorism is through justice. We need international institutions such as a fully empowered and credible world criminal court to define terrorism and dispense justice with impartiality. . . . The world is heading towards disaster if the sole superpower behaves as judge, jury and executioner when dealing with global terrorism.

The news in late 2001 and 2002 of an increasingly intense pattern of extrajudicial, outlaw killings (organized, targeted murders) on both sides of the Israeli-Palestine conflict compounds anxieties about the breakdown of the rule of law, nationally and internationally. This way leads only one way; that is, toward Thomas Hobbes's well-known sixteenth-century metaphor of the "state of nature" in international relations: The "'warre of every one against every one'—life as 'solitary, poore, nasty, brutish, and short.'" Second, a massive effort has to be undertaken to create a new form of global political legitimacy, one that must confront the reasons the West is so often seen as self-interested, partial, one-sided, and insensitive. This must involve condemnation of all human rights violations wherever they occur, renewed peace efforts in the Middle East, talks between Israel and Palestine, and rethinking policy toward Iraq, Iran, Afghanistan, and elsewhere. This cannot be equated with an occasional or one-off effort to create a new momentum for peace and the protection of human rights. It has to be part of a continuous emphasis in foreign policy, year-in, year-out. Many parts of the world will need convincing that the West's interest in security and human rights for all regions and peoples is not just a product of short-term geopolitical or geoeconomic interests.

And, finally, there must be a head-on acknowledgment that the ethical and justice issues posed by the global polarization of wealth, income, and power, and with them the huge asymmetries of life chances, cannot be left to markets to resolve. Those who are poorest and most vulnerable, locked into geopolitical situations that have neglected their economic and political claims for generations, will always provide fertile ground for terrorist recruiters. The project of economic globalization has to be connected to manifest principles of social justice; the latter need to reframe global market activity.

To date the U.S.-led coalition—in pursuing, first and foremost, a military response to the September 11 attack—has chosen *not* to prioritize the development of international law and UN institutional arrangements, and *not* to emphasize the urgency of building institutional bridges between the priorities of social justice and processes of economic globalization, although one or two coalition politicians have made speeches acknowledging the importance of this question. Peace in the Middle East has been singled out as a priority by some coalition leaders, but there is little sign as yet that this is part of a broader rethinking of foreign policy in the Middle East, and of the role of the West in international affairs more generally. These are political choices and, like all such choices, they carry a heavy burden of possibility and lost opportunity.

Of course, terrorist crimes of the kind we witnessed on September 11 may often be the work of the simply deranged and the fanatic, and so there can be no guarantee that a more just world will be a more peaceful one in all respects. But if we turn our backs on this challenge, there is no hope of ameliorating the social basis of disadvantage often experienced in the poorest and most dislocated countries. Gross injustices, linked to a sense of hopelessness born of generations of neglect, feed anger and hostility. Popular support against terrorism depends upon convincing people that there is a legal and pacific way of addressing their grievances. Without this sense of confidence in public institutions and processes, the defeat of terrorism becomes a hugely difficult task, if it can be achieved at all.

Immanuel Kant was right; the violent abrogation of law and justice in one place ricochets across the world. We cannot accept the burden of putting justice right in one dimension of life—security—without at the same time seeking to put it right everywhere. A socioeconomic order in which whole regions and peoples suffer serious harm and disadvantage independently of their will or consent will not command widespread support and legitimacy.

If the political, social, and economic dimensions of justice are separated in the long term—as is the tendency in the global order today—the prospects of a peaceful and civil society will be bleak indeed.

Islam, the Kantian Heritage, and Double Standards

Responsibility for the pursuit of justice does not just fall on the West. It is not simply the United States and Europe that must look critically at themselves in the aftermath of September 11; there is a chronic need for self-examination in parts of Islam as well. The Muslim writer, Ziauddin Sardar, wrote recently in 2001 that

> To Muslims everywhere I issue this *fatwa*: any Muslim involved in the planning, financing, training, recruiting, support or harbouring of those who commit acts of indiscriminate violence against persons . . . is guilty of terror and no part of the *ummah*. It is the duty of every Muslim to spare no effort in hunting down, apprehending and bringing such criminals to justice.
>
> If you see something reprehensible, said the Prophet Muhammad, then change it with your hand; if you are not capable of that then use your tongue (speak out against it); and if you are not capable of that then detest it in your heart. The silent Muslim majority must now become vocal.

Iman Hamza, a noted Islamic teacher, has spoken recently of the "deep denial" many Muslims seem to be in. He is concerned that "Islam has been hijacked by a discourse of anger and a rhetoric of rage." The attacks of September 11 appear to have been perpetrated in the name of Islam, albeit a particular version of Islam. It is this version of Islam that must be repudiated by the wider Islamic community, who need to reaffirm the compatibility of Islam with the universal, cosmopolitan principles that put life, and the free development of all human beings, at their center.

Hugo Young made the same point rather bluntly in *The Guardian* in 2001:

> The September terrorists who left messages and testaments described their actions as being in the name of Allah. They made this their explicit appeal and defence. Bin Laden himself, no longer disclaiming culpability for their actions, clothes their murders and their suicides in religious glory. A version of Islam— not typical, a minority fragment, but undeniably Islamic—endorses the foaming hatred for America that uniquely emanates, with supplementary texts, from a variety of mullahs.

Accordingly, it is not enough for just the West to look critically at itself in the shadow of September 11. Muslim countries need to confront their own ideological extremists, and reject without qualification any doctrine or action that encourages or condones the slaughter of innocent human beings. In addition, they need to reflect on their own failings to ensure minimum standards of living and a decent, free, and democratic life for all their citizens. As Bhikhu Parekh, Chair of the Commission on the Future of Multi-ethnic Britain, put it, Muslims must "stop blaming the West for all their ills" and must grapple with the temptation to locate all the main sources of their problems elsewhere.

The terrorist attack of September 11 can be linked to a new, integrated political crisis developing in west Asia. The crisis has been well analyzed by Fred Halliday:

> In several countries, there has been a weakening, if not collapse, of the state—in the 1970s and 1980s in Lebanon, more recently in Afghanistan and Yemen. . . . It is in these countries, where significant areas are free of government control, or where the government seeks to humor autonomous armed groups, like Al Qaeda, that a culture of violence and religious demagogy has thrived. . . . This is compounded by the way in which the historically distinct conflicts of Afghanistan, Iraq and Palestine have, in recent years, come to be more and more connected. Militants in each—secular nationalist (Saddam Hussein) as well as Islamist (Osama bin Laden)—see the cause of resistance to the West and its regional allies as one.

Hence, Osama bin Laden's first target was the government of Saudi Arabia, to which he later added the governments of Egypt and Jordan (and the Shi'ite Republic of Iran). Only later did he formally connect (via a declared *fatwa* in 1998) his war against these governments to the United States, which he came to see as the key source of, and support for, the corruption of Islamic sovereignty in the Middle East. The fundamental fissure in the Muslim world is between those who want to uphold universal standards, including the standards of democracy and human rights, and want to reform their societies, dislodging the deep connection between religion, culture, and politics, and those who are threatened by this stance and wish to retain and/or restore power to those who represent "fundamentalist" ideals. The political, economic, and cultural challenges posed by the globalization of (for want of a better shorthand) "modernity" now face the counterforce of the globalization of radical Islam. This poses many big questions; but one in particular should be stressed, that is, how far and to what extent Islam—and not just the West—has the capacity to confront its own ideologies, double standards, and limitations. Clearly, the escape from dogma and unvindicated authority—the removal of constraints on the public use of reason—has a long way to go, East and West. The Kantian heritage should be accepted across Islam as well.

It is a mistake to think that this is simply an outsider's challenge to Islam. Islam, like the other great world religions, has incorporated a diverse body of thought and practice. In addition, it has contributed, and accommodated itself, to ideas of religious tolerance, secular political power, and human rights. It is particularly in the contemporary period that radical Islamic movements have turned their backs on these important historical developments and sought to deny Islam's contribution both to the Enlightenment and the formulation of universal ethical codes. There are many good reasons for doubting the often expressed Western belief that thoughts about justice and democracy have flourished only in the West. Islam is not a unitary or explanatory category. Hence, the call for cosmopolitan values speaks to a vital strain within Islam that affirms the importance of rights and justice.

Concluding Reflections

It is useful to return to the passage from Barbara Kingsolver with which I started this essay. It makes uncomfortable reading because it invites reflection on September 11 in the context of other tragedies and conflict situations, and it asks the reader to step outside of the maelstrom of 9/11 and put those events in a wider historical and evaluative framework. Uncomfortable as this request is, we have to accept it if we are to find a satisfactory way of making sense of September 11. To begin with, as the passage suggests, it is important to affirm the irreducible moral status of each and every person and, concomitantly, reject the view of moral particularists that belonging to a given community limits and determines the moral worth of individuals and the nature of their freedom. At the center of this kind of thinking is the cosmopolitan view that human well-being is not defined by geographical and cultural locations, that national or ethnic or gendered boundaries should not determine the limits of rights or responsibilities for the satisfaction of basic human needs, and that all human beings require equal moral respect and concern. Cosmopolitanism builds on the basic principles of equal dignity, equal respect, and the priority of vital need in its preoccupation with what is required for the autonomy and development of all human beings.

Cosmopolitan principles are not principles for some remote utopia; for they are at the center of significant post–Second World War legal and political developments, from the 1948 UN Declaration of Human Rights to the 1998 adoption of the Statute of the International Criminal Court. Many of these developments were framed against the background of formidable threats to humankind—above all, Nazism, fascism, and the Holocaust. The framers of these initiatives affirmed the importance of universal principles, human rights, and the rule of law when there were strong temptations to simply put up the shutters and defend the position of some nations and countries only. The response to the September 11 new form of terrorism could follow in the footsteps of these achievements and strengthen our multilateral institutions and international legal arrangements; or, it could take us further away from these fragile gains toward a world of further antagonisms and divisions—a distinctively uncivil society. At the time of writing the signs are not good, but we have not yet run out of choices—history is still with us and can be made.

Notes

1. Two sections of this essay written especially for *The New Global Terrorism* have been adapted from my previous writings. The first section draws on some material developed at much greater length in my "Law of States, Law of Peoples," *Legal Theory* 8 (No. 2, 2002), forthcoming. The second section draws on my "Violence and Justice in a Global Age" and, with Mary Kaldor, on "What Hope for the Future? Learning the Lessons of the Past." Both these pieces were made available initially through OpenDemocracy.net. I am grateful to Mary Kaldor for

allowing me to draw on our joint essay and to adapt some of the material for this new piece. Her work on old and new wars has been an especially important influence on me here.

2. Yoran Dinstein, "Rules of War," in *The Oxford Companion to Politics of the World,* ed. Joel Krieger (Oxford: Oxford University Press, 1993).

3. David Held, "Law of States, Law of Peoples," *Legal Theory* 8 (No. 2, 2002).

4. Mary Kaldor, *New and Old Wars* (Cambridge: Polity Press, 1998).

5. Frederic Kirgis, "Terrorist Attacks on the World Trade Center and the Pentagon," September 2001, at http://www.asil.org/insights/insigh77.htm (accessed July 2002).

Chapter 21

GLOBAL TERRORISM: PROBLEMS OF CHALLENGE AND RESPONSE[1]

PETER C. SEDERBERG

> *You don't make peace with friends. You make peace with enemies.*
> ISRAELI PRIME MINISTER YITZHAK RABIN, 1993

> *Every nation in every region now has a decision to make: either you are with us or you are with the terrorists.*
> PRESIDENT GEORGE W. BUSH, 2001

Less than ten years ago, on a hopefilled day in Washington, a propitious handshake occurred between Yitzhak Rabin and Yasir Arafat. Chances for a negotiated solution to the festering conflict between Israelis and Palestinians never appeared better. Yet almost exactly eight years later, a grim George W. Bush, speaking to a joint session of Congress while the ruins of the World Trade Center still smoldered, essentially declared war on terrorism, dividing the world into a definitive "us" versus a shadowy, ill-defined "them."

These two events neatly encompass the range of potential response to the problem of terrorism from firm resolve to destroy terrorists wherever they might be found and regardless of whom might be protecting them to the reluctant recognition that terrorist attacks may be symptomatic of underlying problems that must be addressed if the attacks are ever to diminish. Recognition of this range of response, however, offers little guidance as to what might be the appropriate choice to make under particular circumstances.

The puzzle of appropriate response cannot be addressed without first clearing away some rhetorical rubbish that invariably threatens to contaminate discussions of terrorism. Once the conceptual grounds have been policed a bit, then we can better understand the implications of various metaphorical representations of the problem of terrorism and how these in turn shape response. The hidden hand of metaphor often guides our explanatory predilections without our awareness. By making the implicit entailments of our conceptual frameworks more explicit, we can free ourselves from their enthrallment and come to an understanding of the problem of terrorism that expands our repertoire of response.

Clearing the Rhetorical Rubbish

Confusion starts with the conventional language reflected even in the title of this chapter. Who wants to defend doing anything other than hunting down and destroying "terrorists"? Explicitly, the word flattens our perception of people acting in outrageous ways. They are terrorists—evildoers, pure and simple. Implicitly, the term encourages us to think in a neutered present, focusing on specific actors, ignoring both past and future in any detailed sense. As Christopher Hitchens observes, the label "disguises reality and impoverishes language and makes a banality out of the discussion of war and revolution and politics."[2]

Simply moving the rhetoric to the discussion of "terrorism," the act—in distinction to terrorist, the actor—helps to clarify the problem. This simple word change explicitly separates the act from the actor and implies the need to judge the act in some wider context. Since almost every regime and radical challenger group has some acts of terrorism to its (dis)credit, we are compelled to look more closely at distinctions among those resorting to terrorism rather than issuing a blanket condemnation. Once our attention shifts from the actor to the act, we can more easily place terrorist tactics in some perspective. Pursuing the terrorist perpetrators of September 11 by whatever means necessary provided a clarity of mission that rapidly clouded once the agenda expanded into a global "war" against all terrorism. Russians, Israelis, and Indians opportunistically lumped their disparate struggles against dissident populations into America's global campaign, and the Bush administration reluctantly recognized terrorism's complex tangle. The context within which terrorism occurs, while it may not mean everything, certainly means something.

We do not wish to trivialize the damage done by terrorism whether perpetrated by a regime or those challenging its authority, nor do we wish to discount the nightmare that a relatively weak, though desperate, challenger might someday use weapons of mass destruction. Nevertheless, a focus on terrorism as a tactic encourages us to look at just who is using this tactic and why.

This approach, of course, assumes that we can distinguish between acts of terrorism and other violent tactics; otherwise the charge of terrorism becomes merely a rhetorical weapon with which we bludgeon groups that use violence for purposes with which we disagree. Debates over the definition of terrorism may be a form of intellectual onanism—enjoyable, but not especially fruitful. Nonetheless we must make some effort to rescue the concept from the polemicists.[3]

A variety of problems impede our efforts to develop an analytically useful definition of terrorism. First, an understandable, but confusing, tendency to intermingle explanation, justification, and condemnation mars many definitions. Second, the confusion between the action (terrorism), the actor (the terrorist), and the effect (terror) detracts from our ability to distinguish between terrorism and the larger class of coercive behavior of which it is a part. Finally, the option of focusing on various subspecies of terrorism (for example, air piracy; suicide bombings) fails to specify what about these subspecies makes them terrorist. Though we may be able to formulate some policy response to particular terrorist activities, we would be forced to abandon the search for a more general understanding and strategy.

If we are to rescue the concept of terrorism from the polemicists, as well as address the concerns of those who believe it to be an empty rhetorical category, we must specify those characteristics that distinguish terrorism from other coercive tactics used within or between political communities. Two traits, each drawing upon fairly well established rules of war, seem to hold some promise. The most well established limits on the conduct of warfare involve the targets selected and the means chosen to attack those targets. Specifically, the targets of coercive attack should be other combatants, and the weapons used against these targets should be highly discriminating.

The principle of noncombatant immunity and the ban on indiscriminate weapons of destruction are certainly interrelated; nevertheless, they raise distinct issues. Terrorism may be seen as a coercive tactic that deliberately violates these two rules of war: Terrorism deliberately targets noncombatants and uses indiscriminate means. These criteria, then, suggest two propositions and two qualifying exceptions:

- **Proposition One** Discriminating acts of coercion aimed at combatants are not terrorist in nature.
- **Exception One** At some point, attacks on combatants may become so indiscriminate (counterforce nuclear war) that they become terrorist in effect, if not intent.
- **Proposition Two** Undiscriminating and severe coercive attacks deliberately aimed at noncombatants are terrorist in nature.
- **Exception Two** At some point, attacks against noncombatants may become so discriminating in choice of target (e.g., a tyrant) and means, that they are not usefully labeled terrorist.

The value of this definition lies both in its clear specification of what tactics are or are not terrorist and in its explicit identification of the areas where disputes are likely to arise (that is, indiscriminate attacks on combatants; highly discriminating attacks on noncombatants). Moreover, by treating terrorism as a tactic, this approach recognizes all contenders in a political contest may yield to the terrorist temptation.

Two key questions, however, remain open: Who is a noncombatant? And, how indiscriminate is too indiscriminate? These issues cannot be convincingly resolved by definitional fiat. Although they remain open to debate, provisional determinations need not be arbitrary; rather, they should be supported by reasoned elaboration.

The characteristics distinguishing terrorism from other coercive tactics suggest why terrorism commonly spreads fear in excess of the concrete damage done or the probabilities of being a victim. The distinction between combatants and noncombatants is, perhaps, the last firebreak of a civil order. Once it is breached, no one can feel secure. In wartime, widespread use of terror tactics signals a move from limited to total war. Terrorism, moreover, often involves innocuous targets, such as airplanes, railway depots, and office towers, places that people normally consider safe. Terrorist attacks not only cause substantive damage but also undermine the confidence people have in the mundane. Now every place must be viewed with suspicion, if not alarm.

Terrorism, then, is an especially nasty tactic that may be used for a variety of ends by the contenders in a violent political struggle. The hackneyed conundrum that "one person's terrorist is another's freedom fighter" resolves itself into a simple confusion of means and ends. Presumptive freedom fighters have resorted, and will continue to resort, to terrorist tactics to achieve their goals. However laudable the goals of the perpetrators in their own or others' minds, this does not transform the character of the means they choose.

If we abandon the concept of terrorism to the ideologues or ignore the differences between terrorism and other forms of coercion, we hamper the possibilities for successful political action to contain this particular tactic. Only if we have a sensible and reasonably clear idea of the distinctive traits of terrorism can we pursue questions of who uses it and why, and what we should do about it. Our response to terrorist tactics must be informed by the context within which it occurs, including the nature of the groups resorting to terror, the breadth and depth of their support, and, yes, the ends they pursue. To declare an undifferentiated "war" on terrorists or terrorism is to declare war in all these various contexts, a dangerous and daunting escapade.

Cry "Havoc!" and Let Slip the Dogs of Metaphor

Terrorist attacks understandably generate incomprehension and dismay. Why would our adversaries, however aggrieved, deliberately attack school buses, or civilian airplanes, or towers of world trade? When confronted with conundrums of comprehension, we often grope for a more familiar phenomenon with which to compare it. Metaphorical reasoning does not simply satisfy some poetic impulse to vivify dry analysis; often it represents the first step toward developing an explanation and a consequent response. Political metaphors, then, not only invigorate our writing, they also structure the ways we respond to unfamiliar or difficult problems.

In drawing on metaphorical guidance, however, we must remain alert to the ways our linguistic tools can end up using us, rather than the reverse. Any metaphor highlights some aspects of the problem so characterized while drawing our attention away from other elements that the metaphor fails to capture.[4] As long as we recognize the limits of the metaphorical entailments, we can remain sensitive to the potential distortions in our linguistic lens. Sometimes teasing out the tensions among multiple metaphors for the same puzzle will reveal the limits of each perspective. Mixing metaphors, then, may be a stylistic blunder but a methodological necessity.

Clearly, terrorism places a country under some kind of attack, but how should we characterize this assault? How should we respond? Three metaphors have emerged to inform our understanding—terrorism as war; terrorism as crime; and terrorism as disease. Each has certain entailments that add to both our understanding and our confusion.

We should not be surprised that terrorist attacks evoke metaphors of war. We always rally around the rhetoric of war, at least at the beginning. War and the threat of war call for unity and sacrifice; combat often engenders acts of nobility and heroism. When we face a great challenge, a terrible threat, we naturally gravitate toward these images of war to galvanize our community for the struggle ahead.

Sometimes we recognize that our war rhetoric is mere metaphor, poetically invoked to underscore the seriousness of our cause. The war on poverty and the wars on cancer or AIDS come to mind. Other times war metaphors shape our understanding in more specific ways; when we look to the entailments of the metaphor to *define* our actions, as opposed to serving simply as a *call to* action. The war on drugs, for example, leads us down policy paths decidedly different from metaphorically viewing the drug problem as a disease.

The similarities of the terrorist assaults instigated by Al Qaeda and war are compelling—violent attack, thousands dead, an enemy who declared "war." War, however, also suggests front lines, borders, and battle zones that must be defended or pacified. The threat resides in an explicit enemy, commonly another state, who occupies the other side of the battle lines. The differences, then, between these terrorist attacks and conventional war are also telling. The dead are largely civilians; the weapons were our own civilian airplanes; the declared enemy has limited military assets, no territory to hold, and no capital to capture. Indeed, the adversary's assets have already suffused throughout dozens of countries and may well still be lurking within our own.

War, to move from metaphor to reality, needs a physical territory to attack and a regime to defeat. The close association between Al Qaeda and the Taliban regime provided just such targets. A war on Al Qaeda might have been difficult to prosecute; the war against the Taliban, however, proved much more manageable. The collapse of the Taliban regime enabled the United States to pursue more of a policing action against the dispersed Al Qaeda elements located in Afghanistan.

The suggestion that after the defeat of the Taliban regime, the remaining actions against Al Qaeda resembled "policing" reflects the second metaphor—terrorism as crime. Certainly the organization of a transnational extremist organization like Al Qaeda resembles a global crime syndicate with its operatives in many countries, its global communications, and its coordinated flow of money, personnel, and supplies. The way the organization implicates itself within the social order of its target and uses the vulnerabilities of those societies against them also resembles the operations of organized crime.

Unsurprisingly, the policing instruments that states have developed to protect themselves, at least to some extent, from the depredations of organized crime have been mobilized against Al Qaeda and other targeted groups—[money flows have been tracked, assets frozen, surveillance increased, suspects rounded up for interrogation, new legal guidelines developed, and security enhanced.

Of course, telling differences also exist. In fact, global crime syndicates probably dwarf the power of Al Qaeda and similar extremist groups of "global reach," yet they do not engender the response currently mobilized to crush the terrorist criminals. The reason is obvious. Extremist Islamic groups attack the foundation of the established global order; the crime syndicates are parasitical upon it. It's not that they don't stoop to terrorism—Colombia's recent history belies this—rather, they have no interest in killing their host.

The allusion to parasitism segues nicely into the third metaphor for the terrorist challenge, that is, terrorism as disease. We see this metaphor underlying the language of terrorism's contagion across the world; how no country can be secure from this scourge. Like a disease, it respects neither age nor gender nor status. Terrorist "cells" lurk within an apparently healthy body politic, waiting for an opportunity to unleash their poison.

The disease metaphor, to be sure, does not preclude coercive responses. Cancerous cells must be detected and destroyed, though the analogy with cancer also alerts us to the physical cost of putative cures of disease, whether real or metaphorical. Yet the disease metaphor also directs us to find other responses in addition to the vigorous application of "antibiotics." Commentators like Thomas Friedman and Fareed Zakaria draw attention to the fanatical forms of Islam promulgated in the religious schools of Saudi Arabia, Pakistan, and Egypt. They call for action to pressure our erstwhile allies to moderate the teaching of such "infectious" ideas. Zakaria also suggests that many Iranians, having lived under fundamentalist rule for the past two decades, are "now inoculated against its appeal."[5] Indications suggest that Afghanis may have developed similar resistance from their exposure to the Taliban.

The entailments of the war metaphor contrast in one final way with those of the other two metaphors. War advocates generally promise victory over the enemy, a promise that for at least one side in every war proves false. Crime and disease control, however, often entail the management of chronic problems rather than the pursuit of definitive victory. Both crime and disease, like the poor, are always with us, and even the "victory" over smallpox has ironically left us more, not less, vulnerable to its reemergence. Viewed through either of these metaphorical lens, terrorism may become a problem to be contained, perhaps moderated in intensity, but never definitively defeated.

What Is to Be Done? The Range of Relevant Response

Judgments about appropriate response to terrorism often reflect two criteria, *acceptability* to our democratic sensibilities and *effectiveness* in minimizing the problem.[6] Superficially, these criteria might seem reasonably clear, and the problem straightforward. Specifically, what is effective might not be acceptable (for example, turning the country into a police state), and what is acceptable might not be effective (for example, providing those accused of terrorism the full protection of a democratic system of legal rights). How, then, can we find effective solutions that do not damage our fundamental values and institutions?

Unfortunately, several factors further complicate the problem of appropriate response. First, the above–characterization encourages the view that the problem inevitably involves "trade-offs" between our values and security—the challenge of defining responses that effectively cope with terrorism but do minimal damage to our values. We tend to underestimate the possibility that our principles of justice and democracy themselves may suggest effective responses. Negotiation, compromise, and conciliation rest at the heart of democratic political processes, but commentators usually dismiss them as irrelevant or even dangerously ineffective.

An inclination to overvalue the effectiveness of repressive coercion complements the tendency to dismiss the efficacy of democratic responses. Both policymakers and analysts alike seem to feel a little vigorous repression would go a long way to addressing the problem of terrorism, and only grudgingly admit the risks and costs. More thoughtful analysts, however, recognize that external military action or internal police repression may not only damage democratic principles and legal processes; repression may fail to lessen the problem of terrorism and could even inflame it further. In any case, negotiation and conciliation must be judged not against some idealized strategy of perfect coercion, but against what occurs in the real world.

A third complication to the simple criteria of acceptability vs. effectiveness arises from the introduction of notions of time. What works over the short run may not work over the longer term, and vice versa. A reiterated game differs substantially from one conceived as a single round of play. Interestingly, those who oppose short-term concessions argue that, though possibly effective in ending a particular terrorist event, concessions only encourage the perpetrators (and other interested parties) to engage in more terrorism in the future. Consequently, sooner or later, the regime will have to engage in repression or face an escalating terrorist challenge. Less frequently acknowledged is the possibility that repression, too, may work only in the short term, and, sooner or later, the regime will have to undertake forms of conciliation or risk becoming a permanent garrison state.

The impact of time considerations also suggests that what may be inappropriate or even impossible at one stage may become possible, even necessary, over the longer run. A vigorous coercive response may take weeks, even months, to prepare. Programs to reduce the vulnerability of a country to terrorist attacks may take years to implement. Finally, the nature of the threat itself may vary, mutating over time (another entailment of the disease metaphor). As the threat changes, so too will effective response.

Such complexities caution us against impoverishing the range of our repertoire of response. Potential responses to the challenge of terrorism fall into four broad categories:

1. **Defense and destruction leading to deterrence** Coercion, given the dominance of the war metaphor, is the default response to terrorist attacks. Harden the targets of terror and destroy the perpetrators and their patrons. By raising the obvious and immediate costs to the perpetrators and their protectors, coercion effectively deters terrorist attacks in the future. At its most radical, proponents of this strategy argue for preemptive strikes against those contemplating terrorist attacks. Despite the myth of efficacy surrounding this approach, it entails obvious costs and risks. Defense of all potential "soft" targets is impossible, and the destruction of all "terrorists," in willful ignorance of the contexts that generate their extremism and the goals they pursue through terror tactics, may only inflame our insecurity.

2. **Investigation and intelligence leading to interdiction** A successful war strategy against terrorism must have reliable intelligence. A strategy of response that emphasizes the goal of interdiction, though, arises more naturally from viewing the challenge of terrorism as a problem of crime control. Of course crime control involves punishment, but effective management of organized crime places a premium on the penetration of criminal networks, the interruption of criminal activities, and the identification and arrest of criminal kingpins. Effective control of crime through such means, though, presumes a well-organized political community, exactly what is lacking when dealing with transnational terrorist (or criminal) syndicates. Implementation of such strategies on a global scale requires laborious negotiation among largely autonomous states, each pursuing their individual domestic agendas. Military solutions, in contrast, appear to offer greater latitude for unilateral action, though this promise may be illusionary.

3. **Reaction and remediation leading to recovery** If the threat of terrorism is a chronic problem unlikely to be perfectly deterred by coercion, defended against on all points of vulnerability, or interdicted before its implementation, then we must turn our response to reaction and remediation, the strategy most directly entailed by the disease metaphor. The capacity for reaction and remediation grows in importance as terrorist attacks increase in scale. Bioterrorism, interestingly enough, highlights the importance of this approach. An attack using biological weapons needs only a concentration of people to wreak its havoc, an indefinite variety of targets that cannot be effectively defended. Such threats must be addressed through extensive preparations for effective reaction and remediation.

4. **Compromise and conciliation leading to co-optation** Recognition that terrorism is a violent tactic used by groups pursuing a variety of

political agendas leads us to look more closely at the political and social contexts that give rise to extremism. Not all the groups using terrorist tactics, indeed very few of them, embrace an unlimited nihilistic goal of the destruction of Western civilization. Recognition that their goals may reflect deeply embedded needs, aspirations, and conflicts does not excuse the resort to terrorism. However, the nature of their program, the extent to which it represents the aspirations of a wider population, and the breadth of their institutional support all suggest that, at some point, elimination of the threat may not be possible at an acceptable cost. Rather the tactics must be tamed, the agenda moderated, and ultimately the group, or significant portions of it, co-opted into the established order.

The suggestion that "bargaining with terrorists" might under some circumstances be an acceptable, even the most effective, response goes counter to both conventional wisdom ("concessions only encourage further terrorism") and emotional impulse after experiencing a terrorist assault. Nonetheless it deserves serious consideration. If a myth of efficacy amplifies the voices of those advocating force, a myth of inefficacy generally mutes those who call for more conciliatory options.

Considering Conciliation

All three of the metaphors underlying theories of response allow for the possibility of conciliation. My assertion that "wars on terrorism" may ultimately admit the need for conciliation seems the most counterintuitive, so we will turn to it last. The conciliatory implications of the other metaphors appear more obvious.

If terrorism is the disease, coercion may, indeed, be part of the cure. Yet the old saw about an "ounce of prevention" suggests the relevance of other responses entailed by this metaphor. Spinning this entailment out a bit further, most of the advances in public health and longevity have come not from our massive technologies of medical intervention—the medical equivalent of bombardment—but from comprehensive enhancements in sanitation, diet, and vaccination against common childhood killers. The best way to avoid dying from a disease is never to get it. The disease metaphor, then, directs our attention to ameliorating the conditions that increase the appeal of those advocating millenarian goals and extremist means. Programs of social reform increase the resistance of the potential supporters to these infectious ideas. In the absence of such ameliorative measures, one defeated generation of extremists may simply be replaced by the next. Doubters should consider the history of the Palestinian diaspora.

In addition, the disease metaphor, like the crime metaphor discussed subsequently, promotes an understanding of terrorism and other forms of violent discord as a chronic problem to be regulated, rather than a clear-cut foe to be defeated. Sometimes we can prevent an outbreak of a disease; sometimes we can effect a cure. Sometimes we have to manage a chronic health problem. We try to do so by reducing the intensity of its effects. Slowing the transmission of AIDS, for example, may decrease the virulence of the virus through simple natural selection: A virus strain that does not kill its host rapidly will increase its chances of successful transmission and thus survival. Analogously, not all discord or deprivation has to be eliminated. If sufficient channels of effective participation exist, then expressions of grievance can be encouraged to take less destructive paths. All successful bodies politic survive by regulating conflict, not suppressing or resolving all discord, just as all complex organisms live not in perfect harmony but in a dynamic equilibrium with threats from disease or parasites.

Terrorism as crime control also points us toward conciliatory measures, though here the metaphorical entailments may tilt further toward coercion than with the disease metaphor. To combat crime, after all, we create significant police forces and comprehensive penal institutions. Terrorist attacks prompt calls for swift apprehension and severe retribution. If we understand our terrorist adversaries as a criminal network like national or transnational crime syndicates, than a panoply of conventional policing measures can be brought to bear on their apprehension, conviction, and punishment.

Yet the management of normal criminal activity involves more than suppression and retribution. Not all social conditions prove equally conducive to criminal activity; crimes of all sorts rise and fall with the rhythms of economic recession and prosperity. Programs of community policing are often effective in providing integrative institutions in a crime-wracked community. Crime is a chronic problem, and like many diseases, it can only be ameliorated, not eliminated.

The crime metaphor, then, also suggests conciliatory entailments. For example, the demographics of Islamic terrorism resemble those of crime in the United States. Historically, a bulging cohort between the ages of 15 and 35 has repeatedly been associated with increased criminal activity and political discord. Coercion alone is not going to eliminate this potential. Over time we can wait for this cohort to age, again suggesting the chronic nature of the problem of instability that gives rise to terrorism. Meanwhile, recognition of the demographic roots of the problem also suggests strategies of amelioration similar to those entailed by the disease metaphor. Youth who are more successfully integrated into stable social structures may prove less susceptible to the temptations of extremism.

Whatever the conciliatory entailments of the other two metaphors, the currently dominant war metaphor appears to entail a straightforward repressive military response. We might, however, do well to recall some of the other strategic and political entailments of the metaphor. Somewhat simplistically, wars may either be limited or unlimited. Unlimited wars tend to subvert the Clauswitzian principle of the politically instrumental war, for they seek the total destruction of the adversary by whatever means available, up to and including weapons of mass destruction. Indeed, total war inherently tends toward terror tactics. In pre-modern times, an unlimited war might still confront practical limitations in that, though the contestants possess the will, they lacked the means to achieve their unlimited goals. Now we can more effectively pursue unlimited objectives should we so choose.

Alternatively, we may see war as a limited instrument to achieve limited goals. The concept of limited war grows in relevance as the consequences of unlimited war threaten to dwarf any meaningful political objective. Ian Clark notes that the concept of limited war involves two distinct but interrelated problems: how to resolve the conflict, while limiting its impact; and how to limit the impact of the conflict, while working to resolve it.[7] Limited impact and limited duration depend on one another, for if destruction is unlimited, then termination becomes moot; if duration is unlimited, limits on impact become moot.

The overheated rhetoric of the war metaphor, of course, often characterizes these conflicts in unlimited terms. The challengers seek the total destruction of the state; and the state seeks the total elimination of their antagonists. This rhetoric, though, defies reality. Undoubtedly, groups expressing totalistic or nihilistic goals exist (more on this later), but not all the groups using terrorism have unlimited political agendas. Ethnic conflicts fuel much of the terrorism in the world, both internal and transnational. These ethnic groups—whether Sikh, Basque, Northern Irish, or Tamil, and even most Palestinians—do not seek the utter destruction of their adversaries in the regime. Their aims, while hardly benign, are not unlimited.

Moreover, most groups who resort to terrorism do not generate the levels of destruction of which they seem theoretically capable, one reason being that completely gratuitous destruction would likely prove damaging to their own political agendas. Even a revolutionary group that seeks the overthrow of the regime, not merely independence from it, has an interest in containing the level of destruction. After all, someday they hope to inherit the body politic. They benefit little if it's a corpse.

Until recently, regimes seemed more likely to embrace unlimited objectives, a tendency reflected in the magnitude of the body counts attributable to regime terrorism. Nevertheless, many regimes, particularly democratic ones, have been reluctant to use all the weapons at their disposal to extirpate dissident groups, branch, root, and soil. Again, practical considerations about the self-destructive costs of an unlimited counter-terrorism campaign figure greatly in regime restraint, but regimes, too, may seek some accommodation, at least with those who provide support and sympathy for the groups engaged in terrorism, as an effective counter-terrorist measure on its own merits.

Once contenders in a war acknowledge that they fight for limited objectives with limited means, they also tacitly accept that the conflict will end through a political process involving some form of accommodation. Such a process will characterize even those conflicts possessing a clear victor, as long as victory is not total and defeat is not complete. The political process terminating a limited war necessarily entails negotiations that, by their nature, involve the mutual recognition of the adversary's right to exist.

The acceptance of a conflict's limited objectives and the necessity for a process of war termination, however, ultimately lead to something more than the vague acceptance of the opponent's right to exist. Since the adversaries will ultimately become negotiating partners, each gains a vested interest in the capabilities of the other. Neither side wishes any longer to see their partner eliminated either as a tactical military objective or as a result of internal division. Each partner hopes, indeed requires, that the other side can enforce any mutual agreements on their own supporters. In short, neither side in a conflict of limited duration has an interest in destroying the other side's command *or* control. Limited war, ironically, ultimately leads to a kind of tacit interdependence between the antagonists (and an implicit alliance between the extremists in both camps).

Appeasement, ironically, becomes the flip side of limited warfare in the coin of statecraft. Edward Luttwak observes that the purpose of appeasement, properly understood, is "to uncover the incentives to war and to offer, if possible, such benefits as would outmatch their attraction, while advertising with due discretion the disincentives as well."[8] Limited wars for limited objectives, then, are fought with an eye to costs. If the costs of the military solution grow too high, then appeasement might offer the better bargain. These two forms of inducement, Luttwak carefully notes, reinforce rather than undercut one another. Without the willingness to appease, wars become endless; without the willingness to fight, concessions become continuous.

Embracing the war model, then, does not automatically preclude the possibility, indeed the desirability, of negotiations and concessions. Only if the war against terrorism is construed in totalistic terms do conciliatory measures become moot. If the war analogy draws on limited war concepts, then negotiations and concessions come along as part of the political package of war termination. Conciliatory gestures can lead to the transformation of the adversary into a credible partner for conflict management or to the disintegration of the threat posed, as moderate elements are bought off, while the more intransigent are contained or eliminated through policing and, if necessary, conventional combat missions.

Context and the Choice of Response

None of the three metaphors we use to construe the problem of terrorism preclude conciliation as a counter-terrorist strategy. Indeed, interpretations of terrorism that reject conciliation under any circumstances—for example, those that see terrorism as the tool of psychotics or unyielding fanatics resistant to compromise—also raise serious questions about the efficacy of repression short of extermination. Once we conclude that the challenger is either crazy or functions according to "bizarre" beliefs (like in salvation through suicide attacks), then repressive coercion will not produce its expected deterrent effects.

Conciliation, then, cannot be dismissed out of hand; however, we must still determine when it might work. Each challenger group possesses its own political history and character that should shape regime response to it. Moreover, groups change their character. They seldom embody perfect cohesion and consistency. Extremist rhetoric, on both sides, may obscure real possibilities for division or accommodation. Repression and conciliation are not necessarily mutually exclusive counter-terrorist tactics; indeed, the allure of conciliatory carrots often depends on the threat of repressive sticks. Finally, neither repression nor conciliation obviates the need for lessened vulnerability (defense), interdiction of planned attacks (intelligence), or emergency preparedness (recovery).

Regimes, of course, seek more useful guidance than the admonition that each case is unique and the response must be multifaceted. Consequently, we offer some preliminary thoughts on the general conditions and particular factors affecting the relevance of alternative reponses. In this discussion we assume that the adversary represents something more than a bunch of "terrorists;" that is, though they resort to terrorism as a tactic, they also possess some ideological underpinning, a political agenda, an organization, and base of support and sympathy.

1. **The base of support for the adversary** Punitive actions may be most plausible against isolated fringe groups, but an adversary with a broad base of even passive support presents a different problem. Efforts to repress or exterminate a widely supported group may only solidify and expand their base. Unfortunately, a regime's recognition that it cannot eliminate its nemesis often comes only after years of bitter struggle, as the South African and Palestinian cases illustrate. *Proposition 1.1:* The more limited the support for the adversary, the more likely coercive tactics will prove effective. *Proposition 1.2:* Conciliatory strategies increase in relevance as the base of support for the adversary expands.

2. **Time, space, and terrorism** When the challenge of terrorism becomes chronic and its operations dispersed, then a war on terrorism will become a war without end, and the targets for attack multiply indefinitely. The potential for escalation rises, along with the anticipated and unanticipated costs of coercion. The alternatives to living in a constant state of war include efforts at negotiation and compromise as a complement to, and perhaps a replacement for, war fighting. *Proposition 2.1:* As the terrorist threat becomes more dispersed over space and through time, the relevance of conciliatory response will increase.

3. **The diffuseness of the terrorist threat** One of the tactical dilemmas faced when confronting a terrorist threat is how to balance the demands for defense, destruction, interdiction, recovery, and conciliation. Terrorism attacks "soft" targets, and the list, therefore, is essentially unlimited. Improving the defense against one type of attack (airplane hijackings) may displace the attack onto another soft target of opportunity as long as the challenger possesses the capability and interest in attacking. *Proposition 3.1:* The more diffuse the potential targets, the more emphasis

will have to be placed on reaction and remediation. The more limited the targets of opportunity (for example, nuclear reactors, embassies), the more resources should be invested in defense. A geographically centered adversary organization, as noted earlier, presents more clearly defined targets of opportunity for attack. A diffuse global network presents a significantly different challenge. Moreover, the organization of the network complicates the situation further. A highly centralized organization increases the probable success of a tactic of decapitation. A terrorist "franchise" may continue functioning even after its "headquarters" is eliminated. *Proposition 3.2:* The more diffuse and decentralized the terrorist organization, the more emphasis will have to be placed on intelligence and interdiction.

4. **The ideological appeal of the adversary** Groups desiring the total destruction of the established order (nihilists) or its complete transformation (redemptionists) might resist any conciliatory appeal of which the regime is capable. Bruce Hoffman notes some significant differences between secular and religious based ideologies.[9] He argues that religiously motivated challengers are more likely to view their struggle in totalistic terms, see violence as a sacramental act, and resist utilitarian calculations in political decision making. In contrast, more pragmatic aspirations for social justice, greater autonomy within the established political community, or even independence from it when this devolution does not threaten the survival of the existing state (for example, the aspirations for independence by a colony) offer greater promise for a negotiated settlement. Extremist rhetoric may obscure possibilities for compromise; however, members of an adversary movement may not hold their ideas either sincerely or consistently. In addition, attitudes may change over years of fruitless struggle. *Proposition 4.1:* Sincerely held, totalistic ideologies preclude conciliation and compromise. *Proposition 4.2:* Insincerely held ideologies open opportunities to promote pragmatic transformation. *Proposition 4.3:* Inconsistently held ideologies create opportunities to promote disintegration through defections. *Proposition 4.4:* Ideological appeals reflecting concrete objectives (for example, greater autonomy, political representation, material relief) create opportunities for compromise.

5. **The characteristics of the adversary's organization** Kent Oots argues that in addition to their ideological goals, other internal factors and dynamics affect an adversary and the types of demands they make.[10] Among these he includes internal cohesion, competition with other groups, the size of the group, and the nature of the group's leadership. He suggests that sometimes these factors work to escalate the group's political demands and increase the probability of violence. As groups grow in size and diversity, however, cohesion will decline and differences appear over the best way to purse their agenda. The agenda, itself, may evolve over time as the base of support grows. *Proposition 5.1:*

Increasingly complex adversary organizations create opportunities to pursue either their transformation or disintegration through conciliatory measures.

Another organizational factor concerns the role of terrorist tactics in the overall strategy of the adversary. As challenger groups increase their base of support and expand their repertoire of resistance, the relative significance of terrorism usually diminishes as other avenues, including both more conventional coercive tactics and political action, open to pursue their objectives. By rewarding nonviolent expressions of dissent, a regime may encourage the abandonment of terrorism. *Proposition 5.2:* The decreasing significance of terrorist tactics in the overall strategy of the adversary creates opportunities to pursue their transformation.

6. **The political context of negotiation and conciliation** Any regime contemplating conciliation must calculate both the direct costs of compromise and the subsequent risk that terrorism on the part of others might be encouraged. They also must consider how concessions might provoke their original base of support. What may be gained in diminished violence from their adversaries may be lost through new violence from the now disaffected members of the regime. Settler resistance to Algerian independence and a Palestinian state illustrate this dilemma forcefully. Indeed, the DeGaulle government for a time replaced the rebellion and terror tactics of the Algerians with the rebellion and terror tactics of the French colonials in Algeria. *Proposition 6.1:* The more substantive the concessions proposed by the regime, the greater will be the internal political resistance to a strategy of accommodation.

Clearly, moderate elements among the challengers face the same risks with respect to the more radical elements in their coalition. Both the Palestinian and the South African cases give evidence of this problem. Again, widespread weariness with a fruitless struggle often works to minimize these costs. *Proposition 6.2:* Conciliatory strategies that encourage the transformation or defection of the more moderate elements of a challenger movement will tend to increase violence from the remaining radicals.

Another contextual factor concerns the setting for the negotiations. Robert P. Clark, in a sensitive analysis of the Spanish government's attempted negotiations with Basque insurgents, identifies a variety of considerations that seem generally relevant.[11] In addition to the complex political and cultural setting that affects the parties attempting a negotiated settlement, Clark notes that the timing of a cease-fire often presents a roadblock. The possibilities range from the likely regime position of "first truce; then talks," through "truce begins when talks begin," to the more extreme dissident position of "first concessions, then truce." The decade of frustrating negotiations between Israel and the PLO also illustrates this pattern. A third area of dispute involves the definition of the agenda, especially those issues defined as "technical" and resolved promptly and those considered "political" and thus more difficult to negotiate and often postponed. *Proposition 6.3:* Expect negotiations to be frustrated by the challenger's desire to expand the agenda and the regime's desire to narrow it.

Terrorism, Anarchy, and Global Security

At times, President Bush defined America's war on terrorism so broadly as to suggest that at some point we would attack ourselves, since we harbor those accused of acts of terrorism in Central America and Cuba and we continue to produce weapons of mass destruction. At other times, the administration has been more restrained, focusing on terrorist groups possessing "global reach" (meaning they attack America; sorry, Sri Lanka, you're on your own.)

Such paradoxes arise, of course, because we are making war on a tactic, one used by both regimes and challengers including one of our current adversaries, Iraq, and one of our current allies, Russia. Moreover, much of the world's terrorism occurs in local and regional struggles remote from American attention. Finally, the relatively careful way the administration has dealt with the PLO and Iran reflects a deeper understanding of the political complexities that subvert the easy rhetoric of war.

Despite the inadequacy of the metaphor of war to guide our response to the multidimensional terrorist challenge, the problem remains—terrorism is a particularly nasty tactic, especially so now that some extremist groups indicate an interest in escalating its destructiveness. Every political community possesses a strong interest in minimizing this means of political expression. The question is whether the nascent global community has the capability to do so.

We have yet to grasp fully the implications of the many facets of globalization. The speed and density of global exchange grows yearly. The dynamics of global trade, finance, investment, and information exchange may exceed the ability of any nation-state to control its own economic destiny. Globalization, however, also involves global population flows, pollution and disease vectors, criminal syndicates, and, of course, transnational terror organizations. These exchanges—positive, neutral, and negative—dwarf the capability of existing national and international organizations, most of which remain based on principles of national sovereignty, to regulate or meliorate them.

Benjamin Barber observes that we would never tolerate such discord within our national political community. As national citizens we recognize, despite our differences, that a capable government plays an irreplaceable role in providing for the security of the commonwealth, regulating the excesses of the market, and protecting the most vulnerable segments of the population. Yet when we confront consequences of relative global anarchy, we find it difficult to transcend our state-centric blinders even as global forces penetrate and subordinate our sovereignty. In particular, no single state, however powerful, can make an effective response to the problems of global terrorism.

How a viable global security regime might emerge exceeds the limits of this investigation, though dimensions of this puzzle, too, can be captured through metaphor. Daniel Dennet encapsulates the argument over the emergence of biological complexity as being between the advocates of "skyhooks" versus "cranes." The former believe that complexity arose through the intervention of an "intelligent designer," the latter insist that natural selection involving billions of tiny steps (cranes), each building on the one before, cumulatively explain the origins of complex organisms and even the emergence of consciousness.

A similar controversy weaves its way through Western political thought. On one side conservatives like Edmund Burke see political order organically emerging from generations of decisions made in response to immediate problems confronted, each building on the success of past experience. In contrast—from Moses and Solon to the Enlightenment—runs the legend of the lawgiver, the intelligent designer who bestows political order on a ravaged community.

We need both metaphors to grasp the challenge we face. We will be forced to make thousands of decisions about the problems that confront us daily, many perhaps pushing in the direction of a more effective global security community. Yet this process takes both time to build and a leap of faith in the optimality of incrementalism, and both time and faith may be in short supply. Perhaps, then, we should seek guidance from the intelligent designers who two centuries ago defined the goals of their labor:

> We the people of the United States, in order to form a more perfect Union, establish justice, insure domestic tranquility, provide for the common defense, promote the general welfare, and secure the blessings of liberty to ourselves and our posterity, do ordain and establish this Constitution for the United States of America.

Notes

1. Portions of this analysis summarize or expand on several sections of my earlier article, Peter C. Sederberg, "Conciliation as Counter-Terrorist Strategy," *Journal of Peace Research* (August 1995):295–311. A fuller list of citations is included with that article.
2. Christopher Hitchens, "Wanton Acts of Usage," *Harpers* (September 1986):68.
3. See Peter C. Sederberg, *Terrorist Myths: Illusion, Rhetoric, and Reality* (Englewood Cliffs, N.J.: Prentice Hall, 1989), Chapter 2, for an extended discussion of the problems afflicting the definition of terrorism.
4. For an excellent exploration of the use and abuse of metaphor in social understanding, see George Lakoff and Mark Johnson, *Metaphors We Live By* (Chicago: University of Chicago Press, 1980).
5. Fareed Zakaria, "How to Save the Arab World," *Newsweek* (24 December 2001): 22–28.
6. Ronald D. Crelinsten and Alex P. Schmid, "Western Responses to Terrorism: A Twenty-five Year Balance Sheet," in Schmid and Crelinsten, eds., *Western Responses to Terrorism* (Portland: Frank Cass, 1993), pp. 307–340.

7. Ian Clark, *Limited Nuclear War* (Princeton, N.J.: Princeton University Press, 1982), 36.
8. Edward N. Luttwak, "The Traditional Approach to Peace," in *Approaches to Peace: An Intellectual Map,* ed. W. Scott Thompson and Kenneth M. Jensen (Washington, D.C.: U.S. Institute of Peace), 4.
9. Bruce Hoffman, "The Contrasting Ethical Foundations of Terrorism in the 1980s." RAND Paper P 7416, 1988.
10. Kent L. Oots, "Bargaining with Terrorists: Organizational Considerations," *Terrorism* 13 (No. 2), 1990:145–58.
11. Robert P. Clark, "Negotiating with Insurgents: Obstacles to Peace in the Basque Country," *Terrorism and Political Violence* 2 (No. 4, 1990):489–507.